Quick Facts for CHIROPRACTIC BOARDS 3 AND 4

Jeannette B. Gibson, DC
New York Chiropractic College, Class of 1998

George L. Birnbach, DC
New York Chiropractic College, Class of 1998

Appleton & Lange Reviews/McGraw-Hill
Medical Publishing Division

New York Chicago San Francisco Lisbon London Madrid Mexico City
Milan New Delhi San Juan Seoul Singapore Sydney Toronto

The McGraw-Hill Companies

Appleton & Lange's Quick Facts for Chiropractic Boards Parts 3 and 4

4 5 6 7 8 9 0 VGR/VGR 0 9 8 7 6 5 4 3

ISBN 0-8385-0386-1

Notice

Medicine is an ever-changing science. As new research and clinical experience broaden our knowledge, changes in treatment and drug therapy are required. The authors and the publisher of this work have checked with sources believed to be reliable in their efforts to provide information that is complete and generally in accord with the standards accepted at the time of publication. However, in view of the possibility of human error or changes in medical sciences, neither the authors nor the publisher nor any other party who has been involved in the preparation or publication of this work warrants that the information contained herein is in every respect accurate or complete, and they disclaim all responsibility for any errors or omissions or for the results obtained from use of the information contained in this work. Readers are encouraged to confirm the information contained herein with other sources. For example and in particular, readers are advised to check the product information sheet included in the package of each drug they plan to administer to be certain that the information contained in this work is accurate and that changes have not been made in the recommended dose or in the contraindications for administration. This recommendation is of particular importance in connection with new or infrequently used drugs.

The editors of this book were Marinita Timban and Mary Ellen McCourt.
The cover designer was Janice Bielawa.
Victor Graphics was printer and binder.

This book is printed on acid-free paper.

Dedication

This book
is respectfully dedicated
to our family.

Lisa Bloom, DC
Dale Buchberger, DC
Denise Carston, DC
Brian Cunningham, DC
Stacy Davidoff, DC
Greg DeMaille, DC
Lisa DiMarco, DC
Philip Dontino, DC
Russ Ebbets, DC
Lana Feldman, DC
Mark Feldman, DC
Joanne Gjelsten, DC
James Inzerillo, DC
Vincent Loia, DC
Joseph Miller, DC
Hunter Mollin, DC
Michael O'Connor, DC
Dino Patriarco, DC
Julie Plezbert, DC
Eileen Santipadri, DC
Judy Silvestrone, DC
Robert Story, DC

Special thanks to Michael Howard, DC, who provided the idea for this manual.

Contents

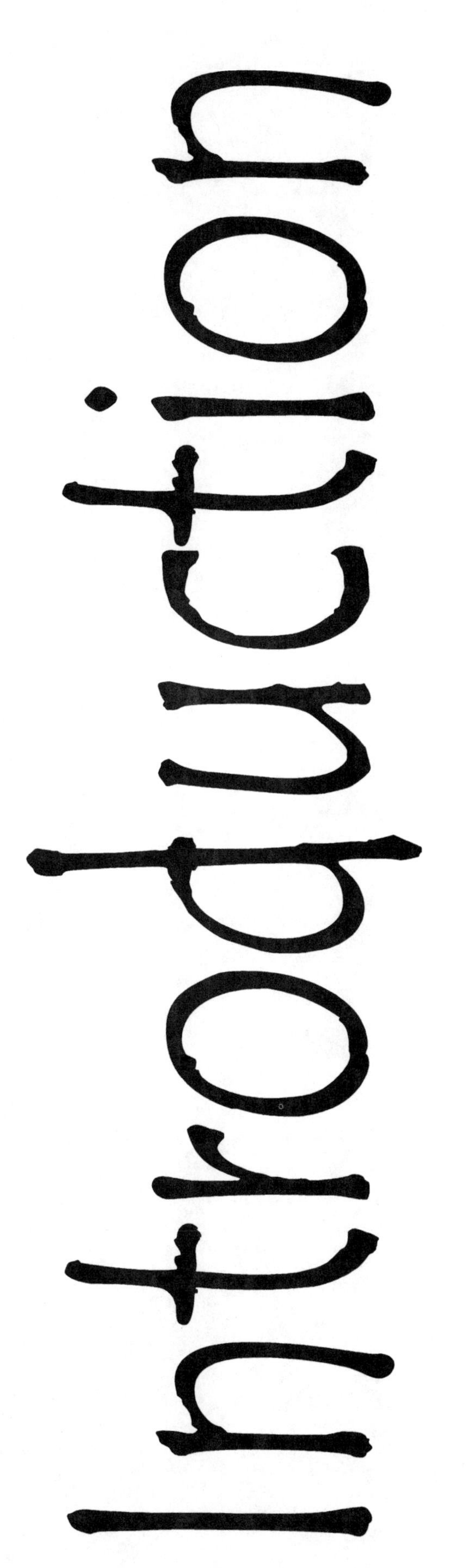

We completed this book while we were still in our last year of chiropractic school at New York Chiropractic College. Looking back now, that was the only time when this information could have been compiled. There is no way to capture in a book the intensity and anxiety of chiropractic school and exams other than to be in the midst of them. We are happy to be graduated and in practice now, and we hope that this book is helpful to you for reaching that goal as well.

This book was written to save you the time of organizing the tremendous volume of information presented to you in school in order to allow you more time to actually practice and learn the material! On each page, every attempt was made to use the references most common in chiropractic colleges today, and to accurately reference each entry. This book may serve you well as a companion for your clinical studies, and help you pace yourself for board exam preparation. We suggest that for board exam preparation, you decide how many weeks you want to devote to your studies, and then cover the appropriate number of pages each week. It's always better to practice clinical skills with a friend than to simply read them.

Good luck with school and boards!

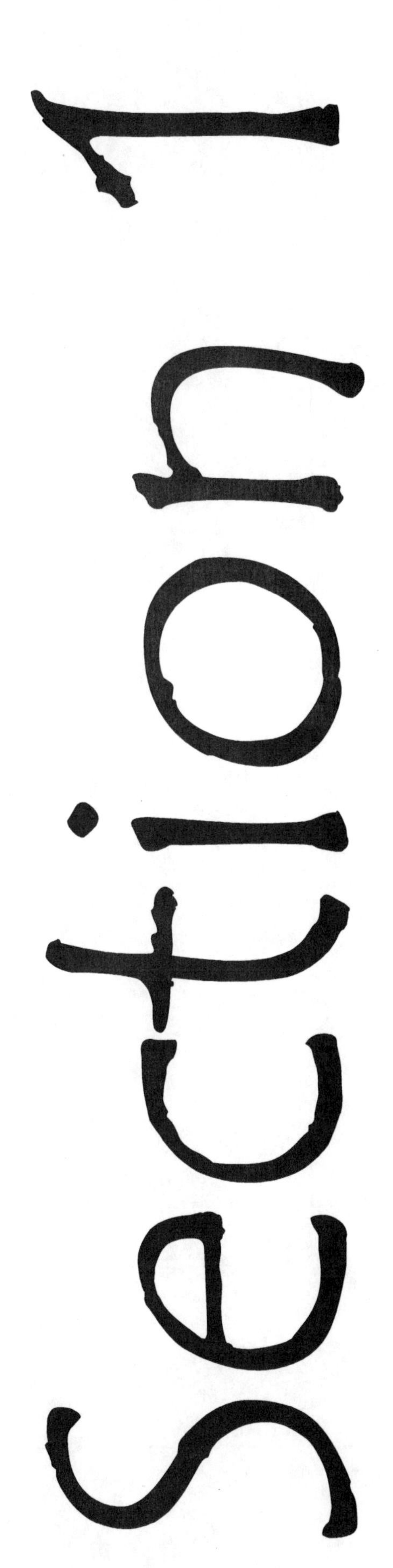
Section 1

CHAPTER 1

Physiotherapy

THE SPECTRA OF THERAPEUTIC MODALITIES (1,2)

ote

- Wavelength is the distance between the peak of one wave and the peak of the wave before or after.
- Frequency is the number of oscillations or vibrations occurring in 1 second (expressed in hertz/Hz).
- Generally, radiations with the longest wavelengths tend to have the greatest depths of penetration, regardless of their frequency.

Therapeutic Modality		Penetration	Clinically Used Wavelength		Clinically Used Frequency
Electromagnetic Radiation	**Electrical Stimulating Currents**	Various	3 x 10^8 Km to 75,000 Km		1-400 Hz
	Diathermy	3 cm	**Shortwave**	22 m	13.56 MHz
				11 m	27.12 MHz
			Microwave	69 cm	433.9 MHz
				33 cm	915 MHz
				12 cm	2450 MHz
	Infrared	1 cm	**Luminous**	28,860 A	1.04 x 10^{13} Hz
			Nonluminous	14,430 A	2.08 x 10^{13} Hz
	Ultraviolet	2 mm	**UV-A**	3200-4000 A	9.38 x 10^{13} – 7.5 x 10^{13} Hz
			UV-B	2900-3200 A	1.03 x 10^{14} - 9.38 x 10^{13} Hz
			UV-C	2000-2900 A	1.50 x 10^{14} – 1.03 x 10^{14} Hz
Acoustic Energy	**Ultrasound**	5 cm	Usually 1 MHz		700,000-1,000,000 Hz

LAWS GOVERNING ELECTROMAGNETIC RADIATION (3)

📖 **ARNDT-SCHULTZ PRINCIPLE** No reactions or changes can occur in the body tissues if the amount of energy absorbed is insufficient to stimulate the absorbing tissues.

📖 **GROTTHUS-DRAPER LAW** If therapeutic energy is not absorbed by the tissues, it must be transmitted to deeper layers.

📖 **COSINE LAW** The smaller the angle between the propagating ray and the right angle, the less radiation reflected and the greater the absorption.

📖 **INVERSE SQUARE LAW** The intensity of the radiation striking a particular surface varies inversely with the square of the distance from the source.

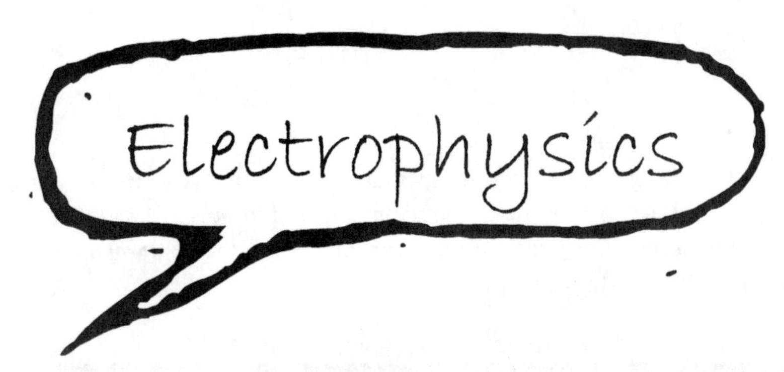

(4,5,6)

Electrical Capacity	Ability of an object to hold an electric charge
Capacitance	Capacity of an object that is charged to a potential of 1 volt by 1 coulomb of electricity, measured in *farads*
Resistance	Impedance to flow of electrons measured in *ohms*
Current intensity	Strength of flow of electrons through a conductor measured in *amperes*
Electrical potential	Electrical properties (condition) measured in *volts*; also called electromotive force
Voltage	The force resulting from an accumulation of electrons at one point in an electrical circuit **NOTE**: low voltage means less than 150 volts; high voltage means several hundred volts
Ohm's law	E = IR where E is electromotive force in volts, I is the intensity of current in amps, and R is the resistance in ohms
Polarity	The cathode is the negative electrode; the anode is the positive electrode

Units of Measurement

Volt	*Electromotive force*
Ohm	*Resistance to current flow*
Coulomb	*The quantity of electricity transferred by a current of 1 ampere in 1 second*
Ampere	*Intensity; indicates the rate at which electrical current is flowing*

Laws

Current flow = Voltage/Resistance (Ohm's law)
Watts = Volts x Amperes

Electrodiagnosis

ote

- Electrodiagnosis is the use of low voltage currents to test the integrity of muscles and nerves.
- Reaction of degeneration is impairment of the conduction of impulses through a peripheral nerve due to disease, trauma to the nerve trunks or anterior roots, or a lesion in the lower spinal cord. Reactive changes usually occur within 10 days after the injury.

Reaction of Degeneration (7,8)

Status		Nerve		Muscle	
		Galvanic	Tetanizing Faradic	Galvanic	Tetanizing Faradic
Normal		Brisk single contraction	Tetanic contraction	Brisk single contraction	Tetanic contraction
Partial Degeneration		Diminished response	Diminished response	Sluggish contraction	Diminished response
Complete Denervation	Full Reaction	No response	No response	Sluggish response	No response
	Complete Reaction	No response	No response	No response	No response

Electrical Muscle Stimulation (7,8)

Rheobase	▪ The smallest amount of current that will produce a muscle contraction if the stimulus is of infinite duration ▪ In denervation, the rheobase may be less than that of innervated muscle
Chronaxie	▪ The duration of shortest impulse that will produce a response with a current of double the rheobase ▪ The chronaxie of the innervated muscle is less than that of denervated muscle

Peripheral Nerve Injuries (8,9,10)

OTE

- The proportion of fibers within a nerve exhibiting electrophysiologically demonstrable changes determines the findings in electromyographic studies. Peripheral nerve injuries are divided into three categories depending on the severity of the injury.

Neurapraxia	First degree injury	▪ Damage causes a temporary conduction block but viability of the axon is maintained ▪ Occurs frequently with pressure or entrapment neuropathies ▪ Transmission of the depolarization impulse is blocked over a short segment, with normal signal propagation possible above and below the area of the block
Axonotmesis	Second degree injury	▪ Local destruction of the axon occurs but the connective tissue of the nerve is intact ▪ Causes failure of axon conduction and loss of motor and sensory evoked response
Neurotmesis	Third degree injury	▪ The whole thickness of the nerve is divided; both the connective tissue structure of the nerve and the continuity of the nerve fibers are disrupted ▪ Recovery is delayed and incomplete; results in degeneration of the axons distal to the site of injury

Electrotherapeutic Currents(11)

Waveforms

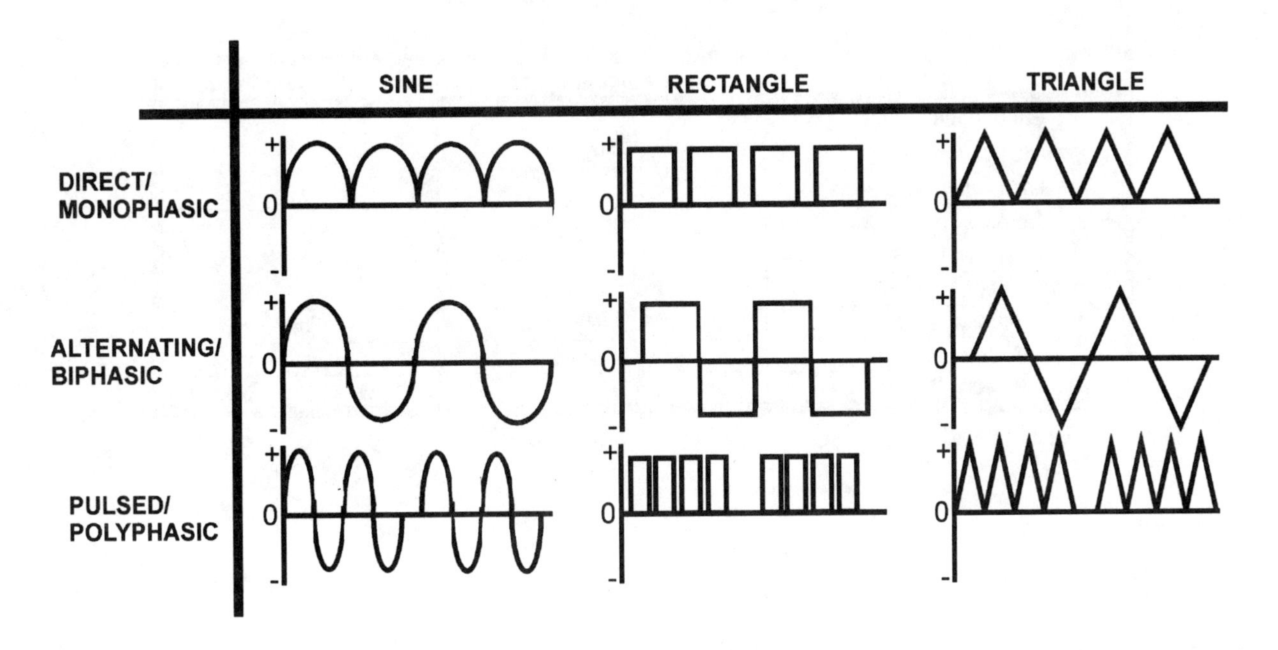

Modulation

- Modulation refers to any alteration in the magnitude or duration of a pulse, or individual waveform.

Modulation	Current	Purpose	
Continuous	Amplitude of current flow remains the same for several seconds or minutes	**Direct current**	Iontophoresis
		Alternating current	Muscle contraction
Interrupted	Current flows during the "on-time" and is turned off during the "off-time"	**Monophasic Biphasic**	Muscle reeducation and strengthening; improving range of motion
Burst	Pulsed current flows for a short duration and then is turned off for a short time in a repetitive cycle	**Monophasic Biphasic Polyphasic**	Pain control
Ramp / Surge	Current amplitude increases or ramps up gradually to some preset maximum and may also decrease in intensity	Elicits muscle contraction	

TREATMENT PARAMETERS (12)

Goal	Pulse Frequency (pps)	Pulse Duration (width)
Enkephalin Release ▪ *Acute conditions* ▪ *Relaxation of muscle spasm*	80 to 150 Hz	
Endorphin Release ▪ *Chronic conditions* ▪ *Analgesic*	1 to 10 Hz	
Muscle Spasm	80 to 120 Hz	Short
Muscle Exercise	15 to 35 Hz	Long / Rest
Muscle Atrophy	5 to 8 Hz	Very Long / Rest

ote (13)

- Increasing the intensity of electrical stimulus causes the current to reach deeper into the tissue.
- Increasing duration while intensity remains the same will stimulate more nerve fibers.
- Polarity can be used with a direct current generator to bring about chemical effects (iontophoresis).
- All or none response: the response of a single nerve fiber is either maximal (depolarization) or non-existent (no depolarization).

THERAPEUTIC USES OF ELECTRIC CURRENT (14,15)

Tissue Stimulated	Physiologic Effect
Innervated Muscle	▪ Muscle reeducation ▪ Muscle pump contractions (stimulation of circulation) ▪ Retardation of atrophy: electric stimulation reproduces the physical and chemical events associated with normal voluntary muscle contraction ▪ Muscle strengthening ▪ Increasing range of motion: electrically stimulating a muscle contraction pulls the joint through the limited range
Denervated muscle	▪ Interrupted direct current (galvanic) causes stimulation of sensory nerves which produces muscle contraction
Sensory nerves	▪ Stimulation of sensory nerves alters the patient's perception of pain (i.e. Gate Control theory)

LOW FREQUENCY CURRENTS (16)

Indications	▪ Adhesions ▪ Circulatory stasis ▪ Edema ▪ Restricted joint motion ▪ Trigger points	▪ Muscle spasm ▪ Muscular atrophy ▪ Pain ▪ Passive exercise
Contraindications	▪ Areas of diminished sensation ▪ Metallic implants ▪ Metastatic carcinoma ▪ Pregnancy	▪ Over or through the heart ▪ Over open wounds ▪ Pacemaker ▪ Transcerebral applications

USE OF LOW FREQUENCY ELECTRIC STIMULATION

Muscle Status	Physiologic Response
Innervated Muscles	▪ Relaxes spastic muscle tissue ▪ Prevents disuse atrophy and re-educates muscle
Denervated Muscles	▪ Enhances the circulation to and nutrition of affected muscle fibers ▪ Retards the development of fascicular agglutination and sclerosis of areolar tissue ▪ Inhibits the progression of disuse atrophy ▪ Assists in correcting arteriovenous and lymphatic stasis within muscle tissue

TYPES OF LOW FREQUENCY ELECTRICAL STIMULATION

Current			Indications
Alternating / Biphasic	Sinusoidal		▪ Used in various modes to create muscular contractions with each impulse
	Faradic		▪ Stimulates contractions in muscles that have normal innervation but poor tonicity; paralyzed muscle will not respond to this current ▪ Tests muscles for reaction of degeneration
Direct/ Galvanic/ Monophasic	Low Volt	Continuous	▪ Iontophoresis: introduction of ions into the body
		Interrupted	▪ Stimulation of neuromuscular components with reaction of degeneration; denervated muscle; myositis

otes on Galvanic Current

PFLUGER'S LAW The closing of a galvanic current on a nerve triggers an increase in irritability at the negative pole (cataelectrotonus), and a decrease in nerve irritability at the positive pole (anaelectrotonus).

The positive pole, or anode:

- *Attracts acids, repels alkaloids*
- *Sclerotic (toughening agent)*
- *Repels positive ions*
- *Analgesic*
- *Vasoconstriction*

The negative pole, or cathode:

- *Attracts alkaloids, repels acids*
- *Sclerolytic (softening agent)*
- *Repels negative ions*
- *Stimulating*
- *Vasodilation*
- *Germicidal effect*

DIRECT LOW VOLT (GALVANISM) (17)

ote

- Great care must be taken to avoid burning the patient.

Indications	▪ Acute trauma ▪ Adhesions ▪ Arthritis	▪ Joint pain ▪ Neuritis ▪ IVD syndromes	▪ Myalgia ▪ Sprain/strain ▪ Sciatica
Contraindications	▪ Impaired cutaneous sensation ▪ Pacemaker, heart area	▪ Metallic joints, pins or IUDs ▪ Over scars, adhesions	▪ Pregnancy ▪ Metastatic carcinoma ▪ Transcerebral
Physical actions	▪ Electrochemical (primary): iontophoresis ▪ Pain control: negative pole is active electrode for treating chronic pain, positive pole is active electrode in treating acute pain ▪ Enkephalin production for pain control		
Treatment	▪ Maximum current intensity is 1 ma per square inch of active electrode or patient tolerance ▪ The electrode placed over the site of treatment is the active electrode; the other is the indifferent electrode and should be large to provide dispersive effects ▪ When the polarity switch of the unit is set at the positive setting, the active electrode is the positive pole and the indifferent electrode is the negative pole. The reverse is true when the unit's polarity switch is set at the negative setting		

IONTOPHORESIS (18,19,20)

ote

- A positively or negatively charged ion is placed under the electrode with the same charge (negative ions go under the cathode). Then a direct continuous current is applied and the ion is electrically propelled into the patient's tissues.

Pathology	Ion Selection	
	Positively Charged	**Negatively Charged**
Pain, inflammation	Hydrocortisone	Salicylate
Spasm	Calcium, magnesium	
Acute pain, myositis, neuritis	Magnesium	
Edema	Magnesium, hyaluronidase	Salicylate
Calcific deposits, bursitis		Acetic acid
Fungal infections	Copper	
Scars, adhesions		Chlorine, iodine, salicylate

Transcutaneous Electrical Nerve Stimulation (TENS) (21)

Parameters	▪ Wave width: 40-500 microseconds or less; interrupted or pulsed ▪ Frequency: 70-150 pps
Indications	▪ Pain control (pads are placed over the painful area)
Contraindications	▪ Pacemaker ▪ Stimulation over the carotid sinus ▪ Stimulation in patient's with arrhythmias or myocardial disease ▪ Pregnancy ▪ Open wounds
Physical actions	▪ Dorsal column stimulator ▪ Gate control theory of pain

Microcurrent (22)

Parameters	▪ Fixed amperage; voltage changes according to skin impedance ▪ Pulse durations are about a half second ▪ Pulse frequency is 0.3 or 0.5 Hz.
Indications	▪ Post traumatic inflammation ▪ Swelling ▪ Atrophy ▪ Fractures ▪ Wound healing
Techniques	▪ Electromassage at the intracellular level ▪ Point stimulation of acupuncture points ▪ Use of pads
Contraindications	▪ Cancer patients ▪ Pacemaker ▪ Patients with suspected heart problems or epilepsy ▪ Over throat muscles and carotid sinus ▪ Transcerebrally or through the heart ▪ Pregnancy
Treatment frequency and duration	▪ 15-20 minutes, daily ▪ Electroanalgesia usually occurs in 3-5 minutes

ote

- The carotid sinus is a slight dilation of the common carotid artery at the bifurcation. It contains baroreceptors that cause bradycardia and a decrease in blood pressure when stimulated.

MEDIUM FREQUENCY CURRENTS (23)

INTERFERENTIAL

- Skin resistance decreases as frequency increases.

Interferential current production		▪ **Frequency difference interferential** One fixed medium frequency sine wave and one variable medium frequency sine wave are crossed simultaneously. The difference between the two frequencies is the beat frequency, and when the electrodes are equally distant from the center they produce a clover leaf pattern. The therapeutic effect of interferential current is due to the beat frequency. When the frequencies cross in the body, they trigger the formation of a third current that radiates from the inside of the body to the outside (endogenous current). Therefore, skin resistance does not dissipate the therapeutic effects ▪ **Premodulated interferential** Both output channels produce an identical carrier frequency of 4000 Hz, but the modulation of bursting occurs within the unit and is delivered to the tissue
Treatment parameters	**Frequency**	▪ 1-10 Hz causes endorphin production (chronic, motor level) ▪ 80-120 Hz triggers enkephalin production for acute pain control
	Dosage	▪ Submitis dose: below sensory level ▪ Dosis mitis: just at sensory level; used for **acute** pain (enkephalin production) ▪ Dosis normalis: intensity set to patient tolerance ▪ Dosis fortis: the strongest intensity the patient can tolerate; used to treat **chronic** cases
	Time	▪ Usually 10-15 minutes; up to 30 minutes in certain cases ▪ The more chronic the case, the longer the therapy time
Indications		▪ Pain control ▪ Tendinitis, synovitis, capsulitis ▪ Post traumatic edema
Contraindications		▪ Over the carotid sinus ▪ Heart area ▪ Pacemaker ▪ Metastatic carcinoma ▪ Pregnancy ▪ Thrombophlebitis ▪ Transcerebral current ▪ Varicosities

RUSSIAN STIMULATION

Medium frequency current of 2500 Hz, premodulated in the range of 40-50 Hz.

Russian stimulation is used for rehabilitation of specific muscle groups and to retrain motor neurons.

Schedule for strengthening: 10 second contraction followed by 50-second rest period for 7-10 repetitions.

HIGH VOLT (24)

- High volt is a unidirectional, monophasic, interrupted current.
- High volt units generate an electromotive force of up to 500 volts. Remember that amperage and not voltage causes patient burns.
- High volt units can achieve higher wave peaks than low volt units without danger of burning the patient because the pulse duration is extremely short (low average current amperage).
- The wave form has twin spikes, as shown at right.

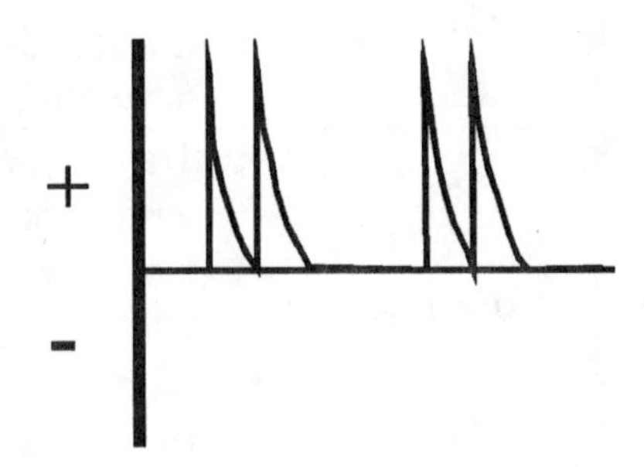

<table>
<tr><td rowspan="5">Physiologic effects
▪ Dependent upon control settings
▪ NOTE: no appreciable iontophoresis</td><td colspan="2">▪ Pain reduction via Gate Control Theory</td><td>▪ 70-110 pps with active electrode over involved site</td></tr>
<tr><td colspan="2">▪ Muscle spasm reduction</td><td>▪ 70-110 pps causes tetany and enkephalin production</td></tr>
<tr><td colspan="2">▪ Muscular exercise and reeducation</td><td>▪ 15 pps for muscle reeducation
▪ 4-5 pps for muscle exercise</td></tr>
<tr><td colspan="2">▪ Circulation enhancement</td><td>▪ Electric stimulation causes local increase in circulation</td></tr>
<tr><td colspan="2">▪ Edema reduction</td><td>▪ Below 10 pps</td></tr>
<tr><td>Contraindications</td><td colspan="3">▪ Applications over the lower back or abdomen during pregnancy
▪ Over neoplasm
▪ Pacemaker
▪ Transcerebral
▪ Extreme caution near the heart or carotid sinus</td></tr>
<tr><td rowspan="2">Polarity</td><td>Positive</td><td colspan="2">▪ Analgesic effect; constriction of blood vessels; mildly germicidal</td></tr>
<tr><td>Negative</td><td colspan="2">▪ Used to treat trigger points, dilate blood vessels, soften adhesions, and exercise and reeducate muscles</td></tr>
</table>

- All high volt units have polarity switches. When the switch is set on positive, the active pads are positive and the indifferent dispersal pad is negative. If the switch is set on negative, the opposite is true.

THERAPEUTIC HEAT (25,26,27)

THE EFFECTS OF HEAT

	Effects	Caution
Physiologic	▪ Analgesic or calming effect ▪ Slight increase in local metabolism ▪ Some sedation of sensory nerves (enkephalin production)	▪ Heat applied for too long or at too high a temperature may cause edema, local congestion and reduced metabolism
Localized	▪ Transient vasoconstriction followed by vasodilation and hyperemia ▪ Increased metabolism of the parts being treated ▪ Removal of toxic wastes with sweating ▪ Patient relaxation	▪ Heat should not be applied to a body part until 48-72 hours after injury, or longer if bleeding or swelling are present
Remote Reflexes	▪ Increased blood flow ▪ Increased metabolism and healing in sites distant from the area of application	
Systemic	▪ Increased oxidation (Van-Hoff's Law) ▪ Tachycardia: for every 1 degree F of temperature increase, there is a corresponding rise in heart rate of 10 beats per minute ▪ Hypotension ▪ Tachypnea (increased respiratory rate) ▪ Polyuria: heat triggers increase in urine production ▪ Alkalemia in the area being treated ▪ Increased plasma blood volume and oxygen consumption	

ote

- VANT-HOFF'S LAW For every temperature rise of 10 degrees C (18F) the velocity of chemical reactions in the body is increased two to three times.
- JOULE'S LAW The conversion of electrical energy to heat is directly proportional to the intensity, resistance, and time.

Forms of Heat Therapy

Superficial

Ultraviolet
Infrared
Hot moist (hydrocollator) packs
Paraffin
Hydrotherapy (whirlpool)
Fluidotherapy

Deep

Shortwave and microwave diathermy
Ultrasound

Laws of Heat Transfer (28)

Type	Definition	Examples
Conduction	▪ Occurs when two or more adjacent objects of unlike temperature are placed in contact and a state of energy exchange affects successive portions of each ▪ Heat moves from the warmer to the cooler body or object	▪ Heating pads ▪ Hot moist packs ▪ Paraffin bath
Convection	▪ Exchange of heat between a surface and a fluid moving over that surface	▪ Whirlpool ▪ Fluidotherapy
Radiation	▪ Heat is transferred between two objects separated by an intervening medium that does not become warmer as a result of the heat transfer	▪ Ultraviolet ▪ Infrared
Conversion	▪ The oscillations of a high-frequency electric current or vibration are converted to heat energy as they pass through a body part ▪ Heat build up is due to friction and molecular bombardment from cell resistance to the current	▪ Diathermy ▪ Ultrasound

Indications and Contraindications to Local Heat (29)

Indications

- *Relaxation of spasticity*
- *Increase suppurative process*
- *Increase vasodilation and hyperemia*
- *Increase local circulatory and metabolic rates*
- *Enhance absorption of exudates*
- *Promote sweating*
- *Sedation and local analgesia*
- *Increase lymph circulation*

Contraindications

- *Deficient vascularity*
- *Areas of diminished sensation*
- *Malignant neoplasm in the area to be treated*
- *Bleeding tendency*
- *Pregnancy*
- *Acute inflammatory process or localized edema*
- *Acute skin conditions*
- *Infants, the elderly*
- *Over recently formed scars or extremely fair skin*
- *Over metal*
- *Over the eyes or contact lenses*

SUPERFICIAL HEAT

ULTRAVIOLET AND INFRARED (30,31)

		Wavelength	Penetration	Physiologic Effects	Indications
Infrared	**Luminous** ▪ Tungsten or calcium filament ▪ Also called "near"	1,500-1,200 millimicrons	5-10 mm	▪ Stimulation of local circulation; hyperemia ▪ Locally increases circulatory and metabolic rates ▪ Relaxation and general sedation ▪ Antispasmodic ▪ Decongestant and analgesic effects	▪ Nonacute arthritis ▪ Catarrhal conditions ▪ Chronic backache ▪ Fractures ▪ Peripheral neuropathy ▪ Sprains/strains/stiffness
	Nonluminous ▪ Incandescent light ▪ Also called "far"	15,000-40,000 millimicrons	0.1-0.2 mm		
Ultraviolet	**UV-A**	3200-4000 A	2 mm	▪ Superficial chemical changes ▪ Tanning effects	▪ Acne ▪ Aseptic wounds ▪ Folliculitis ▪ Pityriasis rosea ▪ Tinea capitum ▪ Septic wounds ▪ Sinusitis
	UV-B	2900-3200 A	2 mm		
	UV-C	2000-2900 A	2 mm	▪ Bactericidal	

ote

- Mottling of the skin due to overexposure to heat radiation is called erythema ab igne.
- Hot packs, paraffin baths, hot and cold whirlpools, and ice packs are forms of radiant energy in the infrared region.
- Laws pertaining to all radiation include:

  - THE INVERSE SQUARE LAW The radiation intensity is inversely proportional to the square of the distance from source to target.
  - THE COSINE LAW The intensity of radiation varies as the cosine of the angle of incidence; the greater the angle at which the radiation strikes the skin, the less the intensity.

ERYTHEMA WITH INFRARED AND ULTRAVIOLET LIGHT (32,33)

- Erythema is a reddening of the skin caused by capillary dilation

	Infrared	Ultraviolet
Appearance	Lighter red, sharp borders	Dark red spots
Development	After several hours	Immediately
Duration	Several hours/ days	Less than one hour
Pigmentation	Diffuse tanning	Mottled

MINIMAL ERYTHEMAL DOSE WITH ULTRAVIOLET LIGHT (34,35)

- The exact exposure necessary to develop erythema determines an individual's degree of intrinsic sensitivity.
- Hot and cold quartz lamps produce ultraviolet light from mercury vapor encased in a quartz envelope and activated by an electric current.

☞ **Sleeve Test**

- Patient is draped so that a small area of the skin is exposed.
- The exposed area is covered with a cloth or cardboard that has five or six one-inch square openings about one inch apart.
- The UV lamp is placed 30 inches from the skin for a hot quartz lamp, and one inch from the skin for a cold quartz lamp.
- The openings are exposed at five-second intervals and then covered one by one; each subsequent opening is therefore exposed five seconds longer than the previous opening. If a cold quartz lamp is used, the interval is reduced to one second.

☞ **Minimal Erythemal Dose**

- This is the patch were the erythema is first perceptible after an eight-hour period and then disappears after 24 hours.
- Dosage: once the MED is known, treatment may be started with increments of 15 seconds at each successive treatment until a maximum is reached (usually 2 minutes).

Degrees of Severity of Erhthema

Dosage	Effect
1 ED (first degree)	Red, itch; this is the MED
2 ED (second degree)	Same as above but exagerrated; resembles a mild sunburn
3 ED (third degree)	Edema, blisters; marked reddening and desquamation
4 ED (fourth degree)	Intense reddening followed by blistering and peeling; AKA bactericidal or destructive dose

Heat Modalities (36,37)

		Treatment	Contraindications
Hot Moist Packs ▪ *Contain silica gel*		▪ The packs should be wrapped with either six or eight layers ▪ Patient should never lie on the packs	▪ Should not be used where there is scar tissue or areas of decreased circulation or diminished sensation
Paraffin ▪ *Contains paraffin and mineral oil in a 7:1 ratio* ▪ *Indicated for non-acute arthritic joints*		▪ Melted paraffin wax is applied by brush or by dipping the part to be treated into the wax and then removing it. The part is immersed from 7-10 times to build up a thick coat of wax ▪ After the wax cools, it is covered and the patient rests for 15-20 minutes. ▪ The wax is then removed and the treated part should be massaged and passively exercised	▪ Should not be used over open wounds, abrasions, acute skin disorders or where there is diminished sensation
Hydrotherapy	**Whirlpool**	▪ Used to treat burns, peripheral vascular disorders; used to exercise a part under water and to provide gentle massage, clean wounds and soften tissues prior to stretching, exercise or manipulation ▪ Treatment time is 15-20 minutes	▪ Extreme care should be used when treating the young or elderly persons ▪ Heart conditions, hypertension ▪ Diabetes ▪ Rashes or dermatologic diseases ▪ Patient becomes dizzy or nauseated or weak
	Hubbard tank	▪ Full immersion therapy	
	Sitz bath	▪ **WARM BATH**: treatment of hemorrhoids, prostatic complaints, sciatica, cystitis, urinary retention, dysmenorrhea, and following pelvic surgery ▪ **COLD BATH**: tones pelvic muscles and viscera; lessens pelvic bleeding	
Fluidotherapy		▪ Patient places affected extremity in a unit which contains solid particles of cellulose (Cellex; finely ground corn cobs) which are rapidly whirled by a high-powered blower ▪ High intensities of heat and micromassage are produced	▪ Acute cardiorenal edema ▪ Chronic venous insufficiency ▪ Vascular disease ▪ Hypesthesia ▪ Malignancy ▪ Acute inflammatory process ▪ Suppurating lesions ▪ Infants or elderly persons ▪ Metal jewelry or implants

Deep Heat

Diathermy (High Frequency) (38,39,40)

	Physiologic Effects	Treatment Time	Indications	Contraindications
Shortwave ▪ ***Frequency***: *10-100 million Hz* ▪ ***Wavelength***: *3-30 meters*	▪ Thermal: increases temperatures within thick muscle, viscera, and paraarticular structures; rapid peripheral vessel dilation accompanied by a rise in body temperature ▪ Analgesic ▪ Sedative effect on irritated motor nerves and sensory nerves	Maximum treatment time of 10 minutes is recommended in most cases	▪ Sinusitis (butterfly electrodes) ▪ Otitis media ▪ Respiratory conditions ▪ Pelvic inflammatory disease ▪ Muscle aches and pains	▪ Acute inflammatory conditions ▪ Implanted cardiac pacemaker ▪ Arteriosclerosis and diabetes ▪ Attached hearing aid ▪ Contact lenses ▪ Hemorrhage ▪ Pregnancy ▪ Rheumatoid arthritis
Microwave ▪ ***Frequency***: *2,450 MHz* ▪ ***Wavelength***: *10-12 cm*	▪ Warms tissues in a much more local area ▪ Little penetration into deeper organs	10-20 minutes	▪ Same as for shortwave; however, may be more effective for localized heating ▪ Bursitis, myositis ▪ Osteoarthritis and rheumatoid arthritis ▪ Sinusitis ▪ Sprains/strains	▪ Pacemakers, metallic implants ▪ Special caution in genital areas ▪ Avoid radiation to the eyes ▪ Edema ▪ Osteomyelitis ▪ Over casts or adhesive tape ▪ Pacemaker

ote

- KIRCHHOFF'S LAW The greatest level of heat will be produced in the area of greatest current density.
- High frequency currents do not stimulate motor or sensory nerves because they do not come in contact with human tissue for sufficient time to cause ion movement.
- Types of electrodes: capacitive (condenser) and inductive (drum)

ULTRASOUND (41,42,43)

ote

- Ultrasound equipment consists of a high-frequency generator and an applicator. The generator produces electric oscillations that cause a transducer in the applicator to vibrate and generate ultrasonic waves.
- Ultrasound vibrations are produces by the rapid contraction and expansion of a crystal subjected to high voltages of electrical energy. The expansion and contraction of the crystal creates longitudinal compression waves, thus transforming electrical energy into mechanical energy and causing the PIEZOELECTRIC EFFECT.
- Ultrasound has the specific effect of building heat and producing a high intensity micromassage where muscles, tendons, and ligaments attach to bone.
- Frequencies up to around 20,000 Hz are audible to humans; ultrasound frequencies occur between 700,000 and 1,000,000 Hz and are therefore inaudible.
- The depth of penetration with ultrasound is much greater than with any of the electromagnetic radiations.
- CAVITATION: deformation and collapse of the molecular structure of loosely bonded substances leads to destruction.
- PHONOPHORESIS: introduction of substances (transmission of molecules) such as hydrocortisone, lidocaine or salicylate into the body by ultrasonic energy.

Coupling Media	▪ Water ▪ Aquagel ▪ Glycerol ▪ Mineral oil
Crystals	▪ Barium titanate ▪ Quartz sulfate ▪ Lithium sulfate
Application	▪ Pulsed: reduction of edema ▪ Continuous: thermal effects ▪ Underwater ▪ Combination with electrical stimulation

GENERAL INDICATIONS AND CONTRAINDICATIONS (44)

Physiologic Effects	Indications	Contraindications
▪ Heat ▪ Specific mechanical action ▪ Micromassage ▪ Tissue alteration: breakdown of collagen and scar tissue ▪ Chemical effects: increased oxidation ▪ Clearing agent: reduction of edema ▪ Analgesia ▪ Antisepsis: increased phagocytic activity ▪ Local histamine release at thermal levels	▪ Spasm ▪ Scar tissue ▪ Ganglia ▪ Myalgia ▪ Neuralgia ▪ Osteoarthritis ▪ Subacute or chronic radiculitis ▪ Strains, tendinitis ▪ Trigger points	▪ Over epiphysis or bony prominences ▪ Fracture ▪ Pregnant uterus ▪ Pacemakers, metallic implants or surgical fixation materials ▪ Caution when patient has sensory loss ▪ Near a hearing aid or metallic implant or pacemaker ▪ Over nerve plexuses ▪ Over the eye, heart or reproductive organs

ULTRASOUND INTENSITY (POWER WATTAGE) (44)

Symptoms	Tissue	Contact Method	Under Water
Acute	Thin	0.5-1.0 W/cm²	1.0-1.5 W/cm²
	Thick	1.0-1.5 W/cm²	1.5-2.0 W/cm²
Chronic	Thin	1.0-1.5 W/cm²	1.5-2.0 W/cm²
	Thick	1.5-2.0 W/cm²	2.0-2.5 W/cm²

MODES OF ULTRASOUND (45)

Mode	Physiologic Effects	Note
Pulsed	▪ Reduction of edema ▪ Micromassage without the production of heat ▪ Mechanical effects associated with soft tissue healing	
Continuous	▪ Thermal effects ▪ Mechanical effects associated with soft tissue healing	▪ Ultrasound head must be kept moving at all times

Note (44)

- Severe tingling, discomfort, or burning sensations during a treatment may indicate periosteal irritation and may be caused by moving the ultrasound head too slowly or not at all; moving the head in a pattern which overlaps too much; or having the intensity setting too high.
- Pain over the area of treatment could indicate a recent fracture.

THERAPEUTIC COLD (46)

Modality	Physiologic Effects	Alleviation of Pain
Cryotherapy **hunting Response**: periods of vasodilation alternating with vasoconstriction due to prolonged exposure to cold	▪ Decreased circulation and metabolism ▪ Decreased inflammation; local vasoconstriction ▪ Decreased pain ▪ Decreased muscle spasm ▪ Decreased enzymatic reaction, nerve conduction ▪ Decreased venous and lymphatic flow; decreased phagocytosis ▪ Increased heart and respiratory rate	▪ Cold affects muscle spindles and Golgi tendon organs directly. At temperatures between 20 and 25 degrees C, the normal discharges from the receptors become irregular, diminish in frequency and stop ▪ Sensory nerve velocity impulses decrease until conduction is totally blocked ▪ Sensory nerve action potentials increase ▪ Motor nerve conduction velocity decreases

Remember (47)

- Ice is applied directly to the patient's skin with a circular or back-and-forth movement on the treatment site. The four stages of cold when performing ice massage include:

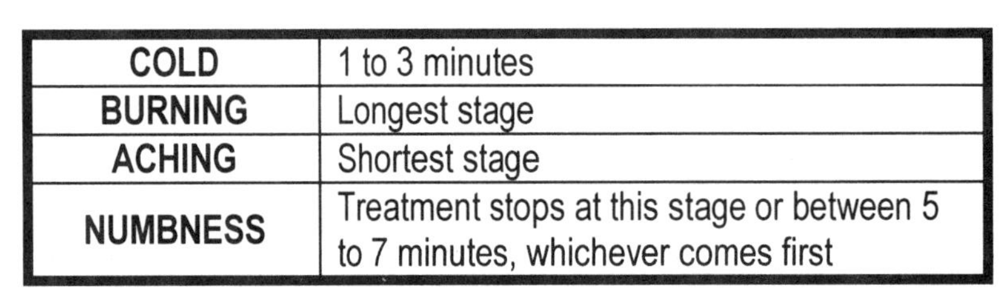

COLD	1 to 3 minutes
BURNING	Longest stage
ACHING	Shortest stage
NUMBNESS	Treatment stops at this stage or between 5 to 7 minutes, whichever comes first

- Cold penetrates deeper than superficial heat because it is not removed as fast by the circulation.

MODALITIES (48,49)

Modality	Application	Treatment time	Contraindicatons
Ice Massage	▪ Ice is applied directly to the patient's skin using a circular motion	Not longer than five minutes; ice application is terminated when the skin becomes numb	
Cold Pack	▪ Commercially available packs contain silicon material to retain coolness ▪ Pack may be applied directly to the skin; wrapped in a dry towel; or wrapped in a moist towel before application	20-30 minutes on and 20-30 minutes off, repeated every two hours	▪ Raynaud's disease ▪ Chilblains ▪ Rheumatoid or gouty arthritis
Cold Whirlpool	▪ Part to be treated is immersed in water at a temperature of 50-60 degrees F ▪ Patient may perform exercises during the treatment	5-10 minutes or until body segment becomes numb	
Spray and Stretch	▪ Vapocoolant (Fluori-Methane) is applied to the skin at an angle of 30 degrees from a distance of 18 inches at a rate of 4 inches/second ▪ The vapocoolant is applied in one direction, covering the entire affected muscle, and traveling toward the area of referred pain and finally covering the area of referred pain ▪ During application of vapocoolant, the affected muscle is passively stretched slowly, with increasing force after the jet stream covers the length of the muscle once; the stretch is held at a point of tolerable discomfort	2-3 stretches of the muscle	▪ When vapocooling the face, the eyes should be covered

MASSAGE TECHNIQUES (50,51)

INDICATIONS AND CONTRAINDICATIONS

Effects of Massage	▪ Assists venous and lymphatic flow ▪ Stretches superficial tissues ▪ Loosens scar tissues
Contraindications	▪ Sprains and strains ▪ Contusions ▪ Chronic adhesions or irritation

TECHNIQUES

Technique	Method of Application	Effect
Friction massage	▪ Friction is administered perpendicularly to the long axis of fibers composing muscle, ligament, and joint capsules ▪ Massage should last 7-10 minutes and should be done every other day	▪ Breaks up adhesions ▪ Reduces local spasm ▪ Increases inflammatory response
Cupping	▪ A rhythmical, rapidly alternation series of brisk blows (tapotement) with the hands cupped	▪ Stimulatory
Trigger point massage	▪ Massage of a trigger point using small, circular motions ▪ Pressure is applied to patient tolerance	▪ Pain reduction
Effleurage	▪ Massage strokes glide over the skin from distal to proximal without attempting to move the deep muscle masses	▪ Improved venous and lymphatic flow ▪ Increased skin circulation
Petrissage	▪ Massage strokes attempt to lift the muscle mass and wring or squeeze them gently; kneading manipulations which press and roll the muscles under the hands ▪ Kneading should progress from distal to proximal, grasping parallel or perpendicular to the muscle fibers	▪ Milks the muscle of waste products ▪ Assists venous return ▪ Breaks up adhesions
Pincement	▪ Rapid, alternating, gentle pinching that picks up small portions of tissue between the thumb and first finger	▪ Stimulatory effect
Tapotement	▪ A series of brisk blows with the ulnar edge of the hand	▪ Stimulatory effect ▪ Increases circulation
Vibration	▪ Fine tremulous movement made by the hand or fingers placed firmly against the affected part	▪ Soothing effect, especially with peripheral neuritis
Myofascial release	▪ Mild combination of pressure and stretch	▪ Frees soft tissue restrictions

SUPPORTS (52)

ote

- Mechanical supports can be divided into four categories: immobilizing; supportive; corrective; protective.

SPINAL BRACING

Effects	▪ Decreased abdominal muscle activity ▪ Decreased intradisc pressure ▪ Decreased lower extremity venous return ▪ IVD immobilization ▪ Placebo effect ▪ Some reversal of abnormal function of spinal curvatures	▪ Increased intra-abdominal pressure ▪ Increased or decreased spinal muscle activity ▪ Increased segmental motion above and below the immobilized area ▪ Transfer of some vertical axis compression load of the spine to other structures
Indications	▪ Acute IVD syndrome ▪ Acute sprain/strain ▪ Degenerative joint disease ▪ Hyperkyphosis ▪ Hyperlordosis ▪ Vertebral collapse	▪ Joint stability ▪ Muscle spasm and guarding ▪ Postural backache ▪ Scoliosis ▪ Spinal fractures
Contraindications	▪ When immobilization promotes muscular atrophy and weakness ▪ When immobilization promotes the organization of inflammatory coagulant and consequent adhesions and/or fibrotic infiltration ▪ When immobilization may produce congestion, ischemia, or vascular stasis ▪ When immobilization may induce unsatisfactory stretching and/or contracture changes	

COMMON SUPPORTS

Cervical	Soft cervical collar
	Firm cervical collar
	Philadelphia collar
Thoracolumbo-sacral	Jewett brace
	Knight-Taylor brace
Lumbar and sacroiliac	Chairback brace
	Williams brace
	Lumbosacral corset
	Knight spinal brace
	Trochanteric belt
Scoliosis	Milwaukee brace
Extremities	Louisiana brace
	Lennox Hill brace
	Cock-up splint

MYOFASCIAL PAIN (53)

Trigger point

- A focus of hyperirritability in a tissue that, when compressed, is locally tender and, if sufficiently hypersensitivity, gives rise to referred pain and tenderness, and sometimes to referred autonomic phenomena and distortion of proprioception

Diagnosis of active myofascial trigger points

- History of sudden onset during or shortly following acute overload stress, or a history of gradual onset with chronic overload of the affected muscle
- Characteristic patterns of pain that are referred from myofascial trigger points; patterns that are specific to individual muscles
- Weakness and restriction in the stretch range of motion of the affected muscle
- A taut, palpable band in the affected muscle
- Focal tenderness to digital pressure at the trigger point
- A local twitch response elicited through snapping palpation or needling of the trigger point

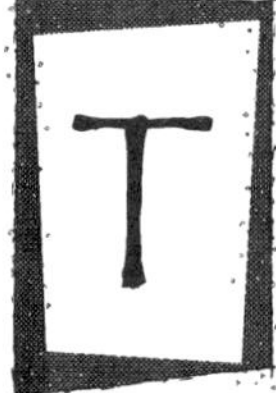

Treatment of trigger points

- ISCHEMIC COMPRESSION: pressure is applied to the trigger point; amount of pressure and time are determined by patient tolerance and physician preference. Usually pressure is applied for no more than one minute. Theories for effectiveness include ischemic nerve block; reflex vasodilation; release of enkephalins/endorphins; pressure causes a specific localized stretch. Named techniques for ischemic compression include: Nimmo technique and Myotherapy
- MUSCLE STRETCH: deactivation of trigger points by separating actin and myosin bridges
- MANUAL RESISTANCE TECHNIQUES: post-facilitation stretch (Janda) and post-isometric stretch (Lewit) both relax muscles for more effective stretching
- Ultrasound and micromassage can be used after ischemic compression to vasodilate and flush toxins from the area

Manual Resistance Techniques

PFS and PIR Stretching (54)

	Post-facilitation Stretch (PFS)	Post-isometric Stretch (PIR)
Purpose	▪ Inhibit muscles ▪ Mobilize joints	▪ Stretch hypertonic muscles ▪ Stretch fascia ▪ Ideal for trigger points, joint mobilization and neuromuscular tension
Contraction	▪ Maximal contraction in neutral position for 7 to 10 seconds	▪ 10% contraction from fully stretched position for 5 to 10 seconds
Stretch	▪ Quick and aggressive as patient relaxes and exhales; hold for 20 seconds	▪ Gentle and gradual as patient relaxes and exhales
Rest	▪ 20 seconds	▪ None
Repeat	▪ 3 to 5 times ▪ Return to neutral after each stretch	▪ 2 to 4 times ▪ Do not give up stretch attained

Ideal Postural Alignment (55)

Posterior View

- The cervical, thoracic and lumbar spines should be straight
- The head should not be tilted or rotated
- The shoulders should be level and neither elevated nor depressed
- The pelvis and hip joints should be level and the hips should be neither adducted nor abducted
- The knees should not have a valgus or varus deformity
- The feet should be parallel or slightly toeing out and neither supinated nor pronated

Lateral View

The plumb line should fall through the following surface landmarks:

- The ear lobe
- The glenohumeral joint (provided arms hang in normal alignment in relation to thorax)
- Approximately midway through the trunk
- The greater trochanter of the femur
- Slightly anterior to the mid-knee
- Slightly anterior to the lateral malleolus

Postural Muscles (56)

Postural Muscles (usually hyperactive)		Phasic Muscles (usually hypoactive)
▪ Triceps surae	▪ Psoas	▪ Tibialis Anterior
▪ Hamstrings	▪ Erector spinae	▪ Gluteus medius and maximus
▪ Adductors	▪ Quadratus lumborum	▪ Rectus abdominus
▪ Rectus femoris	▪ Pectoralis	▪ Lower/middle trapezius
▪ Tensor fascia lata	▪ Upper trapezius	▪ Scaleni/longus colli
▪ Sternocleidomastoid	▪ Suboccipitals	▪ Deltoids

Crossed Syndromes (57)

Syndrome	Facilitated	Inhibited	Posture
Shoulder-Neck Crossed Syndrome	▪ Pectoralis ▪ SCM ▪ UpperTrapezius ▪ Levator Scapula	▪ Deep Neck Flexors ▪ Mid Trapezius ▪ Rhomboids	▪ Flexion of lower cervicals, extension of upper cervicals ▪ May have difficulty swallowing ▪ May have breathing pattern change ▪ Anterior and posterior neck musculature tightness ▪ Look to scalenes and SCM for involvement
Pelvic-Hip Crossed Syndrome	▪ Lumbar Erector Spinae ▪ Hip Flexors	▪ Gluteals ▪ Abdominals	▪ Forward pelvic tilt ▪ Increased lumbar lordosis ▪ Slightly flexed hip ▪ Hamstrings frequently lengthened and taut
Layered Syndrome	▪ Cervical Erector Spinae ▪ Upper Trapezius ▪ Levator Scapula ▪ Thoracolumbar erector spinae ▪ Hamstrings	▪ Lower stabilizers of the scapula ▪ Lumbosacral erector spinae ▪ Gluteus maximus	▪ Overactive Obliquus Abdominus; weak rectus abdominus and transversus abdominus ▪ Poor muscular stability in the lumbosacral region which can predispose to development or perpetuation of low back pain ▪ Normal to slightly hypolordotic cervical curve ▪ No pelvic tilt ▪ Impairment of CNS motor regulation accompanied by poor movement patterns

Treatment (58)

The goal of treatment is to maintain good balance between muscle groups in terms of length and strength, coupled with coordinated, controlled motion and good posture. The exercise program can be broadly divided into the following three stages:

1. Restore normal muscle length to tight, overactive (facilitated) muscles.
2. Strengthening of muscles that are weak due to inhibition.
3. Restoration of optimal motor patterns to protect the spine. For example, for the patient with a pelvic-hip crossed syndrome, the doctor would stretch the lumbar erector spinae and hip flexors and strengthen the abdominals and gluteals.

TRACTION (59)

PHYSIOLOGIC RESPONSES

- *To separate or stretch spinal ligaments and/or extraspinal joint surfaces*
- *To promote distraction and gliding of joint facets*
- *To relieve muscle spasm*
- *To dissipate edema, especially if traction is applied intermittently*
- *To stretch fibrotic tissue and break adhesions*
- *To trigger proprioceptive reflexes*
- *To temporarily immobilize or splint parts (continuous traction)*

WEIGHT POUNDAGE

	Weight	Bilateral angle of pull
Cervical spine	▪ Start at 10 pounds and increase poundage gradually to patient tolerance ▪ Do not exceed 30 pounds	▪ CO-C2: 0 degrees of flexion ▪ C3-C7: head in 25-30 degrees of flexion
Lumbar spine	▪ Apply 25-50% of the patient's total body weight ▪ Do not exceed 120 pounds	▪ Determined by size of pillows and supports used
Intermittent	▪ Use 5-10% of the patient's total body weight ▪ Usual range is from 15-30 pounds	

GENERAL INDICATIONS AND CONTRAINDICATIONS

Indications	Contraindications
▪ IVD protrusion ▪ Degenerative disc disease ▪ Joint hypomobility ▪ Spinal nerve root impingement ▪ Muscle spasm ▪ Compression fractures	▪ Any condition where immobilization is indicated ▪ Osteoporosis, osteomalacia ▪ Pregnancy ▪ Local osseous infection ▪ Uncontrolled hypertension

ote

- Generally, static traction is used in acute cases, and intermittent traction is used in subacute and chronic disorders.

THERAPEUTIC EXERCISE (60)

TYPES OF EXERCISE

Type	Speed	Resistance	Characteristics
Isometric	▪ Fixed	▪ Fixed	▪ Does not produce joint motion ▪ Muscle maintains a fixed length ▪ Strength increases at a joint angle in which the exercise is performed with a 10 to 15 degree overflow
Isotonic	▪ Variable	▪ Fixed/variable	▪ Produced joint movement ▪ Muscle changes length
Isokinetic	▪ Fixed	▪ Variable	▪ Produces joint movement at a controlled rate of speed ▪ Resistance varies to exactly match the force applied at every point in the range of motion

ote

- The application of isometric exercise through a specific range of motion results in about 10 degrees of overflow (benefit to the patient) on each side of the application. Exercising just outside the point of pain in a range of motion provides physiologic overflow into the painful deformation and increases strength and decreases related pain.

TYPES OF MUSCLE CONTRACTIONS

 *Isotonic and isokinetic exercise can be divided into the following types of movement:*

Type of Movement	Characteristics
Concentric	▪ Muscle is contracted from an extended to a shortened position (origins and insertions approximate)
Eccentric	▪ A shortened/contracted muscle is lengthened against resistance (origins and insertions move apart)
Variable Resistance	▪ Specialized equipment permits varying amounts of resistance at specific points in the range of motion ▪ Increases the intensity and efficiency of the exercise

STAGES OF SOFT TISSUE HEALING

Stage	Duration	Signs and Characteristics
Stage 1: Acute, Reactive, Inflammatory	Forty-eight to 72 hours following trauma	▪ Redness, heat, swelling, pain ▪ Possible loss of function, range of motion and strength ▪ **Humoral response**: Blood coagulation, fibrinolytic responses to prevent widespread clotting, kinins to vasodilate blood vessels, and complement phagocytosis to remove cellular debris ▪ **Cellular responses**: mast cells release histamine and serotonin; granulocytes release prostaglandins
Stage 2: Repair and Regeneration	Forty-eight hours to six weeks following trauma	▪ **Repair**: removal of debris, regeneration of endothelial cells, fibroblast production ▪ **Healing**: formation of granulation tissue and tissue regeneration ▪ Increased vascular proliferation to replace disrupted blood vessels ▪ Formation of scar tissue (collagen production)
Stage 3: Remodeling	Three weeks to one year or more following trauma	▪ Remodeling takes place simultaneously with repair and regeneration ▪ Rehabilitative exercise promotes proper collagen healing resulting in a small flexible scar that does not impede functional performance ▪ **Davis' Law**: Soft tissue will model according to imposed demands

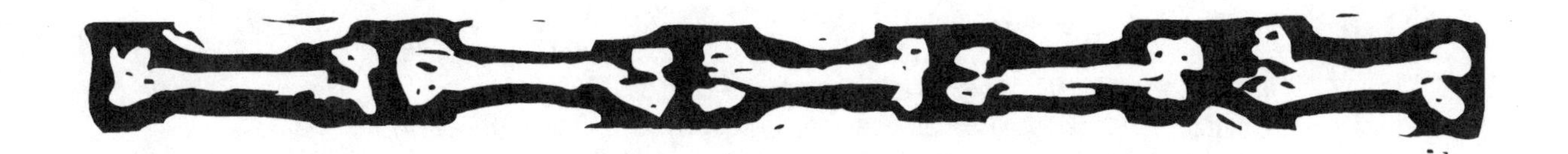

References

1 Prentice WE. Therapeutic Modalities in Relation to the Electromagnetic and Acoustic Spectra. In: Therapeutic Modalities in Sports Medicine. 3rd ed. St. Louis: Mosby, 1994: 1-12.
2 Jaskoviak PA. Applied Physiotherapy: Practical Clinical Applications with Emphasis on the Management of Pain and Related Syndromes. 2nd ed. Virginia: American Chiropractic Association, 1993: 131-134.
3 Prentice WE. Therapeutic Modalities in Sports Medicine. 3rd ed. St. Louis: Mosby, 1994: 5-7.
4 Prentice WE. Basic Principles of Electricity. In: Therapeutic Modalities in Sports Medicine. 3rd ed. St. Louis: Mosby, 1994: 49-71.
5 Forster A, Palastanga N. Clayton's Electrotherapy: Theory and Practice. 9th ed. London: Balliere Tindall, 1985: 1-28.
6 Jaskoviak PA. Applied Physiotherapy: Practical Clinical Applications with Emphasis on the Management of Pain and Related Syndromes. 2nd ed. Virginia: American Chiropractic Association, 1993: 269-277.
7 Jaskoviak PA. Applied Physiotherapy: Practical Clinical Applications with Emphasis on the Management of Pain and Related Syndromes. 2nd ed. Virginia: American Chiropractic Association, 1993: 277-278, 303-304.
8 Forster A, Palastanga N. Clayton's Electrotherapy: Theory and Practice. 9th ed. London: Balliere Tindall, 1985: 87-89, 95-96.
9 Aminoff MJ. Electromyography in Clinical Practice: Electrodiagnostic Aspects of Neuromuscular Disease. 2nd ed. New York: Churchill Livingstone, 1987: 219-220, 339.
10 Johnson EW. Practical Electromyography. 2nd ed. Baltimore: Williams & Wilkins, 1988:96-99.
11 Prentice WE. Therapeutic Modalities in Sports Medicine. 3rd ed. St. Louis: Mosby, 1994: 55-61.
12 Jaskoviak PA. Applied Physiotherapy: Practical Clinical Applications with Emphasis on the Management of Pain and Related Syndromes. 2nd ed. Virginia: American Chiropractic Association, 1993: 51-55.
13 Prentice WE. Therapeutic Modalities in Sports Medicine. 3rd ed. St. Louis: Mosby, 1994: 81, 92-93.
14 Prentice WE. Therapeutic Modalities in Sports Medicine. 3rd ed. St. Louis: Mosby, 1994: 96-106.
15 Forster A, Palastanga N. Clayton's Electrotherapy: Theory and Practice. 9th ed. London: Balliere Tindall, 1985: 82.
16 Jaskoviak PA. Applied Physiotherapy: Practical Clinical Applications with Emphasis on the Management of Pain and Related Syndromes. 2nd ed. Virginia: American Chiropractic Association, 1993: 269-295.
17 Jaskoviak PA. Applied Physiotherapy: Practical Clinical Applications with Emphasis on the Management of Pain and Related Syndromes. 2nd ed. Virginia: American Chiropractic Association, 1993: 288-302.
18 Kahn J. Principles and Practice of Electrotherapy. New York: Churchill Livingstone, 1987: 158.
19 Forster A, Palastanga N. Clayton's Electrotherapy: Theory and Practice. 9th ed. London: Balliere Tindall, 1985: 86.
20 Jaskoviak PA. Applied Physiotherapy: Practical Clinical Applications with Emphasis on the Management of Pain and Related Syndromes. 2nd ed. Virginia: American Chiropractic Association, 1993: 300-302.
21 Jaskoviak PA. Applied Physiotherapy: Practical Clinical Applications with Emphasis on the Management of Pain and Related Syndromes. 2nd ed. Virginia: American Chiropractic Association, 1993: 305-309.
22 Jaskoviak PA. Applied Physiotherapy: Practical Clinical Applications with Emphasis on the Management of Pain and Related Syndromes. 2nd ed. Virginia: American Chiropractic Association, 1993: 381-396.
23 Jaskoviak PA. Applied Physiotherapy: Practical Clinical Applications with Emphasis on the Management of Pain and Related Syndromes. 2nd ed. Virginia: American Chiropractic Association, 1993: 349-380.
24 Jaskoviak PA. Applied Physiotherapy: Practical Clinical Applications with Emphasis on the Management of Pain and Related Syndromes. 2nd ed. Virginia: American Chiropractic Association, 1993: 323-348.
25 McDonald JC, Lundgren KL, Thieme HA. Therapeutic Modalities. 3rd ed. Clinical Education Associates: 1995: IV-1, V-1.
26 Jaskoviak PA. Applied Physiotherapy: Practical Clinical Applications with Emphasis on the Management of Pain and Related Syndromes. 2nd ed. Virginia: American Chiropractic Association, 1993: 132-139, 247.
27 Kahn J. Principles and Practice of Electrotherapy. New York: Churchill Livingstone, 1987: 158.

28 Jaskoviak PA. Applied Physiotherapy: Practical Clinical Applications with Emphasis on the Management of Pain and Related Syndromes. 2nd ed. Virginia: American Chiropractic Association, 1993: 136-138.
29 Jaskoviak PA. Applied Physiotherapy: Practical Clinical Applications with Emphasis on the Management of Pain and Related Syndromes. 2nd ed. Virginia: American Chiropractic Association, 1993: 140.
30 Prentice WE. Therapeutic Modalities in Sports Medicine. 3rd ed. St. Louis: Mosby, 1994: 3, 175, 239-254.
31 Jaskoviak PA. Applied Physiotherapy: Practical Clinical Applications with Emphasis on the Management of Pain and Related Syndromes. 2nd ed. Virginia: American Chiropractic Association, 1993: 147-163.
32 Prentice WE. Therapeutic Modalities in Sports Medicine. 3rd ed. St. Louis: Mosby, 1994: 252.
33 Jaskoviak PA. Applied Physiotherapy: Practical Clinical Applications with Emphasis on the Management of Pain and Related Syndromes. 2nd ed. Virginia: American Chiropractic Association, 1993: 156.
34 Jaskoviak PA. Applied Physiotherapy: Practical Clinical Applications with Emphasis on the Management of Pain and Related Syndromes. 2nd ed. Virginia: American Chiropractic Association, 1993: 157-159, 160-161.
35 Kahn J. Principles and Practice of Electrotherapy. New York: Churchill Livingstone, 1987: 47.
36 Jaskoviak PA. Applied Physiotherapy: Practical Clinical Applications with Emphasis on the Management of Pain and Related Syndromes. 2nd ed. Virginia: American Chiropractic Association, 1993: 163-177, 403-411.
37 Bell GW, Prentice WE. Infrared Modalities. In: Therapeutic Modalities in Sports Medicine. 3rd ed. St. Louis: Mosby, 1994: 175-213.
38 Kahn J. Principles and Practice of Electrotherapy. New York: Churchill Livingstone, 1987: 7-19.
39 Jaskoviak PA. Applied Physiotherapy: Practical Clinical Applications with Emphasis on the Management of Pain and Related Syndromes. 2nd ed. Virginia: American Chiropractic Association, 1993: 184-217.
40 Prentice WE. Therapeutic Modalities in Sports Medicine. 3rd ed. St. Louis: Mosby, 1994: 8.
41 Jaskoviak PA. Applied Physiotherapy: Practical Clinical Applications with Emphasis on the Management of Pain and Related Syndromes. 2nd ed. Virginia: American Chiropractic Association, 1993: 217-241.
42 Prentice WE. Therapeutic Modalities in Sports Medicine. 3rd ed. St. Louis: Mosby, 1994: 10, 255-282.
43 Kahn J. Principles and Practice of Electrotherapy. New York: Churchill Livingstone, 1987: 69-91.
44 Jaskoviak PA. Applied Physiotherapy: Practical Clinical Applications with Emphasis on the Management of Pain and Related Syndromes. 2nd ed. Virginia: American Chiropractic Association, 1993: 217-241.
45 Prentice WE. Therapeutic Modalities in Sports Medicine. 3rd ed. St. Louis: Mosby, 1994: 263.
46 Prentice WE. Therapeutic Modalities in Sports Medicine. 3rd ed. St. Louis: Mosby, 1994: 175-183.
47 Jaskoviak PA. Applied Physiotherapy: Practical Clinical Applications with Emphasis on the Management of Pain and Related Syndromes. 2nd ed. Virginia: American Chiropractic Association, 1993: 134, 249.
48 Prentice WE. Therapeutic Modalities in Sports Medicine. 3rd ed. St. Louis: Mosby, 1994: 184-192.
49 Travell JG, Simons DG. Myofascial Pain and Dysfunction: The Trigger Point Manual. Baltimore: Williams & Wilkins, 1983: 65-70.
50 Tappan FM. Healing Massage Techniques: A Study of Western Methods. Virginia: Prentice-Hall, 1980: 18-23, 44-67.
51 Prentice WE. Therapeutic Modalities in Sports Medicine. 3rd ed. St. Louis: Mosby, 1994: 335-363.
52 Jaskoviak PA. Applied Physiotherapy: Practical Clinical Applications with Emphasis on the Management of Pain and Related Syndromes. 2nd ed. Virginia: American Chiropractic Association, 1993: 451-465.
53 Travell JG, Simons DG. Myofascial Pain and Dysfunction: The Trigger Point Manual. Baltimore: Williams & Wilkins, 1983: 2, 4, 18-19.
54 Liebenson C. Rehabilitation of the Spine. Baltimore: Williams & Wilkins, 1996: 257.
55 Kendall FP, McCreary EK, Provance PG. Muscles: Testing and Function. 4th ed. Baltimore: Williams & Wilkins, 1993: 75, 88.
56 Liebenson C. Rehabilitation of the Spine. Baltimore: Williams & Wilkins, 1996: 26.
57 Jull G, Janda V. Muscles and Motor Control in Low Back Pain: Assessment and Management. In: Twomey LT, Taloer JR (eds). Physical Therapy for the Low Back; Clinics in Physical Therapy. New York: Churchill Livingstone, 1987: 260-263.
58 Jull G, Janda V. Muscles and Motor Control in Low Back Pain: Assessment and Management. In: Twomey LT, Taloer JR (eds). Physical Therapy for the Low Back; Clinics in Physical Therapy. New York: Churchill Livingstone, 1987: 272.
59 Jaskoviak PA. Applied Physiotherapy: Practical Clinical Applications with Emphasis on the Management of Pain and Related Syndromes. 2nd ed. Virginia: American Chiropractic Association, 1993: 421-438.
60 Jaskoviak PA. Applied Physiotherapy: Practical Clinical Applications with Emphasis on the Management of Pain and Related Syndromes. 2nd ed. Virginia: American Chiropractic Association, 1993: 477-483.

CHAPTER 2

X-Ray Positioning

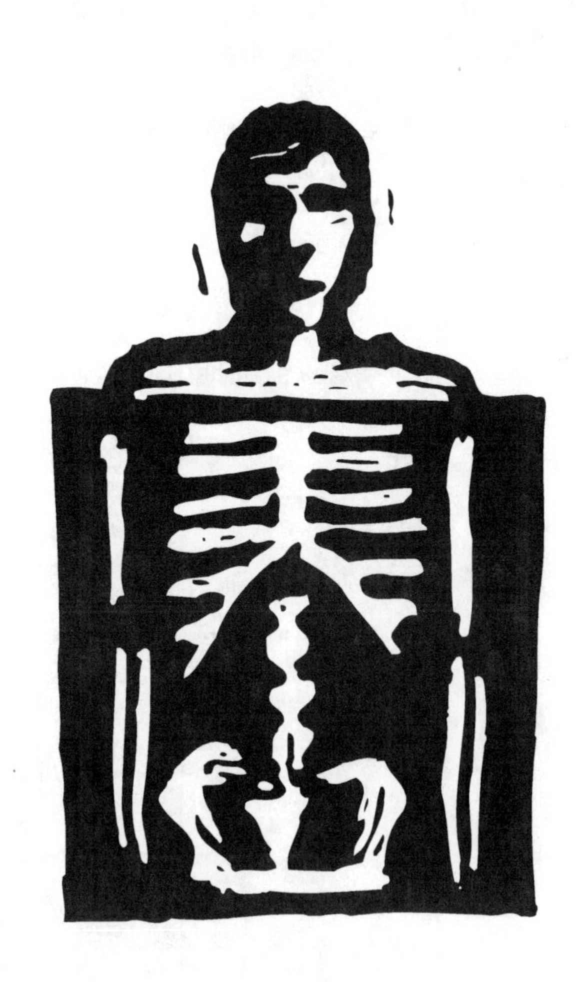

PATIENT PREPARATION

Remember

- Screen the patient for contraindications to radiographs.
- Have the patient remove all jewelry and metal and make sure the patient is properly gowned.
- Make sure the patient's arms are away from the film.
- Seat tall people for cervical shots.
- Use the gray border cassettes for extremity shots.
- The patient should have at least one body part touching the bucky (not necessarily the part being filmed).
- Give the patient instructions ("Don't breathe; don't move").

THE 10-DAY RULE

Elective x-ray examinations involving pelvic irradiation of a female should be done in the first 10 days following the onset of menstruation. (1) In the following example, menses began on day 10 of the month.

Period during which x-ray examination of a female involving irradiation of the pelvis should be conducted.

1	2	3	4	5	6	7
8	9	10 **Onset of Menses**	11	12	13	14
15	16	17	18	19	20	21
22	23	24	25	26	27	28
29	30					

THE CERVICAL SPINE (2)

SHOT	DIST	FILM SIZE	CENTRAL RAY	COLLIMATION	TUBE TILT	NOTES
AP Cervical	40	10 x 12	C4 at the thyroid cartilage	Just below the lip and just (about 1 inch) outside the soft tissues of the neck	15 degrees cephalad	Used to view the von Luschka joints, especially of the lower five vertebrae
APOM	40	8 x 10	Line up the lower border of the upper incisors and the tips of the mastoid processes perpendicular to the film; shoot through the uvula	Below the patient's eyes, and include the mastoid processes and exclude the lower border of the jaw	None	Patient holds suspended expiration
Flexion	72	10 x 12 with cassette holder	C4	Look for the same amount of light on each side of the patient's neck; collimate behind the eyes	None	Patient tucks his or her chin then flexes the head as much as possible
Extension	72	10 x 12 with cassette holder	C4	Look for the same amount of light on each side of the patient's neck	None	Patient looks up with eyes open
Lateral	72	10 x 12 with cassette holder	C4	Top of the ear and just behind the eyes; look for the same amount of light on each side of the patient's neck	None	Patient should hold his or her breath to prevent movement; instructions to patients for all cervical spine shots: "Don't breathe; don't move"
Oblique	72 or 40	10 x 12	C4	Look for the same amount of light on each side of the patient's neck	▪ 15 degrees caudad for **anterior obliques** ▪ 15 degrees cephalad for **posterior obliques**	Turn the patient 45 degrees to the film; turn the patient's head parallel to bucky NOTE: seat tall patients, especially for shots done at 72 inches RPO = left IVF RAO = Right IVF

THE SKULL (2)

SHOT	DIST	FILM SIZE	CENTRAL RAY	COLLIMATION	TUBE TILT	SPECIAL INSTRUCTIONS
Lateral Skull	40	10 x 12 horizontal	Central ray is ¾" anterior to and ¾" superior to the EAM	Make sure entire skull is on the film; ½ inch border all around; the infraorbital meatal line is parallel to the long edge of the cassette, and the interpupillary line is perpendicular to the cassette	None	▪ Take both left and right views ▪ Demonstrates lateral cranial structures closest to the bucky (i.e. sella turcica).
Caldwell's View	40	10 x 12	Central ray should exit through the patient's nose bridge (nasion)	Include the entire skull; frontal bone is in contact with the bucky and the orbital meatal line should be perpendicular to the cassette	15 degrees caudad	▪ Used to see frontal region, sinuses
Town's View	40	10 x 12 with table	Line up the orbital meatal line (tuck the chin to do this) perpendicular to the cassette; central ray passes through the midline at the external auditory meatus	½ inch borders all around	35 degree caudad	▪ Used to visualize posterior structures: occiput, foramen magnum
Water's View	40	10 x 12	Through the nasion	The head is extended such that the orbitomeatal line is elevated 37 degrees relative to the central ray; collimate to film size	None	▪ Instruct the patient to put his or her chin and nose on the midline of the bucky ▪ Demonstrates the maxillary sinuses, ethmoid sinuses, frontal sinuses, orbits, and zygomatic arches

THE THORACIC SPINE (2)

SHOT	DIST	FILM SIZE	CENTRAL RAY	COLLIMATION	TUBE TILT	SPECIAL INSTRUCTIONS
AP	40	14 x 17	Place bucky 2 inches above C7 first, then put the central ray at the center of the bucky	½" vertical border and mid-clavicular line	None	▪ Get down to eye level with the top of the bucky and line up the bucky first ▪ Patient holds his/her breath on inspiration in order to lower the diaphragm
Lateral	40	14 x 17	Place bucky 2 inches above C7 first, then put the central ray at the center of the bucky	Collimate to the size of the thoracic spine	None	▪ Arms crossed in front of the patient; hold breath on inspiration to depress the diaphragm ▪ Don't expose breast tissue
Swimmer's View (Lateral Cervicothoracic Junction)	40	10 x 12	Horizontal central ray at sternal notch; vertical central ray at the SCM or just anterior to the shoulder closest to the tube	½" borders	None	▪ Raise the bucky-side arm high then place on top of head; extend the tube-side arm back and then place on the hip ▪ Instruct the patient to hold his or her breath ▪ Get the shoulders out of the way as best you can without turning the patient into an oblique position; patient's head should look straight ahead

THE LUMBAR (LUMBOPELVIC) SPINE (2)

SHOT	DIST	FILM SIZE	CENTRAL RAY	COLLI-MATION	TUBE TILT	SPECIAL INSTRUCTIONS
AP	40	14 x 17	Place the central ray 1 ½ inches below iliac crest, then line up the bucky with the central ray	½" border all around	None	▪ Patient exhales and holds for shot
Lateral	40	14 x 17	Place the central ray one inch above the iliac crest, with the vertical central ray passing halfway between the ASIS and PSIS then center the film to the central ray	½" border all around	None	▪ Patient exhales and holds for this shot
Oblique	40	14 x 17	▪ **Anterior**: 1 inch lateral to the L3 spinous process ▪ **Posterior**: 1 inch above the iliac crest and 2 inches medial to the ASIS	½" borders top and bottom, open the width according to the patient's lordosis	None	▪ Place patient 45 degrees to bucky with arms away from the film ▪ Patient exhales and holds for shot ▪ Used to visualize facets and pars RAO= left facets RPO= right facets

Lumbopelvic Spot Shots

SHOT	DIST	FILM SIZE	CENTRAL RAY	COLLI-MATION	TUBE TILT	SPECIAL INSTRUCTIONS
Angulated Lumbo-Sacral (AP L5 disc) Spot Shot	40	8 x 10 or 10 x 12	▪ **For P to A**: Palpate the lumbosacral junction, place the central ray at this point then line up the bucky ▪ **For A to P**: Palpate the lumbosacral junction, line up the bucky to the patient, then line up the central ray to the bucky; central ray should be halfway between the umbilicus and the pubic articulation	½" border all around	20 degrees cephalad, or coordinate tube tilt with patient's known lumbosacral lordosis PA-caudad AP-cephalad	▪ You can shoot the lateral lumbosacral view first to determine the patient's angle of lordosis
Lateral L5/S1 Lumbo-Sacral Spot Shot	40	8 x 10 or 10 x 12	Place central ray one inch below the iliac crest then center the film to the central ray	Collimate to size of anatomy	None	▪ Patient lifts arms

The Sacrum and The Coccyx (2)

SHOT	DIST	FILM SIZE	CENTRAL RAY	COLLIMATION	TUBE TILT	SPECIAL INSTRUCTIONS
AP/ PA Sacrum	40	10 x 12	**AP**: place the central ray midway between the pubic symphysis and the ASIS then center the film to the central ray	½" border all around	**A to P**: 15-25 degrees cephalad	▪ Patient holds suspended expiration
Lateral Sacrum	40	10 x 12	Place the central ray at the ASIS level, two inches posterior to the sacral surface then center the film to the central ray	½" border all around	None	▪ Central ray can be lower to see sacrum and coccyx
AP / PA Coccyx	40	8 x 10	**AP**: place the central ray 2 ½ inches above the symphysis pubis then center the film to the central ray	5 x 5 inch box	**A to P**: 5-10 degrees caudad	▪ Patient holds suspended expiration
Lateral Coccyx	40	8 x 10	Two inches in front of the sacrococcygeal junction	8 x 8 inch box	None	▪ Patient holds suspended expiration
A to P Pelvis	40	14 x 17 sideways	Place the central ray midway between the symphysis pubis and iliac crest then center the film to the central ray	½" border all around	None	▪ Palpate the crests; male iliac crests are higher than female iliac crests ▪ Internally rotate the femurs 15 degrees

The Upper Extremity (2)

SHOT	DIST	FILM SIZE	CENTRAL RAY	COLLIMATION	SPECIAL INSTRUCTIONS
Shoulder Internal Rotation	40	10 x 12	Rotate the patient 30 degrees to the bucky, center the coracoid process to the bucky and internally rotate the arm until the epicondyles of the elbow are perpendicular to the film	½" border all around	▪ Patient puts dorsum of wrist on hip for internal rotation ▪ Black border cassette ▪ "Don't breathe; don't move"
Shoulder External Rotation	40	10 x 12	Rotate the patient 30 degrees to the bucky, center the coracoid process to the bucky and externally rotate the elbow until the epicondyles of the elbow are parallel to the film	½" border all around	▪ Patient rotates palm toward film ▪ Black border cassette ▪ "Don't breathe; don't move"
AP Elbow	40	AP elbow and oblique elbow each on ½ of 10x12 on tabletop; use lead shield to mask film	Patient kneels at edge of table, central ray at crease of fully extended elbow, centered on film	½" border on half of film or enough to cover soft tissues	▪ Palm is face up with arm flat and in full extension on the film ▪ Extremity cassette ▪ "Don't move"
Oblique Elbow	40		Central ray at crease of elbow, centered on film; arm is fully extended and forearm is pronated	½" border on half of film or enough to cover soft tissues	▪ Patient rolls shoulder to externally rotate forearm with forearm in full extension; joint is 45 degrees to film ▪ Extremity (gray border) cassette ▪ "Don't move"
Lateral Elbow	40	8 x 10	Patient still kneeling, flex elbow to 90 and place flat on film with the shoulder at the same level as the elbow; point thumb up; palpate lateral epicondyle and place central ray just anterior to the lateral epicondyle	½" border all around	▪ Extremity (gray border) cassette ▪ "Don't move"

The Upper Extremity, Cont'd (2)

SHOT	DIST	FILM SIZE	CENTRAL RAY	COLLIMATION	TUBE TILT	SPECIAL INSTRUCTIONS
PA Clavicle	40	10 x 12 horizontal; no tube tilt	Turn patient's head away from clavicle to be x-rayed in order to place clavicle as close to bucky as possible; midpoint of clavicle is centered to the midline of the bucky and central ray is through the midclavicle and 1 inch above the level of the clavicle at the patient's back	½" border width, include clavicle top and bottom	None	▪ "Don't breath; don't move"
Unilateral AC Joint ▪ *Bilateral AP views are discouraged unless the thyroid is shielded*	40	8 x 10 horizontal; no tube tilt	Acromioclavicular joint is centered to the bucky, and central ray is through the acromioclavicular joint	Collimate to size of anatomy, approximately 5 x 5	None	▪ "Don't breath; don't move"

ote

- The acromioclavicular joint view is taken with and without the patient holding 10 to 15 pound weights to assess the integrity of acromioclavicular and costoclavicular ligaments.

SHOT	DIST	FILM SIZE	CENTRAL RAY	COLLIMATION	SPECIAL INSTRUCTIONS
PA Wrist	40	1/3 of 10 x 12; shield 2/3 of the film each time	Through mid-carpals; have patient make a fist	Don't need to see the entire hand	
Oblique Wrist	40		Patient makes "OK" sign - carpals are 45 degrees to the film; central ray through mid-carpals		
Lateral Wrist	40		Point thumb toward ceiling; central ray through mid-carpals		▪ Keep thumb out of the way of the carpals
PA Hand	40	PA and oblique on 10x12; shield the part of the film not being used	Place the patient's hand in the center of the film, then place the central ray through the third metacarpal head	Include the entire hand and make sure it is flat on the film	
Oblique Hand	40		Make the "OK" sign with hand semipronated to be 45 degrees to the film and place central ray between the second and third metacarpal heads	Include entire hand and make sure the lateral surface and finger tips are touching the film	
Lateral Hand	40	8 x 10		Include entire hand and make sure the lateral surface is flat on the film	
Lateral Thumb	40	8 x 10 for three thumb views; shield the part of the film not being used	Patient lifts fingers off film, holds thumb on film; central ray through the MCP joints	Just outside the soft tissue, but include all parts of thumb	
Oblique Thumb	40		Hand is flat on the film		
AP Thumb	40		Roll hand over, placing thumb nail flat on the film		▪ Make sure thumb is A to P

Remember:

- Use extremity (gray border) cassettes for these shots.

The Lower Extremity (2)

SHOT	DIST	FILM SIZE	CENTRAL RAY	COLLIMATION	TUBE TILT	SPECIAL INSTRUCTIONS
AP Hip	40	10 x 12	Palpate the ASIS, flex patient's knee up to 90, place central ray halfway along crease at the level of the top of the greater trochanter; patient must internally rotate the leg 15 degrees	½" border all around	None	▪ Could use gonadal shields ▪ Black border cassette
Frog Leg	40	10 x 12	Have patient cross leg over opposite knee, place central ray half-way along the crease	½" border all around	None	▪ Have patient hold onto the sides of the bucky to stabilize ▪ Black border cassette
AP Knee	40 on table top	10 x 12	Place the central ray one cm inferior to the apex of the patella then center the film to the central ray	½" border all around; be sure joint is fully extended	None	▪ Extremity (gray border) cassette
Oblique Knee	40 on table top	10 x 12	Patient internally rotates leg 45 degrees to the film	½" border all around	None	▪ Extremity (gray border) cassette
Lateral Knee	40 on table top	8 x 10	Flex the knee 20 degrees; patient lies on side of leg being filmed, crosses top leg over bottom leg; central ray one cm distal to the medial epicondyle	½" border all around	None	▪ Be sure to include patella ▪ Extremity (gray border) cassette
Tunnel View of the Knee	40 on table top	8 x 10	Patient on all fours, with involved knee on film and other leg forward; central ray goes on joint space; create a 25 degree angle between femur and tube (25 degrees off the vertical)	½" border all around	None	▪ For Osteochondritis Dessicans ▪ Extremity (gray border) cassette
Sunrise View of the Knee	40 on table top	8 x 10	Patient lies on his or her stomach, flex knee maximally; central just below patella	5 x 5 box	10 degrees cephalad	▪ To visualize patellofemoral joint ▪ Extremity (gray border) cassette

Remember

- The only shots with tube tilts for the lower extremity are: AP and oblique foot and the Sunrise view of the knee, all with 10 degree cephalad tube tilts.

SHOT	DIST	FILM SIZE	CENTRAL RAY	COLLIMATION	TUBE TILT	SPECIAL INSTRUCTIONS
AP Ankle	40	10 x 12	Between and just proximal to malleoli; bend ankle to 90 degrees	½" borders top and bottom, just outside soft tissue	None	▪ Use the shield if placing more than one shot on one film
Oblique Ankle	40	10 x 12	Internally rotate 45 degrees and dorsiflex 90 degrees; between and just proximal to malleoli	½" borders top and bottom, just outside soft tissue	None	
Lateral Ankle	40	10 x 12 or 8 x 10	Patient bends or lies on side; central ray between and just proximal to malleoli; dorsiflex the foot 90 degrees	½" borders top and bottom, just outside soft tissue	None	

SHOT	DIST	FILM SIZE	CENTRAL RAY	COLLIMATION	TUBE TILT	SPECIAL INSTRUCTIONS
AP foot	40	½ of 10 x 12 lengthwise	Foot flat on film; central ray is centered on film and includes the entire foot	Include entire foot	10 degrees cephalad	
Oblique Foot	40		Internally rotate foot 45 degrees to the film; center foot on film, center the central ray to film	Include entire foot	10 degrees cephalad	
Lateral Foot	40	8 x 10 or 10 x 12	Position foot diagonally on film with the fifth metatarsal in contact with the film; lie patient on side or have patient sit cross legged	Include entire foot	None	

emember

- No tube tilt for ankle shots.
- Extremity cassettes have only one intensifying screen or smaller crystals and less crystal layers; both of these increase detail.

Full Spine Series

SHOT	DIST	FILM SIZE	CENTRAL RAY	COLLIMATION	TUBE TILT	SPECIAL INSTRUCTIONS
AP Cervical	40	10 x 12	C4 at the thyroid cartilage	Just below the lip and just (about 1 inch) outside the soft tissues of the neck	15 degrees cephalad	Used to view the von Luschka joints, especially of the lower five vertebrae
APOM	40	8 x 10	Line up the lower border of the upper incisors and the tips of the mastoid processes perpendicular to the film; shoot through the uvula	Below the patient's eyes, and include the mastoid processes and exclude the lower border of the jaw	None	Patient holds suspended expiration
Lateral Cervical	72	10 x 12 with cassette holder	C4	Top of the ear and just behind the eyes; look for the same amount of light on each side of the patient's neck	None	Patient should hold his or her breath to prevent movement; instructions to patients for all cervical spine shots: "Don't breathe; don't move"
AP Thoracic	40	14 x 17	Place bucky 2 inches above C7 first, then put the central ray at the center of the bucky	½" vertical border and mid-clavicular line	None	▪ Get down to eye level with the top of the bucky and line up the bucky first ▪ Patient holds his/her breath on inspiration in order to lower the diaphragm
Lateral Thoracic	40	14 x 17	Place bucky 2 inches above C7 first, then put the central ray at the center of the bucky	Collimate to the size of the thoracic spine	None	▪ Arms crossed in front of the patient; hold breath on inspiration to depress the diaphragm ▪ Don't expose breast tissue
AP Lumbar	40	14 x 17	Place the central ray 1 ½ inches below iliac crest, then line up the bucky with the central ray	½" border all around	None	▪ Patient exhales and holds for shot
Lateral Lumbar	40	14 x 17	Place the central ray one inch above the iliac crest, with the vertical central ray passing halfway between the ASIS and PSIS then center the film to the central ray	½" border all around	None	▪ Patient exhales and holds for this shot

X-RAY PHYSICS (3)

RADIOGRAPHIC FACTORS

Factor	Primary Factor	Results of an Increase or Decrease	Definition
Contrast (Quality)	kV	▪ The higher the kV, the lower the contrast (longer scale of contrast; more shades of gray) ▪ The lower the kV, the higher the contrast (shorter scale of contrast; less shades of gray)	▪ Refers to the differences between the black, white and gray shadows on a radiograph ▪ High contrast means there will be black and white and little gray; minimal contrast means there will be a lot of gray with little black and white ▪ The greater the kV, the shorter the wavelength and the greater the penetration power of the beam ▪ Quality; determines wavelength of x-rays produced
Density (Quantity)	MAS	▪ The greater the MAS, the greater the density (more boiling off of electrons; more patient exposure) ▪ The lower the MAS, the lower the density	▪ Refers to the amount of light that will pass through the film when it is held to a viewing box ▪ The amount of density is directly proportional to the percentage of blacks and grays compared to whites; the greater the percentage of blacks and grays, the greater the density
Detail	Size of the focal spot	▪ The larger the focal spot, the poorer the detail ▪ The smaller the focal spot, the better the detail	▪ The delineation between structures ▪ Penumbra
Distortion	▪ Film-anode distance ▪ Part-film distance	▪ The greater the film-anode distance, the less the distortion ▪ The shorter the film-anode distance, the greater the distortion ▪ The greater the part-film distance, the greater the distortion ▪ The less the part-film distance, the less the distortion	▪ The misrepresentation of an anatomical structure on a radiograph ▪ Magnification

Density and Contrast (3)

- There is no definite mathematical relationship between the kV and MAS; only rough estimates are possible
- An increase in kV will cause a decrease in contrast even though the MAS may be altered to maintain average density; a decrease in kV results in an increase in contrast even though the MAS is changed to maintain correct density
- If you increase the kV by 16%, you must decrease the MAS by 50% to maintain the same film density
- If you decrease the kV by 16%, you must double the MAS to maintain the same film density

Inverse Square Law (3)

- If you double the tube-film distance, you must increase the MAS four times to maintain the same film density
- If you decrease the tube-film distance by half, you must decrease the MAS to 1/4 of the original value to maintain the same film density

Exposure (3)

- RAD (Radiation Absorbed Dose) = REM (Roentgen Equivalent in Man)
- Occupational MPD (Maximum Permissible Dose) = 5(AGE – 18) RADs
- Weekly maximum exposure = 0.1 RADs
- Maximum public exposure = 0.5 RADs/year
- Lethal dose = n/x where n= % exposed who will die and x=number of days within which they will die.
- INTENSIFYING SCREENS emit light when struck by x-rays. They reduce patient exposure but increase distortion. The fastest screens contain rare earth elements
- The BUCKY AND GRID prevent widely scattered radiation from striking the film. They increase patient exposure but reduce distortion

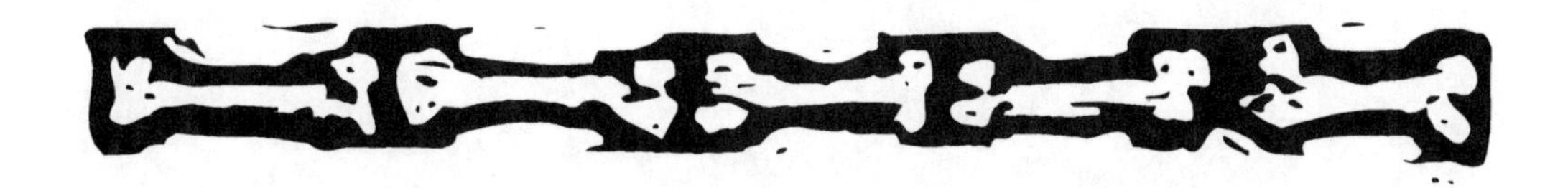

REFERENCES

1 Howe JW, Yochum TR. X-Ray, Pregnancy, and Therapeutic Abortion: A Current Perspective. ACA Journal of Chiropractic; 1985; 19(4):79.

2 Yochum TR, Rowe LJ. Essentials of Skeletal Radiology. Vol. One and Two. 2nd Edition. Baltimore: Williams & Wilkins, 1996: 10-125.

3 McDonnell JJ. A Manual of X-ray Physics. 1st ed. New York: New York Chiropractic College, 1966:27-28, 30-32, 36-38.

CHAPTER 3

X-Ray Diagnosis & Advanced Imaging

SCOLIOSIS (1)

MENSURATION

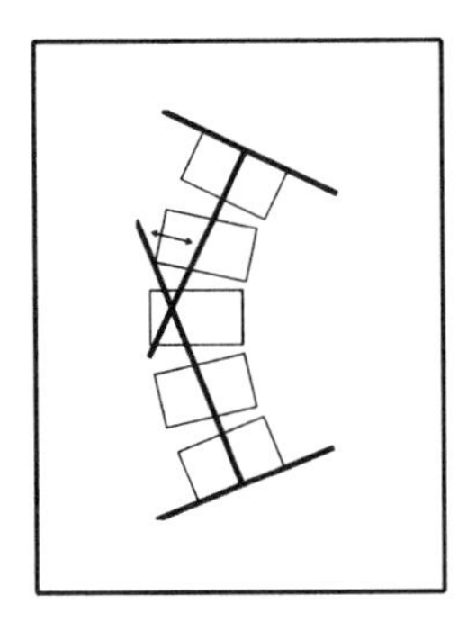

Cobb Method: On an anterior to posterior thoracic or thoracolumbar view, one line is drawn parallel to the superior endplate of the most superior segment involved in the curve and another is drawn parallel to the inferior endplate of the most inferior segment involved. Perpendiculars are drawn from each line and the acute angle is measured.

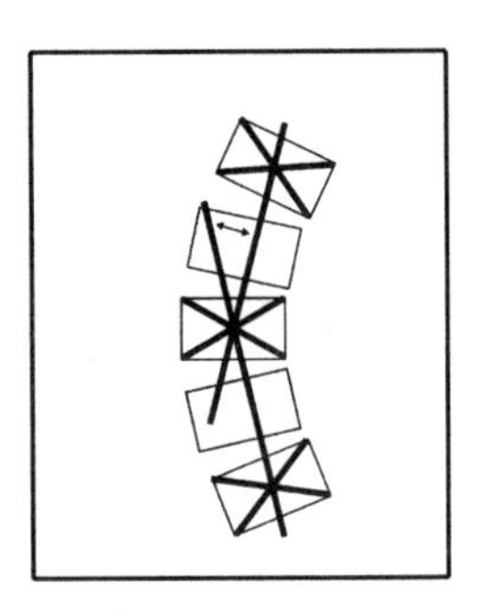

Risser-Ferguson Method: On an anterior to posterior thoracic or thoracolumbar view, the centers of the most superior, the most inferior and the apical vertebrae of the scoliosis are connected and the acute angle is measured. This method produces measurements of approximately 10 degrees less than the Cobb technique.

ROTATION

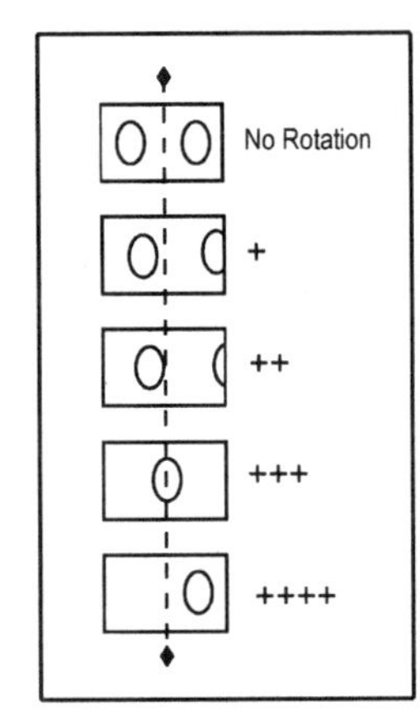

Pedicle Method: The movement of the pedicle on the convex side of the curve is graded between 0 and 4 and is a measure of anterior deformity.

+	Pedicle is midway between the lateral border and the midline
++	Pedicle touches the midline
+++	Pedicle sits in the midline
++++	Pedicle crosses the midline

Skeletal Dysplasias (2)

DYSPLASIA	SPINE	SKULL	PELVIS / THORAX	EXTREMITIES / RIBS
Achondroplasia ▪ Most common cause of congenital dwarfism ▪ Autosomal dominant disturbance in epiphyseal chondroblastic growth and maturation	▪ Narrowing of the spinal canal; narrowed interpedicular distance ▪ Bullet-nosed vertebrae ▪ Posterior scalloping of vertebral bodies	▪ Base of the skull is small; often stenotic foramen magnum ▪ Basilar impression frequent ▪ Prominent frontal bones, small nasal bones	▪ Entire pelvis is small ▪ Ilia are shortened caudally and flattened, with small sciatic notches ▪ Champagne glass pelvis	▪ Symmetric shortening of all long bones ▪ Trident hands
Cleidocranial Dysplasia ▪ Faulty ossification of the intramembranous bones, especially the clavicle, skull and midline	▪ Biconvex vertebral bodies ▪ Spina bifida occulta especially in the cervical and upper thoracic spine ▪ Neural arch defects ▪ Hemivertebra	▪ Multiple Wormian bones ▪ Persistent metopic suture ▪ "Hot cross bun" appearance: widening of sagittal and coronal sutures ▪ Small face due to underdeveloped facial bones ▪ Delayed and defective dentition ▪ Deformed, enlarged foramen magnum ▪ "Light bulb" skull	▪ Anomalous clavicular development (10% completely absent) ▪ Often small, winged or absent scapulae ▪ Early coxa valgus develops into coxa varus	▪ Ribs are normal but chest is narrow and cone-shaped ▪ Elongated second metacarpal ▪ Distal phalanges are hypoplastic and often pointed: "Crayon" appearance
Infantile Cortical Hyperostosis ▪ Presents before age 5 months ▪ Likes mandible, clavicle and ribs; symmetrical involvement ▪ AKA Caffey's disease	▪ Periosteal new bone formation within soft tissue swelling adjacent to the cortex ▪ Laminated appearance of new bone	▪ Thickening of the calvarium or destructive lesions ▪ Mandible usually involved	▪ Clavicle, mandible and ribs are the most commonly involved bones	▪ Cortical hyperostosis is most prominent in the lateral arches of the ribs ▪ Epiphyses spared when long bone involvement occurs ▪ Likes the ulna

DYSPLASIA	SPINE	PELVIS / THORAX	EXTREMITIES / RIBS
Marfan's Syndrome ▪ Problem with collagen formation that involves three systems: skeletal, ocular, and cardiovascular (dissecting aneurysm)	▪ Tall vertebrae ▪ Severe scoliosis or kyphoscoliosis ▪ Widened spinal canal (>50%), especially the lumbosacral region ▪ Posterior scalloping of vertebral bodies ▪ Thinning of pedicles and lamina	▪ Acetabular protrusion, uni- or bilateral (50%) ▪ Pectus excavatum with elongated ribs	▪ Elongations of the extremities; esp. tubular bones of hands and feet (arachnodactyly) ▪ No osteoporosis ▪ Thinned cortices
Fibrodysplasia Ossificans Progressiva ▪ Fibrous tissue becomes ossified; ossification of striated muscle ▪ Hereditary, idiopathic	▪ Vertebral and apophyseal joint fusions ▪ Intervertebral discs are hypoplastic and become calcified		▪ Digits anomalous at birth ▪ Microdactyly of the first toe (75%) ▪ Microdactyly of the thumbs ▪ Hallux valgus

Osteopenic Dysplasias

DYSPLASIA	SPINE	SKULL	PELVIS / THORAX	EXTREMITIES / RIBS
Osteogenesis Imperfecta ▪ Generalized inheritable disorder of connective tissue ▪ Clinical criteria for diagnosis: osteoporosis, blue sclera, abnormal dentition, premature otosclerosis ▪ Congenita (high rate of still borns and infant mortality) and tarda (normal life expectancy) forms	▪ Diffuse decrease in bone density ▪ Pencil-thin cortices ▪ Multiple fractures, especially of the lower extremities ▪ Kyphoscoliosis common from ligamentous laxity ▪ Biconcave vertebrae ▪ Premature DJD	▪ Persistent Wormian bones ▪ Enlarged sinuses ▪ Calvarium is thin and lucent ▪ Platybasia frequent; basilar impression ▪ Abnormal dentition	▪ Protrusio acetabuli ▪ Shepard's crook deformity	▪ Bowing deformities secondary to multiple fractures which are usually transverse and in the lower extremities ▪ Multiple rib fractures

Mucopolysaccharidoses

DYSPLASIA	SPINE	SKULL	PELVIS / THORAX	EXTREMITIES / RIBS
Hurler's Syndrome ▪ Leads to excessive lipid accumulation in the CNS and other viscera ▪ Osteoporosis, otosclerosis ▪ Dwarfism ▪ Mental retardation and decreased life span	▪ Thoracolumbar kyphosis secondary to vertebral body hypoplasia ▪ Beaked vertebrae	▪ Macrocephaly ▪ Frontal bossing ▪ Premature closing of the sagittal and lambdoidal sutures ▪ Hydrocephalus ▪ Enlarged, J-shaped sella turcica ▪ Small facial bones, widened mandible	▪ Flared ilia ▪ Coxa valga or vara common ▪ Widened diaphyses of tubular bones	▪ Ribs are overly wide: paddle ribs ▪ Trident hands
Morquio's Syndrome ▪ Leads to keratosulfaturia ▪ Mild and severe forms ▪ Normal mental capacity ▪ Life span 40-50 years	▪ Slightly rounded vertebrae with small anterior beak seen early in infancy ▪ Platyspondyly with central beaking is pathognomonic by age 2 or 3 ▪ Disc spaces normal or increased ▪ Atlanto-axial instability due to hypoplastic or absent odontoid		▪ Acetabuli and capital femoral epiphyses are hypoplastic and the hips are often unstable ▪ Wide femoral necks; hip dislocation ▪ Coxa vara or valga common ▪ Pectus craniatum ▪ Wine glass pelvis	▪ Long tubular bones are short and thick, esp. upper extremity ▪ Hands and feet are deformed ▪ Bowing deformities ▪ Excessive callus formation

The Sclerosing Dysplasias

DYSPLASIA	SPINE	SKULL	PELVIS / THORAX	EXTREMITIES / RIBS
Melorheostosis ▪ Hyperostotic "candle wax" appearance ▪ Developmental errors of intramembranous and enchondral bone formation			▪ Pelvis often involved	▪ Cortical thickening in a streaked or wavy pattern ▪ Hyperostotic bone protrudes under the periosteum and usually follows along one side of a long bone; medullary cavity spared
Osteopetrosis ▪ Lack of resorption of normal primitive osteochondral tissue ▪ Malignant and benign forms ▪ AKA Albers-Schonberg's disease; marble bone disease ▪ Generalized symmetric sclerosis of skeleton without trabeculation ▪ Pathologic fractures common	▪ Sandwich vertebrae	▪ Calvarial and basilar thickening and sclerosis ▪ Poor sinus development	▪ Ilium demonstrates multiple, dense curved lines paralleling the iliac crest	▪ Long bones have flared and elongated metaphyses ▪ "Erlenmeyer flask" deformity ▪ Hands have a "bone within a bone" appearance
Osteopoikilosis ▪ Small round radiopacities appearing in the juxtaarticular regions of bone ▪ Majority of cases are asymptomatic		▪ Does not involve the skull	▪ Densities found adjacent to acetabulum in pelvis and glenoid in scapula	▪ Multiple small radiopacities (1 to 10 mm) scattered in the epiphyseal and metaphyseal regions ▪ Symmetric lesions, esp. in long tubular bones, carpals and tarsals

emember

- Enchondral bone formation: vertebrae and long bones
- Intramembranous bone formation: flat bones (like the skull) and appositional growth of long bones

The Sclerosing Dysplasias, Cont'd

DYSPLASIA	SPINE	SKULL	PELVIS / THORAX	EXTREMITIES / RIBS
Progressive Diaphyseal Dysplasia ▪ AKA Engelmann's Disease ▪ Usually manifests in the first decade of life ▪ Likes the femur, tibia, radius, ulna and humerus	▪ Sclerosis affects the posterior aspect of the vertebral body and the posterior arches, without causing stenosis	▪ Basilar sclerosis ▪ Calvarial hyperostosis less common	▪ Pelvic bones usually spared	▪ Symmetric distribution with widening of the diaphyseal portions of long bones; metaphysis and epiphysis spared ▪ Carpal and tarsal bones usually spared
Tuberous Sclerosis ▪ AKA Bourneville's Disease ▪ Multi-system disorder of neuroectodermal origin ▪ Characterized by tumors of the skin and CNS ▪ Clinical triad: mental retardation, epileptic seizures, and skin lesions	▪ Osteoblastic deposits of varied size and contour in vertebral bodies and pedicles ▪ Scoliosis	▪ Intracranial calcifications in 50 to 80% of patients ▪ Generalized thickening and hyperostosis of the cranial vault	▪ Pelvis: osteoblastic deposits of varied size and contour	▪ Irregular subperiosteal new bone formation and nodules are common ▪ Small, well-defined cysts are seen in the small tubular bones of the hand ▪ Periosteal warts: cortical excrescences on the tibia

Fractures and Trauma (3)

Skull

Linear fracture	▪ The most common skull fracture ▪ Usually occurs in the parietal and temporal bones ▪ Crosses the sutures (vascular grooves do not cross sutures)
Depressed fracture	▪ Results from a high-velocity impact by a small object ▪ Usually produces multiple fragments, displaced inward
Mandible fracture	▪ Most common site is the body of the mandible ▪ The mandible is the slowest-healing bone in the body

Cervical Spine

Atlas	**Jefferson's fracture / burst fracture**		▪ Fracture through the anterior and posterior arches of atlas due to forceful blow to the vertex of the skull which transmits through the occipital condyles to the lateral masses of atlas ▪ Alters the atlanto-axial alignment and increases the paraodontoid space
	Posterior arch fracture of atlas		▪ The most common fracture of atlas (50% of all atlas fractures) ▪ Bilateral vertical fracture through the neural arch ▪ Mechanism: severe hyperextension injury
	Anterior arch fracture of atlas		▪ Usually horizontal segmental avulsions from hyperextension at the attaachment of the anterior longitudinal ligament and longus colli muscle
Axis	**Hangman's fracture**		▪ Bipedicular fracture of atlas ▪ Mechanism: hyperextension with rotation ▪ Traumatic spondylolysis (Type IV)
	Odontoid process fracture	**Type 1**	▪ Avulsion of the tip of the odontoid process as a result of apical or alar ligament stress ▪ Differentiate from Os Terminale
		Type 2	▪ Fracture at the junction of the odontoid process and the body of axis ▪ The most common odontoid process fracture
		Type 3	▪ Fracture below the base of the attachment of the odontoid process to the vertebral body ▪ Almost as common as Type 2; heals more readily
Vertebral Body	**Clay shoveler's fracture**		▪ Avulsion of lower cervical segment spinous process ▪ Mechanism: hyperflexion injury ▪ Must differentiate from a non-union defect ▪ "Double spinous process" sign
	Teardrop fracture		▪ A displaced, triangular fragment from the anteroinferior body corner ▪ Most common at C2 ▪ Mechanism: hyperflexion (C3,4,5) or hyperextension (C2) ▪ Differentiate from a limbus bone (not common at C2)
	Wedge fracture		▪ Compressed anterior vertebral body fracture ▪ Mechanism: hyperflexion (whiplash) ▪ Differentiate from pathologic fracture

THORACIC SPINE

Compression fracture	▪ Most common type of fracture in the thoracic spine ▪ Mechanism: hyperflexion and axial compression ▪ Due to pathology: see decrease in posterior and anterior body height ▪ Due to trauma: see decrease in anterior body height and anterior cortical offset ▪ Major cause is osteoporosis

LUMBAR SPINE

Chance/seat belt fracture	▪ Horizontal fracture through a single body and posterior arch ▪ "Empty vertebrae" sign
Compression fracture	▪ Mechanism: hyperflexion and axial compression ▪ Acute compression fracture findings: step defect and linear zone of impaction
Transverse process fracture	▪ Mechanism: lateral flexion and hyperextension ▪ Differentiate from non-union defect

PELVIS

Sacral fracture	▪ Horizontal: most common type; usually between the third and fourth sacral tubercle ▪ Vertical: usually due to indirect trauma
Coccyx fracture	▪ Usually transverse ▪ Usually results in anterior displacement of the coccyx
Malgaigne fracture	▪ Most common fracture of the pelvis ▪ Fracture of the inferior pubic ramus with dislocation of the ipsilateral sacroiliac joint ▪ Mechanism: shearing force
Duverney's fracture	▪ Splitting of the iliac wing ▪ Mechanism: direct force from lateral direction
Bucket Handle fracture	▪ Superior and inferior pubic ramus fracture with a fracture or separation of the contralateral sacroiliac joint
Acetabular fracture	▪ Two types: posterior rim fracture and explosion fracture
Avulsion fracture	▪ Most common adolescent athlete fracture ▪ Mechanism: longitudinal force
Sprung pelvis	▪ Separation of the pubic symphysis and both sacroiliac joints

HIP FRACTURES AND DISLOCATIONS

Intracapsular fracture	1. Subcapital: most common 2. Midcervical 3. Basicervical
Extracapsular fracture	1. Intertrochanteric: most common 2. Trochanteric 3. Subtrochanteric
Posterior dislocation	▪ Most common direction of dislocation ▪ Mechanism: force driven anterior to posterior into flexed knee
Anterior dislocation	▪ Mechanism: force driven posterior to anterior through abducted and extended leg
Slipped capital femoral epiphysis	▪ Type I Salter Harris fracture ▪ Evaluated with Klein's Line ▪ Usually affects overweight adolescent males

KNEE FRACTURES AND DISLOCATIONS

Bumper / tibial plateau fracture	▪ Mechanism: femoral condyles are forced into the tibial plateau
Avulsion fracture of the tibial tuberosity	▪ Associated with infrapatellar tendon rupture ▪ Mechanism: force through flexed knee with contracted quadriceps ▪ FBI sign (radiolucent line on top of water density) seen with cross-table lateral view; indicates intraarticular fracture
Patellar fracture	▪ Most common is transverse (through the waist) or slightly oblique ▪ Differentiate from bipartite patella (which usually occurs superolaterally) and tri-/multipartite patella
Patellar dislocation	▪ Usually dislocates laterally

ANKLE FRACTURES

Medial malleolus fracture	▪ Usually transverse
Distal fibula / lateral malleolus fracture	▪ Usually oblique
Bimalleolar fracture	▪ Oblique fracture through the lateral malleolus and a transverse fracture through the medial malleolus
Trimalleolar fracture	▪ Fracture of both malleoli and the posterior aspect of the tibia
Maisonneuve's fracture	▪ Proximal fibula fracture due to an inversion and external rotation injury of the ankle
Toddler's fracture	▪ Distal diaphyseal / metaphyseal spiral fracture of the tibia of an infant
Boot top fracture	▪ Distal diaphyseal / metaphyseal spiral fracture of the tibia and fibula in an adult

FOOT FRACTURES AND DISLOCATIONS

Calcaneal fracture	▪ The most common tarsal to fracture ▪ Mechanism: jumping from heights ▪ Boehler's angle will be less than 28 degrees
Jones'/ Dancer's fracture	▪ Fracture of the base of the fifth metatarsal
Bedroom fracture	▪ Usually occurs in the first and fifth phalanges
Lisfranc's dislocation	▪ Displacement of the second through fifth metatarsal bones with associated fractures

THORAX

Rib fracture	▪ Sometimes occur as an occult fracture ▪ Radiolucent fracture line ▪ Cortical offset ▪ Altered rib orientation ▪ Complications: pneumothorax and subcutaneous emphysema
Clavicle fracture	▪ The most common fracture of childbirth
Scapula fracture	▪ Usually involve the scapular body and neck (80%)

UPPER EXTREMITY FRACTURES, DISLOCATIONS AND SEPARATIONS

Flap fracture of humerus	▪ Avulsion fracture of the greater tuberosity ▪ Often a complication of anterior glenohumeral dislocation
Surgical neck fracture of humerus	▪ Most common site of proximal humerus fracture
Shoulder dislocation	▪ 95% are anterior / inferior due to the orientation of the joint ▪ Complications: Hill-Sachs deformity, flap fracture of the greater tuberosity, Bankart sign
Acromioclavicular joint separation	▪ Grade I: stretching of the AC ligament ▪ Grade II: rupture of the AC ligament and stretching of the coracoclavicular ligament ▪ Grade III: Rupture of both ligaments; requires surgery

FRACTURES AND DISLOCATIONS OF THE ELBOW AND FOREARM

Supracondylar fracture of the humerus	▪ Most common elbow fracture in children
Avulsion fracture / Little leaguer's elbow	▪ Avulsion fracture of medial epicondyle
Comminuted fracture of olecranon process	▪ Second most common adult elbow fracture ▪ Mechanism: direct trauma or an acute flexion avulsion from the triceps insertion
Chisel fracture of the radial head	▪ Most common fracture in adult elbow ▪ Fat pad sign: posterior fat pad is visible
Night stick fracture	▪ Mechanism: direct blow to the ulna
Monteggia's fracture	▪ Fracture of the proximal 1/3 of the ulnar shaft associated with displacement of the radius in any direction
Galeazzi's fracture	▪ Fracture of the radius at the junction of the middle and distal thirds, with dislocation of the distal radioulnar joint

FRACTURES AND DISLOCATIONS OF THE WRIST AND HAND

Colle's fracture	▪ Fracture of the radius with posterior dislocation of the distal fragment
Smith's fracture	▪ Fracture of the radius with anteior dislocation of the distal fragment
Lunate dislocation	▪ "Pie" sign: the lunate appears triangular with the apex pointing distally on the posterior to anterior view ▪ The most commonly dislocated carpal bone ▪ Dislocates anteriorly; seen on lateral view
Barroom fracture	▪ Fourth or fifth metacarpal neck fracture with anterior displacement of the head
Chauffer's fracture	▪ Fracture of the radial styloid
Torus fracture	▪ Most common fracture of the wrist for 6 to 10 year olds
Scaphoid fracture	▪ Most common location for an occult fracture; most common carpal fracture ▪ Mechanism: fall on an outstretched hand ▪ Complications: avascular necrosis, non-union defect
Bennett's fracture	▪ Intraarticular fracture through the base of the first metacarpal, with dorsal and radial displacement of the shaft ▪ Rolando's fracture: comminuted Bennett's fracture
Boxer's fracture	▪ Second or third metacarpal neck fracture with anterior displacement of the head
Pisiform fracture	▪ Mechanism: fall on a hyperextended hand ▪ Use three wrist alignment lines to evaluate carpals on PA view
Gamekeeper's thumb	▪ Avulsion fracture of the proximal phalanx of the thumb ▪ Mechanism: strong abduction stress

STRESS FRACTURES

ote

- There are two types of stress fractures : fatigue (due to repetitive stress) and insufficiency (due to normal stress on a bone with pathology)
- Radiologic signs of a stress fracture include: periosteal response, fracture line and transverse opaque bands

March fracture	▪ Mechanism: repetitive stress ▪ Usually occurs in the second or third metatarsal ▪ Solid periosteal response
Calcaneal fracture	▪ Commonly posterosuperior portion

BATTERED CHILD SYNDROME

- Radiographic hallmark: fractures in different stages of healing
- Multiple closely-approximated fractures
- Metaphyseal corner fractures
- Epiphyseal displacements
- Periosteal new bone

POST-TRAUMATIC MYOSITIS OSSIFICANS

- Heterotrophic bone formation in the soft tissues following trauma
- Two common locations: biceps and quadriceps
- Prussian's Disease: ossification of adductor magnus

Early features	▪ Hazy soft tissue mass ▪ Cloudy ossification
Later features	▪ Round or linear ▪ Smooth, dense outer border ▪ Relatively lucent center ▪ No connection with adjacent bone

EPIPHYSEAL PLATE FRACTURES

SALTER-HARRIS CLASSIFICATION SYSTEM

ote

- The Salter-Harris classification system is based on the mechanism of injury and the relationship of the fracture line to the growing cells of the epiphyseal plate.

Type I	▪ Fracture through the physis (growth plate) ▪ Can complicate metabolic diseases ▪ Radiography usually appears normal with diagnosis made from clinical findings of tenderness over the epiphyseal plate and soft tissue swelling
Type II	▪ Fracture through the physis and metaphysis ▪ Produces a metaphyseal fragment called the "Thurston-Holland" sign ▪ The most common epiphyseal injury (75% of cases) ▪ Most common sites are distal radius (50%), as well as tibia, fibula, femur and ulna ▪ Prognosis is usually favorable
Type III	▪ Fracture through epiphysis and physis ▪ Usually located in the distal tibia
Type IV	▪ Fracture through epiphysis, physis and metaphysis; with or without displacement ▪ Most common sites are lateral condyle of the humerus in patients under 10, and distal tibia in patients over 10
Type V	▪ Compression injury to physis without fracture

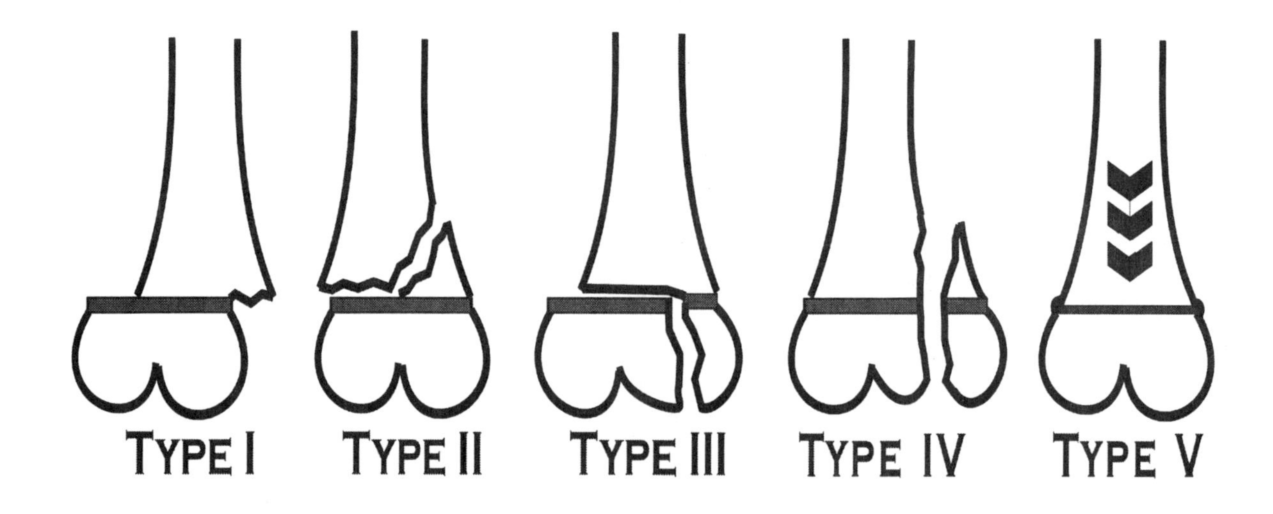

THE MOST COMMON . . .(3)

Location for a skull fracture	Parietal and temporal bones (linear fracture)
Location for an atlas fracture	Posterior arch
Location for an odontoid fracture	Base of the dens (Type 2)
Level for a clay shoveler's fracture	C7
Thoracic spine compression fracture	T11 / T12
Level for degenerative spondylolysis	L4 (usually females)
Type of spondylolysis	Isthmic
Lumbar spine fracture	Compression fracture of T12 / L1
Sacral fracture	Horizontal at level of third and fourth sacral tubercle
Pelvic fracture	Malgaigne fracture
Intracapsular fracture of the femoral head	Subcapital
Extracapsular fracture of the femoral head	Intertrochanteric
Patellar dislocation	Lateral dislocation
Patellar fracture	Transverse (through the waist)
Tarsal fracture	Calcaneus
Fracture of childbirth	Clavicle, especially the middle 1/3
Shoulder dislocation	Subcoracoid
Proximal humerus fracture	Surgical neck
Fracture of the adult elbow	Radial neck and head
Fracture of the child's elbow	Supracondylar
Dislocated carpal bone	Lunate
Fractured carpal bone	Scaphoid

SPONDYLOLYSIS AND SPONDYLOLISTHESIS (4)

THE WILTSE CLASSIFICATION SYSTEM

Type	Description
Type I: Dysplastic	▪ Accompanies congenital abnormality in upper sacrum or neural arch of L5 ▪ No break in the pars
Type II: Isthmic	▪ Involves alteration to the pars; three types A. A lytic or stress fracture of the pars B. Elongated but intact pars C. Acute fracture of the pars
Type III: Degenerative	▪ Secondary to long-standing degenerative arthrosis of the lumbar zygapophyseal joints and discovertebral articulations, **without a pars separation** ▪ Usually occurs at L4
Type IV: Traumatic	▪ Secondary to fracture of part of the neural arch other than the pars
Type V: Pathologic	▪ Occurs in conjunction with generalized or localized bone diseases

PARS ABNORMALITIES

- The best view for diagnosing pars abnormalities above L5 is the oblique, and it should be performed bilaterally.
- The neural arch and its processes on the oblique film are described as looking like a Scottie dog, with the following anatomic counterparts:

Scottie Dog	Anatomic Counterpart
Eye	Pedicle
Nose	Transverse Process
Ear	Superior Articular Process
Foreleg	Inferior Articular Process
Neck	Pars Interarticularis
Body	Lamina

- A pars defect will appear as an irregular linear lucency around the dog's neck ("broken neck" of the Scottie dog)

RADIOGRAPHIC FEATURES

- The inverted Napoleon's hat sign (AKA Gendarme's cap) and bowline of Brailsford (formed by the inferior border of the superimposition of the densities of the 5th vertebral body and transverse processes over the sacral base and alae) are radiographic features of grade 3 or 4 spondylolisthesis viewed on an AP radiograph.
- Meyerding's method for determining the degree of spondylolisthesis results in a grade of 1, 2, 3, 4. With this method, the superior surface of the sacral base is divided into four equal divisions, with 1 at the posterior. The relative position of the posterior-inferior corner of the fifth lumbar body to these segments is determined. The grade of the spondylolisthesis is categorized according to which division the posterior-inferior corner of the body falls into. If the vertebral body has completely slipped off the sacral promontory, the condition is referred to as spondyloptosis.
- Stepladder sign is produced by malalignment of the zygapophyseal joints at the level of the spondylolisthesis.

ARTHRITIC DISORDERS (5)

DEGENERATIVE DISORDERS

<table>
<tr><th>Arthritic Disorder</th><th>Age / Sex</th><th colspan="2">Location</th><th>Radiographic Findings</th></tr>
<tr><td>Degenerative Joint Disease
▪ Most common form of arthritis
▪ AKA osteoarthritis
▪ Primary and secondary forms</td><td>▪ 40 and over
▪ females 10:1</td><td colspan="2">▪ C5-7
▪ T2-4
▪ T9-12
▪ L4-5</td><td>▪ Assymetric distribution
▪ Non-uniform loss of joint space
▪ Osteophytes
▪ Subchondral sclerosis
▪ Geodes (subchondral cysts)
▪ Joint mice
▪ Articular deformities
▪ Joint subluxation
▪ Malum Coxae Senilis
▪ Non-marginal traction spurs
▪ Heberden's nodes (DIP joints); Bouchard's nodes (PIP) joints</td></tr>
<tr><td>Erosive Osteoarthritis
▪ Associated with inflammation</td><td>▪ Females 40-50 years old</td><td colspan="2">▪ DIP joints and PIP joints</td><td>▪ Ankylosis
▪ Gull-wing deformity
▪ Osteophytes
▪ Periostitis
▪ Sclerosis</td></tr>
<tr><td>Diffuse Idiopathic Skeletal Hyperostosis (DISH)
▪ Ligamentous ossification, especially of the ALL
▪ AKA: Forestier's disease</td><td>▪ Males over 50
▪ Up to 20% of patients have diabetes mellitus</td><td colspan="2">▪ Spine: thoracolumbar junction</td><td>▪ Flowing hyperostosis of at least 4 segments; "candle flame" appearance; usually affects anterior longitudinal ligament
▪ Disc height normal
▪ Apophyseal and sacroiliac joints normal
▪ 50% also have ossification of the posterior longitudinal ligament</td></tr>
<tr><td rowspan="2">Neurotrophic Arthropathy
▪ Occurs secondary to loss or impairment of joint proprioception
▪ Painless
▪ AKA Charcot's joint</td><td rowspan="2">▪ Develops secondary to diabetes, syphilis, syringomyelia, others</td><td>Hypertrophic</td><td>▪ Weight-bearing joints</td><td>▪ The 6 Ds: distention, density increase, debris, dislocation, disorganization, destruction
▪ "Bag of bones" appearance</td></tr>
<tr><td>Atrophic</td><td>▪ Non-weight-bearing joints of the upper extremity</td><td>▪ Resorbed articular surface
▪ Tapered bone ends; "licked candy stick" appearance</td></tr>
<tr><td>Synoviochondro-metaplasia
▪ Synovial tissue undergoes metaplastic transformation to produce foci of cartilage</td><td>▪ Males 30 to 50 years old
▪ Males 3:1</td><td colspan="2">▪ Knee, hip, ankle, elbow, wrist
▪ Rare in the spine</td><td>▪ Multiple loose bodies
▪ DJD; extrinsic extraarticular pressure erosions
▪ Primary (idiopathic) and secondary forms, but pathologic alterations are the same</td></tr>
</table>

Inflammatory Disorders

Arthritic Disorder	Age / Sex	Location	Radiographic Findings
Rheumatoid Arthritis ▪ Generalized connective tissue disorder of unknown origin that targets synovial tissue ▪ Course and prognosis are unpredictable ▪ **Felty's syndrome**: leukopenia, splenomegaly and rheumatoid arthritis	▪ Onset between 20 and 60 years of age; peak age between 40 and 60 years ▪ Under 40, females 3:1 ▪ Over 40, males = females	▪ Early: hands and feet; symptoms progress proximally ▪ The spine is rarely affected early, but later the cervical spine is involved in 80% of patients	▪ Bilateral and symmetrical ▪ Periarticular soft tissue swelling ▪ Uniform loss of joint space ▪ Marginal erosions at the bare area ▪ Juxtaarticular osteoporosis ▪ Juxtaarticular periostitis ▪ Large pseudocysts ▪ Joint deformity ▪ Haygarth's nodes: occur at the MCP joints ▪ Most common cause of protrusio acetabuli (Otto's pelvis) ▪ Pannus formation (hyperplastic synovial tissue) ▪ Rheumatoid nodule: soft tissue accumulation of inflammatory cells; presence often indicates that the course of the disease is more severe ▪ Can cause atlanto-axial instability ▪ Soft tissue swelling around the joint ▪ Rat bite lesions ▪ Boutonniere deformity: flexion of the PIP joint and extension of the DIP joint ▪ Swan neck deformity: flexion of the DIP joint and extension of the PIP joint ▪ Lanois deformity: fibular deviation of the digits and dorsal subluxation of MCP joints ▪ Ulnar deviation of the MCP joints ▪ Spotty carpal sign: multiple marginal erosions throughout the carpals ▪ Midcarpal fusion and ankylosis ▪ Arthritis mutilans: severe, polyarticular joint end-stage deformity with severe articular destruction
Juvenile Rheumatoid Arthritis ▪ Unknown etiology ▪ Seronegative form: Still's Disease; associated with visceral dysfunction	▪ Less than 16 years of age	▪ Cervical spine (fusion of C2-4 facets) ▪ Wrist, hands ▪ Knee ▪ Ankles, feet	▪ Soft tissue swelling ▪ Marginal erosions ▪ Bilateral and symmetrical ▪ Periosteal response ▪ Epiphyseal involvement ▪ Can cause growth plate problems

ote

- Atlanto-axial instability is associated with: Down's syndrome, the inflammatory arthritides and trauma.

INFLAMMATORY DISORDERS, CONTINUED

Arthritic Disorder	Age / Sex	Location	Radiographic Findings
Ankylosing Spondylitis ▪ AKA Marie Strumpell's Disease ▪ Enthesopathy (inflammation of ligamentous or tendonous insertion)	▪ 15-35 years of age ▪ Males 10:1	▪ Axial skeleton ▪ Symphysis pubis ▪ Sacroiliac joints	▪ Bilateral and symmetrical ▪ Initial changes occur at the SI joints bilaterally and symmetrically then at the thoraco lumbar junction; reactive sclerosis occurs more on the iliac side because the articular cartilage is thinner ▪ "Ghost joints": ankylosed SI joints ▪ Fluffy periostitis ▪ Shiny corner sign ▪ Marginal syndesmophytes ▪ Barrel vertebrae due to inflammation ▪ Bamboo spine ▪ Carrot stick fractures ▪ Whiskering at iliac crests ▪ Romanus lesions (precursor to syndesmophyte formation) ▪ Dagger sign; trolley track sign ▪ Osteoporosis
Psoriatic Arthritis ▪ 15% of psoriasis patients develop psoriatic arthritis ▪ Difficult to differentiate from Reiter's syndrome on x-ray	▪ Onset between 20 and 50 years old ▪ Male = female	▪ DIP joints and PIP joints ▪ MCP joints and wrist usually spared ▪ Ray pattern can occur in a single digit ▪ Thoracolumbar junction	▪ Asymmetrical ▪ Non-marginal syndesmophytes ▪ Pannus formation ▪ Soft tissue swelling ▪ Bone density is maintained ▪ Marginal erosions and tapered bone ends; "pencil in cup" deformity ▪ Fluffy juxtaarticular periostitis: "mouse ears" ▪ Widened joint space followed by uniform loss of joint space
Reiter's Syndrome ▪ Classic triad: urethritis, conjunctivitis, polyarthritis ▪ Probably sexually transmitted	▪ Between the ages of 18 and 40 ▪ Males 50:1	▪ Likes the lower extremity: knees, ankles and feet ▪ Unilateral sacroiliac joint ▪ Thoracolumbar junction	▪ Asymmetric ▪ Non-marginal syndesmophytes ▪ Marginal erosions ▪ Uniform loss of joint space ▪ Soft tissue swelling ▪ Osteoporosis ▪ Periostitis ▪ Heel spurs: "Lover's heel"

Remember

- The following conditions give positive lab findings for HLA-B27: Ankylosing spondylitis, Reiter's syndrome, Psoriatic arthritis, Enteropathic arthritis, Juvenile Rheumatoid arthritis.
- Seronegative arthropathies include ankylosing spondylitis, enteropathic arthritis, psoriatic arthritis, and Reiter's syndrome.

INFLAMMATORY DISORDERS, CONT'D

Arthritic Disorder	Age / Sex	Location	Radiographic Findings
Enteropathic Arthritis ▪ Associated with diseases of gastrointestinal origin, especially ulcerative colitis and Crohn's disease ▪ Typically resolves in 2-3 months	▪ Young adults	▪ Sacroiliac joints ▪ Knees, ankles, elbows, wrists	▪ Bilateral and symmetric ▪ Marginal syndesmophytes ▪ Erosions, sclerosis, altered joint space ▪ Findings in spine and pelvis are indistinguishable from those of ankylosing spondylitis ▪ Bilateral sacroilitis
Systemic Lupus Erythematosus ▪ Generalized connective tissue disorder involving multiple organ systems ▪ Immunologic abnormalities ▪ Butterfly rash	▪ Predominantly women of childbearing age	▪ Hands ▪ Long bones ▪ Chest	▪ **Hands**: bilateral, symmetrical; reversible ulnar deviation; reversible boutonniere/swan neck deformities; osteoporosis; normal joint space; soft tissue atrophy ▪ Dislocations and deformities ▪ Osteoporosis ▪ Atrophy of overlying musculature and soft tissue calcification
Scleroderma ▪ Idiopathic systemic inflammatory connective tissue disorder involving many systems ▪ Associated with Raynaud's phenomenon	▪ Females 30 to 50 years old ▪ Females 3:1	▪ Hands ▪ First carpo-metacarpal phalangeal joint	▪ Acroosteolysis of the distal phalanges ▪ Bilateral selective involvement of the first carpometacarpal joint of the wrist ▪ Soft tissue calcification ▪ **CREST**: calcinosis; Raynaud's phenomenon; esophageal abnormality; scleroderma; telangiectasia
Osteitis Condensans Ilii ▪ Bilateral, symmetric sacroiliac disorder	▪ Multiparous women between 20 and 40 years old ▪ Females 9:1	▪ Sacroiliac joints	▪ Bilateral, dense, triangle shaped iliac subchondral sclerosis involving the lower half of the joint margin; joint space and margins are normal ▪ Does not affect peripheral joints

ote

- Non-marginal syndesmophytes: psoriatic arthritis, Reiter's.
- Marginal syndesmophytes: ankylosing spondylitis, enteropathic arthritis.

ARTHRITIS IN THE HANDS

Arthritic Disorder	Radiographic Findings	Location	Distribution
Degenerative Joint Disease	▪ Subchondral sclerosing ▪ Decreased joint space	▪ Heberden's nodes at the DIP joints ▪ Bouchard's nodes at the PIP joints	▪ Asymmetrical
Rheumatoid Arthritis	▪ Juxtaarticular osteoporosis ▪ Marginal erosions at PIP joints and MCP joints ▪ Ulnar deviation of the MCP joints ▪ Boutonniere deformity; Swan neck deformity ▪ Periostitis of proximal phalanx ▪ Uniform joint space loss at PIP joints and MCP joints ▪ Soft tissue swelling around the PIP joints and MCP joints	▪ Likes MCP joints and IP joints	▪ Bilateral and symmetrical
Psoriatic Arthritis	▪ Bone density maintained ▪ Ray pattern: affects all joints of a single digit ▪ Soft tissue swelling ▪ Fluffy periostitis ▪ "Pencil in cup" deformity ▪ Marginal erosions and tapered bone ends	▪ Likes DIP joints and PIP joints of hands and feet	▪ Asymmetrical ▪ Uniform loss of joint space
Erosive Osteoarthritis	▪ Gull wing deformity ▪ Osteophytes	▪ DIP joints and PIP joints	▪ Non-uniform loss of joint space
Systemic Lupus Erythematosis	▪ Boutonniere deformity, swan neck deformity (both reversible) ▪ Osteoporosis ▪ Reversible ulnar deviation	▪ No joint destruction	▪ Bilateral and symmetrical

ARTHRITIS IN THE SACROILIAC JOINTS

Arthritic Disorder	Clinical	Radiographic Findings	Location	Distribution
Ankylosing Spondylitis	▪ 15 to 35 years old ▪ Males > females ▪ Elevated ESR ▪ HLA-B27	▪ Hazy margin of sclerosis ▪ Erosions and ankylosis ▪ Marginal syndesmophytes in the spine ▪ Affects the hips and shoulders	▪ Ilium and sacrum	▪ Bilateral, symmetrical
Psoriasis	▪ 20 to 50 years old ▪ females > males ▪ Elevated ESR ▪ HLA-B27	▪ Hazy, minimal sclerosis ▪ Erosions common, ankylosis possible ▪ Non-marginal syndesmophytes in the spine ▪ Common in the hands and feet	▪ Ilium and sacrum	▪ Uni/ bilateral, asymmetrical
Degenerative Joint Disease	▪ 20 to 50 years old ▪ Females > males ▪ No lab findings	▪ Small, hazy sclerosis ▪ No erosions or ankylosis ▪ Osteophytes in the spine ▪ Common in multiple joints	▪ Ilium	▪ Unilateral
Osteitis Condensans Ilii	▪ 20 to 40 years old ▪ Females > males ▪ No lab findings	▪ Triangular, sharp sclerosis ▪ No erosions, no ankylosis ▪ Does not affect the spine ▪ Does not affect peripheral joints	▪ Ilium	▪ Usually bilateral, symmetrical

METABOLIC DISORDERS

Arthritic Disorder	Age / Sex	Location	Radiographic Findings
Gout ▪ Hyperuricemia with acute inflammatory arthritis due to intraarticular deposits of sodium monourate ▪ Family history frequent, especially in females	▪ Males over 40 ▪ Males 20:1	▪ Big toe ▪ Knee ▪ Wrist ▪ Elbow ▪ Sacroiliac joint ▪ Symphysis pubis	▪ Podagra (first MTP joint affected) ▪ Avascular necrosis ▪ Normal bone density ▪ Marginal erosions ▪ "Overhanging margin" sign ▪ Chondrocalcinosis (uncommon) ▪ Normal joint space; uniform loss occurs late ▪ Tophi ▪ "Spotty carpal" sign due to multiple erosions ▪ Large soft tissue masses ▪ Asymmetrical
Calcium Pyrophosphate Dihydrate Crystal Deposition Disease ▪ AKA Pseudogout	▪ Usually over 30 years old ▪ Males = females	▪ Knee ▪ Wrist ▪ MCP joints ▪ Elbow ▪ Shoulder	▪ Soft tissue calcification ▪ Chondrocalcinosis in hyaline and fibrocartilage
Sarcoidosis ▪ Unknown origin; affects multiple organ systems	▪ 20 to 40 years of age ▪ Males = females ▪ Blacks 10:1 ▪ Scandinavians	▪ Peripheral bones of hands and feet ▪ Spinal involvement is rare	▪ Potato nodes ▪ "1-2-3" sign (potato nodes with paratracheal lymphadenopathy) ▪ Diffuse interstitional lung field densities ▪ Bilateral, asymmetrical ▪ Lace-like trabecular patterns due to infiltrate of perivascular granulomas in the Haversian canals

Bone Tumors and Tumorlike Processes

Analysis of a Lesion (6)

Skeletal location and position within bone

- Epiphyseal -- chondroblastoma and giant cell tumor
- Epiphyseal-metaphyseal
- Metaphyseal -- most common site for lesions due to the high metabolic rate and high vascularity of the region
- Metaphyseal-diaphyseal
- Diaphyseal -- usually related to marrow disease such as multiple myeloma and other round cell tumors

Site of origin

- Medullary -- usually central in location
- Cortical
- Periosteal
- Extraosseous

Shape and size

- Useful for differentiating benign from malignant lesions

Margination

- Imperceptible -- wide zone of transition
- Sharp -- sclerotic; narrow zone of transition

Cortical integrity

- Thinning
- Thickening
- Expansion
- Destruction
- Fracture

Matrix

- Fat
- Cartilage
- Osseous
- Fibrous

Soft tissue changes

- Diagnosis of aggressive primary bone tumor is almost certain when there is cortical disruption and an adjacent soft tissue mass

Patterns of bone destruction

- Geographic (soap bubble) -- circumscribed and uniformly lytic; usually solitary, larger than 1 cm and has a sharp margin; usually slow growing
- Motheaten -- multiple; poorly marginated, small or moderately sized (2 to 5 cm) lucencies; margins of each lesion are frequently ragged and irregular; aggressive
- Permeative -- numerous tiny lucencies (less than 1 mm) with a wide zone of transition; very aggressive

Periosteal response

- Solid -- continuous layer of new bone that attaches to the outer cortical surface; caused by slow form of irritation
- Laminated(onion skin) -- alternating layers of lucent opaque densities on the external bone surface; occurs with slow and aggressive tumors and with infection
- Spiculated (brushed whiskers; hair on end; sunburst) -- spicules of bone radiating perpendicularly from a point source in the cortex; suggests aggressive bone tumor
- Codman's triangle (periosteal buttress) -- triangle of periosteal new bone at the peripheral lesion-cortex junction due to subperiosteal extension of the lesion

METASTATIC BONE TUMORS (7)

Causes of Osseous Metastasis

Females
- Lytic: breast (80%)
- Blastic: breast (10%)

Males
- Lytic: lung (75%)
- Blastic: prostate (80%)

Children
- Lytic: neuroblastoma (80%)
- Blastic: Hodgkin's Disease (50%)

Acral Metastasis
- Metastatic lesions of bone rarely occur distal to elbows or knees
- When acral metastasis does occur, the most common site is the foot; the hand is the second most common site
- Sources of acral metastasis in decreasing order: lung, breast, kidney

Pathways of Metastasis
- Direct extension
- Lymphatic dissemination: uncommon
- Hematogenous dissemination: most common; seeding via Batson's Venous Plexus

Causes of Solitary Ivory Vertebrae
- <u>Osteoblastic metastasis</u>: homogenous radiopacity; no cortical thickening or expansion
- <u>Hodgkin's Lymphoma</u>: anterior scalloping
- <u>Paget's Disease</u>: gross expansion, cortical thickening, accented trabecular pattern

Types of Lesions

Lytic
- 75% of all metastatic lesions
- Moth-eaten or permeative pattern of bone destruction

Blastic
- Multiple snowball appearance

Mixed
- Combination of osteolytic and osteoblastic proliferation

Blow-out
- Solitary, large, expansile, bubbly lesion
- Most commonly occurs with carcinoma of the lung, thyroid and kidney

Radiographic Findings of Metastatic Bone Tumors

Tumor	Spine and Pelvis	Skull	Other
Metastatic Bone Tumors ▪ Hot on bone scan ▪ Patients are usually over 40 years old ▪ The only definitive diagnosis is biopsy	▪ Spine and pelvis are the most common locations for metastasis to occur ▪ Vertebral body and pedicle destruction (most common sites); "one-eyed pedicle" sign and blind vertebrae ▪ Altered bone density in one of the destructive patterns ▪ Cortical destruction ▪ Disc space remains intact ▪ Pathologic, uniform collapse in vertebral body height ▪ Endplate disruption (malignant Schmorl's nodes) ▪ Ivory vertebrae	▪ Large and small lesions (multiple myeloma usually has homogenous lesions)	▪ Rare below the elbows and knees (acral mets) ▪ Ribs (extrapleural sign) and sternum (28%) ▪ Proximal femur and humerus
Neuroblastoma	▪ Mixed radiolucencies and radiopacities throughout the spine, sacrum and pelvic bones	▪ Widened sutures ▪ Sunburst spiculation ▪ Lytic lesions	▪ Ends of long bones are common sites

Primary Malignant Bone Tumors

Tumor	Age / Sex	Location	Radiographic Findings
Multiple Myeloma ▪ The most common primary malignant bone tumor ▪ Cold on bone scan	▪ 50-70 years old ▪ Males 2:1	▪ Lower thoracic and lumbar spine vertebral bodies ▪ Ribs ▪ Skull ▪ Pelvis ▪ Scapula ▪ Diaphysis of long bones (humerus and femur)	▪ Diaphysis of long bones ▪ Pedicle sign (pedicle spared, vertebral body collapses) ▪ Diffuse osteoporosis leading to pathological vertebral collapse ▪ Sharply circumscribed osteolytic defect (punched-out lesions) ▪ "Wrinkled" vertebrae (pathologic fracture); vertebra plana ▪ Sclerotic lesions rare but possible: ivory vertebrae ▪ Raindrop skull (widespread lytic lesions) ▪ Pelvic and long bones: diffuse osteolytic round lesions without reactive sclerosis
Solitary Plasmacytoma ▪ Local form of plasma cell proliferation	▪ Age 50 or less (50%)	▪ Mandible ▪ Ilium ▪ Vertebrae ▪ Ribs ▪ Proximal femur ▪ Scapula	▪ Geographic, soap bubbly, highly expansile lesion with endosteal scalloping
Osteosarcoma ▪ Second most common primary malignant bone tumor (20%) ▪ Tumor of undifferentiated connective tissue	▪ 10 to 25 years old (75%) ▪ Males 2:1	▪ Long bones of extremities, esp. femur (42%), tibia (16%), and humerus (15%) ▪ Knee and shoulder	▪ Metaphysis (75%); won't cross a growth plate ▪ Permeative or ivory medullary lesion in the metaphysis of long bones; 50% are blastic, 25% are lytic and 25% are mixed ▪ Sunburst or sunray pattern ▪ Codman's triangle ▪ Cortical disruption with soft tissue mass ▪ "Cumulus cloud" appearance
Chondrosarcoma ▪ Third most common primary malignant bone tumor ▪ Most common primary malignant bone tumor of the hand	▪ Between 40 and 60 years old ▪ Males 2:1	▪ Pelvis and proximal femur (50%) ▪ Proximal humerus ▪ Ribs ▪ Scapula ▪ Distal femur and proximal tibia	▪ Grossly expansile lytic lesion ▪ Cortical disruption; laminated/spiculated periosteal response ▪ Large soft tissue mass ▪ Metaphyseal or diaphyseal lesions ▪ Endosteal scalloping ▪ Popcorn matrix calcification (66%)

ote

- Round cell tumors include multiple myeloma, plasmacytoma, Ewing's sarcoma and Non-Hodgkin's lymphoma.

Tumor	Age / Sex	Location	Radiographic Findings
Ewing's Sarcoma ▪ Most common primary malignant bone tumor to metastasize to bone ▪ Symptoms simulate an infection	▪ 10 to 25 years old ▪ Males 2:1	▪ Long bones (50%), esp. lower extremity ▪ Flat bones (40%)	▪ Diaphysis ▪ Permeative lesion with onion skin periosteal response ▪ Cortical saucerization ▪ Pathologic fracture (5%) ▪ Occasional sunray periosteal response; "trimmed whiskers"
Fibrosarcoma ▪ Produces varying amounts of collagen ▪ Medullary and periosteal forms	▪ 4 to 83 years old, esp. 30 to 50 years old ▪ Males = females	▪ Tubular bones in young patients ▪ Flat bones in older patients ▪ 50% occur around the knee	▪ Metaphysis ▪ Highly destructive medullary lesion ▪ Lytic; moth-eaten / permeative destruction ▪ Eccentric within a long bone ▪ Large soft-tissue mass ▪ Usually no periosteal response ▪ Selectively spreads to the lymphatic system ▪ Cortical destruction, wide zone of transition
Chordoma ▪ Arises from remnants of the notochord	▪ Between 40 and 70 years old ▪ Males 2:1	▪ Ends of the axial skeleton (85% occur at sacrococcygeal and spheno-occipital locations) ▪ The most commonly involved vertebral body is C2	▪ Lytic, expansile lesion with scalloped margins ▪ Soft-tissue mass ▪ Amorphous calcification (50%) ▪ The only primary malignant bone tumor that crosses the joint space
Non-Hodgkin's Lymphoma ▪ Reticulum cell sarcoma	▪ 20 to 40 years old ▪ Males 2:1	▪ Femur ▪ Tibia (40% of tumors are around the knee) ▪ Humerus	▪ Diaphyseal ▪ Permeative, moth-eaten medullary lesion ▪ Minimal laminated periosteal response ▪ Well-defined soft-tissue mass ▪ Pathologic fracture
Hodgkin's Lymphoma of Bone ▪ Occurs secondary to systemic Hodgkin's lymphoma, or, rarely as a primary bone lesion	▪ 20 to 40 years old ▪ Males 2:1	▪ Vertebral bodies of lower thoracic and upper lumbar spine ▪ Pelvis ▪ Scapula ▪ Sternum, ribs ▪ Femur	▪ Usually osteolytic (75%); sclerotic (15%) ▪ Mixed destruction with periosteal response (10%) ▪ Polyostotic lesions (66%) ▪ Anterior or lateral scalloping of vertebral body ▪ Ivory vertebrae ▪ Medullary and cortical destruction

Primary Quasimalignant Bone Tumors

Tumor	Age / Sex	Location	Radiographic Findings
Giant Cell Tumor ▪ 80% benign, 20% malignant	▪ 20-40 years old ▪ Benign form mostly in females 3:2 ▪ Malignant form mostly in males 3:1	▪ Knee: distal femur, proximal tibia ▪ Distal radius ▪ Proximal humerus ▪ Sacrum	▪ Eccentric ▪ Begins in the metaphysis and expands into the epiphysis after growth plates close ▪ Expansile, radiolucent, soap-bubbly lesion ▪ Short zone of transition

Primary Benign Bone Tumors

Tumor	Age / Sex	Location	Radiographic Findings
Osteochondroma ▪ Most common benign bone tumor ▪ Pedunculated and sessile forms ▪ **Hereditary Multiple Exostosis**: multiple osteochondromas; associated with bayonette deformity	▪ Before age 20 ▪ Males 2:1	▪ Long bones: femur (34%), humerus (18%) and tibia (15%) ▪ Pelvis ▪ Scapula ▪ Ribs	▪ Cauliflower exostosis with increased density and calcified cap ▪ Coat hanger exostosis ▪ Metaphysis ▪ Pedunculated stalk points away from the joint (supracondylar process points toward the joint) ▪ Sessile form is a broad-based protruberance
Hemangioma ▪ Most common benign tumor to affect the spine ▪ Composed of newly formed vascular structures ▪ Usually asymptomatic and solitary	▪ Adults over 40 ▪ Females slightly higher than males	▪ Spine and skull (75%) ▪ Thoracolumbar junction ▪ Skull: frontal bone	▪ Corduroy cloth appearance (vertical striations) ▪ No cortical thickening as in Paget's disease ▪ Skull: spoke wheel appearance ▪ Only occurs at one level

ote

- The following can cause striated vertebrae: hemangioma, osteoporosis and Paget's disease.

Tumor	Age / Sex	Location	Radiographic Findings
Osteoma ▪ Arises in membranous bone ▪ **Gardner's syndrome**: multiple osteomas, colonic polyposis and soft tissue fibromas	▪ Unknown	▪ Frontal and ethmoidal sinuses ▪ Outer and inner tables of the skull	▪ Round or oval blastic lesions ▪ Well-circumscribed ▪ Radiopaque; homogeneously opaque ▪ Usually 2 cm in diameter or less; however, giant osteomas occasionally fill the entire sinus cavity
Bone Island ▪ Asymptomatic and clinically insignificant	▪ More common in adults than children	▪ Ischium ▪ Ilium ▪ Sacrum ▪ Femoral neck and intertrochanteric space of proximal femur ▪ Do not occur in the skull ▪ Rare in the spine	▪ Intramedullary, round radiopaque densities aligned with the long axis of the trabecular architecture ▪ Sharply demarcated margins with normal adjacent cortex ▪ Margins can have thornlike radiating spicules of bone ("brush border") ▪ Originates in the epiphysis or metaphysis but never in the diaphysis
Osteoid Osteoma ▪ Pain at night relieved by aspirin	▪ Between 10 and 25 years ▪ Males 2:1	▪ 50% occur in femur and tibia ▪ Femur neck and trochanters ▪ 10% occur in the spine ▪ Ribs and clavicle ▪ Neural arch in the spine	▪ Lucent nidus (geographic lesion) with sclerotic border less than 1 cm in size ▪ Differentiate from Brodie's Abscess which has a nidus larger than 2 cm in diameter ▪ In the spine can cause antalgic scoliosis
Osteoblastoma ▪ Called a kissing cousin of the ABC because they look the same in the posterior vertebral arch (lytic and expansile)	▪ 70% of cases occur before age 20 ▪ Males 2:1	▪ Neural arch of the spine ▪ Lower thoracic spine ▪ Upper lumbar spine ▪ Long bones, especially lower extremity ▪ Hands and feet	▪ Metaphysis and diaphysis of long bones; larger than 2 cm ▪ Expansile, lytic ▪ Thin peripheral cortical rim

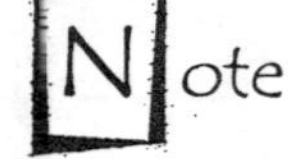

ote

- The following tumors affect the neural arch: osteoblastoma, osteoid osteoma and ABC.
- The following tumors affect the intertrochanteric space: monostotic fibrous dysplasia and bone island.
- The following tumors have sclerotic rings: monostotic fibrous dysplasia, osteoid osteoma, and Brodie's abscess.

Primary Benign Bone Tumors, Cont'd

Tumor	Age / Sex	Location	Radiographic Findings
Solitary Enchondroma ▪ Most common benign tumor of the hand ▪ Arises in cartilage left behind in the metaphysis of growing bones ▪ Malignant potential (to chondrosarcoma) increases when the lesion is closer to the axial skeleton	▪ Between 10 and 30 years old ▪ Males = females	▪ 50% occur in the small tubular bones of the hand, especially the phalanges but the thumb is a rare location ▪ Femur ▪ Humerus ▪ Ribs	▪ Radiolucent ▪ Geographic, expansile lesion with well-defined margins ▪ Cortex is thinned but remains intact ▪ Central in the metaphysis ▪ Stippled matrix calcification ▪ Leads to pathologic fracture
Multiple Enchondromatosis (Ollier's Disease) ▪ Inborn anomaly of enchondral bone formation ▪ **Maffucci's Syndrome**: enchondromatosis of bone with soft tissue cavernous hemangiomas (rare)		▪ Ilium ▪ Around the knee ▪ Hand ▪ Foot	▪ Round or oval radiolucencies that create symmetric widening of bone ▪ Central matrix calcification common
Chondroblastoma ▪ AKA Codman's Tumor ▪ Difficult to differentiate from a giant cell tumor	▪ Between 10 and 25 years old ▪ Males 2:1	▪ Around the knee ▪ Hip ▪ Shoulder ▪ Lower extremity	▪ Epiphyseal region (medullary cavity) of long tubular bones; can extend into the metaphysis ▪ Diaphyseal lesions do not occur ▪ Round or oval and lytic lesions ▪ Most are eccentric and 1 to 10 cm in diameter ▪ 50% have cotton wool calcification of the matrix ▪ Expansile with marginal sclerosis

Primary Benign Bone Tumors, Continued

Tumor	Age / Sex	Location	Radiographic Findings
Chondromyxoid Fibroma	▪ Between 10 and 30 years old ▪ Males = females	▪ Tibia (50%) ▪ Femur ▪ Humerus ▪ Fibula ▪ Ribs ▪ Pelvis ▪ Hands and feet	▪ Metaphyseal origin in long bones ▪ Geographic, eccentric, expansile lesion ▪ Soap bubble appearance ▪ Calcification of the matrix (rare)
Fibrous Xanthoma of Bone: Non-ossifying Fibroma	▪ 4 to 8 years old ▪ Less common than FCD ▪ Males 2:1	▪ Lower extremity, esp. distal tibia ▪ Proximal humerus ▪ Ribs and ilium	▪ Diametaphyseal and eccentric lesion ▪ Solitary, radiolucent and generally ovoid lesion ▪ Thins, and sometimes expands, the cortex ▪ Bubbly appearance ▪ Osteolytic area is 2 to 7 cm and has a narrow zone of transition
Fibrous Xanthoma of Bone: Fibrous Cortical Defect	▪ 8 to 20 years old ▪ 30 to 40% of normal children have FCD ▪ Males 2:1	▪ Lower extremity, esp. distal femur ▪ Proximal humerus ▪ Ribs ▪ Ilium	▪ Diametaphyseal and eccentric lesion ▪ Solitary, radiolucent and generally ovoid lesion ▪ Thins, and sometimes expands, the cortex ▪ Bubbly appearance ▪ Osteolytic area is 2 to 7 cm and has a narrow zone of transition
Simple Bone Cyst ▪ AKA Unicameral bone cyst ▪ Filled with serous fluid ▪ Not painful	▪ 3 to 14 years old ▪ Males 2:1	▪ Humerus and proximal femur (75%)	▪ Metaphyseal origin ▪ Active cysts: central location adjacent to the epiphyseal plate ▪ Latent cysts: displaced from growth plate (less growth potential than active cysts) ▪ Expansile, geographic, pseudoloculated defect ▪ Fallen fragment sign (10%) due to pathologic fracture ▪ Truncated cone appearance
Aneurysmal Bone Cyst ▪ Most common benign bone tumor of the clavicle ▪ Cystic cavity filled with blood ▪ Painful	▪ 5 to 20 years old ▪ 60% occur in females	▪ 80% in femur and tibia ▪ Thoracic and lumbar spine	▪ Metaphyseal origin ▪ Eccentric, sacular protrusion of bone in the long bones ▪ The only benign bone tumor that crosses the epiphyseal plate ▪ Periosteal buttressing at the edge of the lesion

Benign Bone Tumor Differentials

Tumor	Age	Location of Origin	Location	Radiographic Findings
Simple Bone Cyst	▪ 3 to 14 years old ▪ Males 2:1	▪ Metaphysis ▪ Central	▪ Proximal femur ▪ Proximal humerus ▪ Calcaneus	▪ Expansile, geographic ▪ Pseudoloculated
Giant Cell Tumor	▪ 20-40 years old ▪ Benign mostly in females 3:2 ▪ Malignant mostly in males 3:1	▪ Metaphysis prior to fusion of growth plate; ▪ Epiphysis after fusion of growth plate ▪ Eccentric	▪ Femur ▪ Tibia ▪ Radius	▪ Expansile, radiolucent, soap-bubbly lesion ▪ Eccentric ▪ Short zone of transition
Chondromyxoid Fibroma	▪ 8 to 20 years old ▪ Males 2:1	▪ Metaphysis ▪ Eccentric	▪ Tibia ▪ Ribs ▪ Ulna	▪ Expansile ▪ Soap bubble appearance ▪ Rarely calcified ▪ Oval, round
Enchondroma	▪ Between 10 and 30 years old ▪ Males = females	▪ Metaphysis ▪ Central	▪ Metacarpals ▪ Metatarsals	▪ Expansile, geographic ▪ Stippled calcification
Aneurysmal Bone Cyst	▪ 5 to 20 years old ▪ 60% female	▪ Metaphysis ▪ Eccentric	▪ Femur ▪ Tibia ▪ Humerus ▪ Neural arch of spine	▪ More expansile than osteoblastoma ▪ Only benign bone tumor to cross the epiphyseal plate ▪ Periosteal buttressing
Osteoblastoma	▪ 70% of cases occur before age 20 ▪ Males 2:1	▪ Metaphysis and diaphysis of long bones	▪ Neural arch of the spine ▪ Lower thoracic spine ▪ Upper lumbar spine ▪ Long bones, especially in the lower extremity ▪ Hands and feet	▪ Expansile, lytic ▪ May present as a radiopaque lesion (ABC will never be radiopaque); kissing cousin of the ABC

Tumorlike Process	Age / Sex	Location	Radiographic Findings
Paget's Disease ▪ AKA Osteitis Deformans ▪ Osteolysis followed by bone repair ▪ "Great Imitator of Bone Disease" ▪ 90% of patients are asymptomatic ▪ Malignant degeneration (usually to osteosarcoma) occurs at a rate of 0.9 to 2%	▪ Rare before 40 years of age; most patients are over 50 years old ▪ Males 2:1	▪ Axial skeleton (pelvis, femur, skull, spine)	▪ Shepherd's Crook deformity; bowing deformity ▪ Saber shin ▪ Frontal and parietal bossing ▪ Lion face ▪ Basilar invagination ▪ Pathologic fracture ("banana" fracture); usually transverse ▪ Thickened cortex with accented trabecular patterns ▪ Bone expansion and deformity ▪ Skull: "cotton wool" appearance and osteoporosis circumscripta ▪ Spine: picture frame vertebrae (due to cortical thickening) and ivory vertebrae ▪ Pelvis: obliteration of Kohler's teardrop ("Brim" sign) ▪ Femur and tibia: "blade of grass" appearance ▪ Pathologic fracture of the vertebral body is common (decreased posterior body height) ▪ Pseudofractures; Milkman's Syndrome; Looser's lines

ote

- Paget's Disease has four stages:

  I. Osteolytic
  II. Combined
  III. Sclerotic (snowball appearance in the skull)
  IV. Malignant degeneration

Tumor	Age / Sex		Location	Radiographic Findings
Fibrous Dysplasia ▪ Abnormal proliferation of fibrous tissue and poorly-formed trabeculae; arrest of bone development in its immature form ▪ Three forms: monostotic, polyostotic and polyostotic with endocrine abnormalities ▪ **McCune-Albright syndrome** is polyostotic fibrous dysplasia with skin pigmentation and precocious sexual development ▪ "Great Imitator of Bone Disease" ▪ 0.5% degenerate into fibrosarcoma	Monostotic	▪ Around 14 years of age ▪ More common than the polyostotic form	▪ 75% ribs, femur, tibia, skull ▪ FD is the most common benign rib lesion ▪ Pelvis and humerus (10%)	▪ Diametaphyseal origin ▪ Geographic, "smoky" (ground glass) lesion with thick sclerotic margin; occasionally soap bubbly ▪ Expansile ▪ Cortical thinning and scalloping ▪ Café au lait spots rare ▪ Cherubism (fibrous dysplasia of the jaws)
	Polyostotic	▪ Polyostotic form with endocrine disorders: around age 8 ▪ Polyostotic form without endocrine disorders: around age 11	▪ Proximal femur ▪ Skull ▪ Tibia ▪ Humerus ▪ Ribs ▪ Fibula ▪ Radius and ulna	▪ More severe deformities than the monostotic form: coxa vara; extrapleural sign, protrusio acetabuli ▪ Higher incidence of spontaneous fracture than monostotic form ▪ Spinal changes are uncommon ▪ Pseudofractures ▪ Café au lait spots with "Coast of Maine" appearance (30%)
Neurofibromatosis ▪ AKA Von Recklinghausen's Disease ▪ Neuroectodermal and mesodermal dysplasia characterized by café au lait spots, fibroma molluscum and various osseous lesions of the axial and appendicular skeleton	▪ Patient is born with the disorder ▪ Males = females		▪ Spine ▪ Skull ▪ Ribs ▪ Long bones ▪ Extraskeletal: multi-system involvement	▪ Spine: enlarged intervertebral foramen, scoliosis, posterior vertebral scalloping and intrathoracic meningocele ▪ Skull: orbital defects, asterion defect, and macrocranium ▪ Ribs: twisted and irregular ("Twisted Ribbon") appearance ▪ Long bones: pseudoarthrosis, nonossifying fibromas and focal giantism ▪ Café au lait spots with "Coast of California" appearance

THE MOST COMMON . . . (7)

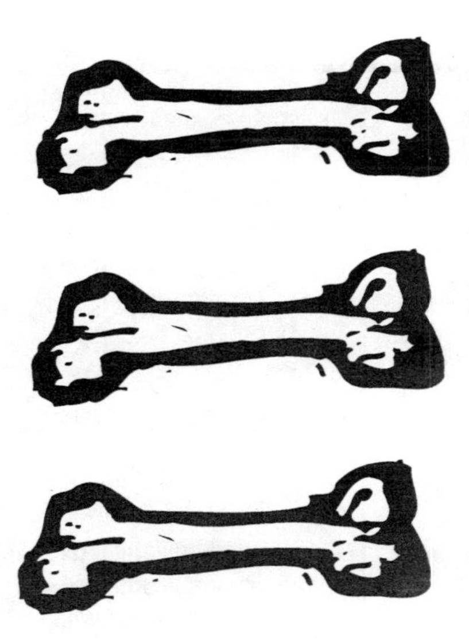

Malignant bone tumor	**Metastatic bone tumor**
Primary malignant bone tumor	**Multiple myeloma**
Primary malignant bone tumor of the hand	**Chondrosarcoma**
Primary malignant bone tumor to metastasize to bone	**Ewing's sarcoma**
Benign bone tumor	**Osteochondroma**
Benign tumor to affect the spine	**Hemangioma**
Benign tumor of the hand	**Solitary enchondroma**
Benign tumor of the clavicle	**Aneurysmal bone cyst**
Benign rib lesion	**Fibrous dysplasia**

INFECTION (8)

Infection	Age/Sex	Location	Radiographic Findings
Suppurative Osteomyelitis ▪ Most commonly caused by Staph Aureus (90%) ▪ Pathways for spread: hematogenous, contiguous source, direct implantation, postsurgery	▪ 2 to 12 years old ▪ Males 3:1	▪ Large tubular bones of the lower extremity, especially the femur	▪ Clinical signs and symptoms precede radiographic findings by 7 to 10 days in the appendicular skeleton and 21 days in the spine ▪ Soft tissue alterations: elevated or obliterated fat planes, increased density and paraspinal edema ▪ Moth-eaten pattern of bone destruction ▪ Usually metaphyseal origin (Ewing's is diaphyseal) ▪ Solid or laminated periosteal new bone formation ▪ Codman's triangle ▪ Sequestrum (dead bone) and involucrum (periosteal collar) ▪ Joint space destruction ▪ Epiphysis usually spared if physis is open ▪ Loss of disc height with spine involvement; vertebral destruction and collapse ▪ Destruction of vertebral endplates on both sides of the disc
Brodie's Abscess ▪ Localized, aborted from of suppurative osteomyelitis ▪ Night pain alleviated by aspirin (mimics osteoid osteoma) ▪ Usually caused by Staph Aureus	▪ Male children	▪ Tubular bones, esp. distal and proximal tibia, distal femur, proximal or distal fibula, distal radius	▪ Metaphysis ▪ Oval or elliptical radiolucency, usually 1.0 cm in diameter (**NOTE**: size is the only feature that allows differentiation between osteoid osteoma and Brodie's Abscess) ▪ Halo or doughnut rim of heavy reactive sclerosis

Infection	Age/Sex	Location	Radiographic Findings
Septic Arthritis ▪ Usually caused by Staph Aureus	▪ Less than 30 years old ▪ Males = females	▪ Knee and hip joints ▪ Shoulder ▪ Hand ▪ Foot and ankle	▪ Radiologic findings occur after clinical symptoms ▪ Loss of subchondral cortical bone ▪ Medullary metaphyseal "moth-eaten" destruction ▪ Laminated periosteal response ▪ Late sequela: complete ankylosis of the affected joint (rare) ▪ Waldenstrom's sign: indicates hip joint effusion ▪ **Tom Smith's arthritis**: osteomyelitis ruptures the metaphyseal cortex, enters the articulation and spreads via synovial fluid to the epiphyseal or subarticular end of the bone. Encountered in the hip, knee, ankle, shoulder and elbow.
Nonsuppurative Osteomyelitis (Tuberculosis) ▪ Usually caused by Mycobacterium tuberculosis (respiratory pathogen)	▪ Immunodeficient persons ▪ Most prevalent before age 30; rare below 1 year ▪ Males = females	▪ Thoracolumbar spine ▪ Extremities	▪ Early tuberculous spondylitis (Pott's Disease): lytic destruction at the anterior subchondral endplate, loss of disc height ▪ Late tuberculous spondylitis: vertebral collapse, obliteration of disc space, Gibbus deformity, abscess formation, multiple segments involved, anterior vertebral scalloping ▪ Early extremities: joint widening, soft tissue swelling, marginal erosions ▪ Late extremities: symmetrical obliteration of joint space, destruction of cortical bone, moth-eaten pattern of destruction, juxtaarticular osteoporosis, occasional ankylosis ▪ Psoas abscess: snowflake density ▪ Kissing sequestrum in a joint: tubercular process involves both surfaces of a joint ▪ Long vertebrae associated with Gibbus deformity
Syphilitic Osteomyelitis ▪ Hutchinson's teeth ▪ Clutton's joints		▪ Congenital: knees, shoulders and wrists; Wimberger's sign ▪ Acquired: skull, tibia, clavicles	**Congenital** ▪ Phase 1: metaphysitis ▪ Phase 2: Periostitis ▪ Phase 3: Osteitis

HEMATOLOGIC AND VASCULAR DISORDERS (9)

HEMATOLOGIC DISORDERS

Disorder	Age / Sex	Location	Radiographic Findings
Sickle Cell Anemia ■ Chronic, congenital, hereditary hemolytic anemia	■ Occurs almost exclusively in Black individuals ■ Clinical onset between 6 months and 2 years of age	■ Long bones	■ Generalized osteopenia ■ Coarsened trabeculae ■ Widened medullary cavity ■ Thin cortices ■ Large vascular channels ■ Epiphyseal ischemic necrosis ■ Spine: fish vertebrae/ H vertebrae (central depression) ■ Long bones: "bone-within-a-bone" appearance of the cortex; laminated or solid periosteal new bone
Thalassemia ■ AKA Cooley's anemia, Mediterranean anemia ■ Hereditary disorder of hemoglobin synthesis	■ Onset in last half of first year	■ Spine ■ Skull ■ Chest abnormalities	■ "Honeycomb" pattern: coarsened trabeculae ■ Cortical thinning ■ Osteoporosis ■ Vascular channel enlargement ■ Widened medullary cavity ■ Erlenmeyer flask deformity ■ Skull: hair on end appearance ■ Sinuses obliterated ■ Rodent facies
Hemophilia ■ Blood coagulation disorders	■ Male predominance	■ Pseudotumors in the lower extremity ■ Knee, ankle, elbow most frequent sites	■ Soft tissue swelling ■ Osteoporosis ■ Subchondral bone cysts ■ Expansile bone lesions ■ Tibiotalar slant deformity ■ Ballooning of the epiphysis due to hyperemia ■ Pseudotumors from hemorrhage into the bone ■ Squaring of the inferior pole of the patella

MYELOPROLIFERATIVE DISEASES

Disorder	Age / Sex	Radiographic Findings
Leukemia ■ Malignant disease of bone marrow ■ Most common malignancy of children 2 to 5 years old	■ Child and adult onset ■ Acute and chronic forms	■ Diffuse osteoporosis ■ Radiolucent submetaphyseal bands ■ Lytic destruction of bone ■ Periosteal new bone formation

Epiphyseal Disorders

Disorder	Age / Sex	Location	Radiographic Findings
Legg-Calve-Perthes Disease ▪ Avascular necrosis of the femoral capital epiphysis before closure of the growth plate	▪ 3 to 12 years old ▪ Males 5:1	▪ 10% of cases are bilateral (rare in females) ▪ Rare in Blacks	▪ Soft tissue swelling due to intraarticular hip effusion ▪ Smaller obturator foramen, increased medial joint space ▪ Small femoral head, wide teardrop, epiphyseal fragmentation, sclerosis ▪ Crescent sign: lytic curvilinear lucency at the end of the epiphysis ▪ Gage's sign: lateral border of the femoral neck becomes convex ▪ Snowcap epiphysis: new trabecular patterns superimposed over the old ones ▪ Mushroom deformity: coxa magna and coxa plana of the femoral head
Osgood Schlatter's Disease	▪ 11 to 15 years old ▪ Much more common in males	▪ Tibial tuberosity	▪ Requires bilateral lateral views with slight medial rotation ▪ Displaced skin contour ▪ Thickened and indistinct patellar ligament ▪ Blurred and opacified infrapatellar fat ▪ Isolated, irregular ossicles ▪ Anterior tuberosity surface irregularities
Scheurmann's Disease ▪ Trauma causes vertebral endplate necrosis	▪ 13 to 17 years old ▪ Slight male predominance	▪ Middle and lower thoracic spine	▪ Anterior wedging of more than 5 degrees or more than three contiguous segments ▪ Irregular end plates; Schmorl's nodes ▪ Loss of disc height ▪ Increased kyphosis (greater than 40 degrees)
Osteochondritis Dissecans	▪ 11 to 20 years old ▪ Male predominance	▪ Knee (most common at the lateral aspect of the medial epicondyle) ▪ Ankle ▪ Elbow ▪ Hip	▪ Dissected fragment may remain in close apposition; can reattach or become a loose body ▪ Fragment is close: arclike radiolucent cleft ▪ Fragment is displaced: concave defect at site of origin ▪ Use Tunnel View to visualize on film

Epiphyseal Disorders (9)

Skeletal Location	Epiphyseal Disorder	Most Common Location
Pelvis	**Van Neck's Disease**	Ischiopubic synchondrosis
Patella	**Sinding-Larsen-Johannsson Disease**	Secondary center of the patella
Tibia	**Blount's Disease**	Medial condyle of tibia
	Osgood Schlatter's Disease	Tibial tuberosity
Foot	**Frieberg's Disease**	Metatarsal head
	Sever's Disease	Calcaneal apophysis
	Kohler's Disease	Tarsal navicular
	Diaz's Disease	Talus
Knee (most common)	**Osteochondritis Dissecans**	Lateral aspect of medial epicondyle
Humerus	**Hass's Disease**	Humeral head
Hand	**Preiser's Disease**	Scaphoid
	Keinboch's Disease	Lunate
	Mauclaire's Disease	Metacarpal heads
Spine	**Scheurmann's Disease**	Thoracic spine

NUTRITIONAL, METABOLIC AND ENDOCRINE DISORDERS (10)

Disorder	Age / Sex		Location	Radiographic Findings
Osteoporosis ▪ Reduction in quantity of bone; quality remains normal ▪ Most common metabolic disease of bone ▪ Generalized, regional and localized forms	**Senile and Postmenopausal Osteoporosis**	▪ Clinical signs in the fifth or sixth decade for women ▪ Clinical signs in the sixth or seventh decade for men ▪ Women 4:1 until age 80 when the ratio equalizes	▪ Spine ▪ Pelvis ▪ Femur	▪ Altered vertebral shape: plana, wedged, biconcave/fish endplates, Schmorl's nodes, "pancake" vertebra ▪ Severe senile kyphosis ▪ Pathological fractures ▪ Pencil-thin cortices ▪ Pseudohemangioma: vertical trabeculae appear accented because they are under the most stress
	Regional Osteoporosis: Reflex Sympathetic Dystrophy	▪ Usually occurs after 50 years of age ▪ History of recent trauma, severe or trivial	▪ Progressive pain, swelling and atrophy distal to the area of trauma	▪ Patchy osteoporosis ▪ Metaphyseal ▪ Late stage: more generalized osteoporosis ▪ Joint disease is not present ▪ Periarticular osteoporosis
	Localized Osteoporosis			▪ Focal losses of bone density are usually due to local disease
Osteomalacia ▪ Quality of bone is altered, usually caused by lack of calcium being deposited in osteoid tissue ▪ Usually calcium, phosphorus or vitamin D deficiency ▪ Adult rickets	▪ Adult		▪ Structure and density of all osseous structures affected	▪ Decreased bone density; osteopenia ▪ Coarse trabecular pattern ▪ Pseudofractures: Looser's lines; Milkman's fractures ▪ Loss of cortical definition ▪ Deformities, especially in the weight-bearing bones ▪ No distinct zone between cortex and medullary bone ▪ Pathologic fracture

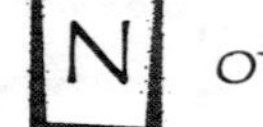

ote

- The following disorders can cause biconcave vertebrae: osteoporosis, osteomalacia, Paget's disease, and hyperparathyroidism.

Disorder	Age / Sex	Location	Radiographic Findings
Rickets ▪ Due to deficiency of vitamin D, calcium, or phosphate	▪ Clinical signs between 6 months and 1 year of age	▪ Systemic	▪ "Rachitic rosary" on anterior rib cage (costochondral bumps) ▪ Generalized osteopenia ▪ "Paintbrush" metaphysis; widened growth plates; cupping of the metaphyseal region ▪ Absent zone of provisional calcification ▪ Bowing deformities ▪ Fractures and pseudofractures ▪ Decreased bone length ▪ Scoliosis
Scurvy ▪ Long-term deficiency of vitamin C	▪ Avitaminosis usually occurs for four months before onset of symptoms ▪ Infants between 4 and 18 months are primarily affected	▪ Systemic	▪ Osteopenia ▪ Dense Zone of Provisional Calcification (White Line of Frankel) ▪ Ring epiphysis (Wimberger's Sign) ▪ Pelken's Spurs (bony protruberances at the metaphyseal margins) ▪ Trummerfeld Zone (radiolucent band below zone of provisional calcification due to disordered osteoid formation) ▪ Subperiosteal hemorrhage
Hyperparathyroidism ▪ Primary, secondary and tertiary forms; can't differentiate on x-ray	▪ 30 to 50 years old ▪ Females 3:1	▪ Hands ▪ Skull ▪ Spine	▪ Accented trabecular patterns ▪ Loss of cortical definition ▪ Brown tumors – usually central, slightly expansile, mimic destructive neoplasm ▪ Subperiosteal bone resorption: "Lace" pattern on side of middle and proximal phalanges due to bone resorption ▪ Osteolysis of distal phalanges ▪ Calcification of vasculature and soft tissue structures due to increases in serum calcium ▪ Salt and Pepper skull ▪ "Rugger Jersey" spine: decreased density in the center of the vertebral body and endplate sclerosis ▪ Widened sacroiliac joints

ote

- The following disorders can cause radiolucent metaphyseal bands: leukemia, rickets, scurvy, syphilis, and normal variations.

Disorder	Age / Sex	Location	Radiographic Findings
Acromegaly ▪ Caused by excessive growth hormone secretion after bone growth plates have closed	▪ Adult	▪ Skull ▪ Hands and feet ▪ Spine	▪ Periosteal appositional new bone with undulating periosteal response ▪ Skull: sella turcica enlargement, sinus overgrowth and malocclusion ▪ Frontal bossing ▪ Hand and foot: widened bone shafts, enlarged distal tufts ("Trident hand"/ "spade-like" hand) ▪ Spine: platyspondyly, hyperostoses, widened disc and facet spaces, posterior vertebral body scalloping ▪ Widened atlantodental interspace ▪ Heel pad thickness increases to more than 20 mm; calcaneal spurs
Cushing's Disease ▪ Excessive glucocorticoid steroids released by the adrenal cortex ▪ Patient can have "moon face," "buffalo hump," hirsutism and truncal obesity ▪ Same clinical and radiologic findings produced by long-term use of therapeutic corticosteroids			▪ Osteopenia: thin cortices, deformities ▪ Biconcave endplate deformities in the spine ▪ Avascular necrosis (osteonecrosis), especially in the femoral heads; more common with corticosteroid use than with Cushing's disease ▪ Pathologic fractures, especially in the spine ▪ Intravertebral vacuum cleft sign ▪ Biconcave endplates ▪ Multiple rib fractures
Heavy Metal Poisoning ▪ Usually lead, phosphorus and bismuth			▪ Linear, transverse densities at the metaphyses ("lead lines")

Disorder		Age / Sex	Location	Radiographic Findings
Histiocytosis X ▪ Abnormal proliferation of reticuloendothelial cells	**Letterer-Siwe Disease**	▪ Children under 3 years old	▪ Skeletal lesions infrequent	▪ Lytic lesions in the calvarium
	Hand-Schuller-Christian Disease			▪ Polyostotic destructive foci ▪ Skull: large, map-like, radiolucent (lytic) lesions ▪ Classic triad (less than 10% of patients) includes: exophthalmus, diabetes insipidus, lytic skull lesions
	Eosinophilic Granuloma	▪ 5 to 10 years old ▪ Male predominance	▪ Skull ▪ Mandible ▪ Pelvis ▪ Long bones ▪ Ribs	▪ Solitary, geographic, round to oval lesions with sharply demarcated borders ▪ Skull: beveled edge sign; "hole-within-a-hole" appearance ▪ Spine: "coin on edge" vertebrae
Gaucher's Disease ▪ Inborn error of lipid metabolism ▪ Three types recognized		▪ Type I: chronic adult form ▪ Type II: acute infantile form ▪ Type III: subacute juvenile form	▪ Hips ▪ Knees ▪ Spine	▪ Avascular necrosis of the femoral and humeral heads ▪ Erlenmeyer flask deformity ▪ Osteoporosis ▪ Medullary expansion ▪ Cortical thinning ▪ Lytic lesions ▪ Periostitis ▪ DJD in the hips and knees

Chest Films

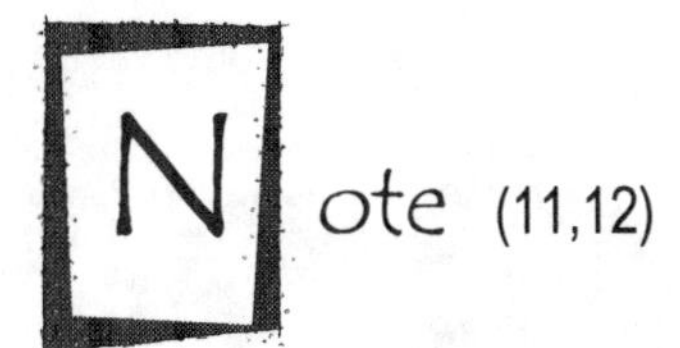

ote (11,12)

- The technique used for chest films has been designed for study of the lungs, with a higher kV value than that used for osseous films in order to create a longer scale of contrast.
- To detect a mediastinal shift, use the trachea (which is normally in the midline), right heart border and aortic knob as landmarks
- Projections include P to A (shoulders rolled forward to move scapulae out of the way; patient inspires); lateral with arms overhead; and lordotic (to visualize lung apices, right middle lobe and lingula segments).

Pathology	Radiographic findings (13)
Pleural effusion	▪ Blunting of angle between diaphragm and rib cage ▪ Upward concave border of fluid level
Pneumothorax	▪ Hyperlucent area in which all pulmonary markings are absent ▪ Visible visceral pleural line ▪ Mediastinal shift away from side of involvement ▪ Visible air-fluid line with no vascular markings above
Emphysema	▪ Flattening of the domes of the diaphragm (looks low) ▪ Increased size and lucency of the retrosternal air space, the distance between the posterior side of the sternum and the anterior wall of the ascending aorta ▪ Barrel chest (increased AP diameter) ▪ Reduction in number and size of peripheral arteries ▪ Bullae (air-containing cystic spaces) ▪ Increased marking patterns
Pneumonia	▪ Silhouette sign (obliteration of heart border by a water density) with right upper lobe pneumonia ▪ Consolidation in the affected segment(s) of the lung(s) ▪ Decreased rib spaces on affected side due to patient's inability to fully inspire
Atelectasis	▪ Local increase in density caused by lack of air in the lung ▪ Displacement of heart, mediastinum and hilum toward the affected portion of the lung ▪ Compensatory overinflation of the unaffected part of the ipsilateral lung
Congestive heart failure	▪ Enlargement of the heart ▪ Kerley B lines (due to created by accumulation of fluid in interlobular septa) ▪ Texas longhorn appearance ▪ Hazing of the lung fields
Sarcoidosis	▪ Bilateral, symmetrical potato nodes in hilar region; indicates lymphadenopathy ▪ Diffuse interstitial pattern that is widely distributed throughout both lungs

Kidney, Ureter, Bladder (KUB) (14,15)

ote

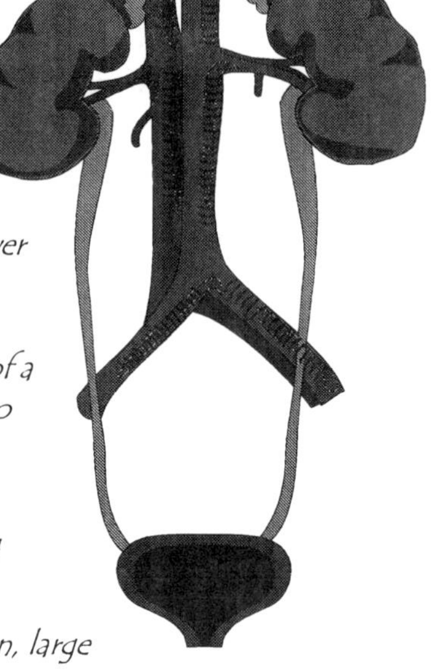

- The KUB is a plain film (no artificially introduced contrast substance).
- From the film you can evaluate

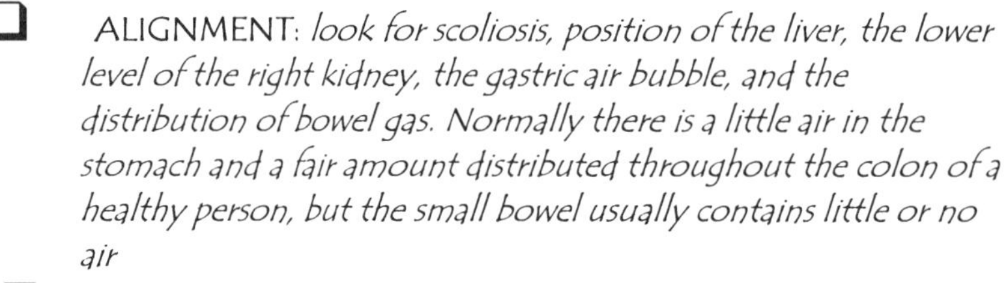

- ❑ ALIGNMENT: *look for scoliosis, position of the liver, the lower level of the right kidney, the gastric air bubble, and the distribution of bowel gas. Normally there is a little air in the stomach and a fair amount distributed throughout the colon of a healthy person, but the small bowel usually contains little or no air*

- ❑ BONE: *spine, pelvis, sacrum, lower ribs*
- ❑ CARTILAGE: *joints and disc spaces, sacroiliac, pubic, hips, and lower costals*

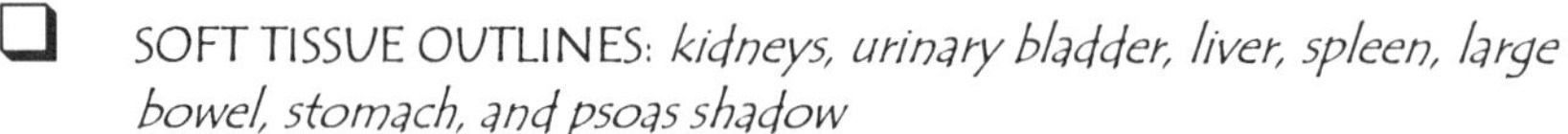

- ❑ SOFT TISSUE OUTLINES: *kidneys, urinary bladder, liver, spleen, large bowel, stomach, and psoas shadow*

Intravenous Urogram (16)

ote

- A plain film to screen for calcifications or stones precedes the conventional intravenous urogram.

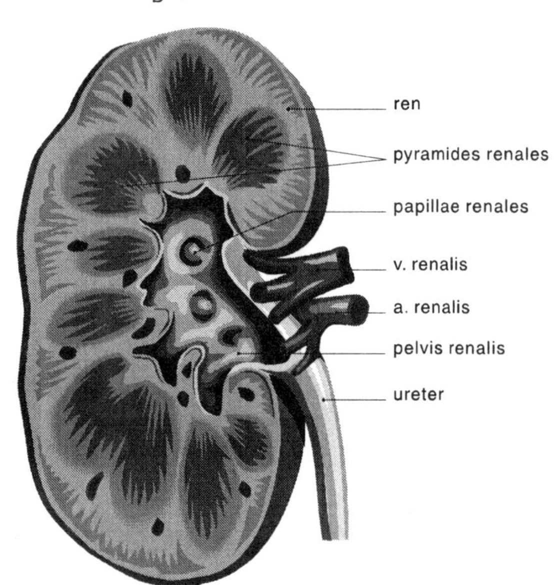

- Then an intravenous infusion of iodinated contrast material is followed by a series of x-ray films that show the opacified kidneys, ureters, and bladder.
- The intravenous urogram is a morphologic rather than functional exam.
- NEPHROGRAM PHASE: occurs less than one minute after the intravenous infusion begins, and is used to evaluate the size and shape of the kidney. In this phase the contrast material, which is excreted almost entirely in the glomerular filtrate, creates enough opacity in the glomeruli and tubules of the renal parenchyma to produce a good kidney shadow. REMEMBER: *the normal length of the kidney is 3.7 times the height of the patient's L2 vertebral body.*
- The calyces, pelves, ureters, and bladder are viewed in sequence during the 20 to 30 minutes after the nephrogram phase.

COMPUTED TOMOGRAPHY (17,18)

ote

- Plain tomography and CT (computed tomography) are not the same thing. Conventional tomography gives you a sharply focused picture of one plane of the patient upon which are superimposed blurred images of structures above and below the area of interest. A CT scan gives a focused picture of one cross-sectional slice of the patient without superimposed images.
- Godfried Hounsfield introduced the first CT equipment in 1972, and won a Nobel prize for medicine in 1979 for the discovery of CT. The original equipment was designed for brain scanning, but an American dentist named Ledley promoted interest in whole-body use of CT to funding for the construction of the first whole-body scanner.

TOMOGRAPHIC SCANNING

CT scanner: rotates around the patient as x-rays are directed to the area of study.

Gantry: houses the x-ray tubes and scintillation detectors. The patient is placed horizontally in the open center; most CT scanners allow angulation of the up to 30 degrees to provide angled slices through the discs.

Photon detector cells housed in the gantry absorb and register attenuated energy (x-rays after they have passed through the patient). The volume of data from the detectors is processed by a computer to form the CT image.

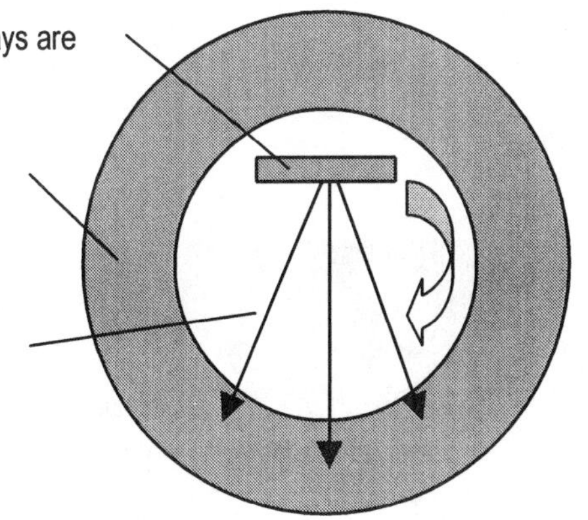

TOMOGRAPHIC IMAGE FORMATION

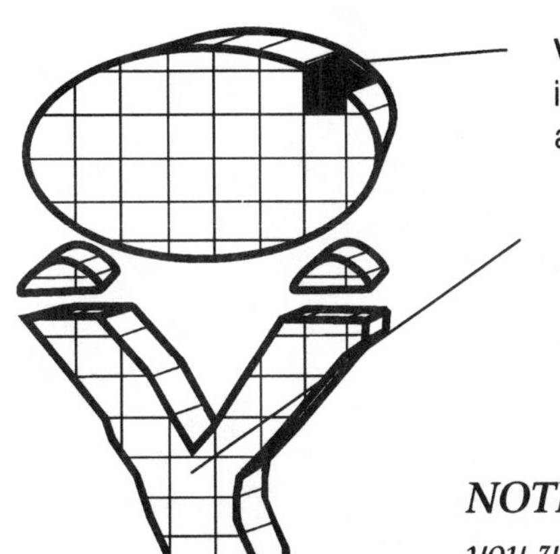

Voxel: The shaded, three-dimensional box represents a voxel, or unit volume, of information. The information is conveyed to a computer, which determines the x-ray absorption for each voxel and assigns an attenuation coefficient of that volume of tissue.

Pixel: The two-dimensional squares represent the attenuation characteristics from the three-dimensional voxels. Each pixel is comprised of multiple attenuation coefficients that are averaged to create a mean measurement of tissue density, which is expressed in Hounsfield units.

NOTE: With computed tomography, you read the film as if you were looking up through the patient's feet; structures on your right are in the left side of the patient's body.

HOUNSFIELD UNITS

The pictorial arrangement of absorption values, expressed in Hounsfield units, makes up the CT image. The Hounsfield unit is the unit of radiographic density in computed tomography. Water was arbitrarily assigned a Hounsfield unit of zero. Denser values more clearly portray bone, which can have a window of +500 or more, and less dense structures range downward through fat to air, which can be –500 or less.

WINDOW LEVEL AND WIDTH

Window Level: an arbitrary number , expressed in Hounsfield Units, selected to limit the shades of gray to optimally display a specific tissue density. The window level is the median density visualized.

Window Width: a preselected range of attenuation values chosen to visualize a range of tissue densities.

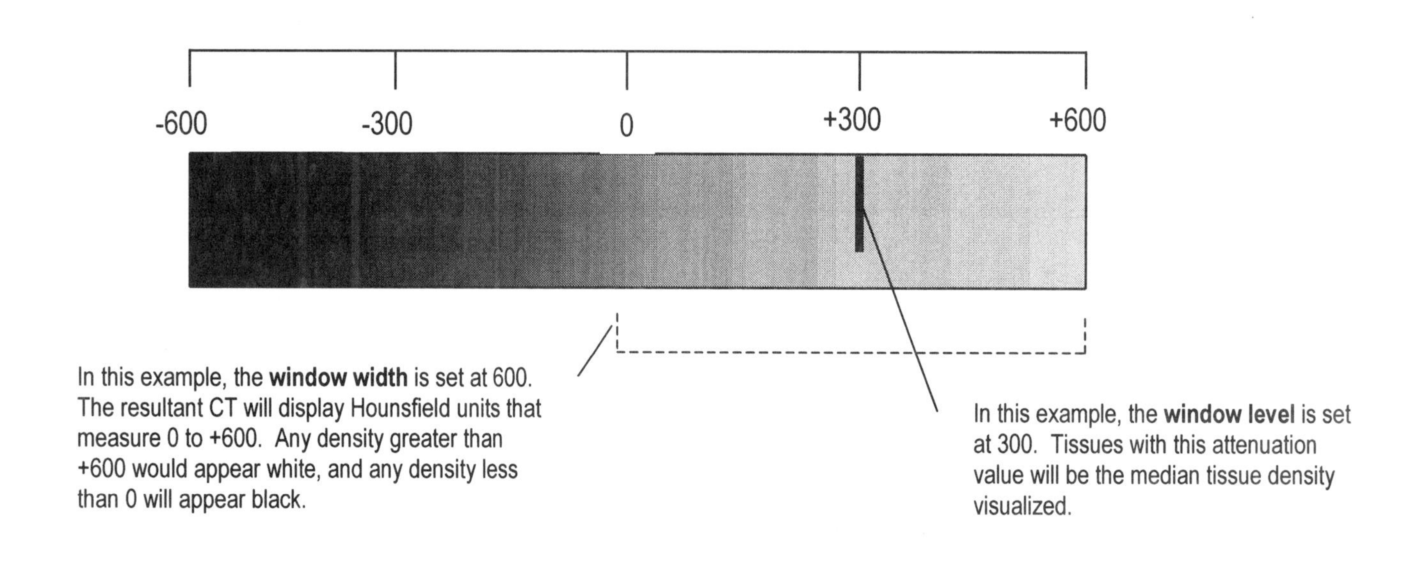

SOFT TISSUE WINDOW

- Window level and width that optimize the attenuation values of soft tissues.

BONE WINDOW

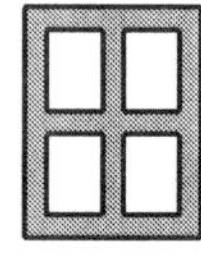

- Window level and width that optimize the attenuation values of bone, allowing cortical and medullary differentiation.

INDICATIONS

Disorder	Example
Trauma	▪ Musculoskeletal lesions that are occult or inadequately demonstrated on plain film
Infection	▪ Discitis ▪ Osteomyelitis ▪ Brodie's abscess ▪ Associated soft tissue involvement ▪ Spinal infection, endplate destruction, paravertebral masses
Vascular	▪ Aneurysms of the intracranial or intrathoracic vessels ▪ Abdominal aortic aneurysms (NOTE: ultrasound is more cost effective and less invasive)
Neoplasms	▪ Osseous characteristics and calcified regions of benign and malignant neoplasms (NOTE: MRI is used to evaluate soft tissue neoplasms)
Congenital Malformations	▪ Congenital anomalies ▪ Congenital spinal stenosis
Arthritides	▪ Degenerative changes in the spine ▪ Spinal canal and lateral recess stenosis
Disc Herniation	▪ Useful to evaluate disc herniation when MRI is not available
Bone Densitometry	▪ Quantitative computed tomography is used in the assessment of bone mineral density with patients who have osteoporosis

CONTRAINDICATIONS

- General precautions for use of ionizing radiation should be observed.
- Hypersensitivity to contrast infusions contraindicates contrast studies.
- Presence of metallic objects near the area to be visualized can result in artifact formation due to scattering of the beam.
- Claustrophobia may occur to a patient when he or she is placed in the gantry.

MAGNETIC RESONANCE IMAGING (19)

ote

- Magnetic resonance imaging (MRI) provides a view of an axial slice of anatomy but does not use ionizing radiation.
- MRI can provide multiplanar images in any orientation without moving the patient's position within the scanner.

THE MAGNET

- MRI uses one of three types of magnets: resistive (electromagnetic), permanent, or superconductive. The latter is the most commonly used system today. Superconducting magnets are maintained at a temperature near absolute zero by liquid cryogens.
- Magnetic strength is measured in **TESLA** or gauss, with one tesla equal to 10,000 gauss.
- The magnet is housed in a gantry and the patient is placed on a couch which remains stationary inside the magnet for the entire exam.

CREATING THE IMAGE

3 After the radiofrequency pulse is removed, the coil records the amount of energy transferred (radiofrequency signal) from the realignment of the protons to the magnetic field. The MR image is produced by computer from the proton-generated radiofrequency signal.

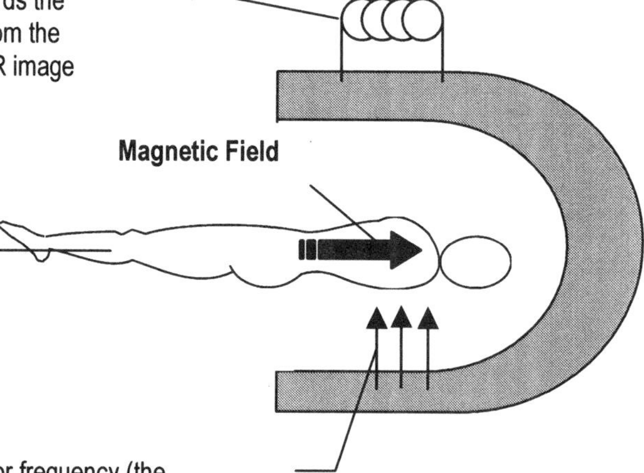

1 The patient is aligned in the gantry with the north-south axis of the magnetic field. The patient's hydrogen atoms will align their magnetic axes in either a parallel or antiparallel orientation.

2 A radiofrequency pulse of the appropriate Larmor frequency (the frequency of rotational motion of a proton as it wobbles about the axis of an external magnetic field) is passed through the patient's body at a 90-degree angle to the magnetic field. This causes hydrogen atoms in the body to move to a higher energy state by altering their orientation relative to the external magnetic field.

SPIN-ECHO SEQUENCES

- MRI image characteristics can be manipulated by altering the interval between radiofrequency pulses (TR; repetition time) and the time between the pulse and the detection of the MR signal (TE; echo time).
- Following a radiofrequency pulse, the excited hydrogen atoms return to alignment with the magnetic field during the relaxation time. Two different relaxation methods – T1 (spin-lattice) and T2 (spin-spin) – occur simultaneously.
- T1 and T2 relaxation times can be altered to give a predominantly T1-weighted image or a T2-weighted image. If the parameters are altered to minimize the effects of T1 and T2 relaxation times, the result is a proton density-weighted image that has characteristics of both sequences.

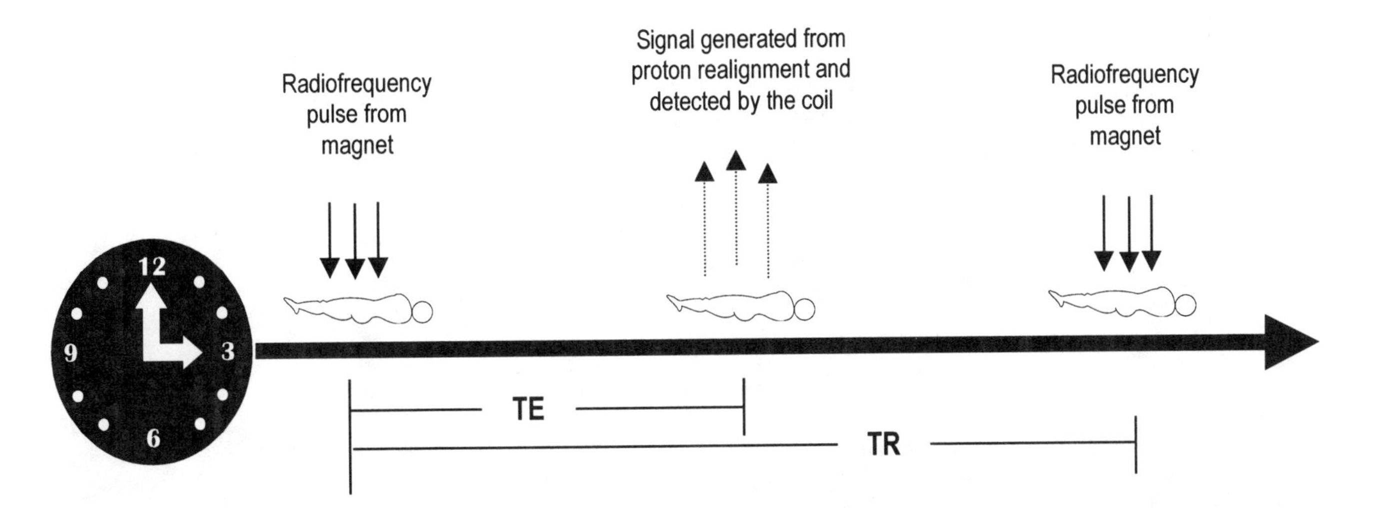

Image	TR	TE	Characteristics
T1-weighted image	Short	Short	▪ Excellent anatomic information ▪ Also called the "fat image" where fat is bright and water densities (intervertebral discs, CSF) are dark
T2-weighted image	Long	Long	▪ Tissues containing mobile hydrogen protons (intervertebral discs, CSF) are bright ▪ Also known as the "water image"
Proton density-weighted image	Long	Short	▪ Provides characteristics of both T1 and T2-weighted images

INDICATIONS

Indication	Example
Spine	▪ Cervical, thoracic and lumbar disc disease ▪ Trauma to vertebral column or spinal cord ▪ Congenital disorders ▪ Early tumor infiltration of bone marrow ▪ Late stages of metastasis ▪ Primary bone neoplasms ▪ Scoliosis ▪ Infectious spondylitis ▪ Spinal cord tumors
Multiple sclerosis	▪ MR imaging is the first and only imaging modality that allows direct visualization of the plaque-like inflammation of the CNS and that characterizes MS
Hip	▪ Common pathologies such as fracture and arthritis
Knee	▪ Meniscal and cruciate and collateral ligament lesions ▪ Chondromalacia patella, Osgood-Schlatter's disease, osteochondritis dissecans, many others ▪ Fracture
Ankle	▪ Injury to tendons and ligaments
Shoulder	▪ Sports- and work-related injuries ▪ Inflammatory processes ▪ Nontraumatic pain
Wrist	▪ Ligamentous injury, occult fracture, carpal tunnel
TMJ	▪ Evaluate structure and function

CONTRAINDICATIONS

- Patients in excess of 300 pounds may be too large to fit into the bore of most scanners.
- Claustrophobia may occur to patients while lying in the gantry; open MRI is an alternative.
- Body inclusions such as metal clips or shards or intraocular foreign bodies contraindicate MR examination.
- Cardiac pacemakers, implanted neurostimulators, some prosthetic heart valves, cochlear implants or other hearing aids, life-support equipment and early pregnancy are contraindications.
- Most surgical clips are not ferromagnetic and do not prevent MR examination.
- Joint prostheses, Harrington rods, and most other orthopedic appliances are not contraindications.

ote

- All ferromagnetic devices and metallic objects must be removed from the patient for MR examination; they may become projectile hazards.

SCINTIGRAPHY: NUCLEAR MEDICINE (20,21)

ote

- In diagnostic nuclear imaging, images are generated as the uptake and distribution of intravenously administered radiopharmaceuticals are detected. Radiopharmaceuticals are deposited in target organs from the circulatory system and are made up of a radionuclide and a pharmacologic agent. A radionuclide emits gamma radiation while undergoing radioactive decay. The half-life of the radiopharmaceutical must be long enough for the gamma camera to detect its emissions and short enough to limit patient radiation to the lowest possible levels.
- Nuclear imaging provides vital information about tissue perfusion, physiology, and biochemistry, but it does not provide the best analysis of structural integrity.
- Scintigraphy is synonymous for a nuclear imaging technique such as single photon emission computed tomography (SPECT), positron emission tomography (PET) and bone scan. The term is derived from the decay of a radionuclide and its resultant gamma radiation or scintillations. A gamma camera detects the scintillations (radiation), a computer processes them and they are displayed as an image.

Nuclear Imaging Method	Radiopharmaceutical	Image Production	Indications
SPECT	Technetium-99m methylene diphosphonate (^{99m}Tc-MDP)	Between 1 and 4 gamma cameras on a rotating gantry are used to provide images in a selected plane. The images may be displayed in a 3-dimensional format like CT or MRI.	▪ Tumor surveillance ▪ Enhances ability to accurately localize and identify a wide range of musculoskeletal lesions ▪ Utility is maximized in spine, TMJ and hip joint
PET	Fluorine-18 (^{18}F) fluorodeoxyglucose (FDG)	Radiation from a positron and electron collision is measured by rings of detectors encircling the patient and displayed as a tomographic image. Image resolution of PET is superior to SPECT. Provides information about distribution and magnitude of glucose metabolism.	▪ Brain physiology and cardiac perfusion, oncologic applications ▪ Allows differentiation of high-grade malignant soft tissue lesions from low-grade and benign neoplasms
Bone Scan	Technetium-99m methylene diphosphonate (^{99m}Tc-MDP)	The most frequently performed nuclear medicine technique. It is very sensitive, but non-specific. Areas of increased gamma emission are hot spots. Areas of decreased emissions are cold spots. Most bone scans are performed in three phases representing the distribution of the tracer (radiopharmaceutical) over time.	▪ Soft tissue, bone and joint disorders

BONE SCAN (20,21)

ote

- The bone scan has great physiologic sensitivity but provides limited anatomic information and diagnostic specificity.
- An injected radioactive isotope is taken up by organs and tissues and emits gamma rays for a brief period of time as it undergoes decay. The number of scintillations detected by the camera correspond to the concentration of the isotope. Physiologic differences between normal and pathologic tissue produce different patterns of radiopharmaceutical uptake and distribution. Areas of increased or decreased gamma emissions are called hot and cold spots, respectively.
- Most radionuclide bone scans are performed in three phases representing the distribution of the tracer over the course of time.

Phase	Description	Time
1	**Flow phase or radionuclide angiogram**: intravenous injection of radiopharmaceutical agent	Rapid sequential images are obtained over the area of interest every 2 to 3 seconds for 30 seconds
2	**Blood-pool phase**: occurs when the tracer is located in the extravascular space	A diffusion pattern is obtained by imaging the whole body or region of interest 5 minutes after injection
3	**Bone scan phase**: delayed images represent clearance of the tracer from the vessels and soft tissues and concentration into the skeleton	Images representing clearance of the tracer from the vessels and soft tissues to the skeleton are produced between 2 and 4 hours following injection

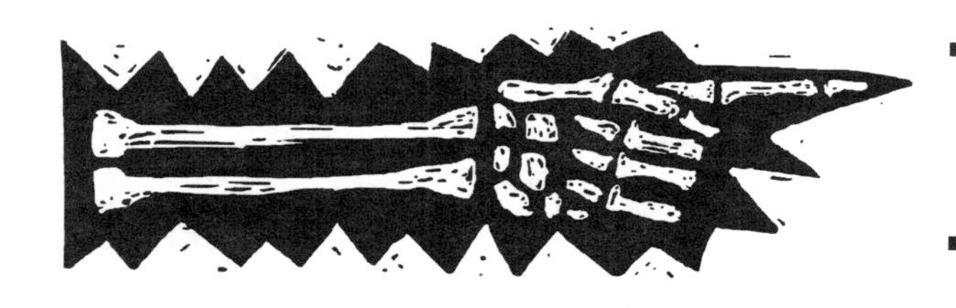

- Multiple myeloma is **COLD** on bone scan. A radiographic skeletal survey is more accurate to diagnose multiple myeloma.
- Metastatic carcinoma is **HOT** on bone scan, which is the imaging modality of choice to detect osseous metastatic carcinoma.

ote

- The ALARA principle states that procedures should not only maintain radiation doses within legal limits, but should be As Low As Reasonably Achievable. This principle helps dictate the choice of radiopharmaceutical.
- Indications and contraindications for the use of bone scan include the following:

Contraindications	Pregnancy	Transplacental transmission of radiopharmaceuticals is possible
	Dehydration	
Indications	Trauma	Occult fracture, stress fracture, acute spondylolysis
	Infection	Osteomyelitis, septic arthritis, cellulitis
	Vascular	Infarction
	Neoplasm	Benign and malignant (metastasis)
	Arthritis	Inflammatory and hypertrophic
	Metabolic	Paget's, fibrous dysplasia
	Other	Prosthesis, course of disease, clinical features of a disease which is unresponsive to therapy or unremarkable on other imaging

ote

- Skeletal scintigraphy has a sensitivity of 95 to 97% in the detection of osseous mets. The typical pattern of mets on bone scan is diffuse multifocal lesions randomly scattered throughout the axial skeleton. Differentials include fracture, Paget's disease, osteomyelitis, metabolic bone disease, and occasionally osteoarthritis.
- MRI is equally sensitive and more specific than bone scan in detecting mets, but does not provide the practical advantage of imaging the entire skeleton in a single examination.

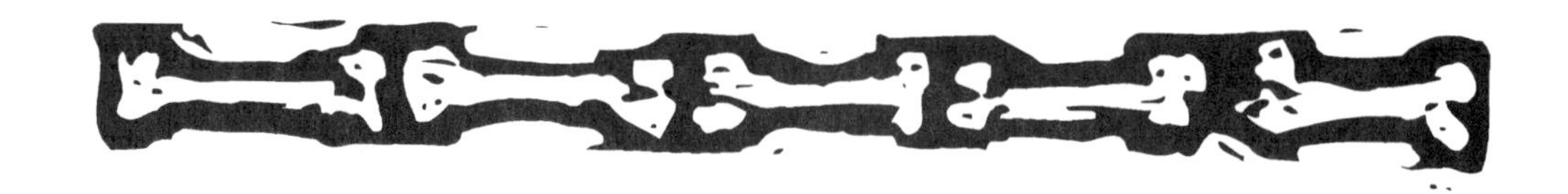

REFERENCES

1 Yochum TR, Rowe LJ. Essentials of Skeletal Radiology. Vol. 1. 2nd Edition. Baltimore: Williams & Wilkins, 1996: 319-320.
2 Seron MA, Yochum TR, Barry MS, Rowe LJ. Skeletal Dysplasias. In: Yochum TR, Rowe LJ. Essentials of Skeletal Radiology. Vol. 1. 2nd Edition. Baltimore: Williams & Wilkins, 1996: 585-651.
3 Rowe LJ, Yochum, TR. Trauma. In: Yochum TR, Rowe LJ. Essentials of Skeletal Radiology. Vol. 1. 2nd Edition. Baltimore: Williams & Wilkins, 1996: 653-793.
4 Yochum TR, Rowe LJ, Barry MS. Natural History of Spondylolysis and Spondylolisthesis. In: Yochum TR, Rowe LJ. Essentials of Skeletal Radiology. Vol. 1. 2nd Edition. Baltimore: Williams & Wilkins, 1996: 331-335, 341, 346.
5 Rowe LJ, Yochum TR. Arthritic Disorders. In: Yochum TR, Rowe LJ. Essentials of Skeletal Radiology. Vol. 2. 2nd Edition. Baltimore: Williams & Wilkins, 1996: 795-973.
6 Yochum TR, Rowe LJ. Essentials of Skeletal Radiology. 2nd ed. Baltimore: Williams & Wilkins, 1996: 563-575.
7 Yochum TR, Rowe LJ. Tumors and Tumorlike Processes. In: Yochum TR, Rowe LJ. Essentials of Skeletal Radiology. Vol. 2. 2nd Edition. Baltimore: Williams & Wilkins, 1996: 975-1191.
8 Rowe LJ, Yochum TR. Infection. In: Yochum TR, Rowe LJ. Essentials of Skeletal Radiology. Vol. 2. 2nd Edition. Baltimore: Williams & Wilkins, 1996: 1193-1241.
9 Rowe LJ, Yochum TR. Hematologic and Vascular Disorders. In: Yochum TR, Rowe LJ. Essentials of Skeletal Radiology. Vol. 2. 2nd Edition. Baltimore: Williams & Wilkins, 1996: 1243-1305.
10 Rowe LJ, Yochum TR. Nutritional, Metabolic and Endocrine Disorders. In: Yochum TR, Rowe LJ. Essentials of Skeletal Radiology. Vol. 2. 2nd Edition. Baltimore: Williams & Wilkins, 1996: 1327-1370.
11 Squire LF, Novelline RA. Fundamentals of Radiology. 4th ed. Cambridge, Massachusetts: Harvard University Press, 1995:32.
12 Yochum TR, Rowe LJ. Essentials of Skeletal Radiology. 2nd ed. Baltimore: Williams & Wilkins, 1996:128-133.
13 Eisenberg RL, Dennis CA. Comprehensive Radiographic Pathology. 2nd ed. St. Louis: Mosby, 1995: 26-27, 34-35, 47, 51-55, 211-212, 353-355.
14 Yochum TR, Rowe LJ. Essentials of Skeletal Radiology. 2nd ed. Baltimore: Williams & Wilkins, 1996: 134-135.
15 Squire LF, Novelline RA. Fundamentals of Radiology. 4th ed. Cambridge, Massachusetts: Harvard University Press, 1995: 156-157.
16 Squire LF, Novelline RA. Fundamentals of Radiology. 4th ed. Cambridge, Massachusetts: Harvard University Press, 1995: 250-251.
17 Yochum TR, Rowe LJ. Essentials of Skeletal Radiology. 2nd ed. Baltimore: Williams & Wilkins, 1996: 473-477, 483, 485, 490.
18 Squire LF, Novelline RA. Fundamentals of Radiology. 4th ed. Cambridge, Massachusetts: Harvard University Press, 1995: 24-26.
19 Yochum TR, Rowe LJ. Essentials of Skeletal Radiology. 2nd ed. Baltimore: Williams & Wilkins, 1996: 374-429.
20 Yochum TR, Rowe LJ. Essentials of Skeletal Radiology. 2nd ed. Baltimore: Williams & Wilkins, 1996: 508-537.
21 Squire LF, Novelline RA. Fundamentals of Radiology. 4th ed. Cambridge, Massachusetts: Harvard University Press, 1995: 29-31.

CHAPTER 4

Physical Diagnosis

VITAL SIGNS (1)

Height and Weight	Use a standing platform scale with a height attachment	
Temperature	**Normal temperature**: ▪ Oral 98.6^{0} F ▪ Rectal and ear 99.6^{0} F ▪ Axilla 97.6^{0} F **Normal range**: ▪ 96-99.5 F or 35-37.5 C	**Factors affecting temperature**: ▪ Gender, age, hormones ▪ Exercise ▪ Stress ▪ Temperature extremes over long periods of time
Pulse	▪ Normal pulse rate is 60-100 beats per minute for adults and 120-160 beats per minute for newborns (decreases with age until adolescence) ▪ Determine if pulse is regular or irregular; if regular, count for 15 seconds; if irregular count for one minute	
Respiratory Rate	▪ Normal rate is 12-20 breaths per minute ▪ Don't let the patient know you are counting	
Blood Pressure *Center the deflated cuff bladder over the brachial artery, just medial to the biceps tendon*	▪ Normal blood pressure for adults is 90-140/ 60-90 mm Hg ▪ Take blood pressure bilaterally; pump the cuff up to 30 mmHg above the palpated systolic pressure to assess the blood pressure ▪ Cuff bladder should be 80% of arm size; if the cuff is too large, it will give a falsely low reading and if the cuff is too small it will give a falsely high reading ▪ Palpate for the systolic pressure to avoid a false reading from an auscultatory gap. Auscultatory gap decreases with constrictive cardiac events ▪ Readings between arms may vary as much as 10 mm Hg and tend to be higher in the right arm. Variation of greater than 10 mm Hg between arms may indicate the need for further evaluation ▪ Korotkoff sounds are low-pitched sounds produced by turbulent blood flow in arteries ▪ Pulse pressure is the difference between the systolic and diastolic pressures. Widens in the instance of systolic hypertension or a drop in diastolic pressure; narrows with constrictive cardiac events	

Measurement	Older Adults	Pregnancy	Infants / Children
Pulse		• Increases during pregnancy; peaks at the 28th week • Returns to pre-pregnancy level within 2 to 6 weeks after delivery	• 1-year-old: 80-160 bpm • 3-year-old: 80-120 bpm • 6-year-old: 75-115 bpm • 10-year-old: 70-110 bpm
Respiratory rate			• Infants: about 40 to 60 breaths per minute
Blood Pressure	• Blood pressure generally increases with age • High blood pressure in the elderly: 170/95	• Decreases slightly in the second trimester; returns to pre-pregnancy level from third trimester on	

THE EYE EXAM (2,3)

The Inner Eye

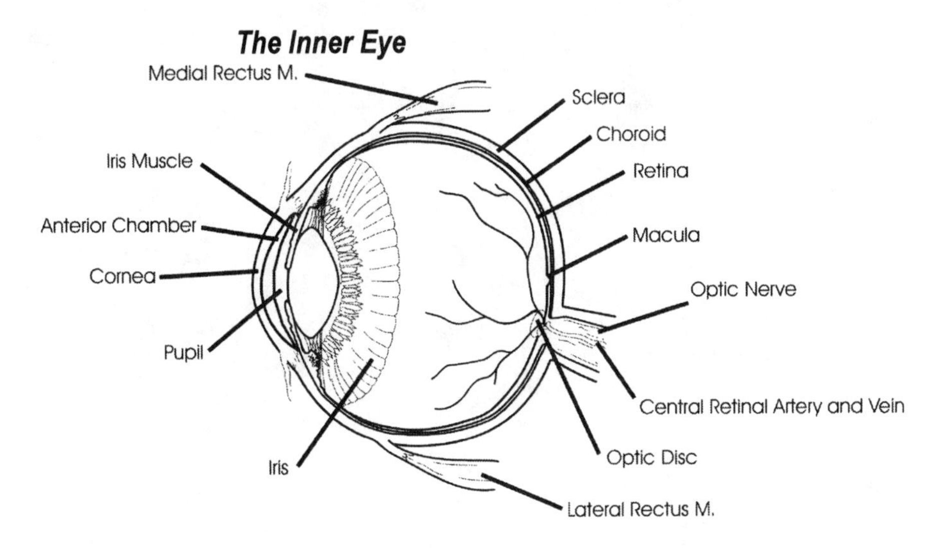

The Outer Eye

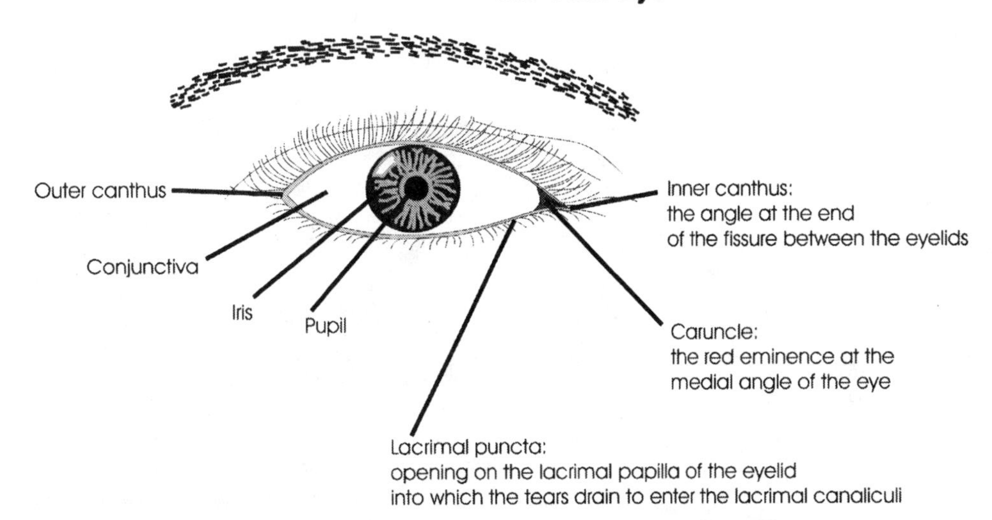

Inspection	▪ Inspect the external structures of the eye ▪ Anterior chamber test: shine a pen light across the eye from lateral to medial. Pen light should not create a shadow on the inner half of the iris; shadow indicates predisposition for narrow angle glaucoma; patient would present with eye pain
Palpation	▪ Palpate around the eyes and press on the eyeballs with patient's eyes closed
Cranial Nerves	1. **CN II** ▪ Visual acuity: Snellen Chart, measurement of central vision ▪ Rosenbaum chart is for near vision and also tests visual acuity ▪ Confrontation test ("wiggle fingers") for peripheral vision 2. **CNs III, IV, VI** ▪ H-pattern (cardinal fields of gaze/ extraocular movements) ▪ Convergence reflex (CN III) ▪ Direct and indirect pupillary light reflex (CNs II and III) ▪ Cover/uncover test for covert strabismus 3. **CNs V, VII** ▪ Corneal reflex: CN V is sensory, CN VII is motor to close the eyes; make sure the patient is looking away from the cotton as it touches the sclera

Rough Sketch of the Normal Fundus

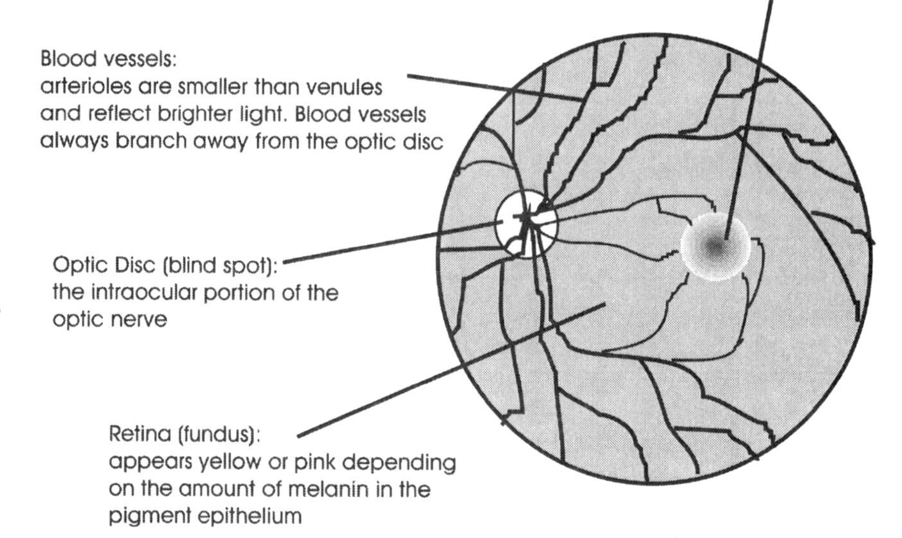

Funduscopic Exam Dim the lights!	1. Use the smallest aperture possible to prevent the pupil from constricting 2. Look for the red reflex: adjust the diopter dial (red/negative for near-sighted patient, green/positive for far-sighted patient), find a vessel and follow it to the optic disc. Examine the disc and cup 3. Follow vessels to all four quadrants 4. Return to the disc, then move the scope medially to look laterally at the macula densa (area void of blood vessels two disc diameters lateral to the disc), or have the patient look into the light directly
The normal fundus	▪ Retina – red/orange color in caucasians ▪ Optic disc and physiological cup – cream colored with distinct margins ▪ Macula – dark area two disc diameters lateral to the disc ▪ Veins (larger and darker) and arteries (smaller and redder), venules and arterioles
Some common expected and unexpected findings	▪ Xanthelasma – small, flat, yellowish skin plaques due to lipid deposition on the eyelids ▪ Hordeolum – sty caused by staphylococcus ▪ Miosis – contraction of the pupil to less than 2mm in diameter ▪ Mydriasis – pupillary dilation of more than 6 mm; failure of the pupils to constrict when exposed to light ▪ Anisocoria – inequality of pupil size; a common variation but may also indicate pathology ▪ Myopia – nearsightedness; hyperopia – farsightedness ▪ Presbyopia – visual deficiency secondary to aging ▪ Papilledema – edema of the optic disc resulting in loss of definition of the disc margin; often caused by increased intracranial pressure; AKA "choked disc" ▪ Corneal Arcus – lipid deposits in the periphery of the cornea; usually seen in patients over 60 years and if seen before 40, indicates hyperlipidemia ▪ Drusen bodies – can appear as small, discrete spots that are slightly pinker than the retina, and which eventually become yellow and blur the disc margins. Consequence of the aging process and considered a normal variant; however, may be a precursor of macular degeneration ▪ Strabismus – condition in which both eyes do not focus on an object simultaneously; caused by impairment of one or more extraocular muscles or their nerve supply ▪ Entropion – the lower eyelid is turned in and eyelashes may cause corneal and conjunctival irritation ▪ Ectropion – the lower eyelid is turned away from the eye and may lead to excessive tearing ▪ Lagophthalmos – the closed eyelids do not cover the globe of the eye
Pathological fundus	▪ Hypertensive retinopathy – hard and soft exudates, flame hemorrhages, AV nicking and tapering ▪ Papilledema – elevated, swollen disc with blurred margins; can be seen with later hypertension ▪ Glaucoma – large cup with disc vessels displaced laterally; pigment ring surrounding disc; hemorrhage at disc margin ▪ Diabetes – neovascularization, hard exudates

THE EAR EXAM (4,5)

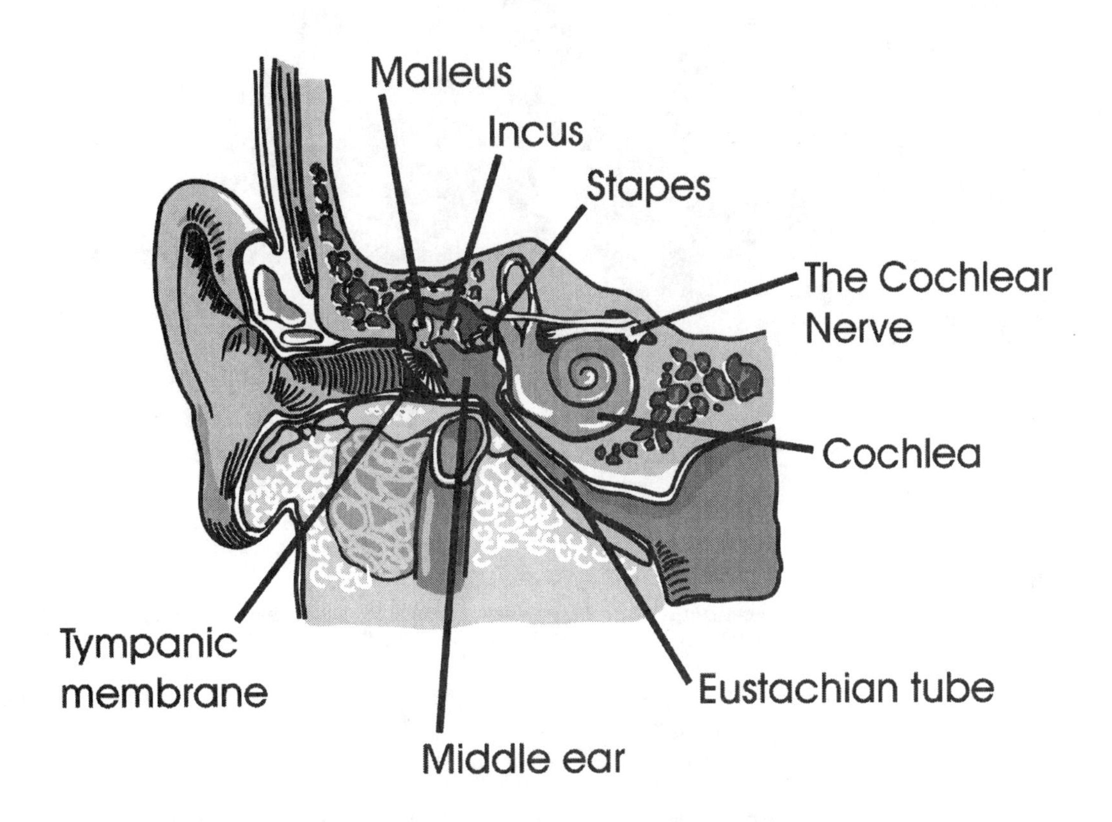

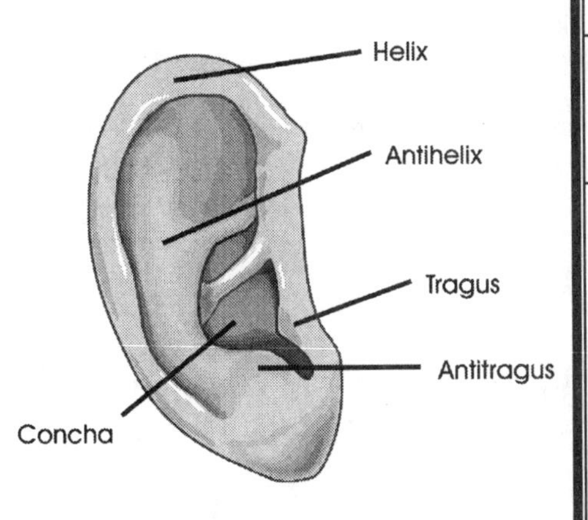

Inspection	▪ Ask the patient to remove his/her glasses ▪ Observe external features of the ear; note any lesions, lumps or malformations ▪ Pull the ear forward and look behind the ear
Palpation	▪ Palpate the entire pinna and lobe between the thumb and index finger, looking for nodules or tenderness ▪ Press on the tragus and gently pull the pinna, looking for discomfort
Cranial Nerve VIII	▪ Weber / Rinne – screens for conduction or sensorineural hearing loss; use 512 Hz tuning fork ▪ Whisper: patient closes off one ear with his/her finger, doctor stands 1-2 feet to the side of the patient and determines if the patient can hear whispered words or numbers without seeing the doctor's lips move. Compare one side to the other. ▪ Ticking watch: patient occludes one ear, doctor positions watch 5 inches away from the patient and determines whether he/she can detect the watch tick. Compare one side to the other. ▪ Cranial Nerve VIII (Vestibular) pathology: test with Barany / Caloric test, Mittlemeyer marching test, Babinski-Weil test and Romberg's test (with eyes closed)

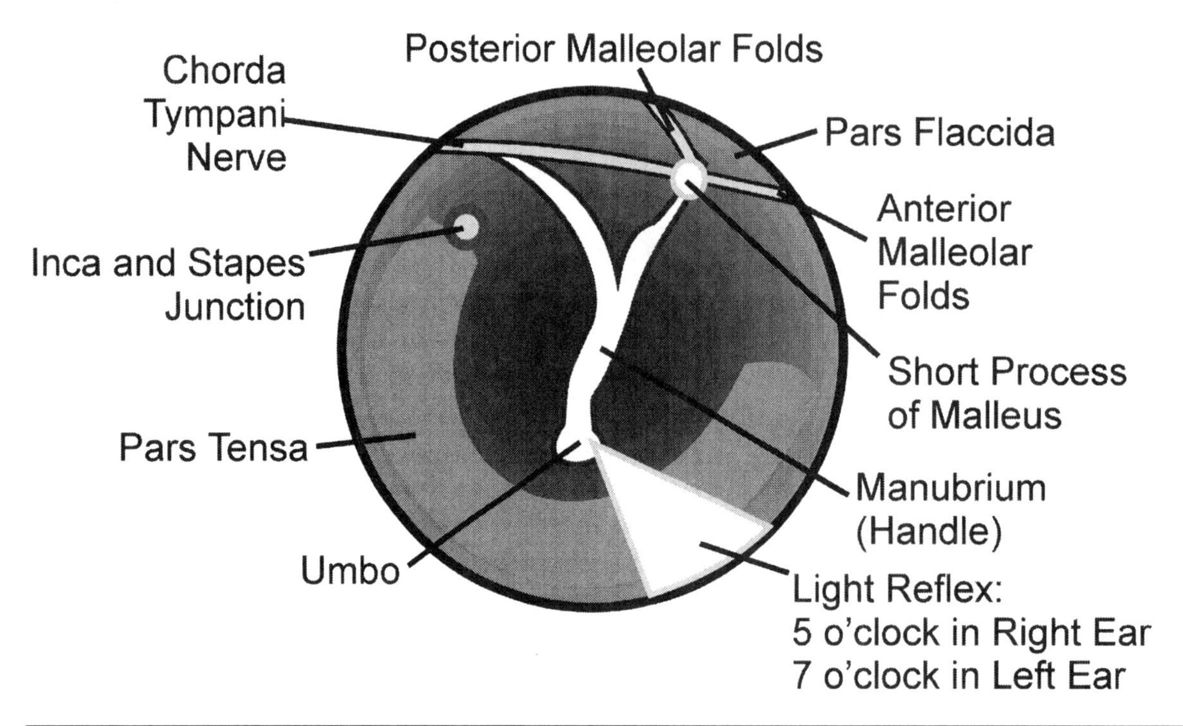

Otoscopic Exam	▪ Observe the canal, the entire surface of the drum, the structures behind the drum and any other findings ▪ Assess mobility of the drum by having the patient hold his/her nose, close his/her mouth and blow (the Toynbee maneuver) ▪ Visible structures include the manubrium, the light reflex (at 5:00 on the right and 7:00 on the left); the umbo and the pars tensa ▪ If the drum is bulging, you will see a loss of bony landmarks and a distorted light reflex ▪ If the ear drum is retracted, landmarks are exaggerated and the light reflex is distorted ▪ Special specula with rounded, soft tips may be used to evaluate children's ears
Ear Pathology Presentation	▪ Acute otitis externa – canal skin is swollen and painful; tympanic membrane may not be visible ▪ Acute otitis media – tympanic membrane is retracted or bulging and red; you may detect a serous effusion or fluid line behind the tympanic membrane ▪ Perforated ear drum (due to infection or trauma) ▪ Presbycussis: loss of upper registers in the elderly

ote (6)

- Select the largest size speculum that fits comfortably into the patient's ear canal in order to obtain the maximum field of view.

Age Group	Speculum Size
Adults	4 or 5 mm
Children	3 or 4 mm
Infants	2.5 or 3 mm

- Special specula with soft material at the distal end may reduce the risk of injury to the ear canal, especially with young children.

THE NOSE (7)

Inspection	▪ Observe contour of the nose, noting irregularities ▪ Determine patency by having the patient close off one nares with his/her finger and breath in through the other. Check both sides
Palpation	▪ Palpate the external portions of the nose, feeling cartilage and bony structures beneath; note any tenderness or crepitus
Speculum Exam	▪ Inspect mucous membranes, turbinates (extensions of the ethmoid bone located along the lateral wall of the nose, covered by mucous membranes) and septum. Patient should extend his/her head and the doctor should traction up the tip of the nose for this exam. ▪ Normal findings include a red nasal mucosa and the middle and inferior concha ▪ Abnormal findings include a perforated septum, lesions, blood or a discharge
Cranial Nerve I	▪ Olfactory nerve: recognition of odors. Test each side individually

THE SINUSES (8,9)

Inspection	▪ Observe the facial areas overlying the frontal and maxillary sinuses noting swelling or redness
Palpation	▪ The areas over the frontal and maxillary sinuses should be gently palpated, pressing to determine if there is swelling or tenderness
Percussion	▪ Percuss the areas over the frontal and maxillary sinuses directly by tapping with two fingers to test for pain and tenderness
Trans-illumination	▪ The room should be darkened ▪ For the frontal sinuses, the patient closes their eyes as the doctor places the tip of the scope under the orbital ridge superior to the inner canthus. Repeat on the other side ▪ For the maxillary sinuses, the patient extends their head back with the mouth wide open. Doctor shines the tip of the scope down through the maxillary sinus toward the roof of the mouth. Compare both sides ▪ If light does not penetrate through the sinuses, then the sinuses are full of secretions or they never developed

THE MOUTH (10,11)

Inspection	▪ Observe the lips: look for fissuring, cracked corners (Riboflavin deficiency/cheilosis), cold sores, ulcers, lesions, etc. ▪ B 12 deficiency can cause a beefy red tongue ▪ Use the penlight and tongue depressor to see all surfaces of the oral cavity ▪ Look for Stenson's ducts and Wharton's ducts ▪ Structures which can be assessed include: frenula of upper and lower lips and tongue, vestibule of mouth, dorsum of tongue, palatine tonsils, uvula, hard palate, soft palate, posterior wall of oropharynx, gingiva and teeth ▪ Fordyce spots: ectopic sebaceous glands on the buccal mucosa and lips; expected variant ▪ Cherry red lips are associated with carbon monoxide poisoning and acidosis ▪ Pallor of the lips is associated with anemia ▪ Circumoral cyanosis is associated with hypoxemia
Cranial Nerves	▪ Glossopharyngeal/ Vagus (gag reflex) ▪ Hypoglossal (patient sticks out his/her tongue)

The Thyroid and Lymph Nodes (12)

Inspection	▪ Observe the neck from the anterior with the patient's head extended. Look for the gland to rise up as the patient swallows
Palpation	▪ Place your index finger on the thyroid cartilage, your middle finger on the cricoid cartilage and your ring finger on the thyroid isthmus (the fingers will be equidistant). Feel the isthmus slide up and down as the patient swallows ▪ Using both hands, position two fingers of each hand on the sides of the trachea just beneath the cricoid cartilage. Ask the patient to swallow and feel for movement of the isthmus. Then displace the trachea to the left, ask the patient to swallow, and palpate the main body of the right lobe. Repeat on the opposite side. ▪ You should feel the thyroid tissue rise beneath your fingers as the patient swallows. It should feel muscular and be free of nodules
Auscultation	▪ Auscultate for vascular sounds if the thyroid gland is enlarged. Blood supply is dramatically increased in a hypermetabolic condition and can cause a vascular bruit or thyroid venous hum
Thyroid conditions	If the patient has a hyperthyroid condition, the following symptoms may be present ▪ Weight loss ▪ Recent onset of heat intolerance ▪ Agitation, nervousness ▪ Tachycardia ▪ Goiter If the patient has a hypothyroid condition, the following symptoms may be present ▪ Constipation, weight gain ▪ Cold intolerance ▪ Lethargy, complacency ▪ No cardiac changes ▪ No goiter ▪ Loss of the lateral 1/3 of the eyebrows
Lymph nodes	Observe, then examine one side at a time, palpating the following lymph nodes: ▪ Occipital, pre-auricular, post-auricular ▪ Tonsilar, submandibular, submental ▪ Posterior cervical, anterior cervical, deep cervical ▪ Supraclavicular, infraclavicular, and axillary ▪ Epitrochlear and inguinal If an enlarged lymph node is observed, note location, size, shape, consistency, contour, motility, and tenderness

ote (13)

- The principal hormones secreted by the thyroid gland are T4 (Thyroxine) and T3 (Triiodothyronine).
- Thyroid function is regulated primarily by variations in the circulating level of pituitary TSH (thyroid-stimulating hormone).
- Children who are hyperthyroid from birth are called cretins.

PULMONARY EXAM (14,15)

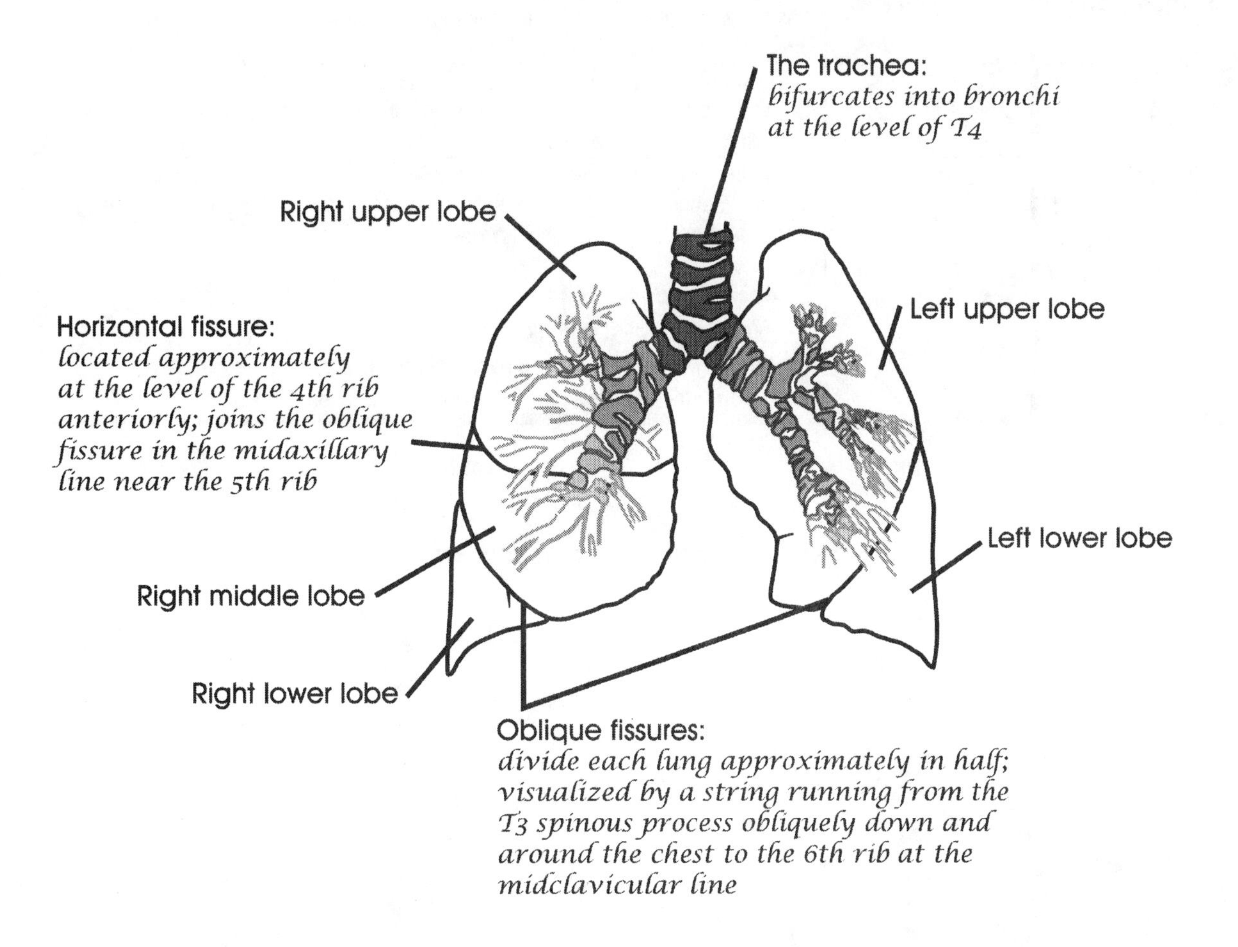

Inspection	▪ Observe lateral chest expansion – place thumbs on the spinous processes with the fingers fanned out laterally ▪ Observe A to P chest expansion – stand at patient's side and place one hand on the sternum and the other hand across the upper thoracic spine

Note

- The term "pink puffer" is associated with persons with pulmonary emphysema.
- The term "blue bloater" is associated with persons with persistent asthma.

Examination *Arms crossed in front for posterior exam!*	Tactile Fremitus	The examiner compares the fremitus of the lung fields from side to side with the ulnar edge of hand. The patient says "99" each time the examiner places a hand down. Fremitus is evaluated at four sites on the posterior lung fields and three sites on the anterior lung fields.
	Chest Percussion	In the healthy patient, the examiner will elicit a resonant note with percussion. Other notes help the examiner determine if the underlying tissues are air-filled, fluid-filled or solid. See locations for evaluation of percussion below.
	Chest Auscultation	The patient breathes deeper than normal in and out through the mouth each time the diaphragm of the stethoscope is placed firmly against the skin. See location for evaluation of auscultation below. Lung sounds include: ▪ **Vesicular**: heard over most of the lung fields; low pitch ▪ **Bronchovesicular**: heard over main bronchus area; medium pitch ▪ **Bronchial/tracheal**: heard only over the trachea; high pitch

Locations for auscultation and percussion

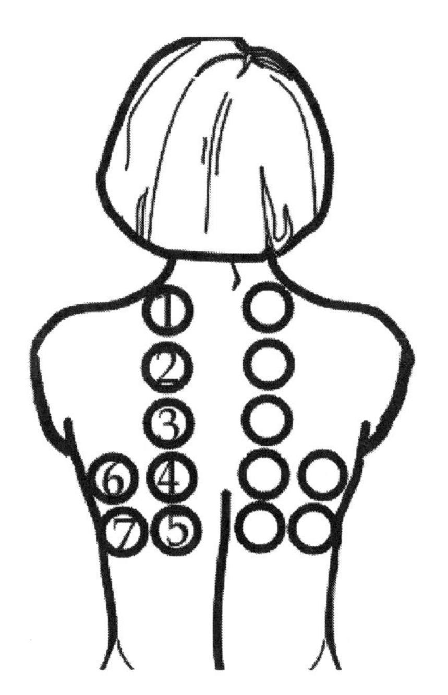

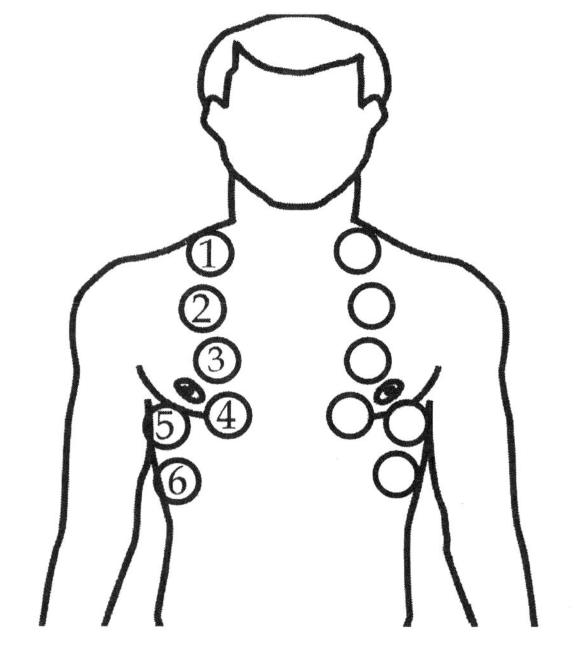

ote

- Bates recommends percussing and auscultating one lung then the other at the locations shown above; Mosby recommends auscultating a greater number of locations in the posterior and anterior lung fields, and comparing each spot side to side.

Diaphragmatic Excursion	1. Patient breathes out fully and holds the breath out while the doctor percusses down the scapular line to where the resonance of the lungs changes to dullness in the flanks. This spot is marked. 2. The patient then inhales as deeply as possible and holds breath in. Doctor percusses down from the mark to where the resonant dullness interface has moved inferiorly. This spot is marked and the distance between the two in the vertical plane is measured and compared on both sides. Three to five centimeters is the normal range.

ABNORMALITIES IN THE LUNGS

	Chronic Bronchitis	Consolidation	Emphysema	Pneumothorax	Pleural Effusion	Asthma
Palpation (Fremitus)	Normal	Increased over involved area	Decreased	Decreased or absent	Decreased to absent	Decreased
Percussion	Resonant	Dull over involved area	Generalized hyperresonance	Hyperresonant or tympanic	Dull to flat over fluid	Normal to hyperresonant
Adventitious Sounds	Prolonged breath sounds; crackles with clear cough	Late inspiratory crackles over involved area	Diminished breath sounds; crackles and wheezes	None	None, except possible pleural rub	Wheezes, crackles

ote

- Adventitious sounds are sounds superimposed on the usual breath sounds. When present, adventitious sounds indicate airway obstruction.

SPECIAL PROCEDURES AND THEIR FINDINGS WITH PNEUMONIA OR CONSOLIDATION

Auscultatory Percussion	1. Doctor listens to the posterior lung fields using one hand to move the stethoscope from side to side along the scapular line and the other hand to directly percuss the manubriosternal joint. 2. To auscultate the anterior lung fields, direct percussion is done on the spinous process of T3.
Broncophony	Patient speaks during auscultation. Examiner will detect increased loudness and greater clearness of spoken sounds with consolidation.
Egophony	Patient says "EEE" each time the examiner places the stethoscope down. "E" will sound like "A" when egophony is present.
Whispered Pectoriloquy	Patient whispers "99" each time the stethoscope is placed down. Whispered sounds will be heard clearly through the stethoscope if consolidation is present.

THE CARDIOVASCULAR EXAM (16,17)

Inspect	▪ The thorax structure: look for cardiac heave (never normal except immediately after aerobic workout) and apical impulse (seen in 50% of population; normal variant), normally located on the left at the 5th intercostal space and mid-clavicular line ▪ Observe for cyanosis or flushing of the skin ▪ Check the nails for capillary refill by compressing the beds gently, then watching for a return of color ▪ Check the nails for clubbing, which would indicate hypoxia
Palpate	▪ The apical impulse is located at the apex of the heart (5th intercostal space at mid-clavicular line) and is caused by left ventricular contraction ▪ Palpate for thrills (a fine, palpable, rushing vibration) over each of the cardiac valve areas: aortic, pulmonic, tricuspid and mitral
Auscultate	▪ Use the diaphragm (firm pressure) of the stethoscope over the four valves sites and Erb's point to assess high-pitched heart sounds for presence of murmurs ▪ Use the bell (light pressure) over each of the five points to auscultate for low-pitched sounds and presence of murmurs
Jugular Venous Pressure	▪ Place the patient supine, elevated approximately 45 degrees. Place a centimeter rule in the vertical plane with the zero end on the patient at the manubriosternal junction. Use a tongue depressor or something with a long straight edge and in the horizontal plane place one end at the top of the jugular vein pulsation and the other end crossing the ruler. Note the vertical distance from the top of the jugular vein pulsation to the manubriosternal junction. Normally this is less than or equal to 2 cm. ▪ Provides a gross indication of the volume and pressure in the right side of the heart.
Bruits NOTE: *Always palpate artery before auscultating*	**NOTE**: a bruit is a whooshing sound heard in an artery due to lack of laminar flow due to aneurysm, atherosclerosis, etc. ▪ Orbital ▪ Temporal ▪ Carotid – patient should hold his or her breath ▪ Subclavian -- patient should hold his or her breath
VBAI screen	▪ George's Test

- Diseased valves either do not open or do not close well. When passages are narrowed by thickened leaflets, forward blood flow is restricted (stenosis).
- When the valve leaflets lose competency, blood is able to flow backward (regurgitation).
- Diastolic murmurs usually indicate heart disease.

ote

- For simplicity, the cardiac cycle is usually discussed as if the events of the cycle were simultaneous on both sides of the heart. In reality, the pressures on the right side (atrium, ventricle, and pulmonary artery) are lower than those on the left side, so the same events occur slightly later on the right side than on the left. Hence, some heart sounds sometimes have two distinct parts, the first of which is produced by the left side and the second produced by the right side. Some heart sounds may be heard to "split" on inspiration, which prolongs ejection of blood from the right ventricle but shortens ejection from the left ventricle.

AUSCULTATORY AREAS

Auscultatory Area		**Location** (place the stethoscope and name each area as you auscultate)	
Aortic Valve	**Semilunar Valves**	Right sternal border	Second right intercostal space
Pulmonic Valve		Left sternal border	Second left intercostal space
Erb's Point (AKA second pulmonic site)		Left sternal border	Third left intercostal space
Tricuspid Area	**AV Valves**	Left sternal border	Fourth left intercostal space
Mitral (Apical) Area		Midclavicular line	Apex of the heart in the fifth left intercostal space

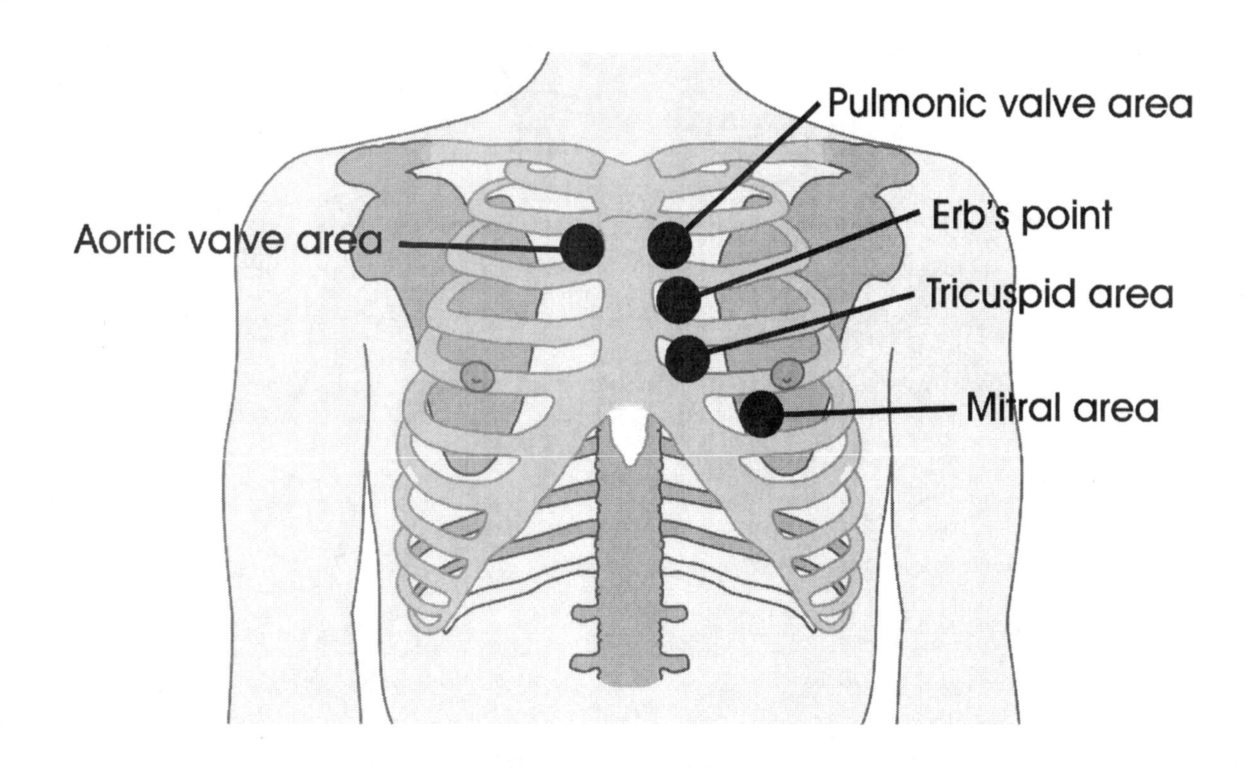

HEART SOUNDS

Heart Sound	Production of the Sound	Diagnosis
S_1	At the beginning of systole, ventricular contraction raises the pressure in the ventricles and forces the mitral and tricuspid valves closed	**NOTE**: S1 is softer than S2 at the base of the heart; S1 is longer in duration and lower in tone than S2
S_2	Closure of the aortic and pulmonic valves; two components ("split S_2") produced by aortic valve closure and pulmonic valve closure can sometimes be heard	**NOTE**: S2 is often but not always louder than S2 at the apex of the heart
S_3	Produced by ventricular filling	▪ Physiologic S3: normal in well-conditioned athletes and frequent in children; common during last trimester of pregnancy ▪ Pathologic S3: presence in people over 40
S_4	Contraction of atria to ensure ejection of all blood	▪ Physiologic: heard occasionally in trained athletes and older age groups ▪ Pathologic: hypertensive heart disease, coronary artery disease, aortic stensosis, cardiomyopathy

THE CARDIAC CYCLE

Blood flow during systole and diastole

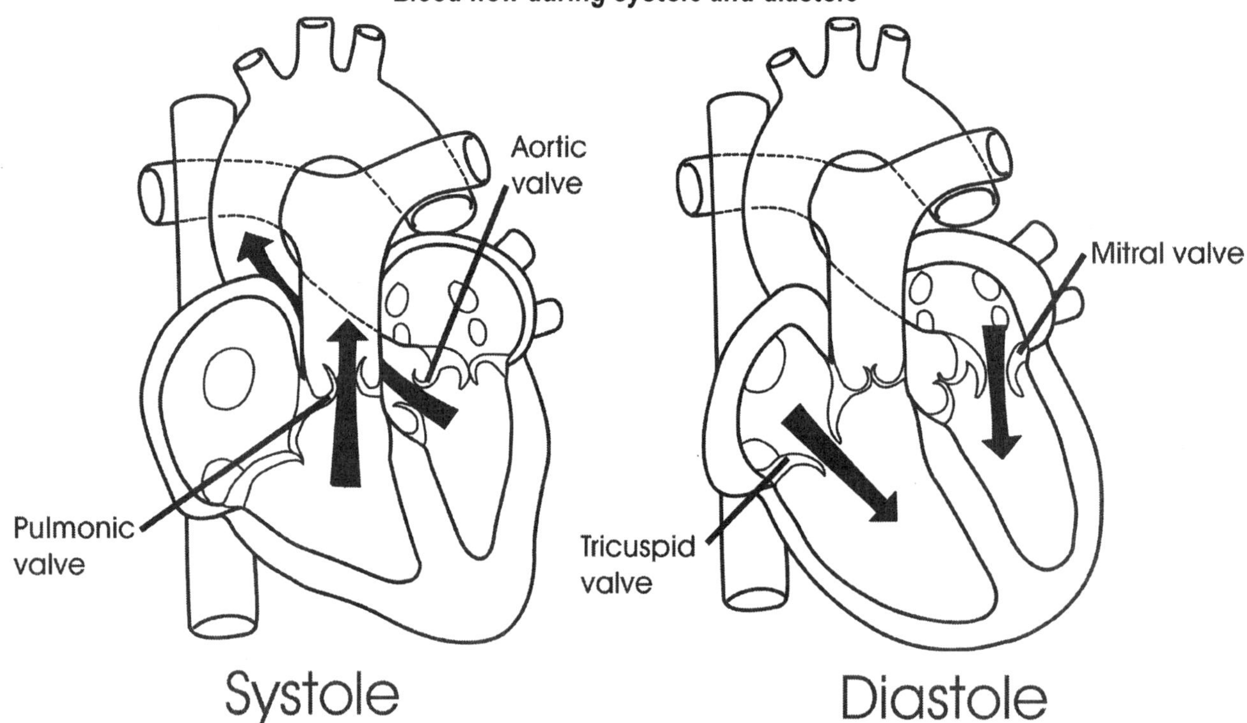

Ventricles contract; S1 heart sound produced by closure of the mitral and tricuspid valves

Ventricles relax, atria contract; S2 heart sound produced by closure of aortic and pulmonic valves

HEART MURMURS

- Heart murmurs are relatively prolonged extra sounds heard during systole or diastole; they can be of no pathologic significance or they may indicate a problem.
- Murmurs are identified by the valve affected and by timing and duration. Systolic murmurs are best described by time of onset and duration; diastolic murmurs are best classified according to time of onset only.
- Use the bell of the stethoscope to auscultate for low-pitched sounds (S3 and S4) and the murmur of mitral stenosis. Use the diaphragm to auscultate for high-pitched sounds (S1 and S2) and the murmur of aortic and mitral regurgitation.

Part of the Cycle Where Murmur is Heard	Aortic/Pulmonic Valves	Mitral/Tricuspid Valves
Systole ▪ Ventricular contraction; closure of semilunar valves (S_1)	Stenosis (forward blood flow restricted)	Regurgitation
Diastole ▪ Ventricles relax, atria contract; aortic and pulmonic valves close (S_2)	Regurgitation (slack openings allow backward flow of blood)	Stenosis

- Water-hammer pulse (jerky pulse with full expansion followed by sudden collapse) associated with aortic regurgitation.
- Pulsus bisferiens (two strong systolic peaks separated by a midsystolic dip) associated with aortic stenosis combined with aortic insufficiency.
- Aortic murmurs are best heard with the patient seated, leaning forward and holding his/her breath on expiration, which enhances detection of aortic insufficiency. Mitral murmurs are best heard with the patient in the left lateral decubitus position, which especially accentuates murmurs of mitral stenosis.

THRILLS

- A thrill is a palpable murmur – a fine, rushing vibration often felt over the base of the heart in the area of the right or left second intercostal space. Thrills generally indicated disruption of the expected blood flow due to defect in closure of one of the semilunar valves, pulmonary hypertension, or atrial septal defect.
- Thrills are usually associated with murmurs of grades 4 through 6 on an intensity scale of 1 (very faint) to 6 (may be heard with the stethoscope entirely off the chest).

PERIPHERAL PULSES (18,19)

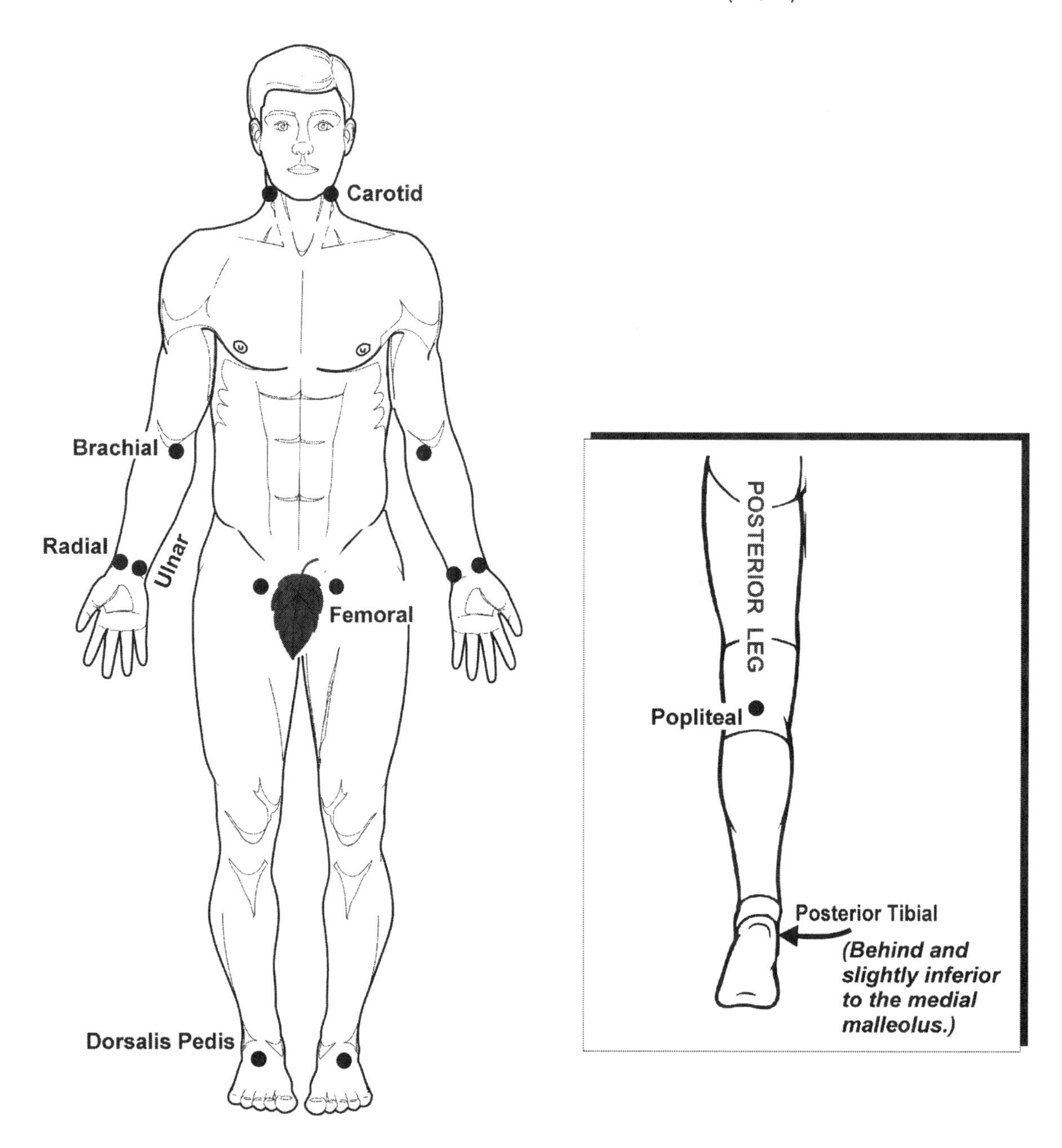

Pulse	Location
Brachial	Just medial to the biceps tendon
Carotid	Just medial to and below jaw; palpate one side at a time and have patient hold his/her breath
Dorsalis Pedis	Medial side of the dorsum of the foot (absent in some well persons)
Femoral	Inferior and medial to inquinal ligament, or midway between ASIS and pubic tubercle
Posterior Tibial	Behind and slightly inferior to the medial malleolus of the ankle
Popliteal	Popliteal fossa
Radial and Ulnar	Lateral and medial ventral wrist, respectively

EVALUATION OF PERIPHERAL PULSES

Peripheral pulses are assigned amplitude values on a scale of 0 to 4.

0	Absent
1	Diminished
2	Normal (expected) finding
3	Increased
4	Bounding

ote

- Compare the pulses and leg temperature side to side; lack of symmetry suggests impaired circulation. Also, inspect the legs for varicosities.
- Tests for vascular insufficiency include Homan's sign (thrombophlebitis); Buerger's test (lower extremity circulation); Allen's test (ulnar or radial arteries); and Wright's test (thoracic outlet syndrome at the Axillary artery).
- The four Ps of arterial occlusion are Pain, Pallor, Pulselessness and Paresthesia.
- A venous thrombosis presents with redness, thickening, and tenderness along a superficial vein.

PITTING EDEMA

Press your index finger over the tibia or medial malleolus for several seconds. Edema (indicated by a depression that does not rapidly refill) could indicate right-sided heart failure, deep venous obstruction, or valvular incompetence

The severity of edema is indicated by a grade of 1 to 4

1+	Slight pitting; disappears rapidly
2+	Pitting disappears in 10 to 15 seconds
3+	Pitting is noticeably deep and may last for one minute; dependent extremity is fuller and swollen
4+	Pitting is very deep and lasts for 2 to 5 minutes; dependent extremity is grossly distorted

ote

- If edema occurs without pitting, suspect arterial disease and occlusion.

THE ABDOMINAL EXAM (20,21)

- Have the patient bend his or her knees
- The exam is performed from the right side of the table only, with the exception of examination of the left kidney
- The patient's hands should be resting at his/her sides or up on his/her chest, not under the head

Inspect		▪ Inspect for contour and symmetry and any surface characteristics **NOTE:** Gastrointestinal disorders often produce secondary skin changes
Auscultate		1. Listening for bowel sounds (5 to 35 minutes); done in all four quadrants using the diaphragm 2. Auscultate for friction rubs over the liver and spleen (patient must breath deeply in and out) 3. Vascular bruits: aorta, splenic artery, renal arteries, iliac arteries, femoral arteries – use the diaphragm
Percuss	**Bowel**	▪ In the presence of ascites, the area around the umbilicus will be tympanic and the lateral aspects of the abdomen will be dull
	Liver	▪ The span of the liver should be 6 to 12 cm in the midclavicular line and 4 to 8 cm in the mid-sternal line; resonance of the lungs changes to dullness over the liver
	Spleen	▪ Find the last intercostal space along the left anterior axillary line and percuss. The note should be tympanic. The patient should take a deep breath as the doctor continues percussing and the note should not change
Palpate	**Bowel**	▪ Superficial bowel: begin with a one-handed light touch ▪ Deep bowel: use one hand to palpate and the other to apply overpressure
	Liver	Palpate under the rib cage with the left hand; patient inhales while doctor palpates the inferior margin of the liver with the right hand; palpate on second inspiration
	Spleen	Doctor reaches across the patient and places the left hand under the left posterior lower costal margin and lifts the rib cage. The right hand palpates below and under the left anterior costal margin as the patient takes a deep breath; palpate on second inspiration
	Kidneys	Doctor's left hand under the right flank area and the right hand just inferior to the right anterior costal margin. The patient inhales deeply and the doctor palpates the kidney by approximating the hands. As the patient exhales, the kidney may be felt slipping out of the doctor's grasp. The left kidney is usually not palpable

- Auscultation precedes percussion and palpation, which may alter frequency and intensity of bowel sounds.

Quadrants and Contents of the Abdomen (20,21)

ote

- The quadrants are created by imaginary lines drawn vertically from sternum to pubis and horizontally through the umbilicus.

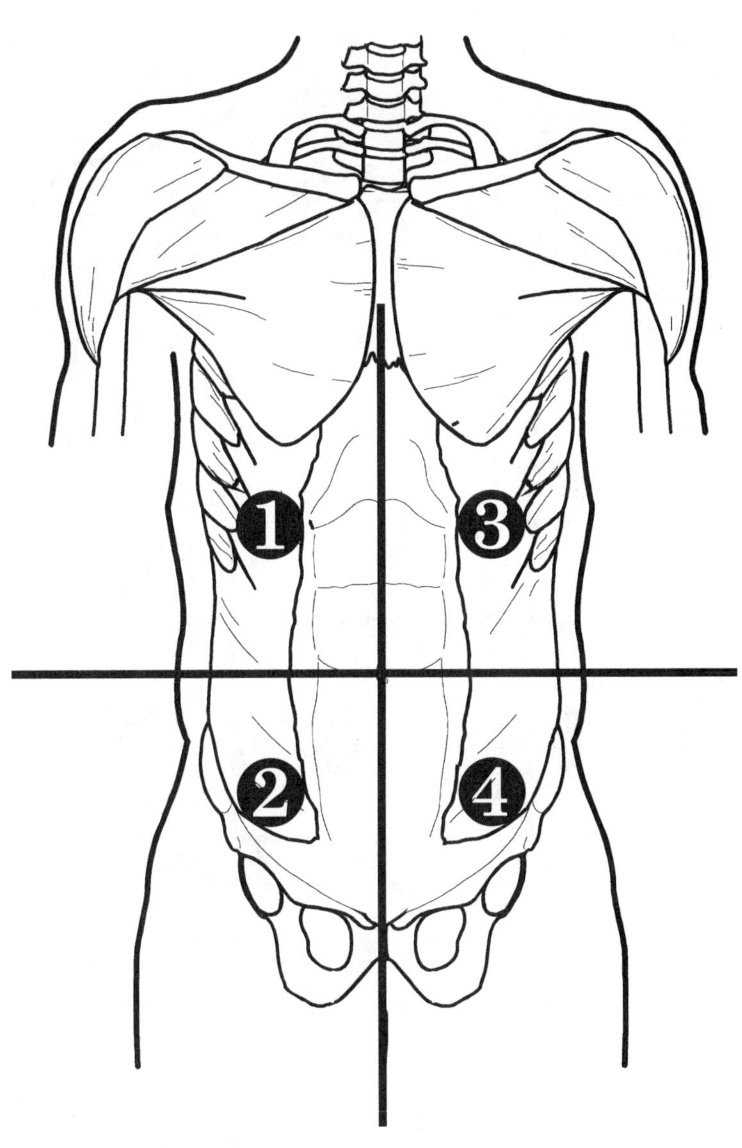

❶ **Right Upper Quadrant**
Contains liver and gallbladder; duodenum, head of pancreas, right adrenal gland; part of right kidney; hepatic flexure of colon; parts of ascending and transverse colon

❷ **Right Lower Quadrant**
Contains lower pole of right kidney; cecum and appendix; part of ascending colon; bladder; ovary and salpinx; right spermatic cord; right ureter; uterus (if enlarged)

❸ **Left Upper Quadrant**
Contains left lobe of liver; spleen; stomach; body of pancreas; left adrenal gland; part of left kidney; splenic flexure of colon; parts of transverse and descending colon

❹ **Left Lower Quadrant**
Contains lower pole of left kidney; sigmoid colon; part of descending colon; bladder; ovary and salpinx; left spermatic cord; left ureter; uterus (if enlarged)

Regions and Contents of the Abdomen (20,21)

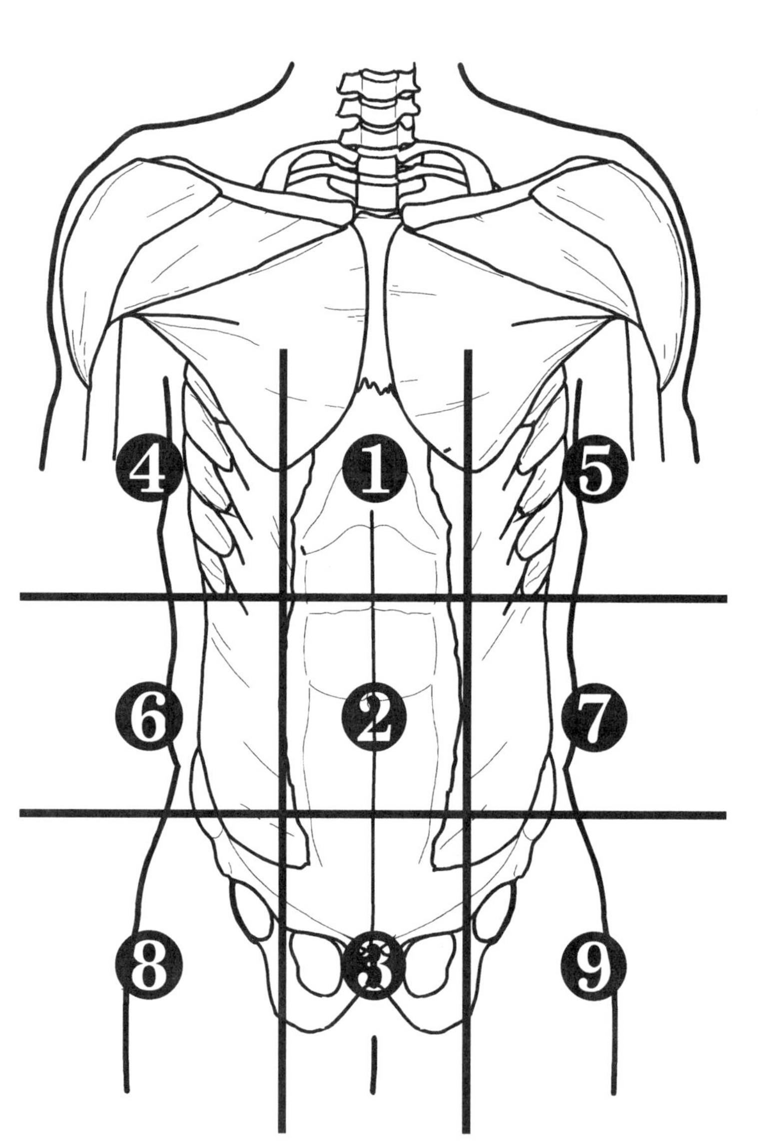

- The nine regions are delineated by two imaginary lines drawn horizontally across the lowest edge of the costal margin and across the iliac crest and by two bilateral vertical lines drawn from the midclavicular line to the middle of the inguinal ligament, approximating the lateral borders of the rectus abdominus muscles.

❶ **Epigastric**: duodenum; pancreas; part of liver

❷ **Umbilical**: lower duodenum; jejunum and ilium

❸ **Hypogastric**: ileum; bladder; uterus (in pregnancy)

❹ **Right hypochondriac**: right lobe of liver; gallbladder; part of duodenum; hepatic flexure; part of right kidney; suprarenal gland

❺ **Left hypochondriac**: stomach; spleen; tail of pancreas; splenic flexure; upper part of left kidney; suprarenal gland

❻ **Right lumbar**: ascending colon; lower half of right kidney; part of duodenum and jejunum

❼ **Left lumbar**: descending colon; lower half of left kidney; parts of jejunum and ileum

❽ **Right inguinal**: cecum; appendix; lower end of ileum; right ureter; right spermatic cord and ovary

❾ **Left inguinal**: sigmoid colon; left ureter; left spermatic cord and ovary

SPECIAL ABDOMINAL PROCEDURES (20,21)

Liver / Gallbladder	**Murphy's Sign**	• Occurs during liver palpation if hepatic or gallbladder inflammation is present. As the doctor palpates the liver, the patient is unable to take in a deep breath due to guarding; classically positive with cholecystitis
Kidney	**Murphy's Punch**	▪ Elicits strong pain in the presence of renal inflammation. The indifferent hand is placed over the flank with the patient seated. The other hand strikes the back of the indifferent hand with the ulnar side of the fist; examiner should tap gently over the involved area at first
Ascites (Abnormal intraperitoneal accumulation of serous fluid) **NOTE:** *Use these tests when the patient has a protuberant abdomen or flanks that bulge in the supine position*	**Shifting Dullness**	▪ Patient is supine; abdomen is percussed from the midline laterally to identify the presence of fluid in the abdominal cavity. The tympanic-dull interfaces should be marked with a grease pencil; the patient then rolls onto his/her side and the abdomen is percussed again. If the interface changes, this indicates shifting dullness
	Fluid Wave	▪ Patient puts knife-edge of hand along midline of abdomen firmly. The doctor places one hand along one of the patient's flanks, while the other hand taps firmly against the opposite flank to create a wave in ascitic fluid
	Auscultatory Percussion	▪ Patient voids urine then stands for 3 minutes to cause fluid to settle. Examiner holds the diaphragm of the stethoscope immediately above the pubic symphysis with one hand and with the other applies percussion to three or more sites from the costal margin downward. With ascites, the percussive note changes above the pelvic border at the fluid level
	Puddle Sign	▪ Tests for fluid pooling with patient on all fours for three minutes. The area is tympanic if no fluid is present and dull if fluid is present
Peritoneal Irritation	**Rebound Tenderness/ Blumberg's Sign**	▪ Doctor gently presses into the abdomen with the fingertips in an area away from the location of complaint. Quickly release the pressure. Sharp pain will occur at the area of peritoneal inflammation as the pressure is released
Appendicitis	**Rovsing's Sign**	▪ Pain in the right lower quadrant during left-sided pressure
	Iliopsoas Muscle Test	▪ Causes pain in the right lower quadrant
	Pain at McBurney's Point	▪ Press in the area at the bisection of a line drawn from the umbilicus to the right ASIS
	Obturator Test / Cope's Test	▪ Patient is supine; ask patient to flex the right leg at the hip and knee to 90 degrees then rotate the leg laterally and medially. Positive finding is pain in the hypogastric region
Conditions which produce abdominal pain	▪ Appendicitis ▪ Cholecystitis ▪ Pancreatitis ▪ Abdominal aneurysm ▪ Intestinal obstruction	▪ Perforated gastric or duodenal ulcer ▪ Diverticulitis ▪ Biliary stones ▪ Pelvic inflammatory disease ▪ Ruptured ovarian cyst
Clinical findings in a patient with peritoneal irritation	▪ Involuntary rigidity of abdominal muscles ▪ Tenderness or guarding ▪ Absent bowel sounds ▪ Abdominal pain with walking or jarring	

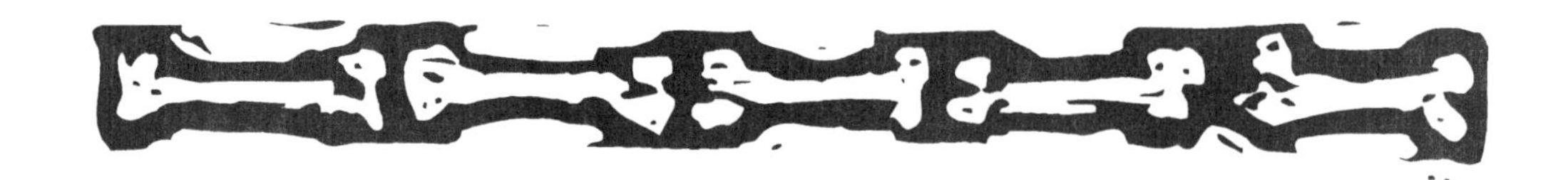

References

1 Seidel HM, Ball JW, Dains JE, Benedict GW. Mosby's Guide to Physical Examination. 3rd ed. St. Louis: Mosby, 1995: 64, 327, 348, 382, 408, 413-415, 422, 425.
2 Seidel HM, Ball JW, Dains JE, Benedict GW. Mosby's Guide to Physical Examination. 3rd ed. St. Louis: Mosby, 1995: 235-268.
3 Bates B. A Guide to Physical Examination. 6th ed. Philadelphia: J.B. Lippincott Company, 1995: 147-154, 168-179.
4 Seidel HM, Ball JW, Dains JE, Benedict GW. Mosby's Guide to Physical Examination. 3rd ed. St. Louis: Mosby, 1995: 269-272, 281-288, 308-309.
5 Bates B. A Guide to Physical Examination. 6th ed. Philadelphia: J.B. Lippincott Company, 1995: 154-156, 179-182.
6 From Welch Allyn's "Guide to the use of diagnostic instruments in Eye and Ear examinations."
7 Bates B. A Guide to Physical Examination. 6th ed. Philadelphia: J.B. Lippincott Company, 1995: 182-184.
8 Seidel HM, Ball JW, Dains JE, Benedict GW. Mosby's Guide to Physical Examination. 3rd ed. St. Louis: Mosby, 1995: 275, 290, 298.
9 Bates B. A Guide to Physical Examination. 6th ed. Philadelphia: J.B. Lippincott Company, 1995: 184, 192-193.
10 Seidel HM, Ball JW, Dains JE, Benedict GW. Mosby's Guide to Physical Examination. 3rd ed. St. Louis: Mosby, 1995: 291-297.
11 Bates B. A Guide to Physical Examination. 6th ed. Philadelphia: J.B. Lippincott Company, 1995: 184-186, 217-226.
12 Seidel HM, Ball JW, Dains JE, Benedict GW. Mosby's Guide to Physical Examination. 3rd ed. St. Louis: Mosby, 1995: 196-201, 219-221, 232.
13 Ganong WF. Review of Medical Physiology. 17th ed. Connecticut: Appleton & Lange, 1995: 291, 299, 301.
14 Seidel HM, Ball JW, Dains JE, Benedict GW. Mosby's Guide to Physical Examination. 3rd ed. St. Louis: Mosby, 1995: 325-366.
15 Bates B. A Guide to Physical Examination. 6th ed. Philadelphia: J.B. Lippincott Company, 1995: 237-251, 256-257.
16 Seidel HM, Ball JW, Dains JE, Benedict GW. Mosby's Guide to Physical Examination. 3rd ed. St. Louis: Mosby, 1995: 367-443.
17 Bates B. A Guide to Physical Examination. 6th ed. Philadelphia: J.B. Lippincott Company, 1995: 259-312.
18 Seidel HM, Ball JW, Dains JE, Benedict GW. Mosby's Guide to Physical Examination. 3rd ed. St. Louis: Mosby, 1995: 405-407, 411, 419-420.
19 Bates B. A Guide to Physical Examination. 6th ed. Philadelphia: J.B. Lippincott Company, 1995: 435-447.
20 Seidel HM, Ball JW, Dains JE, Benedict GW. Mosby's Guide to Physical Examination. 3rd ed. St. Louis: Mosby, 1995: 482-510.
21 Bates B. A Guide to Physical Examination. 6th ed. Philadelphia: J.B. Lippincott Company, 1995: 331-360.

CHAPTER 5

General Diagnosis

The Cardiovascular System

Generalized Disorders (1)

Disease	Definition	Signs/Symptoms	Diagnosis	Notes
Arteriosclerosis	▪ Generalized hypertrophy of the media and subintimal fibrosis with hyaline degeneration in small muscular arteries and arteriololes and large vessels	▪ Generally none until critical stenosis, thrombosis, aneurysm, or embolus develops		▪ Fatty streak evolving into a fibrous plaque
Atherosclerosis	▪ Affects medium and large arteries and is characterized by patchy intramural thickening of the subintima that encroaches on the arterial lumen			
Arterial Hypertension	▪ Primary (essential) hypertension is idiopathic ▪ Mechanism must lead to increased total peripheral vascular resistance (by vasoconstriction) or to increased cardiac output or both	▪ Asymptomatic until complications develop, when complications arise in target organs	▪ 1) Systolic and diastolic blood pressures are usually higher than normal and ▪ 2) secondary causes have been ruled out	▪ **Pheochromocytoma**: tumor of chromaffin cells that secretes catecholamines and causes hypertension; 80% are found in the adrenal medulla and are usually benign; maximum incidence is between 3rd and 4th decades of life
Orthostatic Hypotension	▪ A fall in blood pressure of typically >20/10 mm Hg when the patient stands up	▪ Faintness, light-headedness, dizziness, confusion, visual blurring ▪ In severe cases syncope and generalized seizures may develop	▪ Underlying etiology must be discerned based on patient presentation	
Shock	▪ Widespread hypoperfusion of tissues due to hypovolemia, inadequate cardiac function or vasomotor tone, or combinations ▪ Due to reduction in blood volume or cardiac output, or redistribution of blood	▪ Lethargy, confusion, somnolence ▪ Cold hands and feet ▪ Weak and rapid pulse ▪ Tachypnea and hyperventilation	▪ Requires evidence of insufficient tissue perfusion	
Raynaud's Disease and Phenomenon	▪ Peripheral vascular disorders caused by vasospasm or excessive dilation characterised by spasm of arterioles, usually in the digits, with intermittent pallor or cyanosis of the skin	▪ Disease is most common in young women ▪ Intermittent attacks of blanching or cyanosis of the digits are precipitated by exposure to cold, emotional upsets	▪ Disease is idiopathic, bilateral ▪ Phenomenon secondary to other conditions	▪ Wrist pulses are usually present, but Allen's test frequently positive for occlusion of radial or ulnar artery distal to the wrist

THE ELECTROCARDIOGRAM (2,3,4)

☞ The electrocardiogram (ECG) records electrical activity of the heart as specific waves.

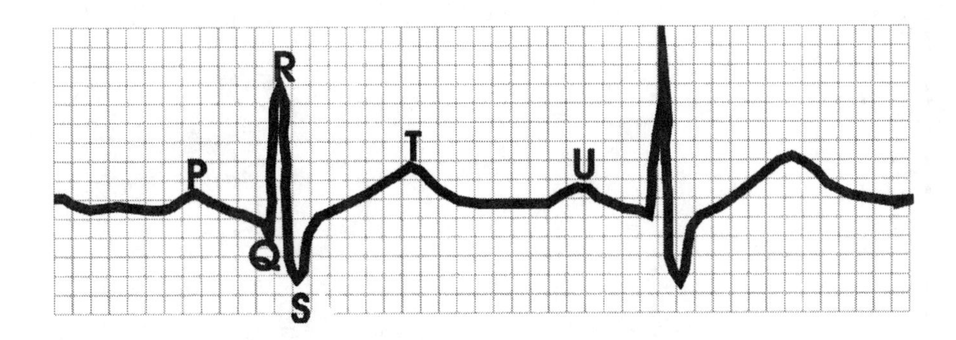

Interval	Cardiac Event	Normal length
P wave	Atrial depolarization	Less than 0.11 seconds
PR interval	Time between initial stimulation of atria to initial stimulation of ventricles	Varies slightly according to age and heart rate; approximately 0.12 to 0.20 seconds
QRS interval	Ventricular depolarization	Less than 0.10 seconds
T wave	Ventricular repolarization	
QT interval		Generally 0.30-0.40 seconds

☞ Myocardial contractions follow the electrical impulses that stimulate them.

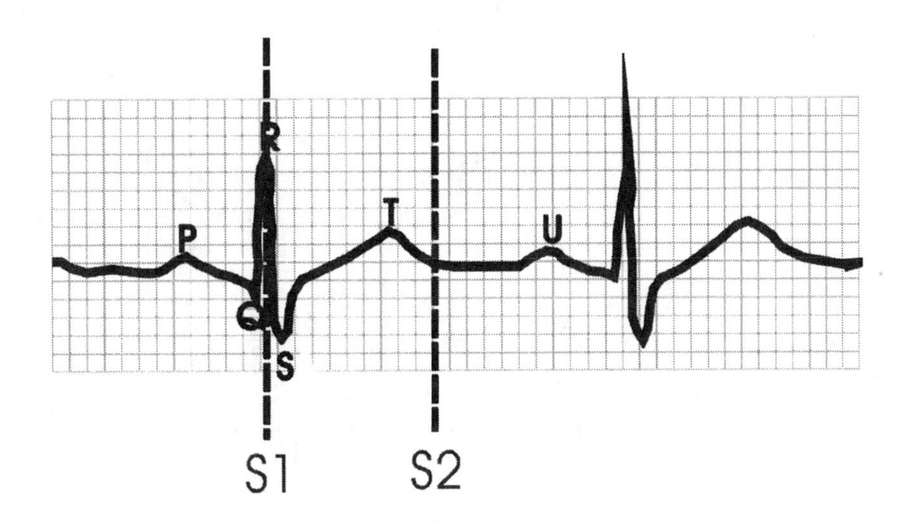

CARDIAC ARRHYTHMIAS (5,6)

Arrhythmia	Description		ECG
Complete (third degree) heart block	Conduction from atria to ventricles is completely interrupted; ventricles beat at a low rate independently of the atria		Atria and ventricles depolarize independently; QRS complexes less frequent (QRS rate slower than P rate)
Incomplete heart block	Conduction between atria and ventricles is slowed but not completely interrupted	▪ First degree heart block: all atrial impulses reach the ventricles but the PR interval is abnormally long	PR interval abnormally long
		▪ Second degree heart block: not all atrial impulses are conducted to the ventricles	A ventricular beat may follow every second or every third atrial beat
		▪ Wenckebach phenomenon: Repeated sequences of beats in which the PR interval lengthens progressively until a ventricular beat is dropped	Wenckebach phenomenon
Bundle branch block	One branch of the bundle of HIS is interrupted; excitation passes normally down the bundle on the intact side and then sweeps back through the muscle to activate the ventricle on the blocked side		Ventricular rate is normal, but the QRS complexes are prolonged and deformed
Circus movement	Defect in conduction allows a wave of excitation to propagate continuously within a closed circuit		
Atrial arrhythmias	▪ Atrial tachycardia		Atrial focus discharges irregularly or there is reentrant activity producing atrial rates up to 220/min
	▪ Atrial flutter: impulses travel in circular course in atria, setting up regular, rapid flutter waves without any isoelectric baseline		Atrial rate of 200-350/min
	▪ Atrial fibrillation: impulses take chaotic, random pathways in atria		Atria beat very rapidly in completely irregular and disorganized manner; P waves absent
Ventricular arrhythmias	▪ Ventricular fibrillation: ventricular muscle fibers contract in a totally irregular and ineffective way because of the very rapid discharge of multiple ventricular ectopic foci or a circus movement		Chaotic ventricular depolarization

Dermatologic Disorders

Skin Lesions (7)

		Lesion	Description		Examples
Primary	Flat, non-palpable	Macule	< 1cm	Flat, discolored spot of varied shape	Freckles, moles, tattoos, port-wine marks and rashes of rubella
		Patch	> 1cm	Similar to a macule	Vitiligo
	Palpable, elevated solid masses	Papule	Usually < 1cm		Many cutaneous diseases begin with papules, i.e. warts, psoriasis
		Plaque	> 1 cm	A plateau-like lesion or a group of confluent papules	
		Nodule	> 0.5 to 1 cm	May or may not be elevated	Keratinous cysts, small lipomas, fibromas, erythema nodosum
		Tumor	> 2 cm	Large nodule	
		Wheal		Transient lesion caused by localized edema	Common allergic reaction to: insect bites, sunlight, cold sensitivity
		Verucae		Warts	
	Fluid-filled lesions	Pustule		Superficial location	May result from infection or a seropurulent evolution of vesicles or bullae; impetigo, acne, furuncles
		Vesicle	< 0.5 cm	Circumscribed and contains serous fluid	
		Bulla	> 0.5 cm	Blister (large vesicle)	Caused by irritants, allergic contact dermatitis, sunburn, viral infections
	Other	Telangiectasia		Dilated superficial blood vessels	Usually idiopathic, but may be seen in rosacea or certain systemic diseases and may result from long-term therapy with topical flouridated corticosteroids
Secondary	Loss of skin surface	Erosion	Loss of part or all of the epidermis		Often seen in infections from herpes viruses and in pemphigus
		Ulcer	Loss of epidermis or part of the epidermis		Often seen with herpes virus and in pemphigus
		Decubitus Ulcer	A "bed sore"		Usually occurs over bony prominences of bedridden patients
	Deposits on skin surface	Crust (scab)	Dried serum, blood or pus		Occurs with various inflammatory and infectious diseases
		Scales	Heaped-up particles of horny epithelium		Psoriasis, seborrheic dermatitis, tinea versicolor, pityriasis rosea, chronic dermatitis of any type
		Ichthyosis	Dry skin		Xeroderma, inherited ichthyoses
	Other	Excoriation	A linear or hollowed-out crusted area		Caused by scratching, rubbing or picking
		Lichenification	Thickened skin with accentuated skin markings		Usually associated with atopic dermatitis and lichen simplex chronicus
		Atrophy	Paper-thin, wrinkled skin		Seen in the elderly, and after some burns
		Scar	Fibrous tissue replacing normal skin structures after destruction of some dermis		

SKIN INFECTIONS (8)

	Infecting Organism	Description of Lesion
Erysipelas	Group A Beta-hemolytic streptococci	The face, an arm or a leg is the most common site of a lesion, which is well-demarcated, shiny, red, edematous and tender; vesicles and **bullae** often develop
Pityriasis Rosea	Unknown	Herald or mother patch, found most commonly on the trunk, usually precedes the generalized eruption by 5 to 10 days. Herald patch is slightly erythematous, rose- or fawn-colored, and circinate or oval; it has a scaly, slightly raised border and resembles a superficial ringworm infection
Rosacea		Chronic inflammatory disorder characterized by telangiectasia, erythema, papules, and pustules appearing especially in the central areas of the face. Most begin in middle age or later
Folliculitis	Usually Staphylococcus aureus	Superficial or deep bacterial infection and irritation of hair follicles
Furuncles	Staphylococci	Acute, tender, perifollicular inflammatory nodules due to infection. Occur most frequently on neck, breasts, face, and buttocks
Carbuncles		A cluster of furuncles with spread of infection subcutaneously, resulting in deep suppuration, often extensive sloughing, slow healing and a large scar
Pediculosis	Lice	May involve the head, body or genital area (crabs). Infestation usually occurs in areas of overcrowding or inadequate personal hygiene
Candidiasis	Candida albicans	Can become pathogenic in a favorable environment or if the host's weakened defenses allow the organisms to proliferate
Tinea Versicolor	Pityrosporum orbiculare	Tan, brown, or white, very slightly scaling lesions that tend to coalesce are seen on the chest, neck, and abdomen and occasionally on the face of young adults

- Upon examination with Wood's light, tinea versicolor may fluoresce golden and erythrasma orange-red. Vitiligo turns ivory-white under Wood's light.

VASCULAR SKIN LESIONS (9,10)

		Description	Distribution
Angioma		Localized vascular lesions of skin and subcutaneous tissues resulting from hyperplasia of blood or lymph vessels	Occur in 1/3 of newborns; usually congenital or appear shortly after birth; most disappear spontaneously
Cherry angioma		Bright red to purple, smooth dome-shaped lesions due to telangiectatic vascular disturbance	Trunk and proximal extremities of the elderly; onset may begin in early adulthood
Discolorations	**Ecchymosis**	Discolorations produced by vascular wall destruction, trauma, or vasculitis	
	Petechia	Round, pinpoint (>5 cm in diameter), non-raised purplish red spot caused by intradermal or subcutaneous hemorrhage due to causes other than injury (i.e intravascular defects or infection)	
	Purpura	Small hemorrhage (larger than 0.5 cm in diameter) in the skin, mucous membrane or serosal surface resulting from intravascular defects or infection	

SKIN TUMORS (11)

	Tumor	Description	Distribution
Benign	**Moles**	Circumscribed pigmented macules, papules, or nodules composed of clusters of melanocytes or nevus cells	During adolescence and pregnancy, more moles may appear and existing ones may enlarge and darken
	Nevi	Congenital lesion of the skin; birth mark	
	Lipomas	Soft, movable, subcutaneous nodules with normal overlying skin	Occur more often in women than men and appear most commonly on the trunk, nape and forearms
	Seborrheic Keratosis	Pigmented superficial epithelial lesions that are usually warty but may occur as smooth papules; round or oval, flesh-colored, brown, or black and may have a waxy, scaling, or crusted surface	Etiology unknown. They occur commonly in middle or old age and most often appear on trunk or temples
Malignant	**Basal Cell Carcinoma**	Most commonly begins as a small shiny papule, enlarges slowly, and after a few months, shows a shiny **pearly border** with prominent engorged vessels on the surface and a central ulcer	Most arise in sun-exposed areas of skin and incidence is related to amount of melanin skin pigmentation (lighter-skinned persons are more susceptible)
	Squamous Cell Carcinoma	Tumor begins as a red papule or plaque with a scaly or crusted surface then becomes nodular, sometimes with a warty surface	Arise from epithelial cells, usually in sun-exposed areas
	Malignant Melanoma	Melanocytic tumor arising in a pigmented area: skin, mucous membranes, eyes, CNS	Most arise from melanocytes in normal skin; 40-50% develop from pigmented moles
	Kaposi's Sarcoma	Neoplasm with vascular skin tumors that may appear in three distinctive forms, one of which is associated with AIDS	Originate from multifocal sites in the mid-dermis and extend to the epidermis.

ote

The following symptoms indicated possible malignant transformation of pigmented nevi:

- Change in size
- Change in color, especially spread of red, white, and blue pigmentation to surrounding normal skin
- Change in surface characteristics, consistency or shape
- Signs of inflammation in surrounding skin

FINGERNAILS (12,13)

	Description	Causes
Clubbing	Nail becomes enlarged and curved, and the distal phalanx of each finger is rounded and bulbous. The proximal nail fold feels spongy upon palpation	Chronic hypoxia, lung cancer
Beau's Lines	Transverse depressions in the nails which emerge from under the proximal nail folds weeks after severe illness and gradually grow out with the nails	Acute severe illness
Koilonychia (Spoon nails)	Fingernails become thin and concave, with edges raised	Associated with iron deficiency anemia
Splinter Hemorrhages	Linear hemorrhages beneath the nails	When located near the base of the nail they are characteristic of subacute bacterial endocarditis; may occur with severe psoriasis
Pitting	Small pits in the nails	Seen most commonly with psoriasis
Onycholysis	Painless separation of the nail plate from the nail bed which starts distally, enlarging the free edge of the nail to a varying degree; several nails are usually affected	
Paronychia	Inflammation of the proximal and lateral nail folds which may be acute or chronic. Nail folds are red and swollen and often tender and the cuticle may not be visible. Multiple nails often affected	People who frequently immerse their nails in water are especially susceptible

ote

- Nail bed color should be variations of pink.
- Yellow discoloration occurs with psoriasis and fungal infections and may occur with chronic respiratory disease.
- Diffuse darkening of the nails may be caused by candidal infection, hyperbilirubinemia, chronic trauma.
- Green-black discoloration is associated with Pseudomonas infection, which is painless.
- Longitudinal white streaks or transverse white bands are indicative of a systemic disorder.

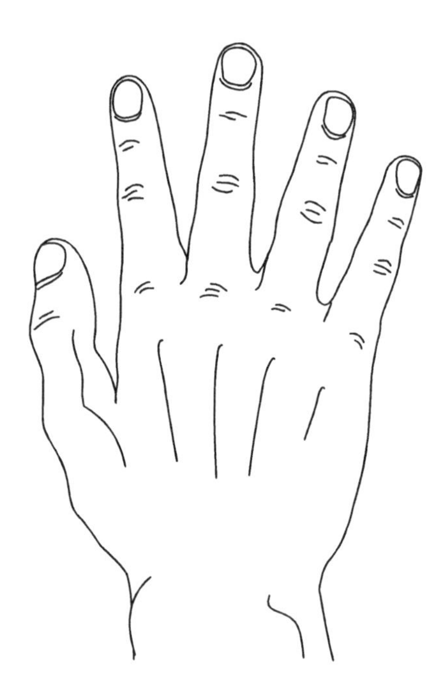

THE ENDOCRINE SYSTEM (14,15)

ote

- The hypothalamus is the highest integrative center of the nervous and endocrine systems.
- Organs with endocrine function include the hypothalamus, pituitary, thyroid, parathyroid, adrenal glands, gonads, pancreas, paraganglia, and the pineal body. The gut and lung also secrete substances that have hormonal function.
- Most tissues that synthesize hormones have a limited capacity to store the completed product due to the unsuitability of hormones to be incorporated into any of the three main storage compartments of the body (lipids, glycogen or protein).
- With few exceptions, hormone deficiencies or excesses cause pathologic effects.

HYPOTHALAMIC CONTROL OF THE ANTERIOR PITUITARY

Hypothalamus		Anterior Pituitary		Target Endocrine Organs
Hypo-thalamus	Thyrotropin-releasing hormone	Anterior Pituitary	Stimulates TSH and PRL	Target Endocrine Organs
	Gonadotropin-releasing hormone		Stimulates LH and FSH	
	Dopamine		Inhibits PRL, LH, FSH, and TSH	
	Corticotropin-releasing hormone		Stimulates ACTH	
	Growth hormone-releasing hormone		Stimulates GH	
	Somatostatin		Inhibits GH and TSH	

THE PITUITARY GLAND (16)

	Hormone	Function	Hormone Production	Disorders
Anterior	Adrenocorticoptropic Hormone (ACTH)	Stimulates adrenal cortex to secrete cortisol, which affects the metabolism of glucose, protein and fats, and several weak androgens	Deficiency	Fatigue, hypotension and intolerance to stress and infection, secondary adrenal insufficiency
			Excess	Cushing's disease
	Thyroid-stimulating hormone (thyrotropin; TSH)	Regulates structure and function of the thyroid gland; stimulates synthesis and release of thyroid hormones (T3 and T4); determines thyroid gland size	Deficiency	Secondary hypothyroidism
			Excess	TSH-mediated hyperthyroidism (due to pituitary tumors or pituitary resistance to thyroid hormone)
	Luteinizing Hormone (LH)	In women, stimulates ovarian cells to produce androgens; in men, primarily responsible for controlling testosterone production in the Leydig cells	Deficiency of gonadotropins	Amenorrhea, regression of secondary sex characteristics and infertility in women; impotence, testicular atrophy, regression of secondary sex characteristics and decreased spermatogenesis with consequent infertility in men
	Follicle-stimulating Hormone (FSH)	In women, stimulates the growth of the granulosa cells of the ovarian follicle and controls estradiol formation in these cells; in men, stimulates sperm production in the seminiferous tubules		
	Human Growth Hormone (GH; somatotropin)	Stimulation of somatic growth and regulation of metabolism	Deficiency	Pituitary dwarfism
			Excess	Leads to pituitary gigantism if hypersecretion starts before closure of the epiphyses; leads to acromegaly if hypersecretion starts after closure of the epiphyses
	Prolactin	Essential for lactation	Excess	Hypogonadism and/or galactorrhea (lactation in men or in women who are not breast feeding an infant)
Posterior	Anti-diuretic Hormone (ADH; vasopressin)	Promotes water conservation by the kidney; important role in maintaining fluid homeostasis and vascular and cellular hydration	Deficiency	Diabetes insipidus (secretion of very dilute urine; excessive thirst)
			Excess	Water retention
	Oxytocin	Stimulates contraction of uterine smooth muscle cells and causes the milk "letdown" reflex of nursing mothers		

ote

- The anterior lobe (adenohypophysis) secretes hormones and the posterior lobe (neurohypophysis) stores and releases neurohormones that it receives from the hypothalamus.
- The anterior pituitary has three target endocrine glands: the gonads, the adrenal cortex, and the thyroid.

The Thyroid Gland (17,18,19)

Hormone	Function	Gland Function	Disorders
T4 (thyroxine, tetraiodothyronine) and T3 (triiodothyronine)	Increase protein synthesis in virtually every body tissue and increase oxygen consumption by increasing the activity of the sodium/potassium pump, especially in liver, kidney, heart and skeletal muscle	Hyperthyroid	▪ Graves' Disease (hyperthyroidism, goiter, exophthalmos, pretibial myxedema) ▪ **NOTE**: Secondary hyperthyroidism due to excess TSH secretion by pituitary tumor
		Hypothyroid (myxedema)	▪ Hashimoto's Thyroiditis (chronic inflammation of the thyroid with lymphocytic infiltration of the gland) is most common cause of primary hypothyroidism; prevalent in women (8:1) between 30 and 50 yrs. ▪ **NOTE**: Secondary hypothyroidism occurs due to deficient secretion of TRH from hypothalamus or lack of secretion of TSH from pituitary
Calcitonin	Inhibits osteoclastic activity and stimulates renal calcium clearance (physiologic antagonist to parathyroid hormone)	Increased levels associated with:	▪ Medullary thyroid cancers ▪ Chronic renal failure ▪ Pernicious anemia

The Adrenal Glands (20,21)

	Hormone	Function	Gland Function	Disorders
Produced in adrenal cortex	**Androgens**	(DHEA) Function as steroids or steroid precursors	Hypofunction	▪ Addison's Disease: characterized by weakness, fatigue, orthostatic hypotension, increased pigmentation early, followed by weight loss, dehydration, hypotension and small heart size in later stages
	Glucocorticoids	(Cortisol) Affects metabolism of proteins, carbohydrates and lipids; stimulates gluconeogenesis by the liver; inhibits effect of insulin, decreases the rate of glucose use by the cells	Hyperfunction	▪ Cushing's Disease: characterized by "moon" facies, truncal obesity (buffalo hump), muscle wasting and weakness, purple striae on abdomen, hypertension, renal calculi, osteoporosis, glucose intolerance
	Mineralocorticoids	(Aldosterone) Causes retention of sodium and chloride and the elimination of potassium and hydrogen; function in maintenance of blood pressure and volume		

Note (22)

- Excess or deficiency of any one of adrenal cortex hormones leads to several well-recognized diseases that are diagnosed by assay of the hormone or its metabolites.

The Parathyroid Gland (23)

Hormone	Function	Gland Function	Disorders
Parathyroid Hormone (PTH)	(Along with Vitamin D) is the principal regulator of calcium and phosphorus homeostasis; increases blood calcium level	Hyperparathyroid	Primary hyperparathyroidism: characterized by hypercalcemia, hypophasphatemia and excessive bone resorption
		Hypoparathyroid	Hypoparathyroidism: characterized by low serum calcium, high serum phosphate and normal alkaline phosphate

The Pancreas (24,25)

	Hormone	Function	Hormone Level	Disorders	
Islets of Langerhans	**Glucagon (Alpha cells)**	Promotes glucose production in the liver (antagonist of insulin)	Increased	▪ Acute pancreatitis ▪ Diabetes mellitus	
			Reduced	▪ Loss of pancreatic tissue due to neoplasm or organ removal ▪ Chronic pancreatitis ▪ Cystic fibrosis	
	Insulin (Beta cells)	Regulates carbohydrate metabolism, together with contributions from the liver, adipose tissue and other target cells; maintains constant blood glucose levels	Deficient insulin production or abnormal insulin release	Diabetes Mellitis	▪ Type I (insulin-dependent) diabetes: begins relatively early in life and is more severe; (blood insulin values will be decreased) ▪ Type II (non-insulin dependent) diabetes: usually begins in middle age or later and affects 80% of diabetics (blood insulin values will be increased)
			Hypersecretion	▪ Pancreatic Beta cell tumor: leads to unregulated hypersecretion of insulin ▪ Insulinoma (islet cell tumor)	

ote (26)

- The pancreas has endocrine and exocrine functions. Pancreatic enzymes consist mainly of starch-digesting amylase, fat-digesting lipase, and protein-digesting trypsin, as well as bicarbonate and other substances, which are secreted into the duodenum via the pancreatic duct.

Central Nervous System Disorders (27)

Disorder	Description		Physical Symptoms
Multiple Sclerosis	▪ Slowly progressive disease of insidious onset resulting in multiple and varied neurologic symptoms, usually with remissions and exacerbations ▪ Plaques of demyelination with destruction of oligodendroglia and perivascular inflammation primarily in the white matter, especially the lateral and posterior columns ▪ No specific therapy and spontaneous remissions may occur		▪ Paresthesias in one or more extremities, in the trunk or one side of the face ▪ Weakness or clumsiness of a leg or a hand ▪ Visual disturbances (retrobulbar neuritis, nystagmus); diplopia, dimness of vision, scotomas ▪ Excess heat may accentuate symptoms and signs ▪ Deep reflexes generally increased; Babinski's sign and clonus often present; superficial reflexes diminished or absent ▪ Intention tremors and ataxic motion ▪ **Charcot's triad**: nystagmus, intention tremor and scanning speech is common advanced stage cerebellar manifestation ▪ Urinary urgency or hesitancy, and other abnormalities ▪ MRI is the most sensitive diagnostic imaging technique
Cerebral Palsy	▪ Motor disorders resulting from prenatal development abnormalities or perinatal or postnatal CNS damage before age 5 ▪ Characterized by impaired voluntary movement	▪ Spastic syndromes: 70%	▪ Hemiplegia, paraplegia, tetraplegia, quadriplegia due to upper motor neuron involvement ▪ Affected limbs are underdeveloped and show increased deep tendon reflexes and hypertonicity, weakness ▪ Scissors gait and toe-walking
		▪ Athetoid or dyskinetc syndromes: 20%	▪ Basal ganglia involvement causes slow, writing, involuntary movements of the extremities or proximal parts of the limbs and trunk ▪ Choreiform movements ▪ Dysarthria present and often severe
		▪ Ataxic syndromes: 10%	▪ Cerebellar involvement causes weakness, incoordination, and intention tremors ▪ Unsteadiness and wide-based gait
		▪ Mixed forms	▪ Usually spasticity and athetosis; less often, ataxia and athetosis
Parkinson's Disease ▪ Parkinson's disease is the antithesis of chorea and athetosis	▪ Idiopathic, slowly progressive, degenerative CNS disorder with mean age of onset 57 years ▪ Caused by depletion of dopamine ▪ Slowness and poverty of movement ▪ Muscular rigidity ▪ Resting tremors ▪ Postural instability		▪ Bradykinesia and akinesia ▪ Pill-rolling tremor of the hand ▪ Masklike face with diminished blinking ▪ Festination gait: patient has difficulty starting to walk, then shuffles with short steps and then quickens the steps to keep from falling ▪ Lead-pipe and cogwheel rigidity ▪ Dementia in 50% of patients
Chorea and athetosis ▪ Both are manifestations of dopaminergic overactivity in the basal ganglia	▪ Chorea: brief, purposeless involuntary movements of the distal extremities and face ▪ Athetosis: writhing, proximal, often alternating postures that blend continuously into a flowing stream of movement		▪ **Huntington's disease**: choreiform movements and progressive intellectual deterioration and psychiatric disturbances; mean age of onset 35 to 50 years old ▪ **Sydenham's chorea**: involuntary, purposeless, nonrepetitive movements that may involve all muscles except the eyes; usually follows Group A beta-hemolytic streptococcal infections; insidious onset and gradual cessation in about 4 months

Central and Peripheral NS Disorders (28)

Disorder	Description	Physical Symptoms
Amyotrophic Lateral Sclerosis	▪ Progressive degeneration of corticospinal tracts and/or anterior horn cells and/or bulbar motor nuclei ▪ Median age of onset is 55 years; incidence greater in males ▪ 50% die within 3 years of onset	▪ Muscular weakness and atrophy ▪ Symptoms of anterior horn cell dysfunction most common in the hands ▪ Visible muscle fasciculations, spasticity, hyperactive deep tendon reflexes and extensor plantar reflexes ▪ Dysarthria and dysphagia ▪ Sensory systems spared

Peripheral NS Disorders (29)

Disorder	Description	Physical Symptoms
Bell's Palsy	▪ Unilateral facial paralysis of sudden idiopathic onset ▪ Possible mechanism is swelling of the facial nerve due to immune or viral disease	▪ Pain behind the ear followed by facial weakness that develops within hours ▪ Involved side is flat and expressionless but no sensory loss is present
Myasthenia Gravis	▪ Episodic muscle weakness, chiefly in muscles innervated by cranial nerves ▪ Autoimmune attack on the acetylcholine receptor of the postsynaptic neuromuscular junction ▪ Predominant in women 20-40 years old ▪ Improved by cholinesterase-inhibiting drugs (endrophonium is used for diagnosis)	▪ Ptosis, diplopia, muscle fatigability after exercise ▪ Ocular muscles affected first in 40% of patients and eventually in 85% ▪ Dysarthria, dysphagia, and proximal limb weakness are common ▪ Normal sensation and deep tendon reflexes ▪ Symptoms fluctuate in intensity over the course of hours or days
Duchenne Muscular Dystrophy	▪ Typically presents in 3 to 7 year old boys with proximal muscle weakness ▪ Progression is steady and most patients are confined to a wheel chair by age 10 or 12	▪ Waddling gait, toe-walking, lordosis, frequent falls and difficulty standing and climbing stairs ▪ Positive Gower's sign ▪ Pseudohypertrophy of the calf muscles due to fatty and fibrous infiltration

Focal Autonomic Nervous System Disorders (30)

Disorder	Description	Physical Symptoms
Reflex Sympathetic Dystrophy	▪ Sympathetically mediated pain following injury to bone and soft tissue ▪ **Causalgia** is a subtype of RSD: usually partial injury to a nerve trunk produces severe, burning pain in the extremity	▪ Autonomic changes including sweating or vasomotor abnormalities and/or dystrophic changes including skin or bone atrophy, hair loss and joint contractures
Horner's Syndrome	▪ Occurs following injury to the sympathetic fibers in either the central or peripheral nervous system ▪ Central lesions disrupt sympathetic pathways between the hypothalamus and upper thoracic cord (C8-T3) ▪ Peripheral lesions damage the cervical sympathetic chain, the superior cervical ganglion, or the sympathetic plexus adhering to the common internal and external carotid arteries.\	▪ Variable ptosis, miosis, and loss of sweating (anhydrosis) develop on the same side of the face as the injury

TUMORS AND TUMORLIKE PROCESSES (31,32)

Disorder	Description	Physical Symptoms	X-ray	Laboratory
Multiple Myeloma	▪ Progressive malignant bone marrow plasma cell proliferation, characterized by overproduction of Bence Jones proteins (free monoclonal light chains) ▪ Patient average age is 60 with 2:1 male predominance	▪ Persistent unexplained skeletal pain in the back, thorax or other area relieved with bedrest and aggravated by weight bearing ▪ Anemia with weakness and fatigue ▪ Renal disease ▪ Recurrent bacterial infections	▪ Spine, pelvis, skull, ribs and scapula are most common sites ▪ Diffuse osteoporosis; pathologic fractures and vertebral collapse ▪ Punched out lesions ▪ Cold on bone scan	▪ Bence Jones proteinuria ▪ ESR often markedly elevated ▪ Hypercalcemia in 1/3 of patients ▪ Serum protein electrophoresis shows an M-spike in 80% of cases
Metastatic Cancer	▪ 70% of all tumors are of metastatic origin ▪ The most common primary sites are breast, lung, prostate, kidney, thyroid, and bowel ▪ Most patients are over 40 years old	▪ History of recent weight loss ▪ Cachexia, anemia and fever in the advanced stages ▪ Nocturnal pain of insidious onset and pathologic fracture	▪ Vertebra plana ▪ One-eyed pedicle sign; blind vertebrae ▪ Ivory vertebrae ▪ 75% are osteolytic	▪ Alkaline phosphatase may be elevated in blastic mets ▪ Acid phosphatase is elevated in prostatic cancer following rupture of the capsule ▪ Elevated ESR
Paget's Disease / Osteitis Deformans	▪ Localized areas of bone experience osteolysis followed by extensive attempts at repair ▪ 2:1 male predominance, usually affects persons over 40 years old	▪ Usually asymptomatic with insidious onset when symptoms occur ▪ Deep, aching pain, stiffness, fatigability, deformity, headaches, decreasing auditory acuity, increasing skull size	▪ Hot on bone scan ▪ Stages: osteolytic, combined, sclerotic, malignant degeneration ▪ Cottonwool skull in advanced stage ▪ Picture frame vertebrae and ivory vertebrae ▪ Cortical thickening and bone expansion ▪ Obliteration of Kohler's teardrop (brim sign)	▪ Elevated serum alkaline phosphatase ▪ Increased urinary excretion of total peptide hydroxyproline ▪ Serum calcium and phosphorus levels are usually normal

ote

- Multiple myeloma is the most common primary malignant bone tumor.
- Metastatic bone tumors are the most common malignant tumors of the skeleton.

Nutritional Disorders

Deficiencies of the B Vitamins (33)

Disorder	Description	Physical Symptoms
Beriberi ▪ Thiamin (B1) deficiency	▪ Caused by severe deficiency of thiamin which depletes stores of the vitamin in the thalamus and brainstem reticular formation ▪ Usually caused by severe alcoholism ▪ **Wernicke-Korsakoff Syndrome** is cerebral beriberi	▪ The most advanced neural changes occur in the peripheral nerves of the legs ▪ Nystagmus or partial ophthalmoplegia ▪ Possible ataxia, confusion, drowsiness or stupor ▪ Clinical defects often appear in other cranial nerve functions ▪ Autonomic dysfunction: sympathetic hyperactivity or hypoactivity
Riboflavin (B2) Deficiency	▪ Primary deficiency associated with inadequate consumption of milk and other animal protein	▪ Oral, ocular, cutaneous and genital lesions
Pellagra ▪ Niacin (B3) deficiency	▪ Caused by severe deficiency of niacin, which plays a vital role in cell metabolism ▪ Can be primary (dietary) or secondary (cirrhosis of the liver or alcoholism)	▪ Cutaneous lesions ▪ Changes in mucous membranes ▪ GI symptoms (diarrhea) ▪ CNS involvement including organic psychosis and encephalopathic syndrome (cogwheel rigidity of the extremities and clouding of consciousness)
Pyridoxine (B6) Deficiency	▪ Primary deficiency is rare; secondary deficiencies can result from malabsorption and other causes	▪ Sebhorrheic dermatosis, glossitis, cheilosis, peripheral neuropathy, lymphopenia
Folic Acid Deficiency	▪ Dietary lack and intestinal malabsorption are common causes of deficiency	▪ Clinical features are those of anemia ▪ Folate deficiency is indistinguishable from B12 deficiency in peripheral blood and bone marrow findings, but with folate deficiency **no neurologic findings occur**
Pernicious Anemia ▪ B12 (cobalamin) deficiency	▪ The atrophic gastric mucosa fails to secrete adequate amounts of intrinsic factor	▪ Anemia develops insidiously and progressively as the large stores of B12 in the liver are depleted ▪ GI manifestations, "burning tongue", weight loss ▪ Neurologic involvement may be present even without anemia and usually involves the peripheral nerves ▪ The next most common neurologic sign is **combined systems disease** which occurs with spinal cord involvement. Symptoms start in the dorsal column (peripheral pins-and-needles paresthesias), followed by lateral column involvement (Babinski's sign and spasticity) ▪ "Stocking and Glove" paresthesia ▪ Positive Schilling test

HEMATOLOGIC DISORDERS

ANEMIA (34)

ote

- Anemia is characterized by a reduction in the number of circulating red blood cells, in the amount of hemoglobin, or in the volume of packed cells (hematocrit), or a combination of these.

CLASSIFICATION OF ANEMIA BASED ON RBC MORPHOLOGY

Microcytic	**Hypochromic**	▪ Chronic iron deficiency (most frequent cause) ▪ Thalassemia ▪ Occasionally in chronic systems disease
	Normochromic	▪ Some cases of chronic systemic disease
Normocytic	**Hypochromic**	▪ Some cases of chronic systemic disease ▪ Lead poisoning
	Normochromic	▪ Many cases due to systemic disease ▪ Many cases associated with pituitary, thyroid, or adrenal disease ▪ Acute blood loss ▪ Hemolytic anemia
Macrocytic	**Hypochromic**	▪ Some cases of macrocytic anemia with superimposed iron deficiency
	Normochromic	▪ B12 or folic acid deficiency or malabsorption ▪ Chronic alcoholism

CLASSIFICATION OF ANEMIAS BASED ON PATHOGENESIS

Anemia Classification	Explanation	Most Common Causes
Factor Deficiency Anemia	Deficiency of vital hematopoietic raw material	▪ Iron deficiency ▪ Vitamin B12 or Folic acid deficiency or combination of both
Production-defect Anemia	Failure of blood-forming organs to produce or to deliver mature RBCs to the peripheral blood	▪ Replacement of marrow by fibrosis or by neoplasm ▪ Hypoplasia of the bone marrow ▪ Toxic suppression of marrow production or delivery without actual marrow hypoplasia (e.g. chronic renal disease)
Depletion Anemia	RBC loss from the peripheral blood	▪ Hemorrhage (acute or chronic) ▪ Hemolytic anemia ▪ Hypersplenism

LEUKEMIA (35)

ote

- Leukemias are malignant neoplasms of blood forming tissues.

Classification	Definition	Signs and Symptoms	Laboratory
Chronic Lymphocytic	▪ Appearance of mature lymphocytes in blood, bone marrow and lymphoid organs	▪ Afflicts older persons with 75% diagnosed at the average age of 60 years; 2 to 3 times more common in men than in women ▪ Onset is usually insidious ▪ Symptomatic patient usually has non-specific signs: fatigue, anorexia, sense of abdominal fullness from an enlarging spleen ▪ At diagnosis, patient presents with generalized lymphadenopathy and minimal-to-moderate enlargement of liver and spleen ▪ Bacterial, viral and fungal infections are features of advancing CLL	▪ Hallmark of the disease is a sustained, absolute lymphocytosis and an increase of lymphocytes in the bone marrow ▪ At diagnosis, there may be moderate anemia and thrombocytopenia ▪ Many patients will have hypogammaglobulinemia
Chronic Myelocytic	▪ Predominance of granulocytic cells of all stages of differentiation in blood, bone marrow, liver, spleen and other organs	▪ Patient may be asymptomatic and the condition may be discovered by incidental CBC, or insidious onset of non-specific symptoms may prompt discovery of the disease ▪ Moderate to severe splenomegaly; possible lymphadenopathy	▪ Absolute increases in numbers of basophils and eosinophils ▪ Leukocytosis ▪ Philadelphia chromosome
Acute Lymphoblastic	▪ The most common malignancy in children, with peak incidence from ages 3 to 5 years	▪ Rapidly progressing leukemias with replacement of normal bone marrow by blast cells of a clone arising from malignant transformation of a hematopoietic stem cell ▪ Presenting symptoms include bleeding, pallor and fever	▪ Anemia and thrombocytopenia ▪ Leukemic blast cells in the blood smear
Acute Myeloid	▪ Occurs at all ages and is the more common acute leukemia in adults		

CONNECTIVE TISSUE DISORDERS (36)

Disorder	Description	Physical Symptoms	Laboratory
Systemic Lupus Erythematosus	▪ Idiopathic inflammatory connective tissue disorder ▪ 90% of cases occur in women, predominantly young women	▪ May begin abruptly with fever or may develop insidiously over months or years with episodes of fever and malaise ▪ 90% of patients complain of articular symptoms (arthralgia; polyarthritis) ▪ **Jaccoud's arthritis**: tendon contractures and secondary joint deformity without x-ray evidence of erosion ▪ Malar butterfly erythema ▪ Discoid lesions ▪ Generalized adenopathy ▪ Kidney damage can become evident (proteinuria) at any time	▪ Screening test is Antinuclear antibody (ANA)
Progressive Systemic Sclerosis	▪ Idiopathic chronic disease with diffuse fibrosis; degenerative changes; and vascular abnormalities in the skin, articular structures, internal organs ▪ About 4 times more common in women; rare in children	▪ Disease varies in severity and progression ▪ Internal manifestations: **CREST syndrome** (Calcinosis, Raynaud's phenomenon, Esophageal dysfunction, Sclerodactyly, Telangiectasia) ▪ Most common initial complaints include Raynaud's phenomenon and insidious swelling of the acral portions of the extremities with gradual thickening of the skin of the fingers; polyarthralgia; GI disturbances or respiratory complaints ▪ Localized form: circumscribed patches (morphea) or linear sclerosis of the integument	▪ RF positive in 1/3 of patients ▪ Serum antinuclear antibodies are present in at least 90% of vases

PERIPHERAL VASCULAR DISORDERS (37)

Disorder	Description	Physical Symptoms
Raynaud's Disease and Phenomenon	▪ Spasm of arterioles, usually in the digits, with intermittent pallor or cyanosis of the skin ▪ Raynaud's disease is idiopathic (60-90% of cases occur in young women); bilateral involvement ▪ Raynaud's phenomenon is secondary to other conditions	▪ Attacks of vasospasm of the digital arteries and arterioles may last from minutes to hours but are rarely severe enough to cause gross tissue loss ▪ Intermittent attacks are precipitated by exposure to cold or by emotional upsets ▪ Triphasic color changes (pallor, cyanosis, redness) or biphasic color changes (cyanosis then reactive hyperemia) ▪ Pain is uncommon but paresthesias are frequent during the attack ▪ Sclerodactyly occurs with long-standing Raynaud's disease ▪ Allen's test frequently shows occlusion of the radial or ulnar arterial branches distal to the wrist
Thromboantitis Obliterans / Buerger's Disease	▪ An obliterative disease characterized by inflammatory changes in small and medium-sized arteries and veins ▪ Occurs predominantly in men 20 to 40 years old who smoke cigarettes	▪ Gradual onset, starting in the most distal vessels of the upper and lower extremities and progressing proximally, culminating in distal gangrene ▪ Patient may complain of coldness, numbness, tingling or burning ▪ Raynaud's phenomenon is common ▪ Intermittent claudication occurs in the affected extremity ▪ Frequent sympathetic nerve overactivity (coldness, sweating)

CHILDHOOD INFECTIONS (38)

	Infection	Infecting Organism	Signs and Symptoms	Laboratory
Bacterial	**Diptheria**	▪ Corynebacterium diphtheriae	▪ Contagious disease characterized by formation of a fibrinous pseudomembrane, usually on the respiratory mucosa, and by myocardial and neural tissue damage secondary to an exotoxin	
Bacterial	**Pertussis / Whooping Cough**	▪ Bordetella pertussis ▪ Transmission by aspiration	▪ B. pertussis invades the mucosa of the nasopharynx, trachea, bronchi, and bronchioles, increasing secretion of mucus. ▪ White blood cell count may be normal or as high as 60,000, usually with 60-80% small lymphocytes	
Bacterial	**Impetigo**	▪ Staphylococcus aureus is most common cause ▪ Ecthyma: ulcerative form	▪ Superficial vesiculopustular skin infection especially on the legs	
Viral	**Measles**	▪ Paramyxovirus ▪ Communicable from droplets from mouth, nose or throat of a person in prodromal stage	▪ Highly contagious, acute disease with fever, cough, coryza, conjuctivitis, enanthem (**Koplik spots**) on the buccal or labial mucosa, and a spreading maculopapular cutaneous rash	▪ Granulocytic leukopenia; virus in blood and nasopharynx
Viral	**Chickenpox**	▪ Varicella-zoster virus ▪ Highly communicable	▪ Moderate fever, headache, malaise, occasional sore throat ▪ Lesions progress from macule to papule to vesicle to crusting	▪ Presence of virus in vesicle fluid
Viral	**Rubella**	▪ Caused by RNA virus ▪ Spread by airborne droplets or by close contact	▪ Malaise, fever, headache, rhinitis, postauricular and suboccipital lymphadenopathy with tender nodes ▪ Fine pinkish macules that become confluent and often scarlatiniform or pinpoint on the second day	▪ WBC count usually normal or slightly reduced; virus in blood and nasopharynx
Viral	**Poliomyelitis**	▪ Enterovirus ▪ Infection through direct contact	▪ Acute infection with varied symptoms including nonspecific minor illness, aseptic meningitis, and flaccid weakness of various muscle groups ▪ Minor illness (recovery in 24 to 72 hours); and major illness (can involve CNS)	▪ With major illness: CSF protein is slightly elevated and peripheral WBC counts may be normal or moderately increased
Viral	**Mumps**	▪ Paramyxovirus ▪ Spread by infected droplets or direct contact with saliva	▪ Acute, contagious, generalized disease, usually causing painful enlargement of the salivary glands, most commonly the parotids	▪ WBC count may be normal, but a slight leukopenia with a reduction in granulocytes is usual
Viral	**Croup**	▪ Parainfluenza virus is most common ▪ Spread is airborne or contact with infected secretions	▪ Acute viral inflammation of the upper and lower respiratory tracts, with inspiratory stridor, subglottic swelling, and respiratory distress that is most pronounced on inspiration	▪ Leukocytosis with increased PMNL cells may be present initially, followed by leukopenia and lymphocytosis
Viral	**Reye's Syndrome**	▪ Idiopathic, but viral agents are associated factors	▪ Syndrome of acute encephalopathy and fatty infiltration of the viscera that tends to follow some acute viral infections	▪ Liver biopsy; increased liver transaminases; increased blood ammonia; prolonged thrombin time

GASTROINTESTINAL DISORDERS (39)

Disorder	Description	Physical Symptoms
Hiatal hernia	▪ Protrusion of the stomach above the abdomen ▪ Can be congenital or secondary to trauma	▪ **Sliding hiatal hernia**: the gastroesophageal junction and a portion of the stomach are above the diaphragm ▪ **Paraesophageal hiatal hernia**: the gastroesophageal junction is in the normal location, but a portion of the stomach is adjacent to the esophagus
Irritable bowel	▪ Motility disorder with no anatomic cause involving the entire hollow GI tract, creating both upper and lower GI symptoms ▪ Women are affected 3:1	▪ Predominant symptoms include variable degrees of abdominal pain, constipation or diarrhea, and postprandial distension ▪ Symptoms occur while the patient is awake and are usually triggered by stress or eating
Diverticulosis	▪ Sac-like mucosal projections through the muscular layer of the colorectum can occur anywhere in the large bowel, but usually in the sigmoid (rarely below the peritoneal reflection of the rectum) ▪ Uncommon in persons under 40 years	▪ Most diverticula are multiple and except for bleeding, they are harmless. Fecal impaction in the sac can cause secondary erosion and inflammation and diverticulitis can follow ▪ **Diverticulitis**: inflammation of the diverticular mucosa with peridiverticulitis, phlegmon of the bowel wall, perforation, abscess, and/or peritonitis

CHRONIC INFLAMMATORY BOWEL DISEASES

Disorder	Description	Physical Symptoms
Crohn's disease / regional enteritis	▪ Nonspecific chronic transmural inflammatory disease that most commonly affects the distal ileum and colon but may also occur in any part of the GI tract from the mouth to the anus and perianal area ▪ Peak incidence between 14 and 24 years	▪ Chronic diarrhea with abdominal pain, fever, anorexia, weight loss, and a right lower quadrant mass or fullness; mimics appendicitis or obstruction ▪ Skip lesions ▪ String sign on radiographs
Ulcerative colitis	▪ Chronic nonspecific inflammatory and ulcerative disease arising in the colonic mucosa ▪ Peak age 15 to 30 years	▪ Bloody diarrhea ▪ Usually begins in the rectosigmoid area and may extend proximally, eventually involving the entire colon ▪ Hemorrhage is the most common local complication ▪ Increased risk of colon cancer with long-standing, extensive ulcerative colitis

AIRWAYS OBSTRUCTION (40)

Disorder	Description	Physical Symptoms
Asthma	▪ Lung disease with airways obstruction that is reversible, either spontaneously or with treatment; airways inflammation; and increased airways responsiveness to a variety of stimuli	▪ Airways obstruction occurs due to spasm of airways smooth muscle; edema of airways mucosa; increased mucus secretion; cellular (eosinophilic) infiltration of the airways walls; injury and desquamation of the airways epithelium ▪ Blue bloaters ▪ Sputum contains Charcot-Leyden crystals originating from eosinophils ▪ Chest x-ray shows increased lung markings
Chronic Obstructive Pulmonary Disease	▪ Combination of chronic obstructive bronchitis and emphysema	▪ Obstruction to expiratory air flow causing a slowing of forced expiration; some wheeze is often noted toward the end of forced expiration ▪ Later stages present with gross pulmonary hyperinflation, prolonged expiration during quiet breathing, depressed diaphragm, stooped posture
Pulmonary Emphysema	▪ Proteolytic enzymes are released from leukocytes participating in the inflammatory process and affect the alveolar walls	▪ Chronic alveolar inflammation (i.e. smoking) encourages development of an emphysematous lesion ▪ Pink puffers

LUNG EXAMINATION (41)

Common Abnormalities With Percussion	▪ Asthma – Normal or hyperresonant ▪ Atelectasis – Dullness over affected lung; tympany over area evacuated ▪ Bronchiectasis – No unusual findings ▪ Hemothorax – Dull over affected side	▪ Bronchitis – Normal ▪ Emphysema – Generalized hyperresonance ▪ Pneumonia – Dullness over involved site ▪ Pneumothorax – Tympany (or hyperresonance) over involved site
Common Abnormalities With Auscultation	▪ Asthma – Wheezes, especially on expiration ▪ Atelectasis – Wheezes, rhonchi, crackles; exaggerated breath sounds over affected lung; absent breath sounds over area evacuated ▪ Pneumothorax – Diminished to absent breath sounds over involved area	▪ Emphysema – Diminished breath sounds; crackles and wheezes ▪ Pneumonia – Variety of crackles; increased breath sounds ▪ Bronchitis – Prolonged breath sounds; crackles which clear with cough ▪ Bronchiectasis – Variety of crackles
Common Abnormalities With Palpation	▪ Increased fremitus – Occurs with presence of fluids or a solid mass in the lungs; pneumonia ▪ Decreased fremitus – Caused by excess air in the lungs; may indicate involved area of pneumonia, hemothorax or pneumothorax	

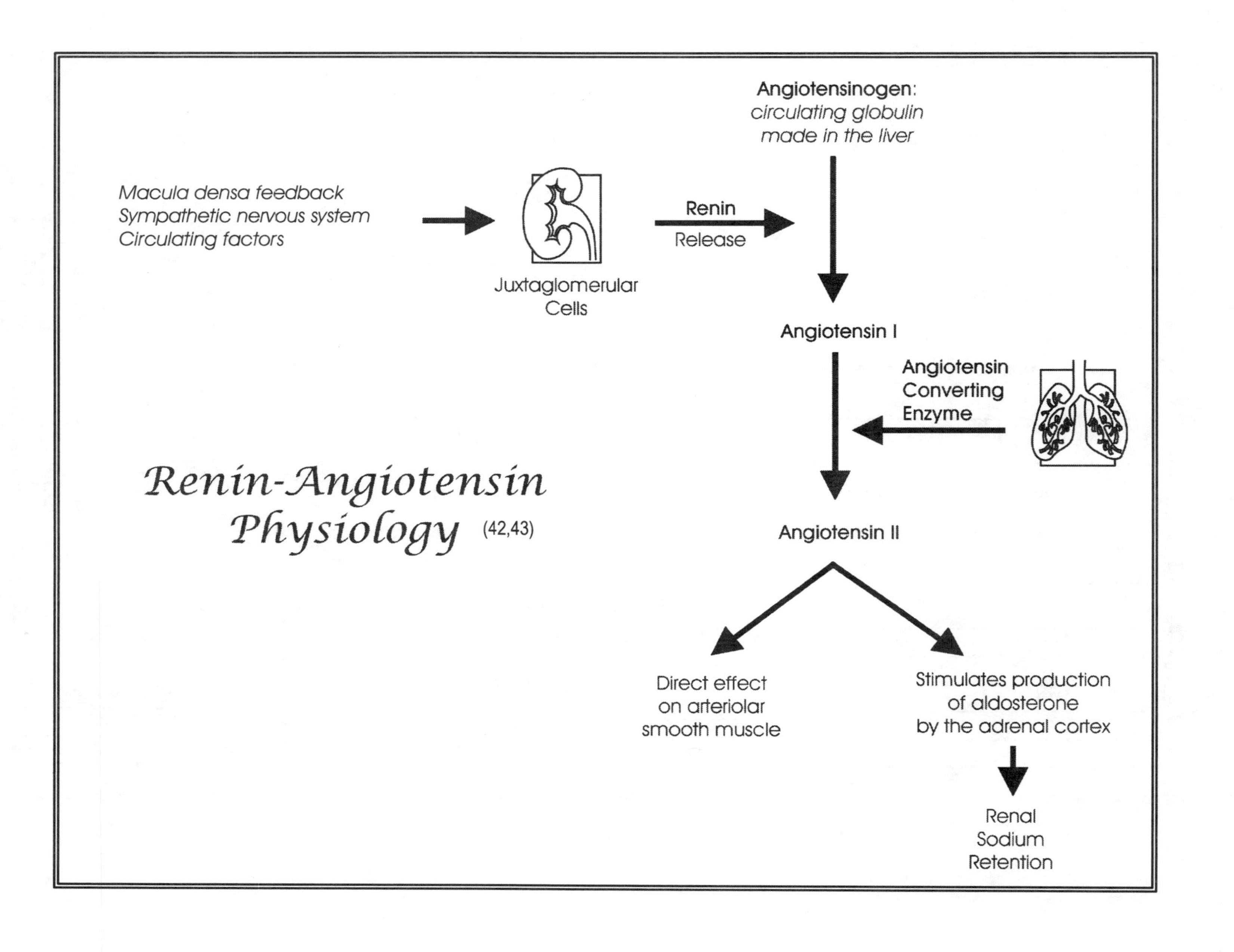

Renin-Angiotensin Physiology (42,43)
Macula densa feedback
Sympathetic nervous system
Circulating factors
Juxtaglomerular Cells
Renin
Release
Angiotensinogen:
circulating globulin made in the liver
Angiotensin I
Angiotensin Converting Enzyme
Angiotensin II
Direct effect on arteriolar smooth muscle
Stimulates production of aldosterone by the adrenal cortex
Renal Sodium Retention

COUGH AND SPUTUM CHARACTERISTICS (44,45)

Diagnosis		Organism	Cough and Sputum Characteristics
Bacterial Infection			Yellow, green, rust, clear or transparent; purulent; blood-streaked
Viral Infection			Mucoid, viscid; usually not blood streaked
Chronic Infectious Disease			Yellow, green, rust, clear or transparent; purulent; possibly blood-streaked mucoid, viscid
Lung Cancer			Dry to productive cough; sputum may be blood-streaked or bloody
Pneumonia	Pneumococcal Pneumonia	Strep pneumonia	Productive cough, pinkish or rusty sputum
	Hemophilus Bronchopneumonia	Hemophilus influenza	Productive cough, rusty sputum
	Mycoplasma Pneumonia (AKA Walking Pneumonia)	Acid fast bacillus	Irritating mucoid cough that produces scant amount of mucoid sputum
	Viral Pneumonia	Adenovirus	Dry, hacking cough with mucopurulent sputum
	Klebsiella Pneumonia	Klebsiella pneumonia	Productive cough with currant jelly sputum

emember

- Acute onset of cough and sputum suggests probable infection.
- Chronicity of symptoms of cough and sputum suggests the possibility of anatomic change (i.e. tumor).

HEADACHES (46)

DIFFERENTIALS

Characteristic	Classic Migraine	Common Migraine	Tension Headache	Cluster Headache	Trigeminal Neuralgia
Age of onset	Usually begins in adolescence or young adulthood	Usually begins in adolescence or young adulthood	Usually begins in young adulthood	Usually middle age (30-50)	Usually occurs in the elderly
Sex	Female 2:1	Female 2:1	Female 2:1	Large male predominance	Female > male
Pain Quality	Usually throbbing	Usually throbbing; often disabling	Often mild/moderate; waxes and wanes; tight, pressure, "band-like"; patient usually remains functional	Excruciating	Severe, lancinating, sudden electric brief and recurrent pains that are intermittent
Location	Usually unilateral	Unilateral (most common) or bilateral	Usually generalized, hat-band or occipital	Periorbital or frontotemporal, unilateral (always same side)	Usually unilaterally involves the second or third division of the trigeminal nerve (rarely the first)
Duration and frequency	One to 6 hours; several headaches per year	May last several hours to 1 to 3 days; frequency variable	Often occur every day or they are constant; duration is extremely variable	Occur in "clusters" of 1 to 3 months and last about 1 hour; occur once to several times each day; often precipitated by alcohol; often nocturnal and can wake the patient from sleep; less common than migraine	Very brief (10 to 45 seconds) but may appear to last 15 to 45 minutes due to "staccato" fashion of presentation; occurs many times per day
Prodromal symptoms	Usually visual and usually last 10 to 30 minutes and disappear with onset of headache	Often absent or may be vague: irritability, insomnia; headache often related to menstruation, psychological stress, etc.	None	None	None
Associated symptoms	Nausea, vomiting, prostration, photophobia	No neurologic findings; photophobia	Occasional muscle spasm and tenderness of occipital and trapezius muscles; general unhappiness	Photophobia, tearing, nasal stuffiness; possible mild Horner's syndrome; agitated, even violent behavior	Trigger points on sensitive areas of the face and gums that may induce an attack when stimulated

URINARY TRACT DISORDERS (47)

Disorder	Description	Physical Symptoms	Laboratory
Glomerulonephritis	▪ Diffuse inflammatory changes in the glomeruli and abrupt onset of hematuria with RBC casts, mild proteinuria and often hypertension, edema and azotemia ▪ Prototypic glomerular disease of acute onset is poststreptococcal glomerulonephritis	▪ Latent period: 1 to 6 weeks between infection and onset of symptoms ▪ Presenting complaints: edema, oliguria, dark urine and possible hypervolemia ▪ 50% of patients are symptom free	▪ Urine appears brown, smoky or frankly bloody ▪ Proteinuria ▪ Urine sediment contains blood cell casts
Pyelonephritis	▪ Acute, patchy, often bilateral pyogenic infection of the renal pelvis and parenchyma	▪ Rapid onset with chills, fever, flank pain, nausea, and vomiting ▪ Symptoms of lower UTI ▪ Tender enlarged kidney and costovertebral tenderness on the infected side	▪ pH of urine may be alkaline ▪ Bacteria and hematuria ▪ WBC casts are pathognomonic of renal inflammation
Nephrotic Syndrome	▪ Severe, prolonged increase in glomerular permeability for protein due to primary glomerula disease or a vast array of systemic diseases	▪ Frothy urine ▪ Anorexia, malaise, puffy eyelids, retinal sheen ▪ Abdominal pain ▪ Edema and focal edema	▪ Proteinuria ▪ Hypoalbuminuria, generalized edema, and lipemia are frequently present
Polycystic Disease	▪ Inherited kidney disorders with many bilateral cysts (dilated portions of renal tubules and glomeruli) that increase kidney size but reduce the functioning renal tissue	▪ Clinical onset in early or middle adult life ▪ Lumbar discomfort or pain ▪ Infection ▪ Hypertension in 50% of patients	▪ Hematuria; pyuria ▪ Grossly bloody urine ▪ Mild proteinuria
Acute Renal Failure	▪ Rapid, steadily increasing azotemia (excess of urea or other nitrogenous compounds in the blood), with or without oliguria	▪ Symptoms depend on degree of renal dysfunction ▪ Bladder outlet obstruction ▪ Enlarged kidney or palpable bladder	▪ Urinary sediment: tubular cells, tubular cell casts, many brown pigmented granular casts ▪ Progressive daily rise in serum creatinine ▪ Progressive azotemia, acidosis, hyperkalemia, hyponatremia
Chronic Renal Failure	▪ Results from a multitude of pathologic processes that lead to derangement and insufficiency of renal excretory and regulatory function	▪ Many patients are asymptomatic ▪ Neuromuscular signs: peripheral neuropathies ▪ GI signs: anorexia, nausea, vomiting ▪ Cardiovascular signs: hypertension	▪ Nitrogen retention ▪ Acidosis usually moderate ▪ Broad waxy casts in urine ▪ Anemia ▪ Elevated urea and creatinine

REFERENCES

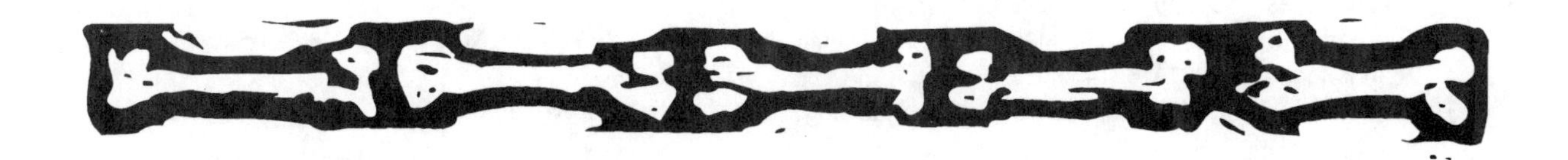

1 Berkow R, Editor-in-Chief. The Merck Manual of Diagnosis and Therapy. 16th ed. New Jersey: Merck Research Laboratories, 1992: 409-418, 434-443, 583-585, 1092.
2 Bates B. A Guide to Physical Examination. 6th ed. Philadelphia: J.B. Lippincott Company, 1995: 267-268.
3 Seidel HM, Ball JW, Dains JE, Benedict GW. Mosby's Guide to Physical Examination. 3rd ed. St. Louis: Mosby, 1995: 374-375
4 Scheidt S. Clinical Symposia: Basic Electrocardiography: Leads, Axes, Arrhythmias. Vol 35, no 2. New Jersey: CIBA Pharmaceutical Company, 1983.
5 Ganong WF. Review of Medical Physiology. 17th ed. Connecticut: Appleton & Lange, 1995: 505-509.
6 Scheidt S. Clinical Symposia: Basic Electrocardiography: Leads, Axes, Arrhythmias. Vol 35, no 2. New Jersey: CIBA Pharmaceutical Company, 1983.
7 Berkow R, Editor-in-Chief. The Merck Manual of Diagnosis and Therapy. 16th ed. New Jersey: Merck Research Laboratories, 1992: 2400-2402, 2445.
8 Berkow R, Editor-in-Chief. The Merck Manual of Diagnosis and Therapy. 16th ed. New Jersey: Merck Research Laboratories, 1992: 2403, 2417-2425, 2432, 2437.
9 Berkow R, Editor-in-Chief. The Merck Manual of Diagnosis and Therapy. 16th ed. New Jersey: Merck Research Laboratories, 1992: 1207, 2454.
10 Seidel HM, Ball JW, Dains JE, Benedict GW. Mosby's Guide to Physical Examination. 3rd ed. St. Louis: Mosby, 1995: 141-143.
11 Berkow R, Editor-in-Chief. The Merck Manual of Diagnosis and Therapy. 16th ed. New Jersey: Merck Research Laboratories, 1992: 2452-2460.
12 Seidel HM, Ball JW, Dains JE, Benedict GW. Mosby's Guide to Physical Examination. 3rd ed. St. Louis: Mosby, 1995: 152-155.
13 Bates B. A Guide to Physical Examination. 6th ed. Philadelphia: J.B. Lippincott Company, 1995: 143-144.
14 Berkow R, Editor-in-Chief. The Merck Manual of Diagnosis and Therapy. 16th ed. New Jersey: Merck Research Laboratories, 1992: 1055-1064.
15 Isselbacher KJ, Braunwald E, Wilson JD. Harrison's Principles of Internal Medicine. New York: McGraw-Hill, 1994: 1883-1888.
16 Isselbacher KJ, Braunwald E, Wilson JD. Harrison's Principles of Internal Medicine. New York: McGraw-Hill, 1994: 1891-1905, 1923-1928.
17 Isselbacher KJ, Braunwald E, Wilson JD. Harrison's Principles of Internal Medicine. New York: McGraw-Hill, 1994: 2149-2150.
18 Berkow R, Editor-in-Chief. The Merck Manual of Diagnosis and Therapy. 16th ed. New Jersey: Merck Research Laboratories, 1992: 1071-1083.
19 Fischbach FT. A Manual of Laboratory & Diagnostic Tests. 5th ed. Philadelphia: Lippincott, 1996: 424-425.
20 Berkow R, Editor-in-Chief. The Merck Manual of Diagnosis and Therapy. 16th ed. New Jersey: Merck Research Laboratories, 1992: 1088-1097.
21 Fischbach FT. A Manual of Laboratory & Diagnostic Tests. 5th ed. Philadelphia: Lippincott, 1996: 359-360, 364-365.
22 Ravel R. Clinical Laboratory Medicine. 6th ed. St. Louis: Mosby, 1995: 503.
23 Berkow R, Editor-in-Chief. The Merck Manual of Diagnosis and Therapy. 16th ed. New Jersey: Merck Research Laboratories, 1992: 1004-1009.
24 Ravel R. Clinical Laboratory Medicine. 6th ed. St. Louis: Mosby, 1995: 453.
25 Fischbach FT. A Manual of Laboratory & Diagnostic Tests. 5th ed. Philadelphia: Lippincott, 1996: 329-330, 337-338.
26 Ravel R. Clinical Laboratory Medicine. 6th ed. St. Louis: Mosby, 1995: 446.

27 Berkow R, Editor-in-Chief. The Merck Manual of Diagnosis and Therapy. 16th ed. New Jersey: Merck Research Laboratories, 1992: 1488-1490, 1495-1497, 2261-2264.
28 Berkow R, Editor-in-Chief. The Merck Manual of Diagnosis and Therapy. 16th ed. New Jersey: Merck Research Laboratories, 1992: 1512-1513.
29 Berkow R, Editor-in-Chief. The Merck Manual of Diagnosis and Therapy. 16th ed. New Jersey: Merck Research Laboratories, 1992: 1510-11, 1524-1527.
30 Berkow R, Editor-in-Chief. The Merck Manual of Diagnosis and Therapy. 16th ed. New Jersey: Merck Research Laboratories, 1992: 1418, 1430.
31 Yochum TR, Rowe LJ. Essentials of Skeletal Radiology. 2nd ed. Baltimore: Williams & Wilkins, 1996: 1003-1004, 1019, 1158.
32 Berkow R, Editor-in-Chief. The Merck Manual of Diagnosis and Therapy. 16th ed. New Jersey: Merck Research Laboratories, 1992: 1254-1256, 1359-1360.
33 Berkow R, Editor-in-Chief. The Merck Manual of Diagnosis and Therapy. 16th ed. New Jersey: Merck Research Laboratories, 1992: 968-973, 1156-1158, 1160-1161, 1396-1397.
34 Ravel R. Clinical Laboratory Medicine. 6th ed. St. Louis: Mosby, 1995:19-20.
35 Berkow R, Editor-in-Chief. The Merck Manual of Diagnosis and Therapy. 16th ed. New Jersey: Merck Research Laboratories, 1992: 1234-11243.
36 Berkow R, Editor-in-Chief. The Merck Manual of Diagnosis and Therapy. 16th ed. New Jersey: Merck Research Laboratories, 1992: 1317-1323.
37 Berkow R, Editor-in-Chief. The Merck Manual of Diagnosis and Therapy. 16th ed. New Jersey: Merck Research Laboratories, 1992: 582-585.
38 Berkow R, Editor-in-Chief. The Merck Manual of Diagnosis and Therapy. 16th ed. New Jersey: Merck Research Laboratories, 1992: 2148-2153, 2163, 2166-2177, 2182-2188, 2198-2201.
39 Berkow R, Editor-in-Chief. The Merck Manual of Diagnosis and Therapy. 16th ed. New Jersey: Merck Research Laboratories, 1992: 750, 830-839, 841-845, 847-850.
40 Berkow R, Editor-in-Chief. The Merck Manual of Diagnosis and Therapy. 16th ed. New Jersey: Merck Research Laboratories, 1992: 646-666.
41 Bates B. A Guide to Physical Examination. 6th ed. Philadelphia: J.B. Lippincott Company, 1995: 246-247, 255-257.
42 Berkow R, Editor-in-Chief. The Merck Manual of Diagnosis and Therapy. 16th ed. New Jersey: Merck Research Laboratories, 1992: 414.
43 Isselbacher KJ, Braunwald E, Wilson JD. Harrison's Principles of Internal Medicine. New York: McGraw-Hill, 1994: 1956-1957.
44 Bates B. A Guide to Physical Examination. 6th ed. Philadelphia: J.B. Lippincott Company, 1995: 72.
45 Seidel HM, Ball JW, Dains JE, Benedict GW. Mosby's Guide to Physical Examination. 3rd ed. St. Louis: Mosby, 1995: 347.
46 Reilly BM. Practical Strategies in Outpatient Medicine. Philadelphia: W.B. Saunders Company, 1984: 185-193.
47 Berkow R, Editor-in-Chief. The Merck Manual of Diagnosis and Therapy. 16th ed. New Jersey: Merck Research Laboratories, 1992: 1661-1668, 1684-1688, 1692-1698, 1710-1712.

CHAPTER 6

Neurologic Exam

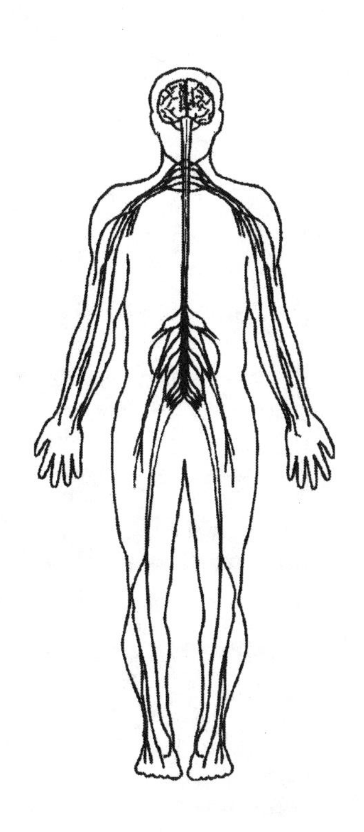

The Cranial Nerves

Summary of the Cranial Nerves (1)

Cranial Nerve	Name	Neuronal Component	Function		Foramen of Exit
I	Olfactory	Sensory	Smell		Cribriform plate
II	Optic	Sensory	Visual input from the eye		Optic canal
III	Oculomotor	Motor	Medial rectus, superior rectus, inferior rectus, inferior oblique muscles of eye; constriction of pupil		Superior orbital fissure
IV	Trochlear	Motor	Superior oblique muscle of the eye		Superior orbital fissure
V	Trigeminal	Motor & sensory	Sensory from the face and general sensation from anterior 2/3 of tongue; motor to muscles of mastication	Opthalmic	Superior orbital fissure
				Maxillary	Foramen rotundum
				Mandibular	Foramen ovale
VI	Abducens	Motor	Lateral rectus muscle of the eye		Superior orbital fissure
VII	Facial	Motor & sensory	Muscles of facial expression; taste to the anterior 2/3 of the tongue; submandibular, sublingual, and lacrimal glands		Internal auditory meatus
VIII	Vestibulocochlear	Sensory	Auditory and vestibular input from the inner ear		Internal auditory meatus
IX	Glossopharyngeal	Motor & sensory	Sensation and taste from posterior 1/3 of the tongue		Jugular foramen
X	Vagus	Motor & sensory	Soft palate and pharynx, autonomic control of thoracic and abdominal viscera		Jugular foramen
XI	Accessory	Motor	Sternocleidomastoid, trapezius		Jugular foramen
XII	Hypoglossal	Motor	Muscles of the tongue, hyoid bone		Hypoglossal canal

Remember (2,3)

- Twelve pairs of cranial nerves emerge from the brain and brain stem.
- The cranial nerves control all motor and sensory functions involving the head, face, and neck, including the special senses.
- Cranial nerve fibers mediating volitional movement arise bilaterally from the precentral gyrus of the cerebral motor cortex and descend along the corticobulbar tract.
- Cranial nerves III, VII, IX, and X are parasympathetic.

Olfactory Nerve (4,5,6)

Neuronal Component
- Sensory for smelling
- Cranial Nerve I is actually a central nervous system tract

Patient History
- Ask the patient if s/he has noticed any change in the ability to smell and/or taste

Tests
- Use two different non-irritating odors (one for each side) to evaluate odor recognition; evaluate each nostril individually with the patient's eyes closed

Physical Diagnosis
- Anosmia can be caused by viral infection, allergy, aging, head trauma (fracture of cribriform plate), tumor compressing the olfactory tract; it is usually not caused by a cortical lesion
- Parosmia is any disease or perversion of olfaction
- Cacosmia is a parosmia consisting of bad smell not related to exposure to a specific odor

Optic Nerve (4,5,6)

Neuronal Component
- Sensory
- The optic nerve arises from ganglion cells in the retina, becomes the optic tract after the optic chiasm and projects to the superior colliculus and lateral geniculate body, which send visual information to the cortex

Patient History
- Note date of last optometric exam
- Note whether the patient wears glasses or contact lenses

Tests
- Test visual acuity (central vision) with the Snellen chart (20 feet from chart), both with and without corrective lenses. Patient covers one eye and reads the smallest line he/she is able to read easily. Progress down the chart until more than two errors are made on a line. The last line with two errors or less indicates his/her vision for that eye. Visual acuity is recorded as a fraction with a numerator of 20 (distance between patient and chart) and a denominator which represents the distance from which a person with normal vision could read the lettering
- Test visual fields (peripheral vision) with the confrontation ("wiggling fingers") test. Patient and doctor cover opposing eyes and patient fixes his/her gaze on the doctor's nose. The patient is instructed to indicate when s/he sees your wiggling fingers (or other object such as a pen) enter his/her field of vision from above, below, medial or lateral. Patient should see your fingers at 50 degrees on the nasal side, 50 degrees to the superior, 90 degrees on the temporal side and 60 degrees to the inferior

Physical Diagnosis
- Definitions: O.D. = ocula dextra (right eye); O.S. = ocula sinestra (left eye); O.U. = ocula unitas (both eyes)
- Legal blindness: 1) The better eye is 20/200 or worse or 2) visual field is 20 degrees or less in the best eye
- Rods see black and white, cones see color

Oculomotor Nerve (4,5,6)

Neuronal Component

- Motor to the superior rectus, inferior rectus, inferior oblique, and medial rectus muscles of the eye
- Motor to levator palpebrae superioris muscle, which opens the eyelid (Facial Nerve closes the eye with orbicular muscle)
- Causes pupillary constriction through ciliary and constrictor pupillae muscles

Patient History

- Ask the patient about any changes or recent changes in vision

Tests

- Check the eye light reflexes: light introduced into the pupil of one eye causes equal reflex constriction of the pupil receiving the stimulus (direct reflex) and the pupil of the other eye (consensual reflex). Use your hand to block spillover of light into both pupils during the test
- Evaluate the near response (patient covers eye and looks far away then uncovers the eye; look for pupillary constriction in the previously-covered eye)
- Accommodation reflex test (eyes become fixated on a single point; "cross-eyed"); reflex occurs when patient voluntarily focuses on an object moving nearer; involves convergence, pupilloconstriction and lens thickening, all accomplished by cranial nerve III
- Check extraocular movements in six cardinal fields of gaze: using a pen light, have patient follow the examiner's movements through the six cardinal planes of gaze (H pattern) without moving his/her head
- Remember LR6SO4: Lateral rectus – VI; Superior oblique – IV; and the rest are Cranial Nerve III

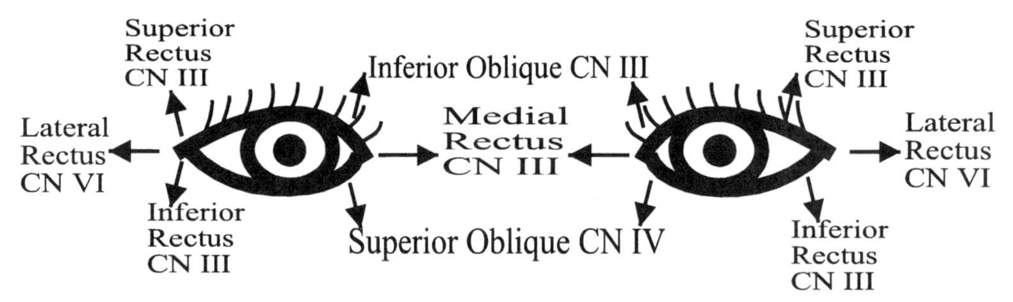

Physical Diagnosis

- Constriction (miosis) of the pupil is caused by the stimulation of parasympathetic fibers (CN III), while dilation is caused by stimulation of sympathetic fibers
- If ocular movement is the same in both eyes, then chances of extraocular muscle paralysis are small
- Strabismus: deviation of one or both eyes
- Diplopia: double vision
- Nystagmus: involuntary eye oscillation
- Ptosis: eyelids droop due to weakness or paralysis of the levator palpebrae superioris muscle

Pupils (8)

- Adie's pupil: reacts to light very slowly, remains constricted longer, then dilates slowly; a benign condition most common in young women.
- Argyll Robertson pupil: reacts only to accomodation (no direct or indirect reaction to light). Can occur as a complication of diabetes or tabes dorsalis.

Trochlear Nerve (5,6)

Neuronal Component

- Motor to the superior oblique muscle of the eye
- The only cranial nerve to exit from the dorsal surface of the brain
- The only crossed cranial nerve

Patient History

- Ask the patient about any changes or recent changes in vision

Tests

- Test with Cranial Nerves III and VI

Physical Diagnosis

- Paralysis causes slight convergent strabismus and diplopia while looking down; causes difficulty descending stairs

Trigeminal Nerve (4,5,6)

Neuronal Components

- Motor to the muscles of mastication and the tensor tympani muscle of the middle ear
- Sensory to the skin and mucosa of most of the head

Motor Tests

- Palpate the masseter and temporalis muscles while the patient clenches his/her teeth and instruct the patient to deviate the jaw sideways against your resistance (lateral pterygoids)

Sensory Tests

- Test patient's response to alternating sharp and dull stimuli over the opthalmic, maxillary and mandibular divisions
- Corneal reflex: the trigeminal nerve synapses with the facial nerve, which closes the eye when a wisp of cotton touches the cornea (move the cotton in from outside the patient's visual field). Contact lenses, if used, should be removed and you should avoid touching the conjunctiva and lashes with the cotton
- Jaw jerk – monosynaptic stretch reflex for the masseter muscle; tell patient to open jaw slightly, put your finger on the jaw, tap your finger to cause a rapid muscle stretch of the masseter muscle

Physical Diagnosis

- Tic Douloureux (trigeminal neuralgia) causes severe, usually unilateral pain in the distribution of one or more branches of the trigeminal nerve
- Jaw paralysis can be caused by upper or lower motor neuron lesions

Abducens Nerve (5)

Neuronal Component
- Motor to the lateral rectus muscle of the eye

Patient History
- Ask the patient about any changes or recent changes in vision

Tests
- Test with Cranial Nerves III and IV

Physical Diagnosis
- Paralysis causes weakness of eye abduction, diplopia

Facial Nerve (4,5,6)

Neuronal Component
- Motor to muscles of facial expression, the platysma muscle and stapedius muscle of the inner ear
- Sensory for taste to the anterior 2/3 of the tongue
- CN VII closes the eye with orbicularis muscle (CN III opens the eye with levator palpebrae muscle)

Motor Tests
- Observe for symmetry and function of muscles of facial expression during the patient history
- Ask patient to make faces; ask patient to close his or her eyes and to keep them closed while you try to open them

Sensory Tests
- Taste to the anterior 2/3 of the tongue (sour, sweet and salty); place a dissolved solution of sugar or lemon on one half of the tongue and ask patient to identify the taste without closing the mouth; repeat on the opposite side

Physical Diagnosis
- Bell's palsy (peripheral facial paralysis) causes flaccid paralysis of all ipsilateral facial muscles. With Bell's palsy, the patient cannot wrinkle the forehead due to loss of control over the frontalis muscle; with a stroke, the patient maintains the ability to wrinkle the forehead
- Bell's palsy can occur as an idiopathic condition or as a complication of diabetes, tumors, AIDS and Lyme's disease

Vestibulocochlear Nerve (4,5,7)

Neuronal Component

- Sensory with auditory (cochlear) and vestibular portions

Patient History

- Ask the patient if s/he has noticed any change in hearing

Auditory Tests

- Weber Test – strike a 512 Hz tuning fork and place on patient's skull midline. Ask patient if he/she hears the sound better in one ear than the other (lateralization of sound)
- Rinne Test – strike the fork again and place on mastoid process; time the interval during which the patient can hear the sound. When patient indicates that sound is no longer audible, move the still-vibrating fork close to the auditory canal. Time the interval during which the patient can hear the sound via air conduction. Air conducted sound should be heard twice as long as bone-conducted sound after bone conduction stops (2:1 ratio)

Conduction Anomalies:

- Air conduction loss: caused by cerumen, foreign object, middle ear infection, perforated tympanum, dislocated ossicles, otosclerosis; AC:BC < 2:1; sound lateralizes to the occluded ear
- Sensorineural loss: caused by drugs, loud noises, congenital loss, inner ear infection, trauma, tumors, aging; AC:BC is 2:1, but both times are shortened

Vestibular Tests

- **BABINSKI-WEIL** – patient takes 7-8 steps forward and backward ten times each way with the eyes shut. The test is positive when patient leans toward side of dysfunction while walking forward and to the opposite side while walking backward
- **BARONY/CALORIC** – patient's semicircular canals are stimulated with warm and cold water and proprioceptive responses noted; "COWS": with Cold water, nystagmus occurs to the Opposite side and with Warm water, nystagmus occurs to the Same side
- **CANTELLI'S "DOLL'S EYES" SIGN**– ask the patient to keep his/her eyes focused on your nose, then rotate the head side to side; the sign is present if the patient's eyes move with the head
- **MITTLEMEYER MARCHING** – patient marches in place; look for falling or deviation to one side. Lesion causes deviation toward the dysfunctional side. Next perform with eyes closed. A vestibular problem will worsen with eyes closed, a cerebellar problem will not
- **PAST POINTING** – examiner stands in front of the patient with index and second finger in the form of a "V"; ask the patient to bring his/her arm above the head and then bring it down to touch the center of the V. Repeat with eyes closed. If the test is positive, the patient's pointing will stray significantly toward the side of vestibular impairment with eyes closed

Differential for vestibular vs. cervicogenic vertigo:

- **SWIVEL TEST** - patient is seated in a swivel chair. Doctor immobilizes the head at the temples. Patient swivels the chair back and forth using his/her legs, with no movement of the head allowed. In a patient with cervical proprioceptive dysfunction, symptoms of dizziness will recur; with vestibular dysfunction they will not

Physical Diagnosis

Vestibular dysfunction symptoms include:

- Vertigo (always accompanies vestibular disease)
- Nausea
- Anxiety
- Unsteadiness
- Nystagmus

Glossopharyngeal Nerve (5,6)

Vagus Nerve (5,6)

Neuronal Component

- Both have sensory and motor components
- Cranial nerves IX and X exit the jugular foramen together so an isolated lesion is uncommon
- Cranial nerves IX and X are usually tested together
- CN IX Innervates stylopharyngeus muscle which elevates the pharynx and larynx
- The Vagus nerve is more important for articulation than the Glossopharyngeal nerve

Motor Tests

- Assess patient's voice for hoarseness or nasal tone
- Determine if there is difficulty swallowing
- Have patient say "AHHH" while looking at the soft palate for bilateral muscle contraction; note deviation of uvula

Sensory Tests

- Assess the gag reflex (depends on cranial nerve IX for sensory component and cranial nerve X for the motor component) by touching the posterior wall of the patient's pharynx with a tongue depressor

Physical Diagnosis

- A lesion causes: aphonia, dysarthria, dysphagia, aphagia, hyper or hyponasal tone

ote (9)

- The olfactory and optic nerves are not true nerves but fiber tracts of the brain; the spinal accessory nerve is derived partly from the upper cervical segments of the spinal cord.
- The remaining nine pairs of cranial nerves relate to the brain stem.

Spinal Accessory Nerve (5,6)

Neuronal Component

- Motor to the sternocleidomastoid muscle and the upper trapezius muscle
- Composed of two parts: the cranial or accessory portion and the spinal portion, which is larger

Tests

- Observe for atrophy or fasciculation of upper trapezius (lower traps are C3/4) and SCM
- Have patient shrug shoulders against resistance to test the upper trapezius and rotate the head against resistance to test the sternocleidomastoid muscle

Hypoglossal Nerve (5)

Neuronal Component

- Motor to muscles of the tongue (genioglossus)

Tests

- Observe the patient's speech
- Observe for tongue atrophy
- Ask patient to stick tongue out, note any deviation (tongue deviates toward side of lesion with a lower motor neuron lesion and to the opposite side with an upper motor lesion)
- Tongue may be muscle tested by having patient press his/her tongue into his/her cheek while doctor palpates the strength of the tongue

Physical Diagnosis

- Paralysis of the tongue

Potentially Confusing Terms

- **Hyperesthesia**: increased sensitivity, particularly a painful sensation from a normally painless touch stimulus
- **Hypesthesia/hypoesthesia**: decreased sensitivity to touch
- **Dysesthesia**: distortion of any sense, especially touch. Also, an unpleasant abnormal sensation produced by normal stimuli.
- **Dyskinesia:** distortion or impairment of voluntary movement
- **Hyperalgesia**: increased sensitivity to pain
- **Paresthesia**: an abnormal touch sensation such as burning or prickling, often in the absence of an external stimulus

- **Dysphasia**: impairment of speech, consisting of a lack of coordination and failure to arrange words in their proper order, due to a central lesion.
- **Dysphagia**: difficulty swallowing
- **Dysarthria:** lack of ability to articulate speech due to disturbances of muscular control resulting from damage to the CNS or ONS.
- **Dysphonia**: any impairment of voice; difficulty speaking

- **Akinesthesia**: absence or loss of movement sense
- **Apallesthesia**: loss of vibration senses

- **Radiculopathy**: direct pressure or irritation of the dorsal root ganglia causes radicular pain; sharp and stabbing pain which radiates along a dermatome
- **Neuropathy:** a functional disturbance or pathologic change in the peripheral nervous system

Descending Tracts (10)

Tract	Function	Origin	Notes
Lateral Corticospinal (Pyramidal)	Voluntary fine motor function to distal musculature	Motor cortex Precentral gyrus	• Contain axons of upper motor neurons • Lesion causes upper motor neuron symptoms
Anterior Corticospinal	Voluntary motor; gross and postural motor function	Motor cortex Precentral gyrus	
Rubrospinal	Role in motor function	Red nucleus (tegmentum)	Branches to cerebellum
Reticulospinal	Modulation of sensory transmission; modulation of spinal reflexes	Reticular formation of brain stem	Gray: pain, sensation White: spinal reflexes, gamma neurons
Vestibulospinal	Extensors' tone; postural reflexes	Vestibular nucleus; brain stem	Quick movements, anti-gravity muscles
Tectospinal	Postural reflexes to sight and sound	Tectum (superior colliculus)	Turns head toward sight and sound

Remember

- Motor cortex neurons descend along the corticospinal tracts, through the brainstem and down the spinal cord, where they terminate at various levels in synapses on their corresponding lower motor neurons; all these lower motor neurons go on to innervate specific muscles. (11)

Ascending Tracts (10)

Tract	Function	Origin	Ending
Fasciculus Gracilus (lower extremity) **Fasciculus Cuneatus** (upper extremity) (Dorsal Columns)	• Vibration • Proprioception • Light touch • Pressure • Two-point discrimination • Stereognosis	• Skin, joints, tendons	• Dorsal column nuclei • Second order neurons project to contralateral thalamus
Posterior Spinocerebellar	• Stretch from spindle cells and pressure • Unconscious proprioception	• Muscle spindles, Golgi tendon organs, touch and pressure receptors	• Cerebellum
Anterior Spinocerebellar	• Stretch from spindle cells and pressure • Unconscious proprioception	• Muscle spindles, Golgi tendon organs, touch and pressure receptors	• Cerebellum
Anterior and Lateral Spinothalamic	• Pain, temperature (on C fibers) • Crude touch	• Skin	• Dorsal horn • Second order neurons project to contralateral thalamus
Spinotectal	• Some pain • Light touch	• Deep somatic structures	• Reticular formation of brain stem

Major Motor System Lesion:
Upper Motor Neuron Lesion

ote (12)

- Control over movement requires interaction of the following major motor components of the nervous system: corticospinal and corticobulbar tracts, basal ganglia, subcortical descending systems and the cerebellum.
- The fibers of the corticospinal (pyramidal) and corticobulbar tracts arise from the sensorimotor cortex around the central sulcus. Lesions can be located in the cerebral cortex, internal capsule, cerebral peduncles, brain stem or spinal cord.

SIGNS OF AN UPPER MOTOR NEURON LESION (13, 14, 15,16)

Muscular Hypertonia and spasticity	▪ Clonus: with a quick stretch on a muscle, you get repeated reflex muscular movements; pathological clonus will cause repeated stretch-reflex contract cycles as long as resistance is applied by the examiner ▪ Hyperreflexia ▪ Knife-clasp phenomenon: doctor's attempts to extend the arm or flex the leg passively elicit increasing resistance that abruptly subsides. When the limb is left in the new position, the resistance reappears
Paralysis or paresis	▪ Affects involved muscles ▪ Forms of paralysis include: hemiplegia, monoplegia, diplegia, paraplegia, quadriplegia and tetraplegia
Presence of Pathologic Reflexes	▪ Gordon's Finger Test: squeeze the patient's pisiform; positive finding is extension of the fingers or the thumb and index finger ▪ Tromner's Test: with patient's wrist in supination, doctor flicks index and middle finger of patient into extension; positive finding is flexion of all fingers and flexion and adduction of the thumb ▪ Hoffman's Test: examiner supports patient's hand in pronation and flicks the third digit into extension; positive finding is flexion of all fingers and flexion and adduction of the thumb ▪ Snout reflex – examiner taps the patient's nose or upper lip sharply; positive finding is exaggerated reflex contraction of the lips or grimace ▪ Chaddock's sign: draw a "C" behind and below the lateral malleolus; positive finding is a Babinski sign ▪ Babinski's Sign: (patient supine) stroke the lateral aspect of the foot from the heel, across the ball of the foot and over to the big toe with a blunt instrument; positive finding is dorsiflexion of the big toe with splaying of the other toes; usually disappears after the stimulus is removed ▪ Schaefer's Test: squeeze the Achilles tendon at the level of the medial malleolus; positive finding is Babinski sign
Absence of Superficial Reflexes	▪ Corneal/Scleral (sensory is CN V, motor is CN VII): examiner touches the patient's cornea with a piece of cotton as the patient looks away; normal response is a brisk, bilateral blink and pain ▪ Gag reflex (CNs IX and X): Assess the gag reflex by touching the posterior third of the tongue with a tongue depressor ▪ Abdominal reflex (above umbilicus T7-10 and below umbilicus T11 to L1): reflex is elicited by gently stroking the four quadrants of the abdomen toward the umbilicus; normal response is jerking of the umbilicus toward the stimulus

Summary of Upper and Lower Motor Neuron Lesions (17)

Lesion	Background	Causes	Symptoms
LMN Lesion	▪ A lower motor neuron consists of a cell body in the anterior gray column and its axon, which passes to the motor end-plates of the muscle by way of the peripheral or cranial nerves ▪ Lesions occur in the ventral roots of the spinal or cranial nerves or from the anterior horn cells out to the myoneural junction	▪ Poliomyelitis – viral disorder that results in the death of motor neurons ▪ Degenerative processes ▪ Compression of ventral roots by disc or tumor ▪ Myasthenia Gravis ▪ Bell's Palsy	▪ Flaccid paralysis ▪ Muscle atrophy ▪ Diminished or absent DTRs ▪ Fasciculations ▪ Absence of pathologic reflexes ▪ Absence of or decrease in superficial reflexes
UMN Lesion	▪ The corticospinal tract passes to the lower motor neurons of the cord; the corticobulbar tract projects to the brain stem nuclei of the cranial nerves that innervate striated muscle ▪ Lesions can be caused by damage to the cerebral hemispheres or the lateral white column of the spinal cord, not including the anterior horn cell	▪ Stroke ▪ Infection ▪ Brain and spinal cord tumors ▪ Cerebral Palsy due to damage to the cerebral cortex in utero or during birth ▪ Encephalitis ▪ Multiple Sclerosis	▪ Spastic paralysis or paresis (weakness); hemiplegia ▪ Early: little or no muscle atrophy; late: disuse atrophy ▪ Loss of cortical inhibition ▪ Hyperactive DTRs ▪ Clonus ▪ Pathologic reflexes present: Babinski's sign ▪ Loss of superficial reflexes

ote

- The only cause of true hyperreflexia is upper motor neuron disease. (18)
- Amyotrophic lateral sclerosis (ALS) selectively attacks both upper motor (the corticospinal tracts) and lower motor neuron cell bodies. It is the most common form of progressive motor neuron disease. (19)
- The ciliospinal reflex, when abnormal, is an unequivocal sign of neurological disease. It tests the cervical nerves (sensory arc) and sympathetics (motor arc). Firmly pinch the skin over the patient's neck to cause brisk, bilateral dilation of the pupils. The reflex is lost with Pancoast tumor, Horner's syndrome and other disorders of sympathetic function. (20)

THE CEREBELLUM

ote

- The cerebellum is the control center for the coordination of voluntary muscle activity, equilibrium and tonus. It does not initiate movement. The cerebellum controls smooth movement by controlling the sequence of muscle contractions. Disturbances of movement caused by cerebellar dysfunction are called asynergia or ataxia. (21) In general, unilateral lesions of the cerebellum lead to motor disabilities ipsilateral to the side of the lesion. (22)

Muscular Hypotonia (23) *Diminished muscle tone*	▪ Rag Doll posture ▪ Pendular reflexes – patient does not have a lot of underlying muscle tone; inertia stops the response (as compared to clonus which is hyperreflexia)
Ataxia (24,25)	▪ Inability to assume position for Romberg's test; sway should not worsen with eyes closed ▪ Inability to perform heel-toe tandem gait ▪ Difficulty with all coordinated muscular contractions required for smooth movements
Dysdiadochokinesia (26) *Inability to perform rapid alternating movements*	▪ **FINGER TAPPING** Patient and examiner stand facing each other and patient is instructed to imitate examiners thumb-finger tapping movements; test is positive when patient cannot maintain a good rhythm with the examiner ▪ **HAND PATTING** Patient rapidly touches the palmar and dorsal surfaces of the hands to the thighs. Test is positive if patient cannot perform test with even amplitude and regular rhythm ▪ **PRONATION/ SUPINATION** Patient extends his/her arms in front and rapidly pronates and supinates the arms as fast as possible. Test is positive if the movements are unequal or the arms drift inward or outward ▪ **FOOT PATTING** Patient taps right and left feet on the ground alternately
Rebound Phenomenon (27)	▪ **HOLMES' SIGN** The examiner tries to extend the patient's flexed elbow by stabilizing the elbow and pulling on the wrist, then suddenly lets go; if the sign is present, the patient's hand will strike his or her face or body, indicating lack of a "check reflex" ▪ **ANDRE THOMAS' SIGN** Tell the patient to raise his or her arm above the head and then suddenly let the arm fall to the head; the sign is present if the arm rebounds off the head and indicates delay in starting/stopping muscle movement ▪ **REBOUND CHECKING** Patient stands with outstretched arms and is instructed to hold them in place while the examiner tries to move them; the examiner then strikes the back of the wrists with enough force to displace the arms; the patient's arms should quickly return to the original position; the sign is present if arms oscillate up and down or if patient loses balance
Accessory Movements (28)	▪ Intention tremors: tremors which arise when voluntary movements are attempted ▪ Nystagmus: rhythmic oscillations of the eyeballs
Dysmetria (29,30,31) *Inability to place an extremity at a precise point is space*	▪ **FINGER TO NOSE** Ask patient to close his/her eyes and touch his/her nose with the index finger of each hand; patient should alternate hands and gradually increase speed. Test is positive when patient cannot touch his/her nose either with eyes open or closed (ability to touch the nose with the eyes open but not with the eyes closed indicates posterior column lesion) ▪ **FINGER TO FINGER** Patient alternately touches his or her own nose and your index finger; change the location of your finger several times during the test. Repeat the test with the opposite hand ▪ **HEEL TO SHIN** Ask patient to run the heel of his or her foot up and down one shin then the other. The test is positive when the patient cannot perform the movement in a smooth, coordinated manner ▪ **TOE TO FINGER** (Supine) patient touches the examiner's finger with his/her great toe and holds it there; examiner moves finger and patient follows the examiner's finger with the toe ▪ **PAST POINTING** Consistent past point may indicate cerebellar disease

THE BASAL GANGLIA

- The basal ganglia are comprised of gray areas at the base of the forebrain: the corpus striatum, subthalamic nucleus, and substantia nigra. (32,33)
- Basal ganglia lesions are also called EXTRAPYRAMIDAL lesions; they are characterized by movement disorders, including: akinesia (poverty of voluntary movement), bradykinesia (abnormally slow movements), and dyskinesia (involuntary, abnormal movement). (34)

Abnormal movement	Characteristics
Parkinsonism (35,36,37) *AKA paralysis agitans*	▪ Progressive disorder associated with loss of dopaminergic neurons in the substantia nigra ▪ Resting tremors ("pill-rolling"): course tremor most often localized in one or both hands ▪ Mask facies: loss of facial expression ▪ Rigidity: i.e. cogwheel (affects joint muscles; passive motion elicits a movement which can be felt by the examiner as a series of catches and releases) ▪ **SOQUE'S TEST** Seat the patient against back support provided by the examiner; suddenly remove the support; positive finding occurs when the patient's extremities do not extend normally or move in an attempt to counteract the loss of balance
Dyskinesias (35,36)	▪ Choreas – a wide variety of rapid, jerky, dyskinetic, involuntary movements of the distal extremity muscles, face and tongue ▪ Athetosis – snake-like movements of the extremites and neck musculature ▪ Hemiballismus – a violent form of dyskinesia characterized by flailing movements of one extremity or the arm and leg of one side ▪ Dystonias – increased muscular tone that causes fixed, abnormal postures ▪ Myoclonus – very brief, involuntary, random muscular contractions

THE DORSAL COLUMN

Remember

- Lesions that affect the sensations carried by the dorsal columns while sparing those carried by the spinothalamic tract (pain, temperature) are likely of spinal cord origin. (38)

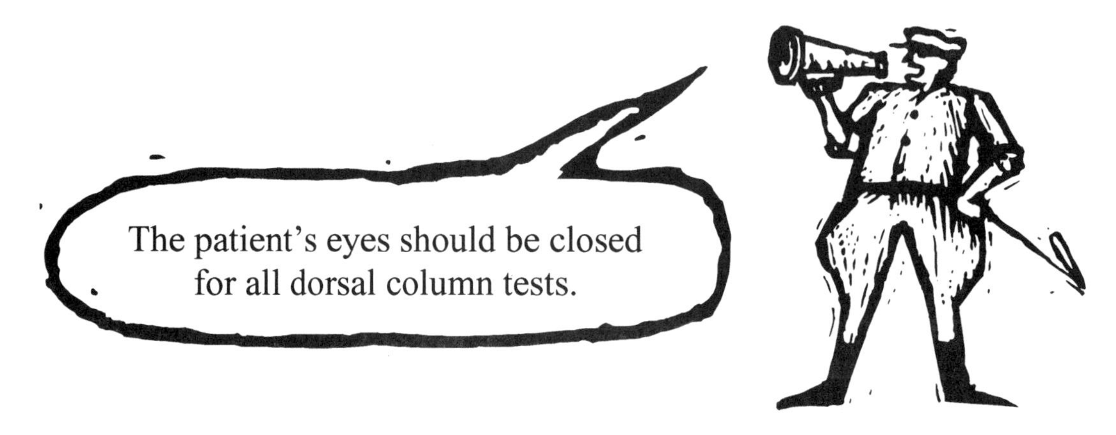

Primary Sensory Functions	**Vibration** (39) Absence = apallesthesia	▪ Use a 128 tuning fork on several bony prominences of the upper and lower extremities, working distal to proximal; ask patient if he/she can tell where the vibration is occurring and when the vibration stops ▪ Tests Fasciculus Gracilus from T6 down ▪ Tests Fasciculus Cuneatus from T6 up
	Proprioception (39,40,41) Absence = akinesthesia	▪ **ROMBERG'S SIGN** Patient stands upright with feet together and arms at sides. If patient can do this, ask him/her to close the eyes; positive finding occurs when patient falls or has to move the feet to retain balance with the eyes closed (a slight amount of swaying is normal) ▪ **POSITIONAL CHANGES OF DIGITS** Doctor contacts the sides of the fingers and moves the patient's fingers into flexion and extension. Patient should describe the direction in which the examiner moves the digit, not the direction the digit is pointing in when it stops
	Deep Pressure (40)	▪ **ABADIE'S SIGN** Examiner squeezes the Achilles tendon; positive finding occurs if the patient feels no discomfort ▪ **BIERNACKI'S SIGN** Examiner compress the patient's ulnar nerve behind the elbow; positive finding occurs if the patient feels no discomfort
Cortical Sensory Functions: multimodal sensations (39)		▪ **STEREOGNOSIS** Identification of a familiar object by touch ▪ **GRAPHESTHESIA** Identification of numbers written on the skin of the palm of the hand with a dull object ▪ **GRAPHOGNOSIS** Identification of letters drawn on the skin of the palm of the hand with a dull object ▪ **POINT LOCATION/TOUCH LOCALIZATION** Ask patient to identify where you apply a brief stimulus to the skin; there should be no difficulty locating the area stimulated

Motor, Reflex, and Sensory Evaluation

The Upper Extremity (42)

Reflex

Muscle	Innervation	Peripheral Nerve
Biceps	**C5**, C6	Musculocutaneous
Brachioradialis	**C6**, C7, C8	Radial
Triceps	C6, **C7**	Radial

Motor

Muscle	Innervation	Peripheral Nerve
Deltoid	**C5**, C6	Axillary
Biceps	**C5**, C6	Musculocutaneous
Wrist Extensors	**C6**, C7	Radial
Wrist Flexors	C6, **C7**, C8, T1	Median and Ulnar
Finger Flexors	C7, **C8**, T1	Median and Ulnar
Interossei	C8, **T1**	Ulnar

Cervical Disc Herniations

Disc Level	Nerve Root Affected	Muscles Affected
C4 / C5	C5	Deltoid, Biceps
C5 / 6	C6	Brachioradialis, Wrist Extensors
C6 / C7	C7	Triceps, Wrist Flexors, Finger Extensors
C7 / T1	C8	Finger Flexors, Hand Intrinsics
T1 / T2	T1	Interossei

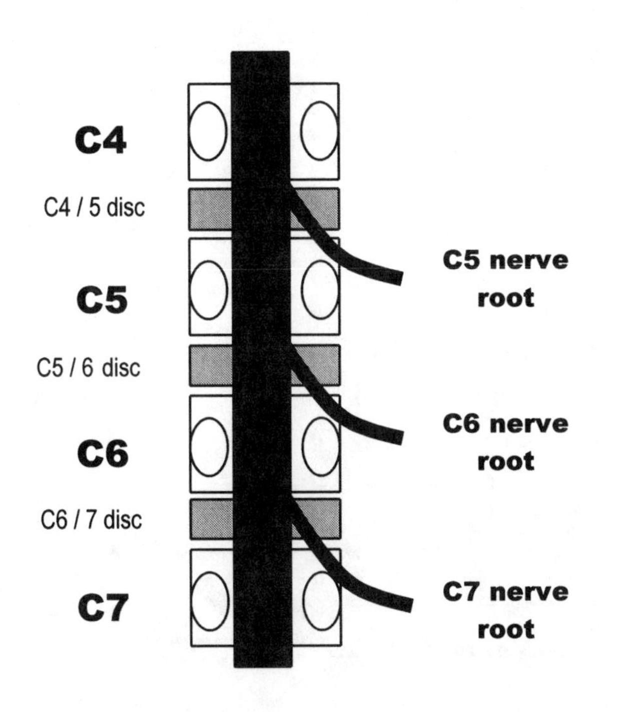

The most commonly herniated disc in the cervical spine is the C5/6 disc

Sensory (42)

Dermatome	Location
C5	Lateral arm
C6	Lateral forearm, thumb, index finger
C7	Middle finger
C8	Distal medial forearm, ring, and small finger
T1	Medial arm and forearm
T2	Axilla

Pure Patch	Location
Axillary	Lateral aspect of deltoid muscle
Musculocutaneous	Lateral forearm
Radial	Posterior web space between thumb and index finger
Ulnar	Palmar surface of the tip of the little finger
Median	Palmar skin of the tip of the index finger

Note

- All spinal nerves except C1 supply branches to the skin.
  A dermatome is an area of skin that provides sensory input to the dorsal roots of one pair of spinal nerves or to one spinal cord segment. (43)

Anterior and Posterior Dermatomes of the Upper Extremity (44)

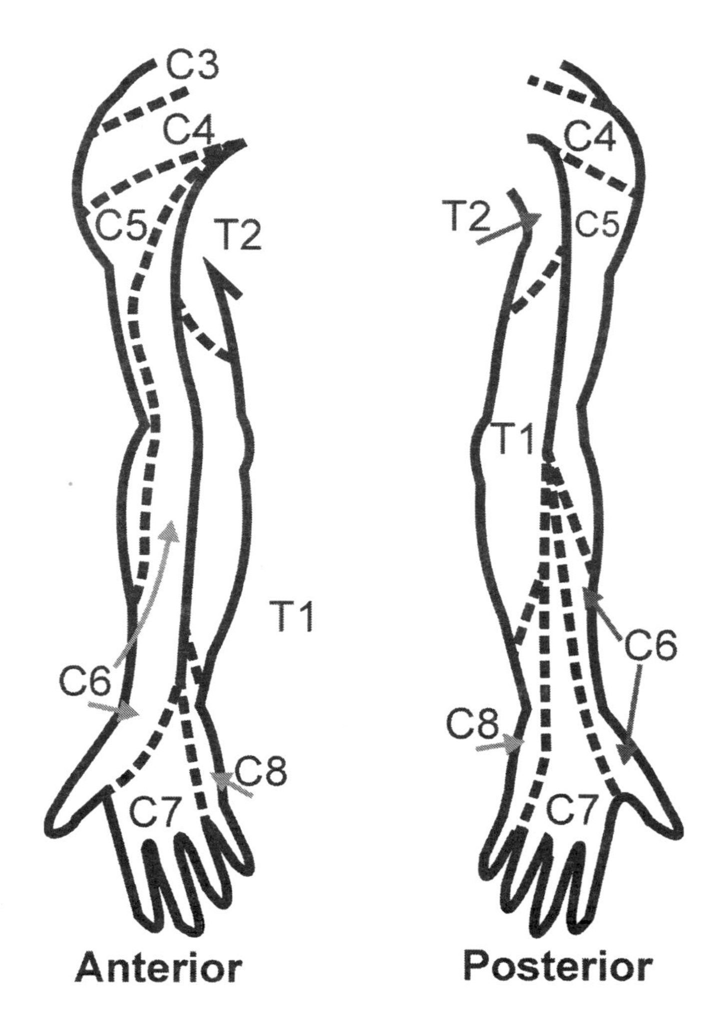

Cutaneous Nerves of the Upper Extremity (45)

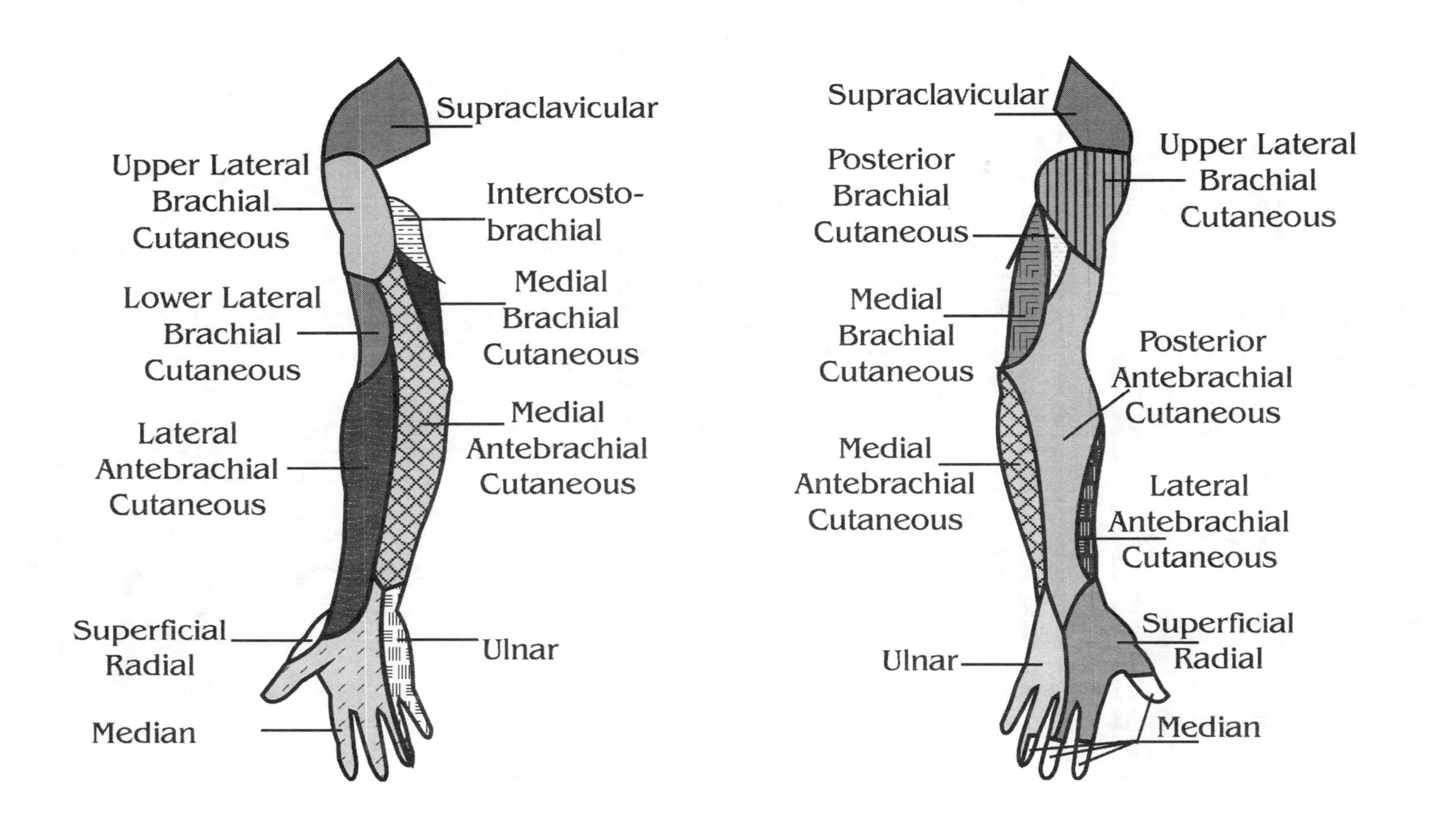

The Lower Extremity (46)

Reflex

Tendon or Muscle	Innervation	Peripheral Nerve
Patellar	L2, L3, **L4**	Femoral
Achilles	**S1**, S2	Tibial
Medial Hamstrings	L4, **L5**, S1	Sciatic nerve, tibial portion
Lateral Hamstrings	L5, **S1**, S2	Sciatic nerve, tibial portion

Motor

Muscle		Innervation	Peripheral Nerve
Hip Flexors	**Iliopsoas**	T12, L1, L2, L3	
	Rectus Femoris	L2, L3, L4	Femoral
Hip Adductors		L2, **L3**, L4	Obturator
Quadriceps		L2, L3, **L4**	Femoral
Tibialis Anterior		**L4**, L5	Deep Peroneal
Extensor Digitorum Longus		**L5**, S1	Deep Peroneal
Extensor Hallucis Longus		**L5**, S1	Deep Peroneal
Gluteus Medius and Minimus		L4, **L5**, S1	Superior Gluteal
Peroneus Longus and Brevis		L5, **S1**, S2	Superficial Peroneal
Gluteus Maximus		L5, **S1**, S2	Inferior Gluteal
Gastrocnemius and Soleus		S1, S2	Tibial

Lumbar Disc Herniations

Disc Level	Nerve Root Affected	Muscles Affected
L3 / L4	L4	Tibialis Anterior
L4 / L5	L5	Extensor Hallucis Longus
L5 / S1	S1	Peroneus Longus and Brevis, Gastrocnemius and Soleus

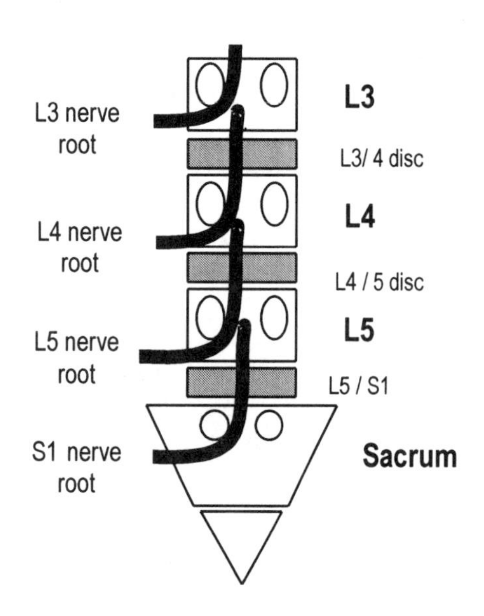

The most commonly herniated disc in the lumbar spine is the L5/S1 disc

Sensory (46)

Dermatome	Location
L1	Crosses the anterior superior thigh in an oblique band
L2	Crosses the anterior middle thigh in an oblique band
L3	Covers the anterior thigh immediately at and above the knee joint in an oblique band; the knee joint divides the L3 and L4 dermatomes
L4	Crosses the anterior medial knee and continues down the medial leg to the medial malleolus and medial side of the foot; the sharp crest of the tibia is the dividing line between the L4 and L5 dermatomes
L5	Crosses the anterior lateral knee, lateral leg and the dorsum of the foot
S1	Lateral side of foot and a portion of the plantar surface of the foot

Anterior and Posterior Dermatomes of the Lower Extremity (47)

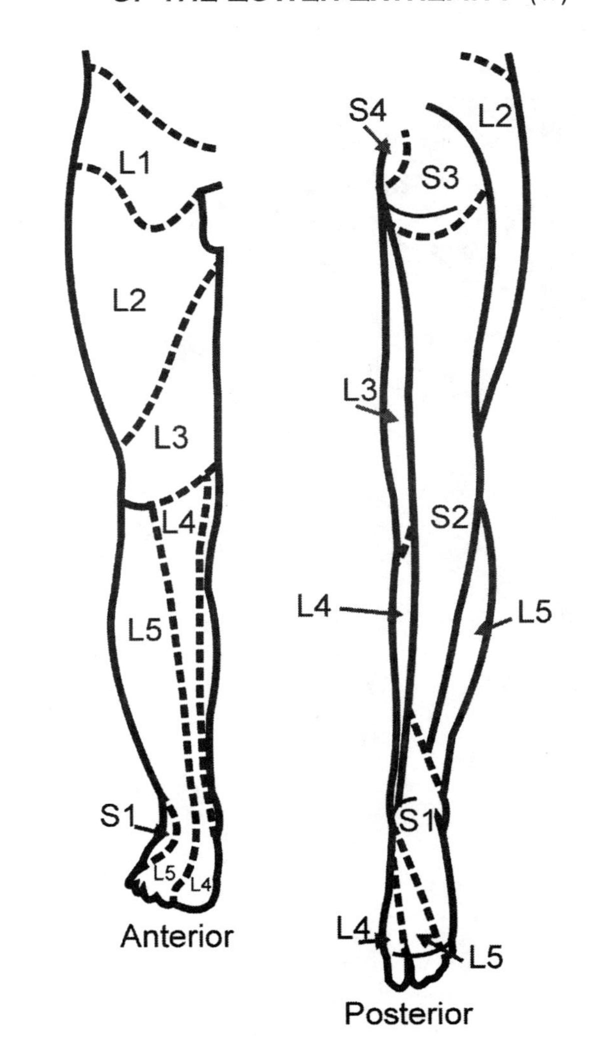

Cutaneous Nerves of the Lower Extremity (48)

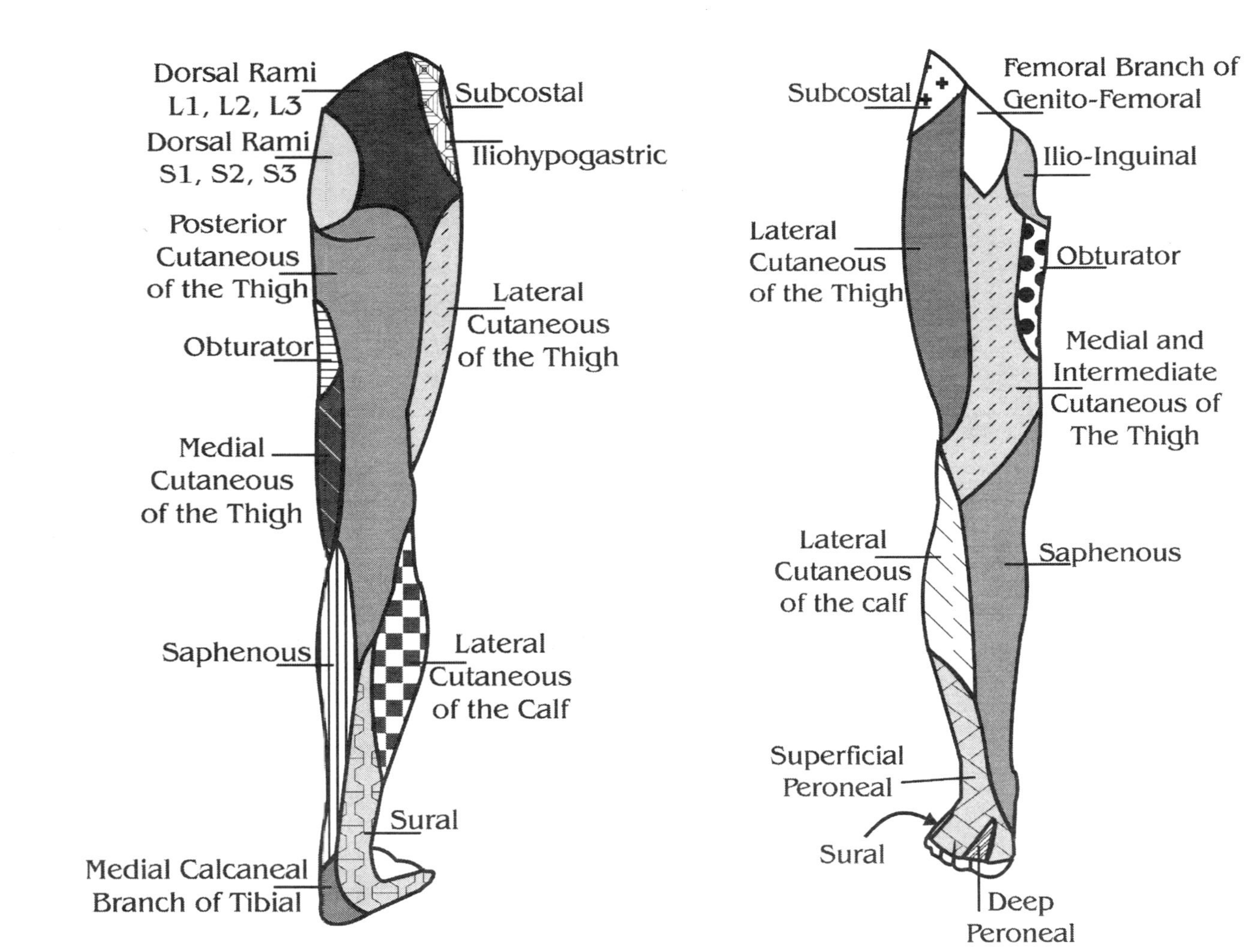

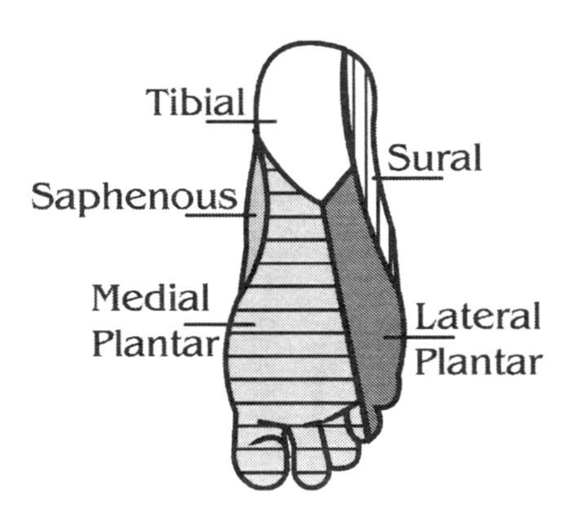

NEUROLOGIC EVALUATION (49)

❶ Decide whether the lesion involves the CNS (upper motor neuron lesion) or the PNS (lower motor neuron lesion)

Test	Upper Motor Neuron Lesion	Lower Motor Neuron Lesion
Deep Tendon Reflexes	• Hyperreflexia	• Hyporeflexia or areflexia
Paralysis/Paresis	• Spastic paralysis: marked by an inability to move an extremity and increased deep tendon reflexes • Cogwheel rigidity	• Flaccid paralysis: accompanied by loss of muscle tone and absence of tendon reflexes in the paralyzed part
Clonus	Yes	No
Babinski Reflex	Yes	No
Fasciculations	No	Yes

❷ If the lesion is a lower motor neuron lesion, decide if the defect is at the nerve root or in the peripheral nerve.

- Orthopedic tests for nerve root tension or peripheral nerve neuropathy.
- Pain in a root lesion will also be noted from the spine to below the elbow or knee in a dermatomal pattern, whereas pain and numbness of a peripheral lesion begins at the site of entrapment and does not follow a dermatomal pattern.

❸ If the lesion involves the CNS, decide whether the spinal cord or brain is the primary site.

	Spinal Cord Lesion	Cerebrum	Cerebellum / Brain Stem
Presentation	• UMNL findings • Localized to a cord segment • Dissociation of sensory function in the extremities	• CN deficit and hemiplegia or hemiparesis on same side of body • May not cause CN palsies due to crossover of their nerve fibers • Altered mental status • Produce contralateral deficit	• CN deficit contralateral to side of hemiparesis or hemiplegia → brain stem • Cerebellar lesions tend to produce ipsilateral loss and intention tremors
Lesions	• Brown-Sequard syndrome • Disc herniation • Tumor • Metastasis • Syringomyelia • Myelopathy (i.e. canal stenosis)	• Vascular diseases (ischemia, hemorrhage, aneurysm) • Tumor (esp. gliomas) • Trauma	• Brain stem: usually due to vascular disease or tumor; i.e. gliomas, meningiomas

The Dorsal Column and Spinothalamic Tracts (50)

	Function	Pathway	Decussation
Dorsal Column / Medial Leminiscal System	▪ Fine touch ▪ Vibration ▪ 2-point discrimination ▪ Proprioception from skin and joints	▪ Ascends, without crossing, in the dorsal white column of the spinal cord to the lower brain stem	▪ Decussates in the medulla
Spinothalamic Tract	▪ Sharp pain ▪ Temperature ▪ Crude touch	▪ Enters the spinal cord via the dorsal root and ascends for one or two segments at the periphery of the dorsal horn (Lissauer's tract), then synapses with one or more dorsal column neurons, crosses to the opposite side of the spinal cord and ascends within the spinothalamic tracts	▪ Crosses at every segmental level in the spinal cord

ote

- The pattern of decussation of the dorsal columns and spinothalamic tracts allows for differentiation between brain stem and spinal cord lesions.

Brain Stem (or higher) Lesion	Deficits of pain perception, touch, and proprioception are all contralateral to the lesion
Spinal Cord Lesion	Deficit in pain perception (spinothalamic tract) is contralateral to the lesion while other sensory deficits (dorsal column) are ipsilateral

- BROWN SEQUARD SYNDROME is caused by unilateral lesions or transsections of the spinal cord. Symptoms include ipsilateral weakness and loss of position and vibration sense below the lesion as a result of transsection of the lateral corticospinal tract and dorsal columns. Pain and temperature sense are usually lost a few segments below the level of the lesion on the contralateral side due to damage to the spinothalamic tract.

THE PHYSIOLOGY OF PAIN (51)

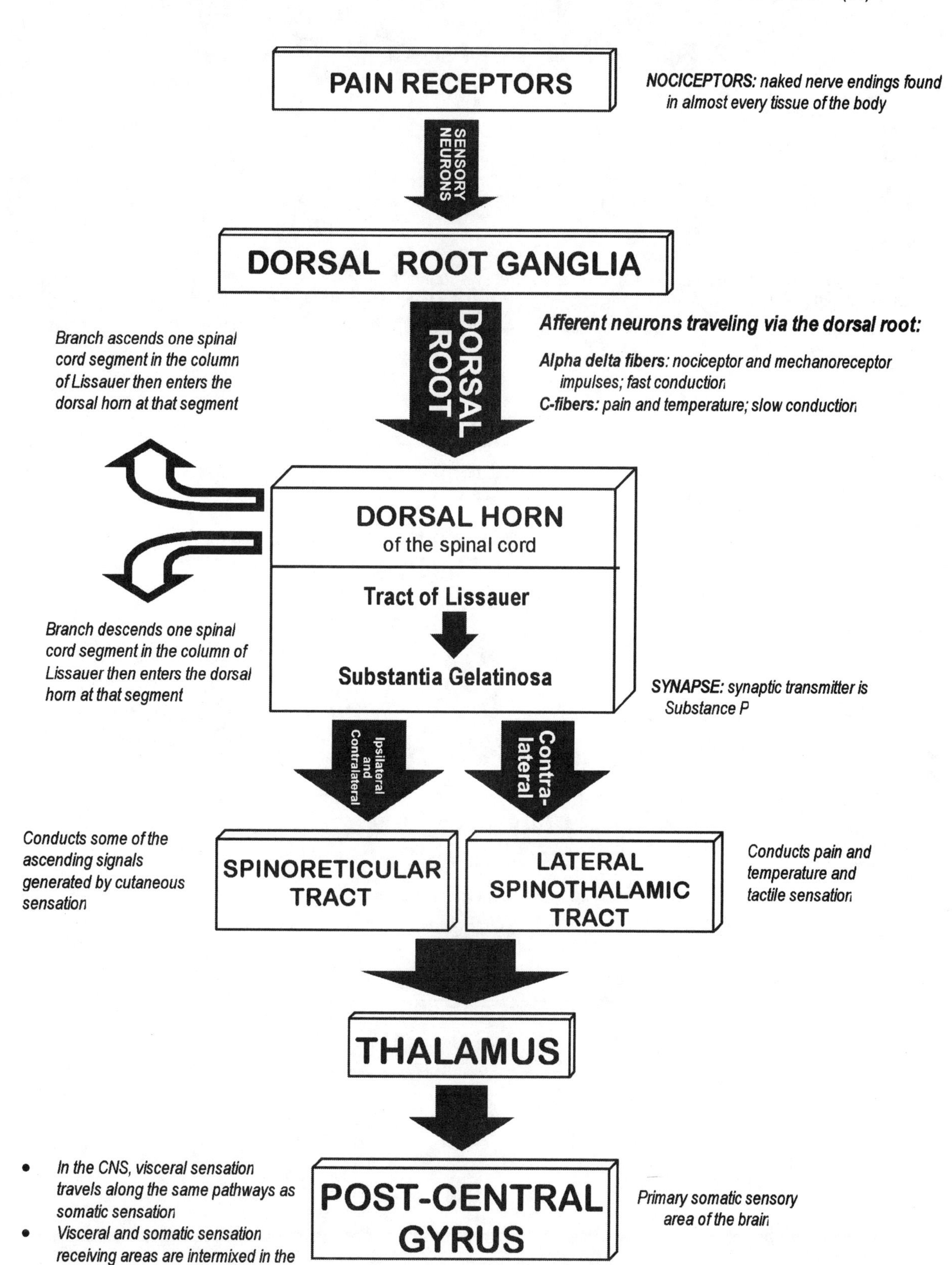

Perception of Pain

Gate Control Theory

- The transmission of impulses for pain to the brain is altered by dorsal root afferents for other sensory modalities. Trains of non-nociceptive (i.e. mechanoreceptor) impulses coming through the larger fibers cause synaptic inhibition (decrease in the rate of firing) of the spinothalamic tract cells concerned with nociception. (52) The following chart is a simplified illustration of the gate control theory of pain: (53)

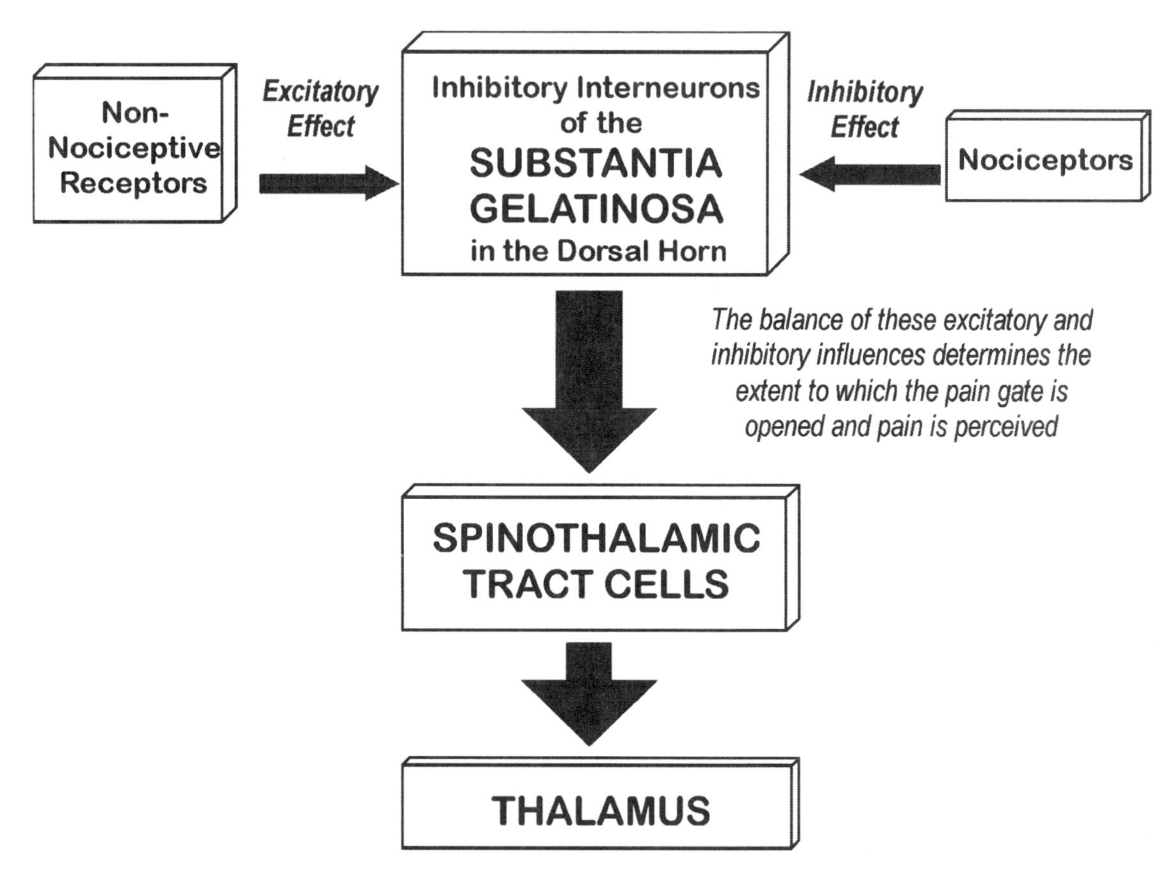

Remember (54)

- Endorphins and enkephalins are the body's own natural opiates. They are produced in certain tissues in response to pain, stress, electrical stimulation and other stimuli.

LOVETT MUSCLE GRADING (55)

5 - Normal	Complete range of motion against gravity with full resistance
4 - Good	Complete range of motion against gravity with some resistance
3 - Fair	Complete range of motion against gravity
2 - Poor	Complete range of motion with gravity eliminated
1 - Trace	Evidence of slight contractility; no joint motion
0 - Zero	No evidence of contraction

Remember (56)

- Bring the muscle into an antigravity position to test it.
- Stabilize just proximal to the part to be tested.
- The optimal test position for a one-joint muscle is at the complete range of motion.
- To evaluate a two-joint muscle, lengthen the muscle over one joint to get the greatest power of contraction over the second joint. The optimal test position for a two-joint muscle is within the mid-range of its overall length.

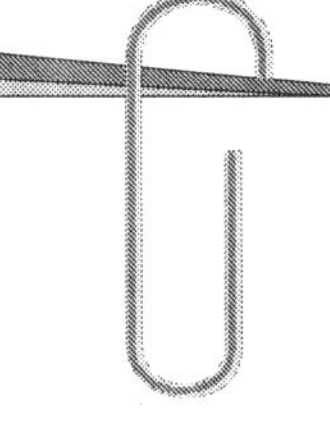

Deep Tendon Reflex Grading (57)

0	No response
1	Sluggish or diminished
2	Active or expected response
3	More brisk than expected, slightly hyperactive
4	Brisk, hyperactive, with intermittent or transient clonus

Wexler Reflex Grading for DTRs

0	No reflex
1	Hyporeflexic – LMN lesion
2	Normal
3	Hyperreflexic – UMN lesion
4	Hyperreflexic with transient clonus – UMN lesion
5	Sustained clonus – UMN lesion

- WESTPHAL'S SIGN: Loss of a deep tendon reflex, especially the knee-jerk reflex; indicates a lower motor neuron lesion. (58)
- JENDRASSIK'S MANEUVER: A technique of cortical distraction to help elicit a reflex; the patient interlocks his/her fingers and tries to pull them apart while the doctor simultaneously tests for a muscle stretch reflex. (59)

ANTALGIA (60)

- Relief or aggravation of pain with lateral flexion may indicate whether the patient has a medial or lateral disc protrusion.

Patient posture for relief of left sciatica due to disc protrusion lateral to the nerve root

Patient posture for relief of left sciatica due to disc protrusion medial to the nerve root

TYPES OF PAIN

Dermatogenous	Pain occurs along the sensory distribution of a nerve root
Sclerotogenous	Pain arises from structures derived from embryological sclerotomes
Myotogenous	Pain originates in a muscle
Radiating	Caused by direct pressure or irritation of a dorsal nerve roots or DRG; it radiates along a narrow band and is accompanied by sensory or motor deficits
Referred	Pain along a scleroderm of origination; involves more than one kind of tissue

PERIPHERAL NEUROPATHIES (61,62,63)

Nerve	Function		Clinical Features
Median	Sensory	▪ Lateral part of palm, including thenar eminence and lateral 3 ½ digits ▪ Distal dorsum of lateral 3 ½ digits	▪ Carpal tunnel syndrome: characterized by nocturnal parasthesias of radial 3 ½ digits ▪ Pronator teres syndrome ▪ Anterior Interosseous syndrome
	Motor	▪ Superficial flexors except flexor carpi ulnaris ▪ Pronator Teres ▪ Flexor pollicus longus ▪ Pronator quadratus ▪ Half of flexor digitorum profundus	
Radial	Sensory	▪ Dorsal surfaces of the lateral 3 ½ digits except the tips	▪ Wrist drop ▪ Crutch/Saturday night palsy: wrist drop and triceps paralysis; parasthesia in dorsum of radial 3½ digits ▪ Cheiralgia parasthetica ▪ Supinator syndrome ▪ Inability to extend the MCP joints
	Motor	▪ Extensors of the forearm, wrist, hand and fingers	
Ulnar	Sensory	▪ Skin on medial palm ▪ Skin over hypothenar eminence ▪ Skin on posterior surface of medial 1½ digits	▪ Claw hand ▪ Cyclist's palsy ▪ Weakness of finger adduction and abduction ▪ Interosseous atrophy
	Motor	▪ Flexor carpi ulnaris ▪ Ulnar portion of flexor digitorum profundus ▪ Interossei	

emember (64)

- Erb Duchenne Paralysis: Upper Brachial Plexus injury (C5/6); causes "Waiter's Tip" position; usually caused by birth injury.

- Klumpke's Paralysis: Lower Brachial Plexus Injury (C8/T1); usually caused by birth injury, or upward pull on the shoulder.

Nerve Plexuses

The Cervical Plexus

ote (65)

- The cervical plexus is formed by the ventral primary rami of the first through fourth spinal nerves, with a small contribution from the fifth spinal nerve.
- Peripheral nerves derived from the cervical plexus innervate most of the anterior and lateral muscles of the neck and supply sensory fibers to part of the head and much of the neck.

Muscles	Spinal Segment		Peripheral Nerve
Sternocleidomastoid	Ventral Primary Ramus	C(1), 2, 3	
Levator Scapulae		C3, 4, 5	Dorsal scapular (plus direct)
Trapezius (upper, middle, lower)		C2, 3, 4	
Scalenes (anterior, middle, posterior)		C3, 4, 5, 6, 7, 8	
Longus Colli		C2, 3, 4, 5, 6, (7)	
Rectus capitis anterior and lateralis		C1, 2	
Diaphragm		C3, 4, 5	Phrenic
Head and neck extensors	Dorsal Primary Ramus	C1-8	

THE LUMBAR PLEXUS (66)

			Muscles	Spinal Segment
Ventral primary ramus of lumbar plexus		Lumbar plexus	Quadratus lumborum	L1, 2, 3
			Psoas major	L1, 2, 3, 4
			Psoas minor	L1, 2
		Iliohypogastric	Internal oblique, transversus abdominus	T12, L1
Anterior Division	Obturator	Anterior	(Pectineus), adductor brevis, adductor longus, gracilis	L(1), 2, 3, 4
		Posterior	Obturator externus, adductor magnus	L(1), 2, 3, 4
Posterior Division	Femoral		Iliacus, sartorius, quadriceps, pectineus	L(1), 2, 3, 4

THE SACRAL PLEXUS (67)

			Muscles	Spinal Segments
Ventral primary ramus			Piriformis	L(5), S1, 2
			Gemellus superior, obturator internus	L5, S1, 2
			Gemellus inferior, quadratus femoris	L4, 5, S1, (2)
Anterior Division	Sciatic	Tibial branch	Biceps (long head)	L5, S1, 2, 3
			Semimembranosus, semitendinosus	L4, 5, S1, 2
	Tibial	Tibial	Plantaris	L4, 5, S1, (2)
			Gastrocnemius	S1, 2
			Popliteus	L4, 5, S1
			Tibialis posterior	L(4), 5, S1
			Soleus	L5, S1, 2
			Flexor digitorum longus	L5, S1, (2)
			Flexor hallucis longus	L5, S1, 2
		Medial Plantar	Flexor digitorum brevis, abductor hallucis, flexor hallucis brevis, lumbricales I	L4, 5, S1
		Lateral Plantar	Abductor digiti minimi, quadratus plantae, flexor digiti minimi, opponens digiti minimi, adductor hallucis, plantar interossei, dorsal interossei	S1, 2
			Lumbricales II, III, IV	L(4), (5), S1, 2
Posterior Division	Sciatic	Peroneal branch	Biceps (short head)	L5, S1, 2
	Gluteal	Superior	Gluteus medius and minimus, tensor fascia lata	L4, 5, S1
		Inferior	Gluteus maximus	L5, S1, 2
	Common Peroneal	Superficial	Peroneus longus and brevis	L4, 5, S1
		Deep	Tibialis anterior, extensor hallucis longus, extensor digitorum longus, peroneus tertius, extensor digitorum brevis	L4, 5, S1

THE BRACHIAL PLEXUS

ote (68)

- The ventral rami of C5-C8 plus the greater part of T1 plus a communicating loop from C4 to C5 successively form the roots, trunks, divisions, cords (lateral, medial and posterior) and branches of the brachial plexus. The branches become peripheral nerves. Other peripheral nerves exit directly from various components of the brachial plexus and some directly from the ventral rami.
- The posterior cord branches to become the axillary and radial nerves. The medial cord receives a branch from the lateral cord and becomes the ulnar nerve. One branch of the lateral cord becomes the musculocutaneous nerve and the other unites with one from the medial cord to form the median nerve.

PERIPHERAL NERVES (68)

Section of the Brachial Plexus	Peripheral nerves		Nerve Root Levels
Roots	Long thoracic nerve		C5, 6, 7, (8)
	Dorsal scapular nerve		C4, 5
Superior Trunk	Nerve to subclavius		C5, 6
	Suprascapular nerve		C4, 5, 6
Divisions	No peripheral nerves exit this section		
Cords	Posterior	Upper subscapular	C(4), 5, 6, (7)
		Thoracodorsal	C(5), 6, 7, 8
		Lower subscapular	C5, 6, (7)
	Lateral	Lateral pectoral	C5, 6, 7
	Medial	Medial pectoral	C(6), 7, 8. T1
Branches	Axillary (from posterior cord)		C5, 6
	Radial (from posterior cord)		C5, 6, 7, 8, T1
	Musculocutaneous (from lateral cord)		C(4), 5, 6, 7
	Ulnar (from medial cord)		C7, 8, T1
	Median (from medial and lateral cords)		C5, 6, 7, 8, T1

MUSCLES INNERVATED BY THE BRACHIAL PLEXUS (68)

	Peripheral Nerve	Muscles	Spinal Segments
Roots	Long thoracic	Serratus Anterior	C5, 6, 7, (8)
	Dorsal scapular	Rhomboid Major and Minor	C4, 5
Superior Trunk	Nerve to subclavius	Subclavius	C5, 6
	Suprascapular	Supraspinatus and infraspinatus	C4, 5, 6
Posterior cord	Upper subscapular	Subscapularis	C 5, 6, 7
	Thoracodorsal	Latissimus dorsi	C 6, 7, 8
	Lower subscapular	Subscapularis and teres major	C5, 6, 7
	Axillary (branch from posterior cord)	Deltoid and teres minor	C5, 6
	Radial (branch from posterior cord)	Triceps	C6, 7, 8, T1
		Anconeus	C7, 8
		Brachialis (small part), brachioradialis	C5, 6
		Extensor carpi radialis longus	C5, 6, 7, 8
		Extensor carpi radialis brevis	C6, 7, 8
		Supinator	C5, 6 (7)
		Extensor digitorum, extensor digiti minimi, extensor carpi ulnaris, abductor pollicis longus, extensor pollicis brevis and longus, extensor indicis	C6, 7, 8
Medial cord	Ulnar (branch from medial cord)	Palmar and dorsal interossei, adductor pollicis, flexor pollicis brevis (deep head)	C8, T1
		Flexor carpi ulnaris, flexor digitorum profundus III and IV	C7, 8, T1
		Palmaris brevis, abductor digiti minimi, opponens digiti minimi, flexor digiti minimi, lumbricales III and IV	C(7), 8, T1
	Medial pectoral	Pectoralis major (lower) and pectoralis minor	C(6), 7, 8, T1
Lateral cord	Musculocutaneous (branch from lateral cord)	Biceps and brachialis	C 5, 6
		Coracobrachialis	C6,7
	Lateral pectoral	Pectoralis major (upper)	C5, 6, 7
		Pectoralis major (lower)	C6, 7, 8, T1
Medial and Lateral cord	Median (branch from medial and lateral cords)	Pronator teres	C6, 7
		Flexor carpi radialis	C6, 7, 8
		Palmaris longus, flexor pollicis longus, lumbricales I and II	C(6), 7, 8, T1
		Abductor pollicis brevis, opponens pollicis, flexor pollicis brevis (superior head)	C6, 7, 8, T1
		Flexor digitorum superficialis, flexor digitorum profundus I and II, pronator quadratus	C7, 8, T1

Peripheral Nerve	Thumb Muscles
Radial	Abductor pollicis longus, extensor pollicis longus and brevis
Ulnar	Flexor pollicis brevis (deep head), adductor pollicis
Median	Flexor pollicis longus, abductor pollicis brevis, opponens pollicis, flexor pollicis brevis (superior head)

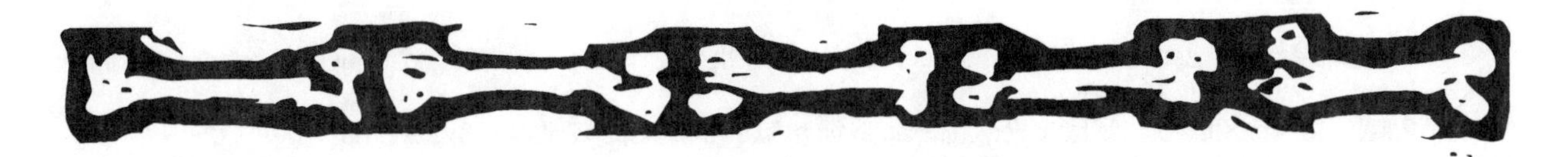

References

1 Waxman SG, deGroot J. Correlative Neuroanatomy. 22nd ed. Connecticut: Appleton & Lange, 1995:106-126.
2 Ferezy JS. The Chiropractic Neurological Examination. Maryland: Aspen Publishers, 1992: 15.
3 Waxman SG, deGroot J. Correlative Neuroanatomy. 22nd ed. Connecticut: Appleton & Lange, 1995: 106.
4 Seidel HM, Ball JW, Dains JE, Benedict GW. Mosby's Guide to Physical Examination. 3rd ed. St. Louis: Mosby, 1995: 75, 247, 287, 736-741.
5 Ferezy JS. The Chiropractic Neurological Examination. Maryland: Aspen Publishers, 1992: 15-38.
6 Waxman SG, deGroot J. Correlative Neuroanatomy. 22nd ed. Connecticut: Appleton & Lange, 1995: 106-122.
7 Mazion JM. Illustrated Reference Manual of Ortho/Neuro/Physio Clinical Diagnostic Techniques. 4th ed. Arizona: Imperial Litho/graphics, 1980: 23, 26, 27, 43, 113, 125.
8 Ferezy JS. The Chiropractic Neurological Examination. Maryland: Aspen Publishers, 1992: 21.
9 Waxman SG, deGroot J. Correlative Neuroanatomy. 22nd ed. Connecticut: Appleton & Lange, 1995: 106.
10 Waxman SG, deGroot J. Correlative Neuroanatomy. 22nd ed. Connecticut: Appleton & Lange, 1995: 52-57.
11 Ferezy JS. The Chiropractic Neurological Examination. Maryland: Aspen Publishers, 1992: 39.
12 Waxman SG, deGroot J. Correlative Neuroanatomy. 22nd ed. Connecticut: Appleton & Lange, 1995: 191-200.
13 Ferezy JS. The Chiropractic Neurological Examination. Maryland: Aspen Publishers, 1992: 37, 83, 84-89.
14 Waxman SG, deGroot J. Correlative Neuroanatomy. 22nd ed. Connecticut: Appleton & Lange, 1995: 200-201.
15 Isselbacher KJ, Braunwald E, Wilson JD, Martin JB, Fauci AS, Kasper DL. Harrison's Principles of Internal Medicine. 13th ed. New York: McGraw-Hill, Inc., 1994: 117.
16 Mazion JM. Illustrated Reference Manual of Ortho/Neuro/Physio Clinical Diagnostic Techniques. 4th ed. Arizona: Imperial Litho/graphics, 1980: 22, 45, 86, 148, 151.
17 Waxman SG, deGroot J. Correlative Neuroanatomy. 22nd ed. Connecticut: Appleton & Lange, 1995: 63-64, 199-201.
18 Ferezy JS. The Chiropractic Neurological Examination. Maryland: Aspen Publishers, 1992: 82.
19 Isselbacher KJ, Braunwald E, Wilson JD, Martin JB, Fauci AS, Kasper DL. Harrison's Principles of Internal Medicine. 13th ed. New York: McGraw-Hill, Inc., 1994: 2280.
20 Ferezy JS. The Chiropractic Neurological Examination. Maryland: Aspen Publishers, 1992: 85.
21 Waxman SG, deGroot J. Correlative Neuroanatomy. 22nd ed. Connecticut: Appleton & Lange, 1995: 98.
22 Waxman SG, deGroot J. Correlative Neuroanatomy. 22nd ed. Connecticut: Appleton & Lange, 1995:102.
23 Waxman SG, deGroot J. Correlative Neuroanatomy. 22nd ed. Connecticut: Appleton & Lange, 1995: 102.
24 Seidel HM, Ball JW, Dains JE, Benedict GW. Mosby's Guide to Physical Examination. 3rd ed. St. Louis: Mosby, 1995: 743-746.
25 Waxman SG, deGroot J. Correlative Neuroanatomy. 22nd ed. Connecticut: Appleton & Lange, 1995: 102.
26 Mazion JM. Illustrated Reference Manual of Ortho/Neuro/Physio Clinical Diagnostic Techniques. 4th ed. Arizona: Imperial Litho/graphics, 1980: 63, 126, 133.
27 Mazion JM. Illustrated Reference Manual of Ortho/Neuro/Physio Clinical Diagnostic Techniques. 4th ed. Arizona: Imperial Litho/graphics, 1980: 17, 87, 139.
28 Waxman SG, deGroot J. Correlative Neuroanatomy. 22nd ed. Connecticut: Appleton & Lange, 1995: 102-103.
29 Mazion JM. Illustrated Reference Manual of Ortho/Neuro/Physio Clinical Diagnostic Techniques. 4th ed. Arizona: Imperial Litho/graphics, 1980: 66, 82-83, 161.
30 Seidel HM, Ball JW, Dains JE, Benedict GW. Mosby's Guide to Physical Examination. 3rd ed. St. Louis: Mosby, 1995: 741, 743.
31 Waxman SG, deGroot J. Correlative Neuroanatomy. 22nd ed. Connecticut: Appleton & Lange, 1995: 103.
32 Waxman SG, deGroot J. Correlative Neuroanatomy. 22nd ed. Connecticut: Appleton & Lange, 1995: 150.
33 Barr ML, Kiernan JA. The Human Nervous System. 6th ed. Philadelphia: J.B. Lippincott Company, 1993: 210.
34 Waxman SG, deGroot J. Correlative Neuroanatomy. 22nd ed. Connecticut: Appleton & Lange, 1995: 201.
35 Waxman SG, deGroot J. Correlative Neuroanatomy. 22nd ed. Connecticut: Appleton & Lange, 1995: 201.
36 Isselbacher KJ, Braunwald E, Wilson JD, Martin JB, Fauci AS, Kasper DL. Harrison's Principles of Internal Medicine. 13th ed. New York: McGraw-Hill, Inc., 1994: 122, 123.

37 Mazion JM. Illustrated Reference Manual of Ortho/Neuro/Physio Clinical Diagnostic Techniques. 4th ed. Arizona: Imperial Litho/graphics, 1980: 49, 153.
38 Ferezy JS. The Chiropractic Neurological Examination. Maryland: Aspen Publishers, 1992: 65.
39 Seidel HM, Ball JW, Dains JE, Benedict GW. Mosby's Guide to Physical Examination. 3rd ed. St. Louis: Mosby, 1995: 748-749.
40 Mazion JM. Illustrated Reference Manual of Ortho/Neuro/Physio Clinical Diagnostic Techniques. 4th ed. Arizona: Imperial Litho/graphics, 1980: 9, 34, 143.
41 Isselbacher KJ, Braunwald E, Wilson JD, Martin JB, Fauci AS, Kasper DL. Harrison's Principles of Internal Medicine. 13th ed. New York: McGraw-Hill, Inc., 1994: 135.
42 Hoppenfeld S. Orthopaedic Neurology. Philadelphia: J.B. Lippincott Company, 1977: 7-38.
43 Tortora GJ, Grabowski SR. Principles of Anatomy and Physiology. 7th ed. New York: Harper Collins, 1993: 401.
44 Williams PL, Warwick R, eds. Gray's Anatomy. 36th ed. Philadelphia: W.B. Saunders Company, 1980: 1117.
45 Williams PL, Warwick R, eds. Gray's Anatomy. 36th ed. Philadelphia: W.B. Saunders Company, 1980: 1096-1097.
46 Hoppenfeld S. Orthopaedic Neurology. Philadelphia: J.B. Lippincott Company, 1977: 45-74.
47 Williams PL, Warwick R, eds. Gray's Anatomy. 36th ed. Philadelphia: W.B. Saunders Company, 1980: 1117.
48 Williams PL, Warwick R, eds. Gray's Anatomy. 36th ed. Philadelphia: W.B. Saunders Company, 1980: 1108, 1112, 1114.
49 Wyatt LH. Handbook of Clinical Chiropractic. Maryland: Aspen Publishers, 1992:85.
50 Waxman SG, deGroot J. Correlative Neuroanatomy. 22nd ed. Connecticut: Appleton & Lange, 1995: 54-55, 57.
51 The chart is derived from the following references:
- Barr ML, Kiernan JA. The Human Nervous System: An Anatomical Viewpoint. 6th ed. Philadelphia: J.B. Lippincott company, 1993: 294.
- Ganong Wf. Review of Medical Physiology. 17th ed. Connecticut: Appleton & Lange, 1995: 126-127.
- Gertz DS. Neuroanatomy Made Easy and Understandable. 5th ed. Maryland: Aspen Publishers, Inc., 1991: 10.
- Jaskoviak PA. Applied Physiotherapy: Practical Clinical Applications with Emphasis on the Management of Pain and Related Syndromes. 2nd ed. Virginia: American Chiropractic Association, 1993: 22-23.

52 Barr ML, Kiernan JA. The Human Nervous System: An Anatomical Viewpoint. 6th ed. Philadelphia: J.B. Lippincott company, 1993: 299.
53 Barr ML, Kiernan JA. The Human Nervous System: An Anatomical Viewpoint. 6th ed. Philadelphia: J.B. Lippincott company, 1993: 299.
54 Jaskoviak PA. Applied Physiotherapy: Practical Clinical Applications with Emphasis on the Management of Pain and Related Syndromes. 2nd ed. Virginia: American Chiropractic Association, 1993: 51.
55 Kendall FP. Muscles: Testing and Function. 4th ed. Baltimore: Williams & Wilkins, 1993: 188-189.
56 Kendall FP. Muscles: Testing and Function. 4th ed. Baltimore: Williams & Wilkins, 1993: 179-180.
57 Seidel HM, Ball JW, Dains JE, Benedict GW. Mosby's Guide to Physical Examination. 3rd ed. St. Louis: Mosby, 1995: 751.
58 Dorland's Medical Dictionary, 28th ed.
59 Mazion JM. Illustrated Reference Manual of Ortho/Neuro/Physio Clinical Diagnostic Techniques. 4th ed. Arizona: Imperial Litho/graphics, 1980: 91.
60 Cox JM. Low Back Pain. 5th ed. Baltimore: Williams & Wilkins, 1990: 47.
61 Netter FH. Atlas of Human Anatomy. New Jersey: Ciba Corporation, 1989: 448, 449, 451.
62 Hollinshead WH, Rosse C. Textbook of Anatomy. 4th ed. Philadelphia: Harper & Rowe, 1985: 244-245, 258-263.
63 Isselbacher KJ, Braunwald E, Wilson JD. Harrison's Principles of Internal Medicine. 13th ed. New York: McGraw-Hill, 1994: 2377-2378.
64 Hollinshead WH, Rosse C. Textbook of Anatomy. 4th ed. Philadelphia: Harper & Rowe, 1985: 187.
65 Kendall FP. Muscles: Testing and Function. 4th ed. Baltimore: Williams & Wilkins, 1993: 384,389.
66 Kendall FP. Muscles: Testing and Function. 4th ed. Baltimore: Williams & Wilkins, 1993: 386, 393.
67 Kendall FP. Muscles: Testing and Function. 4th ed. Baltimore: Williams & Wilkins, 1993: 387, 393.
68 Kendall FP. Muscles: Testing and Function. 4th ed. Baltimore: Williams & Wilkins, 1993: 385, 389.

CHAPTER 7

Orthopedic Exam

ORTHOPEDIC TESTS

ote

- Only the positive finding indicated by your reference is a positive finding for any orthopedic test. If you elicit results other than those of the positive finding, then the orthopedic test was negative with a significant other finding of the result(s) produced.

THE CERVICAL SPINE

	Test	Procedure	Positive Finding
Nerve Root Compression / Encroachment	Jackson's Lateral Compression (1)	Examiner laterally flexes the patient's head and applies downward pressure	Exacerbation of local or radicular pain
	Foraminal Compression (1,2)	Examiner applies downward pressure to patient's neutrally-positioned head and notes report of localized or radicular pain. Next, examiner rotates the patient's head toward the side of complaint, applies downward pressure and notes reproduction of complaint. Repeat on the opposite side	Localized or radicular pain
	Maximal Foraminal Compression (1,2)	Patient actively rotates and hyperextends the head. Perform the test bilaterally	Pain on the side of head rotation indicates nerve root compression or facet pathology. Pain on the opposite side indicates muscle strain
	Spurling's (1)	1 Seated patient actively rotates the head from side to side; examiner notes localization of pain. Next, examiner laterally flexes the head toward the symptomatic side and applies gradual downward pressure to the head; reproduction of symptoms is a positive test and the rest of the test is not performed 2 Otherwise, from the laterally flexed position, examiner applies gradual downward pressure to the head; reproduction of radicular symptoms suggests nerve root compression while localized pain suggests facet involvement 3 Finally, vertical blows are delivered to the cranium with the patient's head in a neutral position, followed by lateral flexion and extension. The test is meant to simulate nerve root irritation caused by disc disease or cervical spondylosis	
	Bakody Sign/ Shoulder Abduction (1,2)	Patient abducts and externally rotates the symptomatic shoulder in order to place the hand on the top of the head	Hand-on-head position relieves radicular pain
	Cervical Distraction (1,2)	Examiner cups the patient's mandible and occiput in order to distract the patient's head	Relief of localized or radicular symptoms **NOTE**: *Increase in pain indicates muscle spasm*
Space-occupying Lesion	Valsalva's (1,2)	Examiner instructs seated patient to take a deep breath and bear down to create greater pressure on the cervical region	Reproduction of radicular pain
	Triad of Dejerine (1)	Patient reports aggravation of radicular symptoms with coughing, sneezing and straining during defecation	Aggravation of radicular symptoms
	Nafzigger's (1)	Examiner occludes the right and left jugular veins of the seated patient simultaneously for 30 to 40 seconds	Radicular or localized pain in the spine
	Swallowing (1)	Examiner instructs seated patient to swallow (examiner may provide a glass of water)	Pain or difficulty swallowing indicates space-occupying lesion at the anterior cervical spine; sprain; strain; or fracture

Test		Procedure	Positive Finding
Myelopathy	L'hermitte's Sign (3)	Examiner flexes the head and neck of the seated patient	Sharp, radiating pain or paresthesia along the spine or into one or more extremities **NOTE**: *This test may or may not be positive with multiple sclerosis, which has a predilection for the lateral and dorsal columns*
Sprain / Strain	O'Donoghue's Maneuver (3,4)	Examiner moves the cervical spine of the seated patient through resisted range of motion then through passive range of motion	Pain during resisted range of motion (isometric contraction) indicates muscle strain. Pain during passive range of motion indicates ligamentous sprain
Osseous or Soft Tissue Lesion	Rust's Sign (3)	Patient spontaneously holds the weight of the head with both hands when lying down or when arising from a recumbent position	Indicates severe sprain; rheumatoid arthritis; fracture; or severe cervical subluxation
	Soto-Hall Sign (3,4)	Patient lies supine with legs fully extended and arms extended over the head. Examiner stabilizes the patient's chest at the sternum and flexes the head to the chest	Pain localized to the cervico-thoracic spine indicates subluxation; exostoses; disc lesion; sprain; strain; or vertebral fracture **NOTE**: *See Meningitis*
	Spinous Percussion (3,4)	Seated patient actively flexes his/her cervical spine to make spinous processes more prominent; examiner percusses each spinous process. Next, examiner percusses the paravertebral soft tissues	Localized pain with spinous process percussion suggests fracture or severe sprain; radiating pain suggests an intervertebral disc syndrome. Pain elicited in the soft tissues suggests muscular strain or highly sensitive trigger points **NOTE**: *This test is non-specific*
Brachial Plexus Neuritis	Bikele's Sign (3)	Seated patient abducts the shoulder to 90 degrees, externally rotates the shoulder and fully extends the elbow	Presence of radicular pain
Nerve Root / Dural Sleeve Adhesions	Shoulder Depression (3,4)	Examiner slowly depresses the symptomatic shoulder of the seated patient while laterally flexing the head away from the shoulder	Production or aggravation of radicular pain

MENINGITIS

Test	Procedure	Positive Finding
Soto-Hall (3)	Patient lies supine with legs fully extended and arms extended over the head. Examiner stabilizes the patient's chest at the sternum and flexes the head to the chest	While the head is flexed toward the chest, a reflex flexion of the knees and thighs is equivalent to a Kernig's or Brudzinski's sign and suggests meningitis
Kernig's (3,4)	Examiner flexes the hip and knee of one leg of the supine patient each to 90 degrees then attempts to completely extend the leg	Sign is present when patient pain prevents the examiner from completely straightening the leg. Often the sign is accompanied by involuntary flexion of opposite knee and hip
Brudzinski's (3,4)	Examiner flexes the head of the supine patient	Sign is present if flexion of both knees occurs. Frequently the sign is accompanied by flexion of both hips

ote

- Bacterial meningitis is an inflammatory response to bacterial infection of the pia-arachnoid and the cerebrospinal fluid of the subarachnoid space. Approximately 25,000 cases of bacterial meningitis occur annually in the U.S., of which about 70% occur in children under 5 years of age. (5)

VERTEBROBASILAR ARTERY INSUFFICIENCY (6,7)

☞ **Do a complete patient history and physical exam. Risk factors include:**

- Vascular bruits in the carotid or subclavian arteries
- Significant difference in bilateral pulse volumes and/or blood pressures
- Pre-existing atherosclerotic disease
- Use of anti-coagulants
- Family history of stroke or cardiovascular disease, hypertension, bleeding disorders, cervical spondylosis or arthrosis
- Birth control pills
- Diabetes
- Hypertension
- Smoking

☞ **The vertebral artery is most susceptible to trauma at the following areas:**

- The posterior atlanto-occipital membrane
- The space between the occiput and posterior arch of the atlas, especially during extension
- Between the lateral mass of the atlas and the transverse process of the axis, especially during extension and rotation

☞ **While performing the tests look for the following signs, which indicate a positive test:**

- Nausea
- Vertigo
- Syncope
- Dizziness
- Visual changes (diplopia, blurring)
- Tinnitus
- Nystagmus
- Faintness

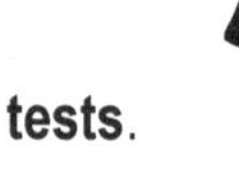

☞ **Be prepared to catch the patient if he or she becomes dizzy during the tests.**

VERTEBROBASILAR ARTERY ASSESSMENT

Test	Description
Vertebrobasilar Artery Functional Maneuver (6,7)	Examiner auscultates the subclavian and carotid arteries for bruits, then palpates the arteries for pulse assessment. If bruits are present, the test is positive and the balance of the test is not completed. If no bruits are detected, the patient rotates and hyperextends the head and neck toward each side while the examiner observes for signs of vertebrobasilar artery compromise.
Barre-Leiou Sign (6,7)	The patient rotates his/her head maximally while seated, holding each head rotation for 15 to 30 seconds. Repeat on the opposite side. Positive finding indicates VBAI on the ipsilateral side of head rotation.
Maigne's Test / George's Test (7)	The patient rotates and extends the head maximally while seated, holding each head rotation/extension for 15 to 30 seconds. Repeat on opposite side. Positive finding indicates vertebral, basilar or carotid artery stenosis.
Hautant's Test (6,7)	Patient seated with head in neutral position. Examiner asks patient to bring his/her arms into 90 degrees of flexion with palms up. Next, examiner instructs patient is to extend and rotate his/her head to one side. Look for pronator drift of the arms indicating vertebral, basilar or carotid artery stenosis or compression. Repeat on opposite side.
Dekleyn's Test (6,7)	Patient is supine with his/her head extended off the table. Examiner asks patient to further extend (hyperextend) the head and rotate to one side, and hold this position for 15 to 45 seconds. Repeat on the opposite side. Positive finding indicates VBAI on the ipsilateral side.
Underberg's Test (6,7) **NOTE:** Be prepared to catch the patient!	Patient stands with eyes open, arms at sides and feet close together. First, patient closes his/her eyes and elevates the extended arms forward 90 degrees with hands supinated. Next, patient extends the neck and rotates the head to one side while keeping eyes closed. Finally, patient attempts to maintain the head rotation and extension, arm elevation and hand supination while marching in place. Perform test bilaterally and observe for loss of equilibrium with each step of the test. Loss of balance, dropping or drifting of the arms or pronation of the hands indicates VBAI or carotid artery stenosis or compression.
Hallpike Maneuver (6) **NOTE:** Use Caution!	Patient lies supine. Examiner supports the weight of the patient's head while bringing the head into positions of extension, rotation and lateral flexion on both sides and holding each position for 15 to 45 seconds. Positive finding indicates VBAI.

THE CIRCLE OF WILLIS

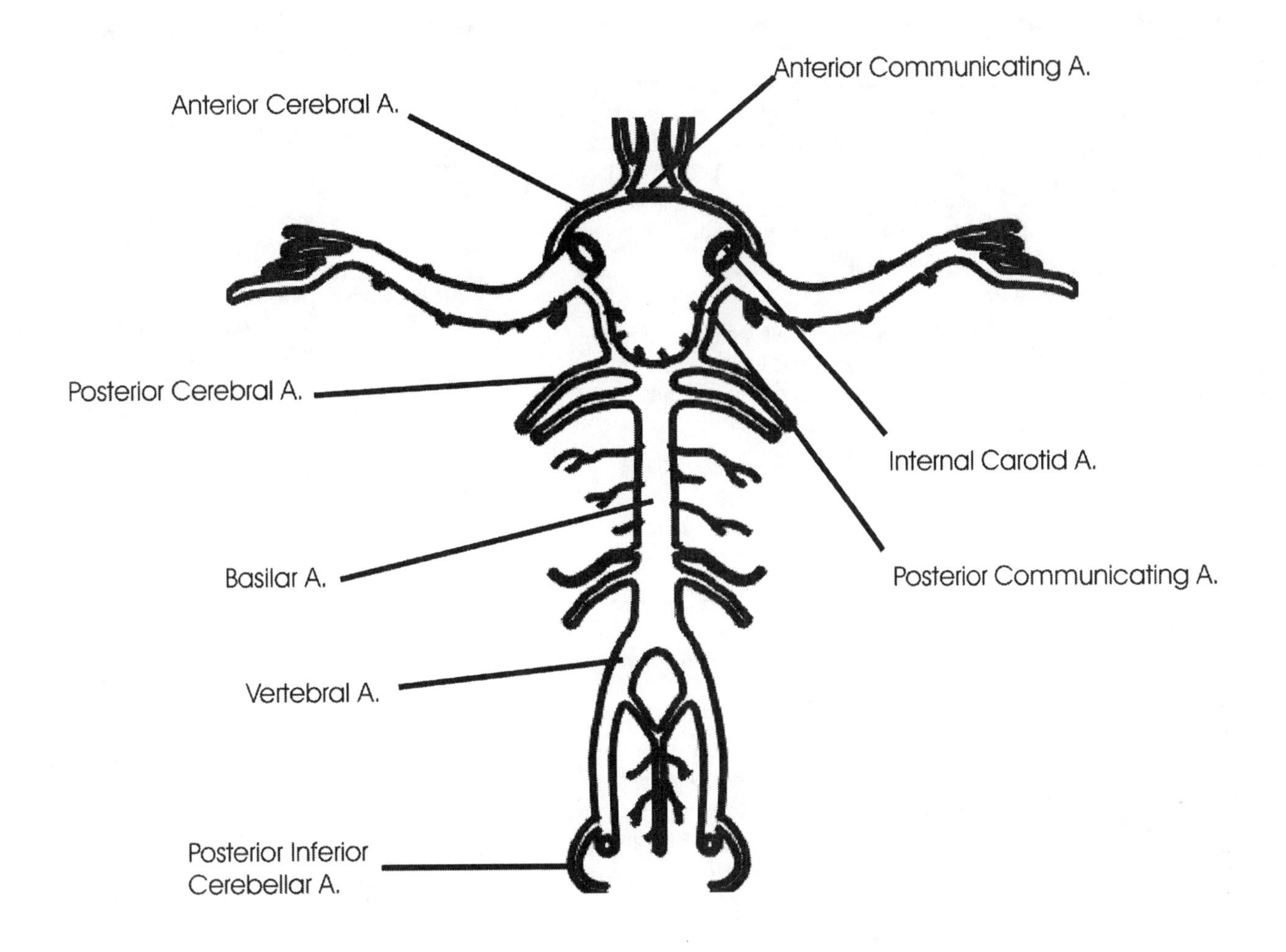

The **Circle of Willis** is formed by the posterior cerebral, posterior communicating, internal carotid, anterior cerebral, and anterior communicating arteries. Also shown are the Basilar, Vertebral and Posterior Inferior Cerebellar arteries.

Note (8)

- The arterial blood for the brain enters the cranial cavity via the vertebral arteries and the internal carotid arteries. The vertebral arteries, from the subclavian arteries, supply the brain stem, cerebellum, occipital lobe, and parts of the thalamus. The carotid arteries, from the common carotids, supply the remainder of the forebrain.

THE THORACIC SPINE

Test / Sign		Procedure	Positive Finding
Scoliosis	**Adam's Position** (9)	While patient is standing, examiner notes any spinal asymmetry, winging of the scapula or other abnormality. Examiner then instructs patient to bend forward with arms hanging toward the floor and palms together and observes the thoracolumbar spine for deformity, rib humping or muscular atrophy	A positive sign occurs when the scoliosis does not improve with forward flexion, indicating a structural scoliosis **NOTE**: *If a spinal curvature straightens when the spine is flexed forward, the sign is negative and indicates a functional scoliosis*
Myelopathy	**Beevor's Sign** (9,10)	Examiner instructs the supine patient to lift his/her head off the examining table. Observe for the umbilicus to move or drift up or down	If the umbilicus is drawn upward (due to weakened lower abdominal muscles) the sign is positive and is associated with a spinal cord lesion at the T10-12 level. If the umbilicus moves inferiorward, then a bilateral T7-10 nerve root lesion is suspect
Rib Integrity	**Rib Motion** (9)	Patient lies supine and examiner places his/her hands over the chest. Examiner instructs patient to inhale and exhale and palpates for movement of the ribs, noting any restrictions. Next, test middle and lower ribs. Test restricted ribs individually	An elevated rib stops moving in relation to the other ribs during exhalation. A depressed rib stops moving in relation to the other ribs during inhalation
	Schepelmann's Sign (9,10)	Patient is seated and raises his/her arms overhead then bends laterally	Pain on the side the patient is bending toward indicates intercostal neuritis. Pain on the side the patient is bending away from indicates intercostal myofascitis, which must be differentiated from pleurisy
Osseous or Soft Tissue Lesion	**Spinous Percussion** (9,10)	Patient is seated and bends forward to flex the thoracic spine. Examiner percusses the spinous processes then percusses the paraspinal musculature with a reflex hammer	Localized pain indicates a possible fractured vertebra or ligamentous sprain. Radicular pain is evidence of a possible disc lesion or muscle strain **NOTE**: *This test is non-specific*
Ankylosing Spondylitis	**Chest Expansion** (9,10)	Examiner places a tape measure around the patient's chest at the level of the fourth intercostal space. Examiner instructs patient to exhale deeply and records the circumference of the chest. Next, examiner instructs the patient to inhale deeply and records the circumference of the chest	The normal difference between the circumference of the chest on expiration and inspiration is 5.75 cm to 7.62 cm. A positive test occurs if the measurement is less than 3 centimeters
	Forestier's Bowstring (9)	Examiner instructs the standing patient to laterally bend and observes for tightening and contracture of the ipsilateral paraspinal muscles	Normally, the contralateral paraspinal musculature tightens with lateral bending; positive sign occurs when the ipsilateral musculature contracts

THE LUMBAR SPINE

IVD Syndrome	Sciatica	IVF encroachment	Dural adhesions	Spinal cord tumor	Spinal neuropathy	Sprain / strain	Femoral nerve	Hamstring spasm	Test / Sign	Procedure	Positive Finding
✓	✓	✓	✓						**Bechterew's** (11)	Examiner instructs the seated patient to extend first one leg then the other, making sure the patient does not flex the hip. If a positive response is elicited, examiner instructs patient to extend both legs simultaneously	Back pain or sciatic pain is increased or the patient cannot extend one or both legs
					✓				**Bowstring Sign** (11,12)	Examiner places the leg of the supine patient on his/her shoulder, causing hip flexion. Examiner exerts firm pressure near the insertion of the hamstring muscles. If this is painful for the patient , examiner applies pressure to the popliteal fossa	Pain in the lumbar region or radicular pain with compression of the popliteal fossa is a positive sign for nerve root compression
✓	✓			✓	✓			✓	**Bragard's Sign** (11,12)	If the SLR test is positive, examiner lowers the patient's leg just below the point of discomfort and sharply dorsiflexes the patient's foot	Increased pain **NOTE**: *Dull posterior thigh pain indicates tight hamstring muscles*
✓						✓			**Double Leg Raise** (11)	Examiner performs a straight leg raise on each of the supine patient's legs, noting the angle at which the pain is produced. Examiner then lifts both legs at the same time, noting the angle at which pain is produced	A positive sign occurs when pain is produced at an earlier angle by raising both legs at the same time and indicates lumbosacral joint involvement in the case of disc disease with resulting vertebral instability
					✓		✓		**Ely's Sign** (11) ***Also for hip lesion**	Examiner approximates the heel of the prone patient to the contralateral buttock and hyperextends the thigh. Perform bilaterally	▪ Iliopsoas irritation: lack of thigh extension ▪ Inflamed lumbar nerve roots: radicular pain ▪ Nerve root adhesions: upper lumbar pain
✓	✓		✓						**Fajersztajn's / Well Leg Raise** (11)	Examiner performs a straight leg raise on the asymptomatic leg. Examiner lowers the leg just below the point of discomfort and sharply dorsiflexes the foot	Test causes pain on the symptomatic side, indicating sciatic nerve root involvement
					✓		✓		**Femoral Nerve Traction** (11)	Patient lies on the asymptomatic side with the asymptomatic leg slightly flexed at the hip and knee. Examiner extends the knee of the symptomatic leg while gently extending the hip about 15 degrees. Examiner then slightly flexes the knee to further stretch the femoral nerve	Radiating pain down the anterior thigh. Indicates radiculopathy involving L2, 3, 4

IVD Syndrome	Sciatica	IVF encroachment	Dural adhesions	Spinal cord tumor	Spinal neuropathy	Sprain / strain	Femoral nerve	Hamstring spasm	Test / Sign	Procedure	Positive Finding
✓		✓			✓	✓			**Kemp's** (13)	Examiner performs the test first on the seated patient by supporting the patient and directing him/her to lean forward to one side and then around until s/he is bending obliquely backward. Next, perform the same test on the standing patient, causing the trunk to rotate and extend under increased downward pressure	If the maneuver, seated or standing, causes or aggravates radicular pain in the thigh and leg the sign is positive and indicates nerve root compression. Local pain is not a positive test, and may indicate sprain/strain **NOTE**: *The seated position increases intradiscal pressure while the standing position stresses the facet joints maximally*
✓	✓	✓	✓	✓					**Laseque** (13,14)	Patient supine with legs fully extended. Examiner flexes patient's hip and knee to 90 degrees, respectively. Next, examiner fully extends the patient's knee	Knee extension elicits pain **NOTE:** *Can also indicate a sacroiliac lesion*
					✓				**Laseque Differential Sign** (13)	Patient lies supine with legs fully extended. Examiner performs a SLR on the symptomatic leg and notes the angle at which sciatic pain is produced. Examiner then flexes the thigh and knee, relieving the stretch on the sciatic nerve	If pain is relieved with knee and thigh flexion, the sign is present **NOTE**: *This sign indicates neural rather than hip articular pain, and rules out a hip lesion*
✓									**Laseque Rebound** (13)	Patient supine with both legs extended. Examiner performs a straight leg raise on the symptomatic leg. When the leg is elevated to the point where pain is produced, the examiner suddenly removes support from the elevated leg, allowing it to drop to the examining table	Marked increase in back pain, sciatic neuralgia and muscle spasm
	✓							✓	**Lewin Standing** (13)	Examiner stabilizes the patient's pelvis on the symptomatic side with one hand, then quickly pulls the knee of the symptomatic leg into extension. Repeat on the opposite side. Next, the examiner pulls both knees sharply into extension	Pulling the knee into extension causes pain and is followed by a snapping back of either knee into flexion
✓	✓								**Lewin Supine** (13)	Patient supine with legs fully extended. Examiner applies firm downward pressure on the patient's legs and instructs patient to sit up without using his/her hands	Test is positive if patient cannot sit up. Patient can frequently localize the origin of the pain **NOTE**: *Can also indicate a sacroiliac lesion*
	✓				✓				**Lindner's Sign** (13,14)	Patient seated or supine. Examiner flexes the patient's head onto the chest	Pain in the lumbar spine and sciatic nerve distribution **NOTE**: *Differentiate from Kernig's/Brudzinski's test*

IVD Syndrome	Sciatica	IVF encroachment	Dural adhesions	Spinal cord tumor	Spinal neuropathy	Sprain / strain	Femoral nerve	Space-occupying lesion	Test / Sign	Procedure	Positive Finding
✓				✓				✓	**Milgram's** (15,16)	Patient supine with legs extended. Examiner instructs patient to raise both legs to a position where his/her heels are about six inches off the examining table	Patient experiences low back pain that prevents raising the legs more than 2 or 3 inches, if at all **NOTE**: *If patient can hold this position for any length of time without pain, pathologic intrathecal process can be ruled out*
✓						✓			**Minor's Sign** (15,16)	Examiner asks patient to rise from a seated position and observes how the patient performs this task	Patient supports weight on the asymptomatic side by balancing on the unaffected leg, placing one hand on the back, and flexing the knee and hip on the affected side to decrease tension on the sciatic nerve **NOTE**: *Can also indicate sacroiliac lesion*
✓	✓								**Neri's Sign** (15)	Examiner instructs standing patient to bow forward	Sign is present if patient flexes knee on affected side **NOTE**: *Can indicate a low back or sacroiliac lesion*
✓	✓	✓			✓			✓	**Prone Knee Flexion / Pheasant's** (15,17)	Examiner hyperflexes the knees of the prone patient, producing lumbar extension. Patient remains in this position for approximately 45 to 60 seconds	Examiner is unable to flex the patient's knees or the test produces unilateral pain, indicating an L2 or L3 nerve root lesion. Test also stretches the femoral nerve
	✓				✓				**Sicard's Sign** (15,16)	Patient supine with legs extended. Examiner performs a straight-leg raise on the symptomatic side to the point where pain occurs. Examiner then lowers the leg slightly and sharply dorsiflexes the great toe	Toe dorsiflexion reproduces symptoms
✓						✓			**Spinous Percussion** (15,16)	Patient stands and flexes the lumbosacral spine. Examiner percusses the spinous processes of each vertebra then percusses the paravertebral soft tissue	Localized pain elicited with spinous process percussion is evidence of fracture or severe sprain; radiating pain suggests intervertebral disc syndrome. Pain elicited with percussion of soft tissue suggests muscle strain or highly sensitive trigger points
								✓	**Triad of Dejerine** (15)	Patient reports aggravation of radicular symptoms with coughing, sneezing and straining during defecation	Aggravation of radicular symptoms
	✓								**Turyn's Sign** (15)	Patient supine with legs extended. Examiner dorsiflexes the patient's great toe	Pain is elicited in the gluteal region.
								✓	**Valsalva's** (15,16)	Seated patient is instructed to take a deep breath and bear down to create greater intraabdominal pressure but concentrating the stress on the lumbar region	Reproduction of radicular pain

The Straight Leg Raise

Test	Procedure	Interpretation
Straight Leg Raise (SLR) (18,19) ✓	Patient supine with legs fully extended. Examiner places one hand under the ankle of the symptomatic leg and the other on the knee to prevent flexion of the knee. Examiner then flexes the thigh to the point at which symptoms are reproduced and instructs the patient to flex the cervical spine. If this maneuver is limited due to pain, the test is positive for sciatica	▪ In patients with lateral protrusion, SLR causes patient to experience leg pain ▪ Medial protrusion causes back pain ▪ Intermediate (subrhizal) protrusion causes both back and leg pain **NOTE**: *If the patient feels pain before the examiner lifts the leg 15 degrees off the table,* ***Demianoff's sign*** *is present and indicates strain of the iliocostalis lumborum muscle*
Bonet's Phenomenon (19)	Adduction and internal rotation of the leg while a straight leg raise is performed	▪ Brings out pain response more readily
Well Leg Raise (Fajersztajn) (18,19) ✓	Straight leg raise and dorsiflexion of the foot on the asymptomatic side of a sciatic patient. If this test causes pain on the symptomatic side, the sign is present, indicating sciatic nerve root involvement	▪ Increased sciatica in the symptomatic leg on raising the well leg is associated with a lumbar disc herniation in 97% of patients ▪ With lateral disc protrusion, raising the well leg actually pulls the nerve root away from the disc and can relieve back or leg pain ▪ With medial disc protrusion, raising the well leg pulls the nerve root into the disc bulge and causes radiculopathy down the symptomatic leg

ote (20)

- The SLR is more useful for identifying L5-S1 disc lesions, since the pressures are highest at this level. On SLR, the pressure between the disc and the nerve root at L4/5 is half that at L5-S1.
- No movement on the nerve root occurs until the SLR reaches 30 degrees.
- No movement of the L4 nerve root occurs during the SLR.

Stretch on the Sciatic Nerve during the Straight Leg Raise (21)

The straight leg raise primarily stretches the L5, S1, and S2 level nerve roots.

- If pain begins between 0 and 35 degrees of hip flexion, extradural sciatic involvement is suspect.
- Between 35 and 70 degrees of flexion, the sciatic nerve roots tense over the disc, and pain at this level suggests sciatic nerve root irritation by disc pathology.
- Pain between 70 and 90 degrees of flexion suggests lumbar joint pain.

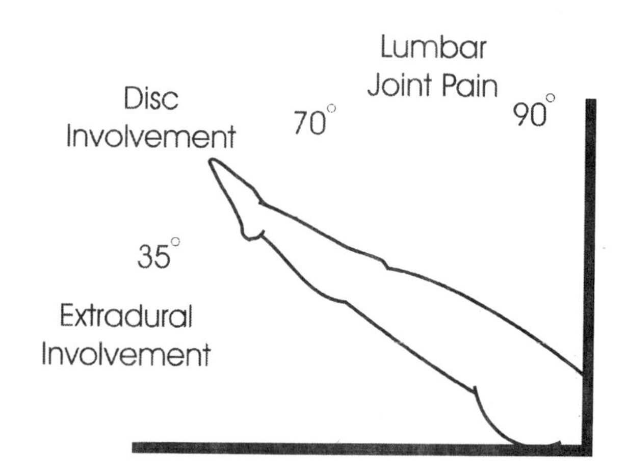

THE SACROILIAC JOINTS

Sacroiliac pathology	Lumbosacral syndrome	Sprain	Subluxation	Fracture	Test / Sign	Procedure	Positive Finding
✓	✓				**Belt / Supported Adam's** (22,23)	Standing patient flexes the dorsolumbar spine by bending forward; examiner notes amount of movement needed to cause pain. Next, examiner stabilizes patient's iliac crests by bracing a hip against the patient's sacrum. The patient then bends forward	If the lesion is in the pelvis, flexing the dorsolumbar spine while the pelvis is stabilized will decrease symptomatology. If the lesion is in the spine, the pain will be aggravated with or without stabilization of the pelvis
✓					**Erichsen's Sign** (22)	Examiner places his/her hands over the dorsa of the patient's ilia and gives a firm, sharp thrust toward the midline	Production of pain over the sacroiliac area
✓	✓				**Gaenslen's** (22,23)	Patient supine with symptomatic side of pelvis off the side of the table. The patient flexes the asymptomatic thigh toward the abdomen while the examiner hyperextends the affected thigh by gradually increasing the pressure of one hand on top of the knee. Perform bilaterally	Pain in the sacroiliac area or referred down the thigh. If the test is negative, suspect a lumbosacral lesion **NOTE**: *The test is usually contraindicated in geriatrics*
✓	✓				**Goldthwait's Sign** (22,23)	Patient is supine. Examiner places one hand under the lumbosacral portion of the patient's spine and palpates the L5 and S1 spinous processes throughout the test. The examiner elevates the symptomatic leg as if performing an SLR	If pain is produced before the L5-S1 spinous processes separate, the lesion involves the sacroiliac joint. If the pain is produced as the L5 and S1 spinous processes separate, a spinal lesion is more likely **NOTE**: *(Cipriano) Radiating pain is indicative of sciatic nerve compression at the following levels: 0-35 degrees indicates extradural nerve compression lesion; 35-70 degrees indicates sciatic nerve root irritation; 70 to 90 degrees indicates lumbar joint pain*
✓		✓	✓		**Hibb's** (22,23)	Patient prone. Examiner stabilizes the unaffected side of the pelvis with one hand. With the other hand the examiner grasps the ankle of the affected leg and flexes the knee to its maximum without elevating the thigh from the examination table. Examiner slowly pushes the leg laterally (internal rotation of the femoral head)	Sacroiliac joint pain **NOTE**: *A pathologic condition of the hip will produce hip pain*
✓		✓	✓	✓	**Iliac Compression** (22,23)	Patient side-lying on a table with a firm surface. Examiner places both hands over the upper part of the superior iliac crest and exerts downward pressure	Patient experiences an increased feeling of pressure in either sacroiliac joint

Sacroiliac pathology	Lumbosacral syndrome	Sprain	Subluxation	Fracture	Test / Sign	Procedure	Positive Finding
✓		✓	✓		**Laguerre's** (24)	Patient supine. Examiner flexes, abducts and externally rotates the patient's hip, applying overpressure at the end of the range of motion. Examiner stabilizes the pelvis on the opposite side by holding the opposite ASIS down	Pain in the sacroiliac joint on the symptomatic side **NOTE**: *Perform with caution for patient's with pathologic hip conditions*
✓		✓	✓		**Lewin-Gaenslen's** (24,25)	Patient side lying with asymptomatic side down and knee and hip of the asymptomatic leg flexed. Examiner abducts the affected leg slightly, supporting its weight with one hand. Examiner's other hand fixes the pelvis to the table with firm downward pressure. Examiner extends affected leg	Pain in the sacroiliac joint **NOTE**: *The further the patient flexes the unaffected leg, the less extension of the affected leg is necessary*
✓	✓				**Nachlas** (24,25)	Patient prone with legs extended. Examiner fully flexes the knee of the affected leg to the ipsilateral buttock	Pain in the sacroiliac area or the lumbosacral area, or radiating down the thigh or leg **NOTE**: *Pain over the anterior thigh indicates tight quadriceps*
		✓	✓		**Resisted Abduction** (25)	Patient side lying with the downside limb slightly flexed for balance during the test and upside limb extended and abducted. Examiner places pressure on the abducted limb and patient resists	Pain in the ipsilateral sacroiliac joint **NOTE**: *Pain in the buttock or lateral thigh indicates a strain of the tensor fascia latae and gluteus group*
✓	✓				**Smith-Petersen's** (24)	Patient supine. Examiner stands on the side of the symptomatic leg. The examiner places one hand under the patient's lumbar spine and palpates the L5-S1 spinous processes. While maintaining contact, the examiner performs a straight leg raise on the affected leg. Perform bilaterally	If pain occurs before the L5-S1 spinous processes separate, a sacroiliac lesion is present. If pain occurs as the L5-S1 spinous processes separate, either a sacroiliac or lumbosacral lesion may be present
		✓			**Squish** (24)	Patient supine, examiner places both hands on the patient's anterior superior iliac spines and iliac crests and pushes down at a 45-degree angle	Pain indicates a positive test **NOTE**: *Stresses the posterior sacroiliac ligaments*
✓		✓	✓		**Yoeman's** (24,25)	Patient prone. With one hand the examiner stabilizes the affected sacroiliac joint and flexes the knee of the affected leg to 90 degrees with the other hand. Examiner then hyperextends the thigh of the affected leg by lifting it off the table and maintaining pressure on the sacroiliac joint	Increased sacroiliac pain on the ipsilateral side **NOTE**: *Lumbar pain indicates lumbar involvement*

The Hips

Fracture	Coxa pathology	Iliotibial Band	Hip flexion contracture	Test / Sign	Procedure	Positive Finding
✓	✓			**Anvil** (26,27)	Patient supine. Examiner elevates symptomatic leg while keeping knee extended. Examiner strikes the calcaneus with a fist	Localized pain in the thigh indicates a femoral fracture or a severe pathologic condition involving the joint. Localized pain in the leg indicates a tibial or fibular fracture. Pain localized to the calcaneus indicates calcaneal fracture **NOTE**: *Very symptomatic patients may be tested with the leg resting on the table*
	✓			**Gauvain's Sign** (26,27)	Patient side lying with asymptomatic side down. The symptomatic leg is extended and the examiner slightly abducts the symptomatic leg. Examiner cautiously externally rotates the leg (internal rotation of the femoral head) then internally rotates the leg while palpating the patient's abdomen	Abdominal muscular contraction occurring on the same side indicates reflex muscle spasm due to tuberculosis of the hip
		✓		**Ober's** (26,27) ✓	Patient side-lying on asymptomatic hip with legs extended. Examiner slightly abducts the symptomatic leg, stabilizes the pelvis with one hand and grasps the ankle of the affected leg with the other hand. Examiner flexes knee to 90 degrees, abducts and extends the thigh	Test is positive if the leg remains abducted, indicating iliotibial band or tensor fascia latae contracture
	✓			**Patrick's** (26) ✓	Patient supine with legs extended. Examiner flexes the hip, abducts the thigh and crosses the ankle over the contralateral knee (causing external rotation of the hip). Next, examiner extends the hip further by applying downward pressure on the flexed knee while stabilizing the contralateral side of the pelvis to the table	Pain during abduction and external rotation
	✓		✓	**Thomas** (26,27) ✓	Patient supine on examination table with asymptomatic thigh actively flexed toward the abdomen and held there by the patient. Lumbar spine should flatten and the opposite leg should remain flat on the table	Lumbar spine maintains a lordosis and the symptomatic leg flexes, and if the patient is unable to lay the leg flat on the table (indicates shortened iliopsoas)
✓				**Trendelenberg** (26,27)	Patient is instructed to stand and raise the leg of the asymptomatic side off the floor	If the test is positive, the iliac crest will be high on the standing side and low on the side of the elevated leg, indicating weakness of gluteus medius on the standing side

Leg Lengths

Test	Procedure	Positive Finding
Allis' Sign (28)	Patient supine with knees flexed, feet flat on the examination table and toes and malleoli lined up. From the foot of the table, examiner observes the height of the patient's knees. From the side of the table, the examiner observes the position of the patient's knees	From the foot of the table, if one knee is lower than the other, it indicates a femoral deficiency that is due to a pathologic condition of the ipsilateral coxa or it may indicate a tibial length discrepancy. From the side of the table, if one knee is ahead of the other, it indicates femoral length discrepancy or ipsilateral coxa pathology
Actual Leg Length (28,29)	**EVANS**: Patient supine with feet together and legs extended. Use a tape measure to measure the length of the symptomatic leg from the apex of the anterior superior iliac spine to the medial malleolus. Compare the measurement to that of the opposite leg **CIPRIANO**: Patient standing. Examiner measures each leg from the anterior superior iliac spine to the floor	Actual leg length shortening (**anatomical short leg**) is caused by an abnormality above or below the trochanteric level
Apparent Leg Length (28,29)	Patient supine with legs extended. Examiner measures the length of each leg from the medial malleolus to the umbilicus	Difference in leg lengths indicates a **functional leg length deficiency**, which may be caused by muscular or ligamentous contracture deformities

Vascular Evaluation for the Lower Extremity

Test	Procedure	Positive Finding
Homan's Sign (30,31)	Patient supine with knees extended and legs resting on the examining table. Examiner elevates symptomatic leg to 45 degrees and squeezes the calf firmly. Calf pressure is maintained while the examiner dorsiflexes the foot	Deep calf or leg pain during this maneuver indicates thrombophlebitis
Moses's (30)	Patient prone. Examiner flexes the patient's knee to 90 degrees. Examiner grasps and squeezes the calf of the symptomatic leg	Pain suggests phlebitis
Buerger's (30,31)	Patient supine. Examiner elevates the patient's leg to 45 degrees while the knee is fully extended. Patient actively dorsiflexes the foot then plantar flexes the foot for at least 2-3 minutes. Patient then sits at the edge of the examining table and dangles the leg	The test is positive if the foot is blanched and the veins are collapsed or it takes more than 1-2 minutes for the circulation to return to the dangling leg

THE KNEE

	Test	Procedure	Positive Finding
Cruciate Ligaments	**Drawer** (32,33)	Patient supine with knee flexed to 90 degrees and hip flexed to 45 degrees. Examiner holds the patient's foot on the table by sitting on it. Examiner places hands around the tibia to ensure that the hamstring muscles are relaxed and draws the tibia forward on the femur. Normal amount of movement is about 6 mm. Next, examiner moves the tibia posteriorly on the femur	Excessive anterior movement of the tibia on the femur indicates potential injury to one or more of the structures which give anterior stability to the knee (i.e. anterior cruciate ligament). Excessive posterior movement of the tibia on the femur indicates potential injury to one or more of the structures which give posterior stability to the knee (i.e. posterior cruciate ligament)
	Lachman's (32)	Patient supine with symptomatic leg beside the examiner. Examiner holds the patient's knee between full extension and 30 degrees of flexion. Examiner stabilizes the patient's femur with one hand, and moves the proximal aspect of the tibia forward with the other hand	Positive sign occurs when there is a mushy end feel when the tibia is moved forward on the femur and the infrapatellar tendon slope disappears. Sign indicates potential damage to the anterior cruciate ligament, the posterior oblique ligament or the arcuate-popliteus complex
	Slocum's (32,33)	Patient seated with knees flexed and hanging over the examination table. Examiner internally or externally rotates the foot and applies an anterior force to the tibia to test anterior rotary stability or posterior force to test posterior rotary stability	Examiner should note whether the movement is excessive on the medial or lateral side of the knee compared to the normal knee. Excessive movement indicates cruciate ligament instability. Other structures that give stability to the knee may be involved **NOTE**: *If the anterior drawer sign is positive while the patient is in this position, it is likely that the lateral capsule or lateral collateral ligament is also damaged*
Collateral Ligaments	**Abduction/valgus Stress** (32,33)	Patient supine with knees extended. Examiner stands on ipsilateral side and places one hand against the lateral aspect of the patient's knee at the joint line. With the other hand gripping the ankle, the examiner draws the leg laterally to open the medial side of the knee joint	Production or increase of pain, especially above, below or at the joint line suggests medial collateral ligament injury. Other structures that give stability to the knee may be involved
	Adduction/varus Stress (32,33)	Patient supine with knees extended. Examiner stands on the ipsilateral side and places one hand against the medial aspect of the patient's knee at the joint line. With the other hand gripping the ankle, the examiner pushes the leg medially, to open the lateral side of the knee joint	Production or increase in pain that is above, below or at the joint line is evidence of lateral collateral ligament injury. Other structures that give stability to the knee may be involved
	Apley's Distraction (32,33)	Patient prone with legs extended. Examiner anchors the patient's thigh to the table by placing a knee in the popliteal space. Examiner then strongly distracts the patient's knee joint by lifting the foot straight up	Pain elicited is significant for non-specific collateral ligament tear or instability

Test		Procedure	Positive Finding
Meniscus	**Apley's Compression** (34)	Patient prone with legs extended and ankles hanging over the table edge. Examiner grasps the foot, extends the leg to 90 degrees then applies strong downward pressure while internally rotating the leg. Repeat the maneuver while the leg is strongly rotated externally	Production of pain is significant for meniscus tear
	McMurray's (34)	Patient supine. Examiner flexes the thigh and leg each to 90 degrees. Examiner places one hand on the knee, the other grasps the patient's heel. Examiner internally rotates the lower leg, then slowly extends the knee while applying valgus pressure to the joint. Examiner then externally rotates the leg, then slowly extends the leg	Test is positive if, at some point in the arc, a painful click or snap is heard. Test is significant for meniscal injury. **NOTE**: *If the click is noted with external rotation, the medial meniscus is involved. If the click is heard with internal rotation, the lateral meniscus is involved*
	Bounce Home (34)	Patient supine. Examiner holds patient's ankle and flexes the patient's knee with the other hand. Examiner releases the knee and allows the leg to extend	If extension is not complete or if it has a rubbery end feel, this indicates a torn meniscus

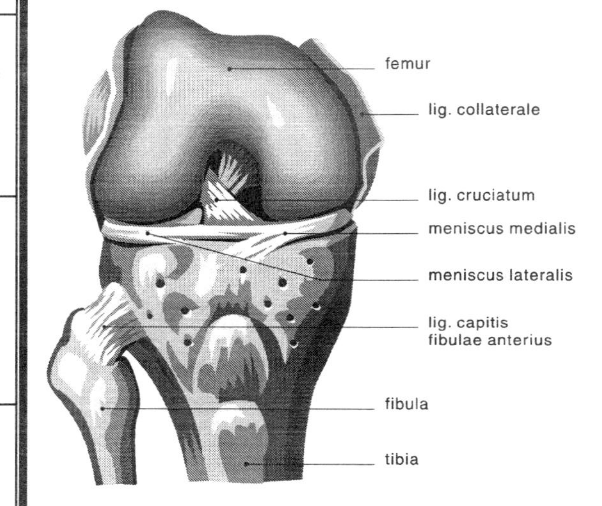

Test		Procedure	Positive Finding
Patella	**Patellar Ballottment/tap** (34,35)	Patient supine with legs extended and relaxed. Examiner applies pressure over the patella	If the patella "floats" this is an indication of significant swelling around the knee
	Patella Grinding (34)	Patient supine with legs extended. Examiner moves the patella medially and laterally while exerting downward pressure	Pain in the knee joint indicates either chondromalacia patella or retropatellar arthritis
	Apprehension (34,35)	Patient seated with knee flexed to about 30 degrees over the examiner's leg. Examiner carefully and slowly pushes the patella laterally	Patient will contract the quadriceps if s/he perceives that the patella will dislocate as the patella is pushed laterally by the examiner. This positive sign indicates vulnerability for recurrent dislocation of the patella
	Dreyer's Sign (34,35)	Patient supine with knee extended. Patient attempts to raise the leg. If the patient cannot raise the leg without pain or difficulty, the examiner applies a forceful, circumferential grasp to the thigh with the hands in order to anchor the quadriceps. The patient attempts to lift the leg	Sign is present when the patient can lift the leg with minimal stress while the examiner anchors the quadriceps. Sign indicates fracture of the patella

Test			Procedure	Positive Finding
Foot	Tarsal Tunnel Syndrome	**Tourniquet** (36,37)	Patient prone with legs extended, feet dangling off the end of the table and calf musculature relaxed. Examiner applies a blood pressure cuff to the leg, near the ankle, above the area of complaint and inflates the cuff to 20 mm above the patient's resting diastolic pressure. Examiner may need to increase pressure to reach blanching of the distal extremity	Foot pain is exacerbated or elicited, indicating compromise of the tarsal tunnel
		Tinel's Foot Sign (36,37)	Patient prone. Examiner percusses the posterior tibial nerve (in the tarsal tunnel) with a reflex hammer	Paresthesia that is elicited distal to the percussion indicates tarsal tunnel syndrome
	Morton's test (36)		Patient supine. Examiner grasps the affected forefoot with one hand and applies transverse pressure to the metatarsal heads	Sharp pain in the foot indicates metatarsalgia or neuroma
	Thompson's (36,37)		Patient prone. Examiner flexes the knee of the symptomatic leg to 90 degrees and grasps the patient's calf with both hands. Examiner squeezes the calf musculature at a point just distal to the widest part of the leg	Foot does not flex; indicates rupture of the Achilles tendon
	Duchenne's Sign (36)		Patient supine with legs extended. Examiner grasps the lower tibia with one hand and with the thumb of the other hand applies pressure to the head of the first metatarsal. Patient plantar flexes the foot as the examiner maintains pressure on the first metatarsal	Sign is present when the medial border of the foot dorsiflexes, the lateral border of the foot plantar flexes, and the arch of the foot disappears. Sign indicates paralysis of the peroneus longus muscle that is due to a lesion of the superficial peroneal nerve
Ankle	**Anterior/Posterior Drawer** (36,37)		Patient seated or supine. Examiner places one hand around the lower tibia, slightly above the ankle mortice joint. Examiner grips the calcaneus and talus in the palm of the other hand and pushes the tibia posteriorly while drawing the calcaneus anteriorly. Next, examiner draws the tibia anteriorly while pushing the calcaneus and talus posteriorly	Sign is present if excessive gapping is detected in the ankle mortice joint, indicating talofibular ligament instability
	Lateral/ Medial Stability (37)		Patient seated or supine. Examiner grasps the patient's foot and passively inverts and everts it	Suspect a tear of the anterior talofibular and/or calcaneofibular ligament if excessive gapping occurs with inversion. Suspect a tear of the deltoid ligament if excessive gapping occurs with eversion

ote

- TARSAL TUNNEL SYNDROME is compression of the posterior tibial nerve beneath the flexor retinaculum of the ankle. The tarsal tunnel contains the flexor digitorum longus tendon, the posterior tibial artery, the posterior tibial nerve, and the flexor hallucis longus tendon behind the medial malleolus of the foot.

Thoracic Outlet Tests

Test	Procedure	Positive Finding
Adson's (38,39)	Patient seated with arms at sides. Examiner slightly abducts the symptomatic arm and palpates the radial pulse. Patient rotates the head toward the affected shoulder and then extends the head while the examiner rotates and extends the shoulder slightly. Examiner instructs patient to take a deep breath and hold it	Disappearance of pulse indicates compression of the vascular component of the neurovascular bundle by the scalenus anticus or a cervical rib. Paresthesias or radiculopathy in the upper extremity indicate compression of neural component of neurovascular bundle. **NOTE**: *If the test is negative, test is repeated with patient turning head away from symptomatic side*
Allen's (38,39)	Patient seated with elbow flexed and forearm supinated. Examiner occludes radial and ulnar arteries, one with each thumb. While the radial and ulnar arteries are occluded, the patient opens and closes the hand repeatedly to force blood out of the tissue. Patient then opens the blanched hand and the examiner releases pressure from one of the arteries and notes the time it takes for the hand to flush with blood. Repeat with other artery	If circulation fails to return within 5 seconds or less, this indicates vascular compromise
Costoclavicular Maneuver (38,39)	Patient seated comfortably with arms at sides. Examiner palpates radial pulse bilaterally then extends the patient's shoulders as the patient flexes the cervical spine	Test is positive if radial pulse of symptomatic arm disappears
Halstead Maneuver (38,39)	Patient seated with arms at sides. Examiner palpates the radial pulse of the symptomatic arm. Examiner applies downward traction on the symptomatic arm while the patient hyperextends the neck	Disappearance of the radial pulse **NOTE**: *If the pulse does not disappear, the test is repeated with the patient's head rotated to the opposite side*
Reverse Bakody Maneuver (38)	Patient seated. Patient abducts and externally rotates the symptomatic shoulder in order to place the hand on top of the head	Increase in pain in this position is a positive sign and indicates interscalene compression of the lower branches of the brachial plexus
Roos' s (38)	While seated, patient abducts both arms to 90 degrees and flexes the elbows to 90 degrees (palms facing forward). Patient repeatedly opens and closes the hands for three minutes	Affected arm weakens
Traction Test (39)	Patient seated with arms at sides. Examiner slightly abducts the symptomatic arm and palpates the radial pulse. While maintaining contact with the pulse with one hand, examiner applies traction from the patient's elbow with the other hand. Perform on both sides	Pulse is decreased or obliterated on one side compared to the other. **NOTE**: *A decreased or obliterated pulse on one side is only diagnostic if the test reveals no change in pulse quality on the opposite side*
Wright's (38,39)	Patient seated with arms at sides. Examiner palpates the radial pulse of the symptomatic arm then abducts the arm to 180 degrees, noting the angle at which the radial pulse diminishes or disappears. This angle is compared with the same test on the opposite side	Decrease or cessation of the radial pulse at a lesser angle on the symptomatic side, the test is positive for hyperabduction thoracic outlet syndromes. **NOTE**: *If the asymptomatic arm demonstrates radial pulse dampening or cessation at the same approximate angle of abduction, the test is not positive*

Thoracic Outlet Syndrome

The following are compression sites for thoracic outlet syndrome:

- Between the anterior and middle scalene muscles;
- In the space between the clavicle and the first rib;
- In the axilla if the axillary artery is compressed by either the pectoralis minor muscle or the coracoid process.

Causes of Thoracic Outlet Syndrome	Orthopedic Tests (41,42)
Loss of arterial supply to the upper extremity	▪ Allen's test ▪ ROOS/ elevated arm stress test
Compression of the neurovascular bundle by the scalene muscles (40) ▪ The lower roots (C8-T1; ulnar nerve) are at a higher risk for compression due to their location in the plexus ▪ Symptoms include: pain in the fingers, hand etc; paresthesia especially in the C8 and T1 dermatomes.	▪ Adson's test – entrapment of the subclavian artery and/or brachial plexus in the scalene triangle ▪ Reversed Adson's to test for compression under scalene medius ▪ Halstead Maneuver
Cervical rib	▪ Traction test ▪ Halstead Maneuver
Costoclavicular compression	▪ Costoclavicular Maneuver ▪ Roos' test
Hyperabduction compression	▪ Wright's test ▪ Reverse Bakody

Note (43)

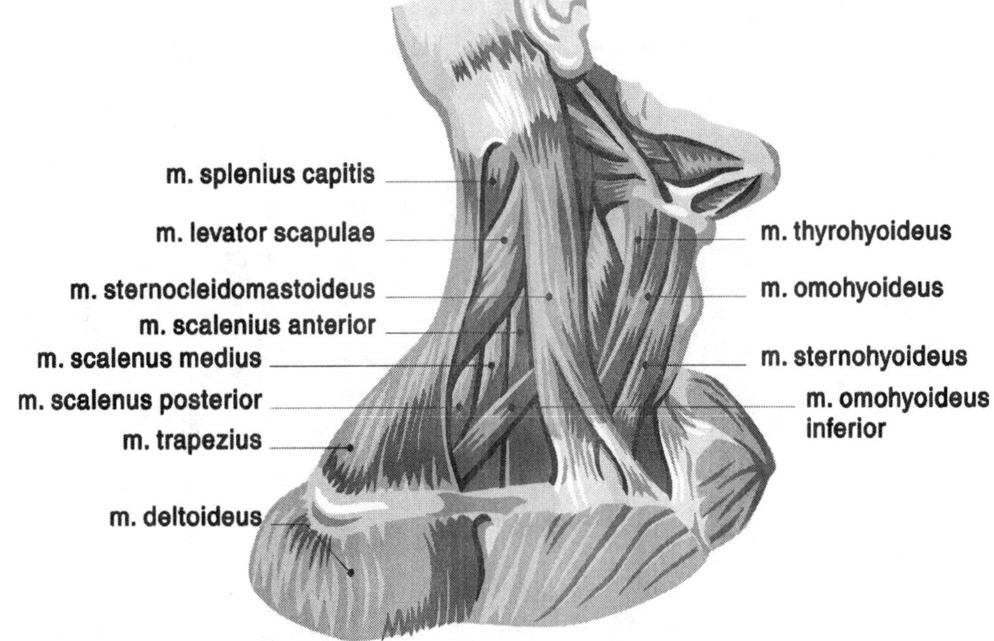

- All three scalene muscles originate from the transverse processes of the cervical vertebrae. The anterior scalene muscle attaches to the transverse processes of C3 to C6 and inserts on the first rib. The medial scalene muscle originates on the transverse processes of C2 to C7 and inserts on the first rib. The anterior and medial scalene muscles forma groove over the first rib for the subclavian artery. The posterior scalene originates from the lowest two or three cervical vertebrae and inserts on the second and sometimes the third rib.

Test		Procedure	Positive Finding
Biceps Tendon	**Yergason's** (44,45)	Patient seated with the elbow of the symptomatic arm flexed. Patient resists examiner's attempts to extend the arm. Examiner resists the patient's attempts to supinate the forearm	Pain develops or is aggravated over the intertubercular groove. Indicates tenosynovitis or involvement of the transverse humeral ligament
	Abbott-Saunder's (44,45)	Patient seated. Examiner fully abducts the patient's arm then externally rotates the arm. While maintaining the externally rotated position, the examiner then lowers the arm to the patient's side	A palpable or audible click or pop indicates a subluxation or dislocation of the biceps tendon
	Speed's (44,45)	Patient seated. Patient flexes and supinates a fully extended arm and the examiner provides resistance while palpating the bicipital groove	Increased tenderness in the bicipital groove
Bursitis	**Dawbarn's Sign** (44,45)	Patient seated with arms at sides. Examiner palpates the symptomatic shoulder and discovers a local, tender pain at the subacromial bursa. While maintaining contact with the painful spot, the examiner abducts the patient's arm with the other hand	Sign is present when the painful spot disappears as the arm is abducted. Abduction causes the deltoid to come between the examiner's palpating hand and the subacromial bursa. Sign is significant for subacromial bursitis
Glenohumeral Dislocation	**Dugas's** (44,45)	Patient seated with arms at sides. Patient places the hand of the symptomatic shoulder on his/her opposite shoulder and attempts to touch the chest with the elbow	If patient cannot touch the chest wall with the elbow, the examiner confirms this by gently applying pressure to the elbow, attempting to approximate it to the chest. Presence of the sign indicates shoulder subluxation or dislocation
	Apprehension (44,45)	Patient seated in front of examiner. Examiner slowly abducts and externally rotates the patient's symptomatic shoulder	Patient will feel apprehension or alarm and will resist this maneuver **NOTE**: *Perform this test slowly to prevent risk of dislocating the patient's shoulder*
Rotator Cuff	**Codman's / Drop Arm** (44,45)	Patient seated in front of examiner. Examiner abducts the patient's symptomatic arm to slightly above 90 degrees. Examiner suddenly removes support, forcing the patient's deltoid to contract. Alternative test: examiner instructs patient to slowly lower the abducted arm and watches for smooth movement as the arm lowers	Shoulder pain and a hunching of the shoulder indicates a positive test and is due to absence of rotator cuff function **NOTE**: *Significant for rotator cuff tear*
	Impingement Sign (44)	Patient seated with arms at sides. Examiner slightly abducts the patient's affected arm and moves it through forward flexion, causing jamming of the greater tuberosity against the anteroinferior acromial surface	Shoulder pain **NOTE**: *Significant for overuse injury to the supraspinatus and sometimes the biceps tendon*
	Supraspinatus Tendinitis (45)	Patient seated. Examiner instructs patient to abduct his/her arm against resistance	Pain over the insertion of the supraspinatus tendon indicates degenerative tendinitis
	Apley's Scratch (44,45)	Patient seated. Patient is instructed to place the hand of the symptomatic arm behind the head and touch near the opposite scapula. Next, patient places hand of symptomatic shoulder behind the back and attempts to touch near the opposite scapula	If either position exacerbates the patient's pain, this indicates degenerative tendinitis of one of the tendons (usually supraspinatus) of the rotator cuff

THE ROTATOR CUFF

☞ Scaption is a term used to describe abduction in the coronal plane in alignment with the orientation of the scapula. This position is commonly recommended as the testing position of muscles rather than the straight coronal abduction movement of abduction.(46)

Muscle	Origin (47)	Insertion (47)	Action (47)	Position for Muscle Testing (48)
Supraspinatus	▪ Supraspinatus fossa of the scapula	▪ Upper part of the greater tubercle of the humerus (travels under the acromion process and the lateral clavicle to get there)	▪ Arm abduction ▪ Prevents downward displacement of the head of the humerus at rest	▪ **"Empty Can" test**: With the thumb pointing down and the arm in scaption (about 90 degrees abduction and 30 degrees anterior from coronal plane), patient resists Dr.'s attempt to push the wrist toward the floor ▪ "Full Can" test: Place patient's arm at 90 degrees abduction in scaption with 45 degrees external humeral rotation
Infraspinatus	▪ Medial two-thirds of the infraspinous fossa below the spine of the scapula and from adjacent fascia	▪ Posterior aspect of the greater tuberosity of the humerus	▪ Externally rotates the humerus with the arm in any position ▪ Helps stabilize the head of the humerus in the glenoid cavity during upward movement of the arm ▪ Upper fibers help to abduct the arm ▪ Lower fibers help to adduct the arm	Tested in combination: A Place the patient's arm at his/her side and internally rotate the humerus 45 degrees B Place the patient's arm at 90 degrees abduction in scaption with the elbow at 90 degrees; there is no humeral rotation
Teres Minor	▪ Dorsal surface of the scapula near its axillary border ▪ Aponeuroses which separate it from the infraspinatus and teres major muscles	▪ Lowermost impression on the greater tubercle of the humerus	▪ Externally rotate the arm at the shoulder in any position ▪ Helps to stabilize the head of the humerus in the glenoid cavity during arm movement ▪ Weak adduction	
Subscapularis	▪ Most of the inner (anterior) surface of the scapula, filling the subscapular fossa	▪ Passes across the front of the shoulder joint via a tendon, which attaches to the lesser tubercle on the anterior aspect of the humerus	▪ Internally rotates the arm ▪ Adducts the arm ▪ Helps hold the head of the humerus in the glenoid fossa ▪ Counteracts the deltoid's tendency to upwardly displace the humerus during abduction	▪ Patient's arm is positioned in scaption with no external rotation and the elbow at 90 degrees; he/she attempts to internally rotate against resistance

ORTHOPEDIC EXAMINATION OF THE SHOULDER

LOCATION OF PAIN IN THE SHOULDER (49)

ote

- With superficial lesions, pain location may help determine the site of the lesion.

Area of Shoulder Pain	Possible Shoulder Lesion
Superior shoulder	▪ Acromioclavicular joint
Lateral shoulder	▪ Supraspinatus ▪ Deltoid ▪ Occassionally teres minor or infraspinatus
Posterior shoulder	▪ Teres minor / infraspinatus ▪ Posterior deltoid ▪ Capsule
Anterior shoulder	▪ Anterolateral – supraspinatus ▪ Anterior – subacromial bursa or biceps ▪ Anteromedial – capsule, subscapularis, pectorals
Deep shoulder	▪ Capsule ▪ Labrum ▪ Sometimes rotator cuff tear
Inferior shoulder	▪ Long head of triceps
Upper medial scapula	▪ Levator scapula syndrome
Superior scapula	▪ Supraspinatus or upper trapezius

Structure	Possible Lesion Site
Coracoid	▪ Pectoralis minor ▪ Short head of the biceps ▪ Coracobrachialis ▪ Coracoacromial ligament ▪ Coracohumeral ligament
Between coracoid and AC joint	▪ Coracoacromial ligament
Lesser tuberosity	▪ Subscapularis
Greater tuberosity	▪ Anterior: supraspinatus ▪ Posterior: infraspinatus / teres minor
Bicipital groove	▪ Long head of biceps ▪ Latissimus dorsi ▪ Pectoralis major

ote (50)

- Before beginning orthopedic tests, rule out serious damage due to trauma or suspicious history.
- Many orthopedic tests may not be possible if the patient has a limited range of motion due to pain.
- Orthopedic tests can be used to classify shoulder injuries into one of two categories:
    - I. Instability
    - II. Impingement. Instability and impingement may occur at the same time.

I *Instability Tests (51)*

The following orthopedic and muscle tests are part of the protocol of shoulder evaluation taught by Dale J. Buchberger, DC, DACBSP at New York Chiropractic College since January 1997.

Category	Dysfunction	Test			Positive Findings
Load and Shift Maneuvers	**Anterior instability**	Seated	**Drawer tests**	▪ Patient is forward flexed with elbow at side ▪ Dr. stabilizes the spine of the scapula and coracoid with one hand ▪ The other hand pushes and pulls the humerus anterior, posterior and inferior	▪ Laxity in one direction or multidirectional instability
	Posterior instability				
	Inferior instability				

	Category	Patient Position	Description of the Test	Positive Findings
Posterior instability	**Push / pull test**	Supine	▪ Flex patient's elbow to 90 degrees ▪ Externally rotate and abduct the patient's arm to 90 degrees ▪ Dr. pulls on the wrist to distract the shoulder while the other hand pushes posteriorly at the proximal humerus	▪ Subluxation may occur ▪ As the arm is taken out of horizontal adduction into neutral, the head may slip back into place
	Jerk test (Seated Norwood test)	Seated	▪ The patient's arm is forward flexed to 90 degrees with the elbow bent 90 degrees. ▪ Dr. directs a force from P to A through the shoulder ▪ While maintaining the posterior load, the Dr. horizontally adducts the arm	▪ Subluxation or dislocation is likely ▪ Apprehension is less likely
Protzman test For anterior instability		Seated	▪ Abduct and support the patient's shoulder to 90 degrees of abduction ▪ Dr. pushes the posterior humeral head anteriorly while the other hand palpates for anterior movement	▪ Anterior movement
Feagan test for inferior and multidirctional instability		Seated	▪ Dr. abducts the patient's shoulder to 90 degrees and rests it on Dr.'s shoulder ▪ Dr. uses both hands to push down on the proximal humerus	▪ Reproduction of subluxation or ▪ Palpable bounce

Test	Description of the Test			Positive Finding
Apprehension Test for instability	**Part I: Seated exam:**		▪ Arm at side and elbow at 90 degrees flexion ▪ Apply passive external rotation at the following angles: 0 degrees of abduction, 45 degrees of abduction, 90 degrees of abduction, 120 degrees of abduction while applying P to A pressure at the posterior glenohumeral joint	▪ Patient experiences sense of apprehension that shoulder will slip out of place (dislocate) ▪ Reproduction of pain
	Part II: Supine exam *Bring about external rotation with various contact points*	**Crank test**	▪ Patient supine with arm at 90 degrees of abduction and elbow flexed to 90 degrees ▪ Dr. uses the patient's elbow and wrist to passively externally rotate the humeral head	
		Fulcrum test	▪ Same patient position as above ▪ Dr. externally rotates the humerus by using the posterior shoulder as the fulcrum	
		Rowe test	▪ Patient supine with arm at 90 degrees of abduction, elbow at 90 degrees flexion, and patient's hand under his/her head ▪ Dr. uses posterior shoulder as a fulcrum to apply P to A pressure on the posterior glenohumeral joint with the fingers	

Category	Patient Position	Description of the Test	Positive Findings
Relocation Test *Follows positive apprehension test* *Can be performed at any phase of the supine apprehension test that is painful or produces apprehension*	Supine *Determines whether external stability provided by the Dr. alleviates sense of apprehension or pain*	▪ Patient's shoulder at 90 degrees of abduction ▪ Dr. externally rotates the patient's shoulder while applying an A to P force to the proximal humerus (creating the opposite humeral head movement of the apprehension test)	▪ Relief of pain or apprehension

<table>
<tr><th>Category</th><th>Test</th><th colspan="2">Description of the Test</th><th colspan="2">Positive Findings</th></tr>
<tr><td rowspan="3">Glenoid Labrum Signs / Tests
Usually associated with damage to the capsule</td><td>Clunk Test(54)</td><td>Supine</td><td>▪ Abduct the shoulder to 120 degrees or more
▪ Dr. applies an A to P force to the humeral head while circumducting and/or rotating the shoulder</td><td rowspan="2">Both tests should be performed several times</td><td>▪ A clunk or click is felt by the patient, usually deep in the shoulder
▪ Often there is a painful catch before the clunk sensation</td></tr>
<tr><td>Kocher Maneuver (54)</td><td>Seated</td><td>▪ Dr. distracts the patient's arm from the bent elbow while maintaining slight external rotation and abduction
▪ Dr. then passively adducts the arm at the elbow followed by internal rotation</td><td>▪ A clunk or click is often felt in the presence of a glenoid labrum tear</td></tr>
<tr><td>Superior Labrum A to P (SLAP) test (55)</td><td>Seated</td><td>▪ Patient's shoulder is abducted and externally rotated (palm up) with elbow extended
▪ Downward pressure is applied to the proximal forearm as the patient resists</td><td colspan="2">▪ Reproduction of symptoms
▪ Snapping, clicking or giving way secondary to pain</td></tr>
</table>

II Impingement Tests

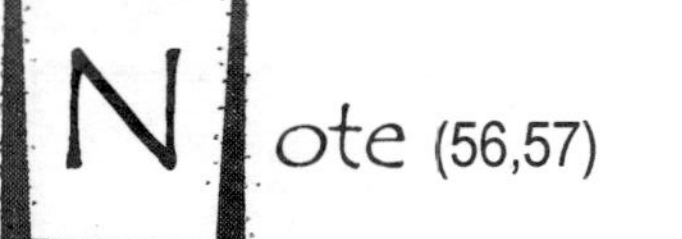

ote (56,57)

- The subacromial space or arch is bordered by the acromion and coracoacromial ligament anterosuperiorly and the superior aspect of the humeral head inferiorly. It contains the tendons of the rotator cuff and biceps and the subacromial bursa.
- The coracoacromial arch is formed by the coracoacromial ligament. It creates a functional space that is occupied by the tendons of the rotator cuff, biceps, and the subdeltoid bursa.
- Impingement occurs against the anterior edge and undersurface of the anterior third of the acromion, the coracoacromial ligament, and sometimes the acromioclavicular joint.
- Impingement is increased by internal rotation of the humerus, which jams the greater tuberosity under the coracoacromial arch.

Category	Description of the Test		Positive Findings
Painful Arc (58)	Seated	▪ Passively or actively abduct the arm through a range of no abduction to maximal abduction	▪ Pain through a range of 70 to 110 degrees with less or no pain before and after this range
Neer's Test (58)	Seated	▪ Passively flex and externally rotate the patient's arm with elbow extended to end range while attempting to jam the humerus up under the acromial arch	▪ Pain, primarily at the end range ▪ Indicates **subacromial impingement**
Hawkins-Kennedy Test (58)	Seated	▪ Patient's arm is forward flexed to 90 degrees with the elbow bent to 90 degrees and internally rotated so that it is parallel with the floor. Dr. supports the arm at the elbow with one hand while the other applies more internal rotation by pressure on the patient's dorsal wrist	▪ End-range pain felt anteriorly ▪ Indicates **coracoacromial impingement**

Orthopedic Tests that Focus on Specific Muscles

ote (59)

- Location of a shoulder lesion can be narrowed down further with specific muscle testing.
- Scaption is a term used to describe abduction in the coronal plane in alignment with the orientation of the scapula. This position is commonly recommended as the testing position of muscles rather than the straight coronal abduction movement of abduction.

Muscle(s)	Description of the Test			Positive Findings
Supraspinatus / infraspinatus tendonitis	**Jobe's test** (60)	Seated	▪ Patient's arm is forward flexed to 90 degrees with the elbow bent to 90 degrees and internally rotated so that the forearm is parallel with the floor ▪ Dr. applies downward pressure over the dorsal wrist as the patient resists	▪ Reproduction of symptoms
Biceps	**Speed's test** (61)	Seated	▪ Patient's shoulder is forward flexed to 90 degrees with elbow extended and forearm supinated ▪ Dr. attempts to further extend the forearm (push the extended arm down to the floor) while patient resists	▪ Reproduction of symptoms due to impingement
	Transverse humeral ligament test (62)	Seated	▪ Dr. subluxates the patient's biceps tendon from the bicipital groove by abducting the arm 90 degrees, flexing the elbow 90 degrees and bringing the shoulder into external rotation. The Dr. palpates the biceps tendon and internally rotates the shoulder, which replaces the biceps tendon in the groove	▪ Palpable clicking, pain or movement of the biceps tendon

Category	Description of the Test			Positive Findings
Subscapularis	**Lift off test** (63)	Seated	▪ Patient actively places the back of his or her hand against the small of the back, with the forearm parallel to the floor ▪ Ask the patient to actively lift the forearm straight off his or her back, keeping the forearm parallel to the floor	▪ Ability to lift off with pain indicates tendonitis or dysfunction ▪ Inability to lift off indicates disruption or the subscapularis tendon
	Gerber push-off test (64)	Seated	▪ Patient actively places the back of his or her hand against the small of the back, with the forearm parallel to the floor ▪ Patient actively internally and externally rotates the forearm while Dr. resists	▪ Pain indicates subscapularis strain/ tendonitis/ dysfunction, rupture, or capsular tear
Scapulo-humeral coordination	**Field goal test** (64)	Prone	▪ Place patient's shoulders at 90 degrees of abduction and 90 degrees of flexion, parallel to the floor ▪ In sequence, the patient actively retracts the scapula together, then horizontally extends the arms then externally rotates the shoulders	▪ Inability to retract the scapula fully or to perform the three required motions in sequence ▪ Pain at any point during the test

ote

- The AC joint is stressed in most full end-range positions of elevation, forward flexion and horizontal adduction.

THE ACROMIOCLAVICULAR JOINT (65)

Category	Description of the Test			Positive Findings
AC Joint	**Shultz test**	Seated	▪ Patient's arm is at his or her side with elbow flexed to 90 degrees and Dr. supporting the elbow ▪ Dr. directs pressure upward along the long axis of the humerus while stabilizing the AC joint with the other hand	▪ Movement with second or third degree AC separation ▪ Pain, especially with osteoarthritis
	Squeeze test *Follows Neer test*	Seated	▪ Dr.'s hands are cupped over the involved shoulder, with one hand over the spine of the scapula and the other over the clavicle, and squeezed together to approximate the AC joint	▪ Pain may indicate acute inflammation or chronic osteoarthritis ▪ Unusual movement or relief of symptoms may indicate an acute or chronic separation
	Adduction stress test (crossover test)	Seated	▪ Dr. horizontally adducts the patient's arm to end range	▪ Compression causes pain in the area of the AC joint

	Test	Procedure	Positive Finding
Lateral Epicondylitis	**Cozen's** (66,67)	Patient seated with affected elbow slightly flexed and pronated and hand in a fist. Patient actively dorsiflexes the hand and wrist. Examiner applies steady pressure against dorsum of the patient's hand in an attempt to flex it while patient resists	Pain elicited at or near the lateral epicondyle
	Mill's (66)	Patient seated while examiner passively and fully flexes the elbow, wrist and fingers in supination in that order. Examiner then maintains wrist and finger flexion while extending the patient's elbow. At maximum elbow extension, the wrist and fingers remain flexed and the forearm is pronated	Pain at the lateral epicondyle **NOTE**: *Perform all test movements in a smooth, continuous manner*
Medial Epicondylitis	**Golfer's elbow** (66)	Patient seated with elbow slightly flexed. The hand and wrist are supinated. Examiner applies steady pressure to the hand in an attempt to extend the elbow while patient resists this movement	Pain elicited at or near the medial epicondyle
Neuritis / Neuroma	**Tinel's Sign** (66,67)	Patient seated with elbow flexed to 90 degrees. Examiner percusses the radial nerve at the lateral epicondylar groove. Repeat the same procedure with the ulnar nerve in the medial epicondylar groove	Tingling that radiates down the lateral forearm indicates regeneration associated with superficial radial nerve palsy. Pain radiating down the lateral forearm is associated with injury and superficial radial nerve degeneration
Ligaments	**Ligamentous Instability** (66,67)	Patient seated with elbow flexed 20 to 30 degrees and hand and arm in supination. Examiner stabilizes the elbow while applying abduction (valgus) force to the distal forearm. Procedure is repeated with adduction (varus) force applied to the distal forearm	Pain with either abduction or adduction indicates sprain **NOTE**: *Abduction force tests the medial collateral ligaments. Adduction tests the lateral collateral ligaments*

ote

- The common extensor tendon of the lateral epicondyle of the humerus includes extensor carpi radialis brevis; extensor digitorum; extensor digiti minimi; and extensor carpi ulnaris. Supinator partially originates from the lateral epicondyle of the humerus, but not from the common extensor tendon.
- The common flexor tendon of the medial epicondyle of the humerus includes pronator teres; flexor carpi radialis; palmaris longus; flexor digitorum superficialis; flexor carpi ulnaris.

Test		Procedure	Positive Finding
Carpal Tunnel	**Tinel's Sign** (68,69)	Examiner slightly dorsiflexes the patient's wrist and hand and percusses the anterior surface of the wrist over the carpal tunnel with a reflex hammer or tuning fork	Tingling along median nerve distribution (first 3 ½ fingers) indicates carpal tunnel syndrome **NOTE**: *Percussion at the Tunnel of Guyon reveals the condition of the ulnar nerve as it passes into the hand*
	Phalen's / Prayer Sign (68,69)	Patient seated with both elbows flexed and arms pronated. Wrists are flexed and the dorsal surfaces of the hands are approximated to each other. The position is maintained for at least 60 seconds. A reversed position for this test is with the patient's wrists extended and the palms of the hands approximated to each other. Maintain this position for 60 seconds	Median nerve paresthesia with the wrists flexed indicates carpal tunnel syndrome due to neural ischemia. Median nerve paresthesia with the wrists extended indicates carpal tunnel syndrome due to neural stretch
	Tourniquet (68)	Examiner occludes the circulation of the extremity manually until the hand is blanched	Arm and hand pain, paresthesia, and muscle weakness appearing in less than 5 minutes indicate arterial insufficiency
Synovitis	**Finkelstein's** (68,69)	Patient seated with elbow flexed and forearm pronated. Examiner tucks the affected thumb into the palm of the patient's hand, and patient makes a fist over the thumb. Examiner moves hand and wrist into sharp ulnar deviation	Pain elicited at the abductor pollicis longus and the extensor pollicis brevis tendons distal to the styloid process indicates stenosing synovitis (de Quervain's disease)
Ulnar Nerve	**Froment's Paper Sign** (68)	Patient's elbow is flexed and the forearm is pronated. Patient abducts the fingers from each other. Examiner places a sheet of paper between any two fingers and the patient adducts the fingers, gripping the paper	Failure to maintain this grip as the examiner tugs on the paper suggests ulnar nerve paralysis
RA	**Bracelet** (68)	Patient seated with elbow flexed. Examiner grasps the affected wrist and applies lateral compression to the distal radius and ulna. While the examiner is applying pressure, the patient attempts to make a fist	Pain indicates rheumatoid arthritis of the wrist. Patient may be able to localize pain, which will intensify when s/he makes a fist
Vascular Occlusion	**Allen's** (68)	Patient seated with elbow flexed and forearm supinated. Examiner occludes radial and ulnar arteries, one with each thumb. While the radial and ulnar arteries are occluded, the patient opens and closes the hand repeatedly to force blood out of the tissue. Patient then opens the blanched hand and the examiner releases pressure from one of the arteries and notes the time it takes for the hand to flush with blood. Repeat with other artery	If circulation fails to return within 5 seconds or less, this indicates vascular compromise

ote

- The Tunnel of Guyon is bordered by the hook of the hamate laterally and the pisiform bone medially. The tunnel transports the ulnar nerve and artery to the hand.

Malingering (70)

Test	Procedure and Explanation	Positive Result
Hoover's Sign	Patient supine with legs extended. Examiner places one hand under the heel of the asymptomatic leg. Patient attempts to lift the symptomatic leg off the table. If the symptomatic leg were organically paralyzed, the patient would press the asymptomatic leg firmly downward when attempting to flex the paralyzed hip. Because the malingerer is not trying, there is no downward pressure placed on the asymptomatic leg.	Counterpressure is absent on the asymptomatic leg
Plantar Flexion	Patient supine. Patient is instructed to raise the extended, affected leg until pain is felt in the low back or in the leg. Examiner notes the angle at which pain occurs. Patient then lowers the leg to the table. Examiner places one hand under the patient's knee and one hand under the ankle and elevates the leg, keeping the knee slightly flexed. The leg is elevated to a point below the production of original pain. Examiner plantar flexes the foot (opposite of Braggard's), which should reduce pain.	Patient reports pain when the foot is plantar flexed by the examiner
Flexed Hip	Patient is supine. Examiner palpates the spinous processes of L5 and S1 with one hand and maintains contact with these landmarks. Examiner passively flexes the knee to 90 degrees and then flexes the hip to 90 while palpating for separation of the L5 and S1 spinouses.	Low back or leg pain is experienced before the L5 and S1 spinouses separate
Axial Loading	Patient is in the standing position. Examiner presses downward on the patient's head with both hands carefully and without disturbing any antalgic posture. The axial loading may elicit pain in the neck, but should not elicit pain in the low back.	Report of low back pain indicates lack of organic basis for low back complaint
Trunk Rotation	Patient stands with arms folded across the chest. Examiner instructs patient to rotate the trunk, while making sure that the pelvis is rotated simultaneously, which prevents movement of the lumbar vertebrae.	Patient reports pain with trunk rotation
Burn's Bench	Examiner instructs patient to kneel on the table or a stool approximately 18 inches from the floor. Examiner then instructs patient to flex the trunk forward and attempt to touch the floor. This maneuver does not affect the lumbar tissues to any significant degree, and patient with low back pain should be able to perform this maneuver.	Patient declines to perform the test and indicates that s/he cannot do it
Flip Sign	Patient supine. Examiner performs a straight leg raise on the symptomatic side, noting the limitation of movement due to pain or muscle spasm. Next, examiner instructs patient to sit at the side of the table, with legs dangling over the edge. The examiner pretends to be examining an uninvolved joint of the symptomatic leg and fully extends the knee, effecting a straight leg raise sciatic stretch maneuver.	The seated straight leg raise sciatic stretch maneuver does not elicit pain
Mannkopf's Sign	Test may be applied to any area of musculoskeletal pain. Examiner palpates patient's resting radial pulse. Examiner then applies firm pressure over the area of pain. The examiner again palpates the patient's radial pulse. If the patient is really experiencing pain, the pulse rate should increase 10 or more beats per minute.	No increase in pulse rate with stimulation of area of complaint
Magnuson's	Patient may be standing or seated. Examiner directs patient to point to the site of low back pain and marks or notes the site. Later in the examination the patient is instructed again to point to the location of pain, which should not have moved.	Patient identifies any site other than the originally identified site of pain

Active Range of Motion
Cervical Spine

ote (71)

- Approximately 50% of head flexion and extension occurs between the occiput and C1. The remaining 50% is relatively evenly distributed throughout the cervical spine from C2 to C7.
- Approximately 50% of head rotation occurs between C1 and C2. The remaining 50% of head rotation is relatively evenly distributed throughout the cervical spine from C3 to C7.
- Lateral bending of the head does not occur as a pure motion; it occurs in conjunction with elements of rotation.

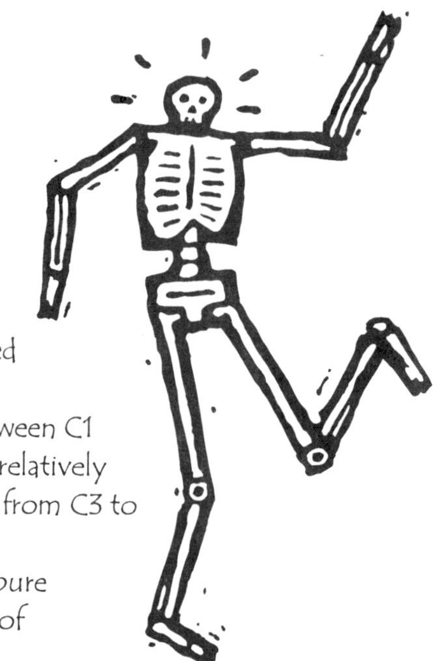

	Hoppenfeld (72)		**Evans** (73)	
Flexion	Look for a smooth arc of motion	Patient should be able to touch chin to chest	**Max.**	80 to 90 degrees
			Min.	40 degrees or less or retained flexion indicates impairment of neck function in activities of daily living (ADLs)
Extension		Patient should be able to look directly at the ceiling above	**Max.**	70 degrees
			Min.	50 degrees or less of retained extension indicates impairment of function in ADLs
Rotation		Patient should be able to almost align chin with shoulder on both sides	**Max.**	70 to 90 degrees to each side
			Min.	60 degrees or less or retained rotation to each side indicates impairment of function in ADLs
Lateral Flexion	Patient should be able to tilt head about 45 degrees toward each shoulder		**Max.**	20 to 45 degrees to the right and left
			Min.	30 degrees or less of retained lateral flexion to each side indicates impairment of function in ADLs

THE THORACIC SPINE

	Range of Motion According to Evans (74)
Flexion	▪ Examiner measures the length of the spine from C7 spinous process to T12 spinous process while the patient is standing and while the patient is bending forward ▪ A minimum of 2.7 cm difference between the two measurements is normal (about 20 to 45 degrees)
Extension	▪ Examiner measures the length of the spine from C7 spinous process to T12 spinous process while the patient is standing and while the patient is bending backward ▪ A difference of 2.5 cm difference between the two measurements is normal (about 25 to 35 degrees)
Rotation	▪ Approximately 35 to 50 degrees to each side
Lateral Flexion	▪ Approximately 20 to 40 degrees to each side

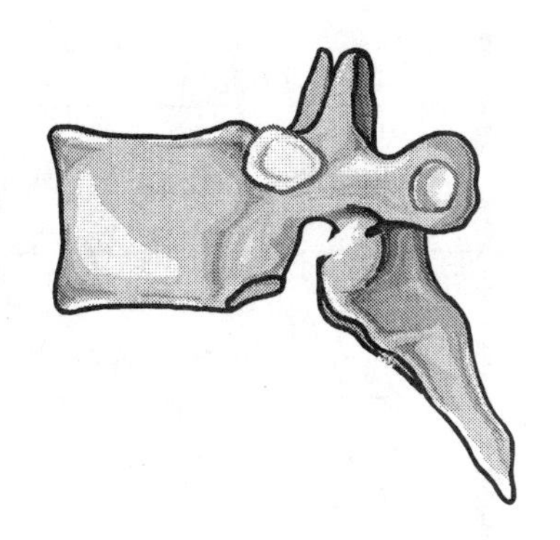

THE LUMBAR SPINE

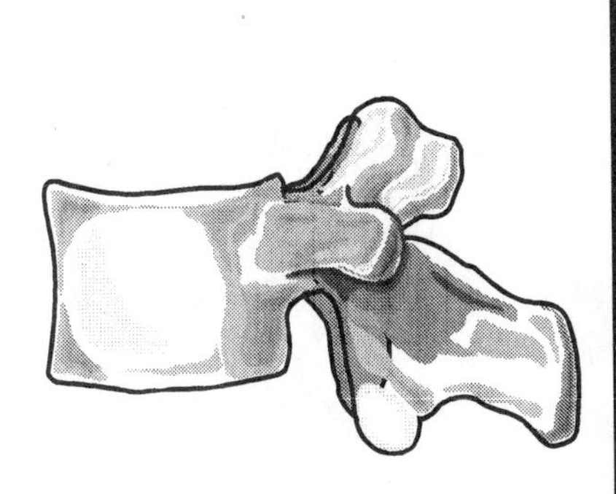

	Range of Motion According to Evans (75)	
Flexion	*Measured with an inclinometer*	▪ 80 degrees is normal ▪ Flexion of 60 degrees or less indicates impairment in activities of daily living (ADLs)
Extension		▪ 35 degrees ▪ Extension of 20 degrees or less indicates impairment in ADLs
Lateral Flexion		▪ 25 degrees to each side ▪ Lateral flexion of 20 degrees or less indicates impairment of function in ADLs
Rotation	*Can't be quantified with an inclinometer*	▪ 3 to 18 degrees ▪ Loss of rotation is not identified as an impairment of the lumbar spine in ADLs

The Shoulder

	Hoppenfeld (76)	**Evans** (77)
Abduction	▪ Approximately 120 degrees without external rotation; 180 degrees with external rotation ▪ Occurs in the glenohumeral joint and scapulothoracic junction in a 2 to 1 ratio	▪ 180 degrees ▪ A retained abduction range of 160 degrees or less indicates impairment of function of activities of daily living (ADLs)
Adduction	▪ 45 degrees	▪ 50 degrees ▪ A retained adduction range of 30 degrees or less indicates impairment of function in ADLs
Extension	▪ 45 degrees (examiner stabilizes scapula)	▪ 50 degrees ▪ A retained extension range of 40 degrees or less indicates impairment of function in ADLs
Flexion	▪ 90 degrees (examiner stabilizes scapula)	▪ The arm can be flexed to 110 degrees at the shoulder and carried up to 180 degrees in circumduction flexion ▪ A retained flexion range of 160 degrees or less indicates impairment of function in ADLs
Internal rotation	▪ 55 degrees	▪ Approximately 90 degrees ▪ A retained internal rotation range of 60 degrees or less indicates impairment of function in ADLs
External rotation	▪ 40 to 45 degrees	▪ Approximately 90 degrees ▪ A retained external rotation range of 60 degrees or less indicates impairment of function in ADLs

When assessing ranges of motion (78)

✓ Make sure you position yourself so that you can best see the motions you are assessing. Stand to the patient's side for flexion and extension assessment.

✓ Give the patient instructions in plain language. Don't say, "Please laterally flex your head."

✓ Use landmarks on the patient's body to compare the ranges of motion from side to side. For thoracic lateral flexion, note how close to the knee the patient's fingertips come on each side.

✓ Make sure the patient performs the active motions correctly. The patient should not lift or shrug his or her shoulders while performing cervical lateral flexion.

PASSIVE RANGE OF MOTION (79)

- Active movements are done before passive movements.
- Any movements that are not painful are done last if possible.
- Passive range of motion is tested to determine the end feel of each movement.
- With passive movement, the joint is put through a range of motion by the examiner while the patient is relaxed. The examiner should evaluate the end feel of the joints in each range of motion.

CLASSIC DESCRIPTIONS OF END FEEL

End Feel		Description
NORMAL	**Bone to bone**	▪ Painless, unyielding sensation ▪ Example: elbow extension
	Soft –tissue approximation	▪ Yielding compression that stops further movement ▪ Examples: elbow and knee flexion
	Tissue stretch *Most common type of end feel*	▪ Hard or firm (springy) type of movement with a slight give and elastic resistance at the end of range of motion ▪ Examples: lateral rotation of the shoulder and knee
ABNORMAL	**Muscle spasm**	▪ Sudden arrest of movement often accompanied by pain ▪ Invoked by movement
	Capsular	▪ Range of movement is reduced ▪ Hard and soft capsular end feels
	Bone to bone	▪ Restriction occurs before the normal end of range of movement would normally occur
	Empty	▪ Considerable pain is produced by movement; pain makes the movement impossible ▪ Examples: subacromial bursitis or neoplasm
	Springy block	▪ Rebound effect; tends to be found in joints with menisci ▪ Example: torn knee meniscus

CAPSULAR VS. NON-CAPSULAR PATTERNS

	Capsular pattern	Non-capsular pattern
Pattern of limitation	▪ Results from a total joint reaction ▪ Each joint has a characteristic pattern of proportional limitation	▪ Limitation exists but does not correspond to the classic capsular pattern for the affected joint ▪ Total capsular reaction is absent
Affected joints	▪ Only joints that are controlled by muscles have a capsular pattern	

Disc Herniations

The Cervical Spine (80)

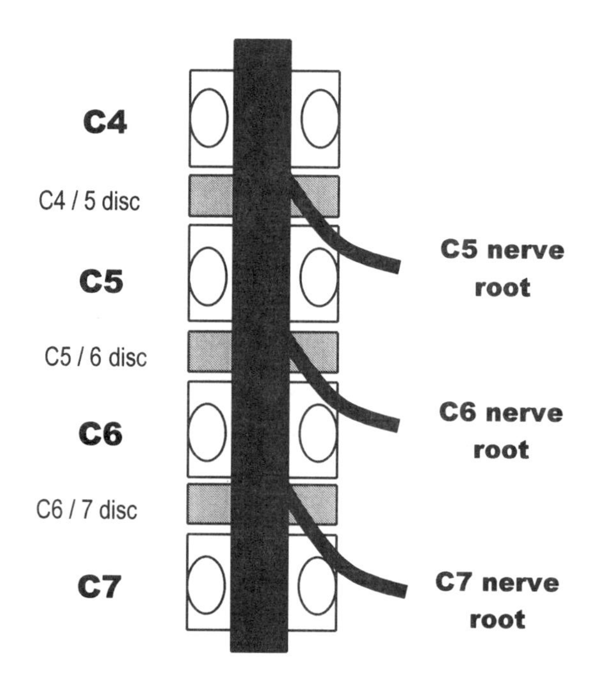

Herniated Disc	Nerve root affected
C4 / 5	C5
C5 / 6 *The most commonly herniated cervical disc*	C6
C6 / 7	C7
C7 / T1	C8

The Lumbar Spine (81)

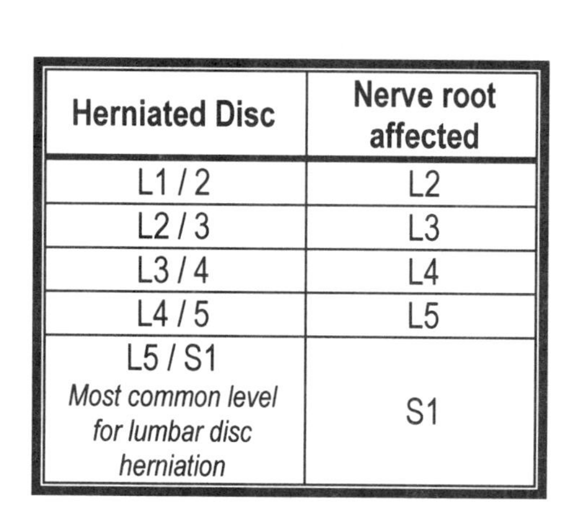

Herniated Disc	Nerve root affected
L1 / 2	L2
L2 / 3	L3
L3 / 4	L4
L4 / 5	L5
L5 / S1 *Most common level for lumbar disc herniation*	S1

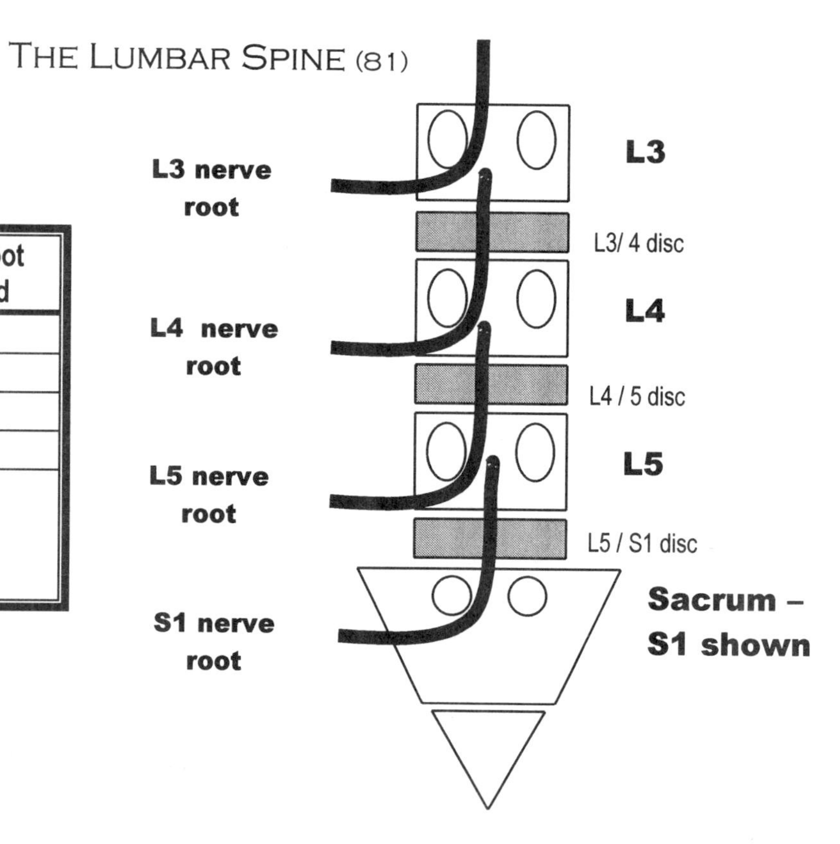

PATHOLOGIC GAITS

For each of the following gaits:

- Know what causes each gait
- Be able to demonstrate each gait

SUMMARY OF GAIT EXAMINATION

Gait	Cause	Level/area
Foot Slap (82)	Weak foot dorsiflexors	L4 / L5
Foot Drop Gait (82)	Weakness of tibialis anterior	L4
Flat Foot Gait (82)	Weakness of gastrocnemius and soleus	S1 / S2
Steppage Gait (82)	Weak ankle dorsiflexors cause the patient to excessively flex the hip in order to clear the floor with the foot	L4 / L5
Peroneal Muscle Weakness (82)	Foot is varus during swing phase	S1
Back Knee Gait (82)	Weak quadriceps	L2, 3, 4
Gluteus Maximus Lurch (82)	Patient thrusts trunk posteriorly in order to maintain hip extension	S1
Circumduction Gait (82)	Hemiplegia or gluteus medius weakness	L5
Gluteus Medius Lurch (82)	Body weight is thrown over the involved hip causing a big swing of the lateral trunk	L5
Scissors Gait (83)	**SPASTIC DIPLEGIA** Patient uses short steps and drags the ball of the foot across the floor. The patient's legs are extended and the thighs cross forward over each other with every step	CNS
Waddling Gait (84)	**MUSCULAR DYSTROPHY** Patient's legs are spread widely apart and waddling develops due to weak gluteal muscles	Muscle
Festination Gait and Retropulsion Gait (85)	**PARKINSON'S DISEASE** Initial steps are short so that the feet barely clear the ground and the soles of the feet scrape the floor. The steps become successively more rapid.	Melanin-containing nerve cells of the brain stem

PALPATION (86,87)

THE UPPER EXTREMITY

Shoulder

- Coracoid process – directly below inferior end of clavicle; pops forward with protraction of the shoulder
- Bicipital groove – between greater and lesser tubercles
- Greater tubercle – inferior to the acromion process' lateral edge
- Lesser tubercle – (externally rotate the humerus to facilitate palpation) anterior to the greater tubercle
- 2nd rib: medial to the superior angle of the scapula
- 7th rib: medial to the inferior angle of the scapula
- Root of the spine of the scapula is on line with spinous process of T3
- Teres minor – along lateral border of scapula
- Rhomboids – along vertebral border of scapula
- AC joint – follow clavical out laterally; have patient flex and extend his or her arm to ensure correct contact
- Acromion process

Elbow

- Medial epicondyle
- Medial supracondylar ridge
- Groove for ulnar nerve
- Trochlea – goes with the ulna
- Olecranon and olecranon fossa
- Ulnar ridge
- Cubital fossa contents from lateral to medial: Brachioradialis M.; Biceps T.; Brachial A.; Median Nerve; Musculocutaneous Nerve; Pronator Teres M.
- Ulnar and radial styloids

Hand and Wrist

- Ulnar styloid
- Radial styloid
- Anatomical snuffbox and tendons: lateral - extensor pollicis brevis and abductor pollicis longus (most lateral); medial - extensor pollicis longus
- Capitate
- Hamate
- Hook of the hamate
- Lunate
- Triquetrum
- Pisiform
- Navicular/Scaphoid – floor of the anatomical snuff box
- Lister's tubercle – follow the third metacarpal ray proximally through the capitate, lunate and then Lister's tubercle

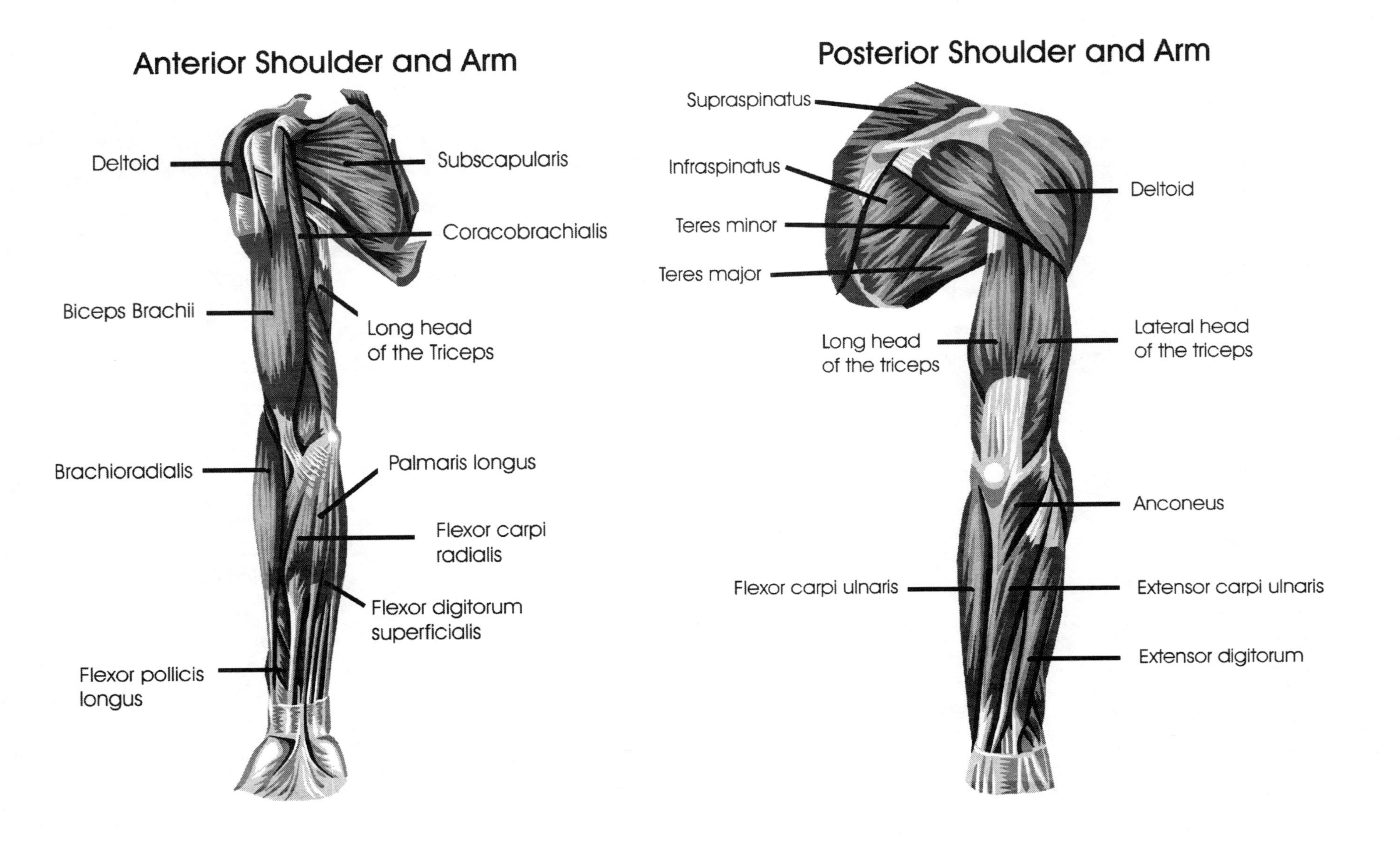
Anterior Shoulder and Arm
Deltoid
Subscapularis
Coracobrachialis
Biceps Brachii
Long head
of the Triceps
Brachioradialis
Palmaris longus
Flexor carpi
radialis
Flexor digitorum
superficialis
Flexor pollicis
longus
Posterior Shoulder and Arm
Supraspinatus
Infraspinatus
Deltoid
Teres minor
Teres major
Long head
of the triceps
Lateral head
of the triceps
Anconeus
Flexor carpi ulnaris
Extensor carpi ulnaris
Extensor digitorum

Anterior Shoulder

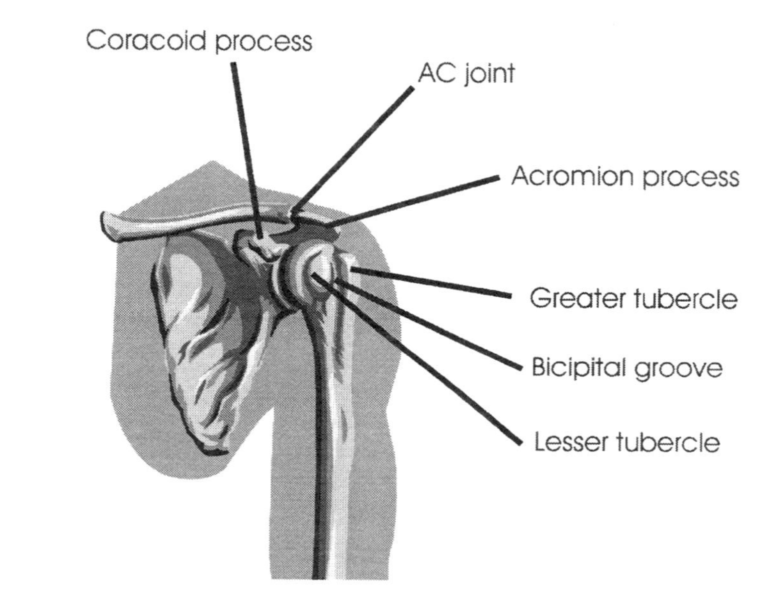

Posterior Shoulder

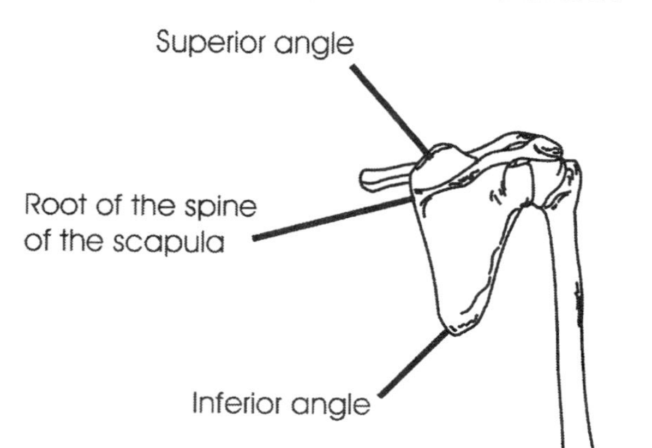

Anterior Elbow

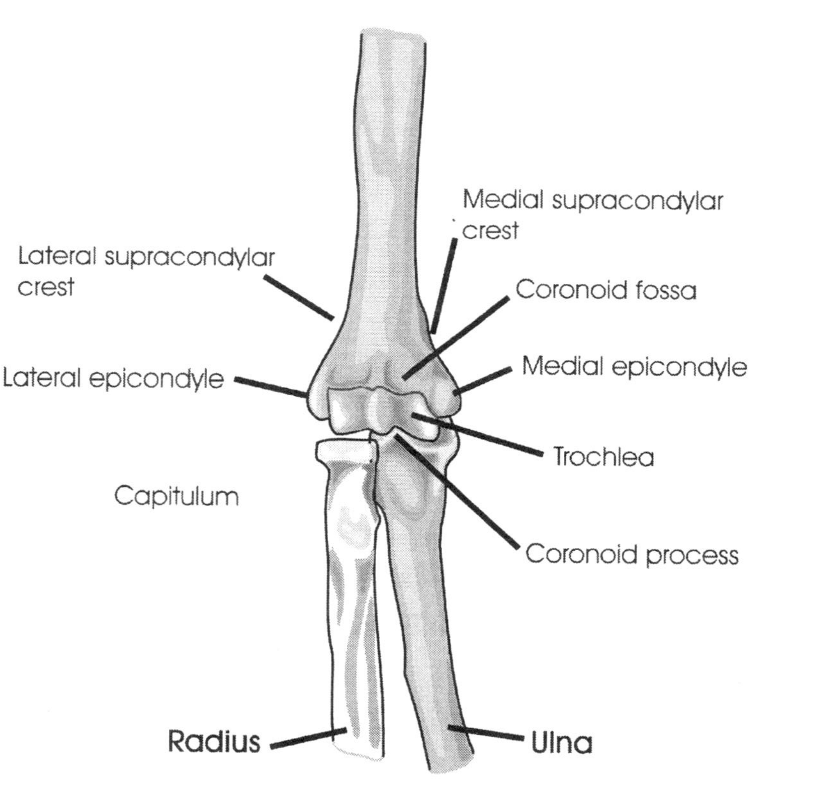

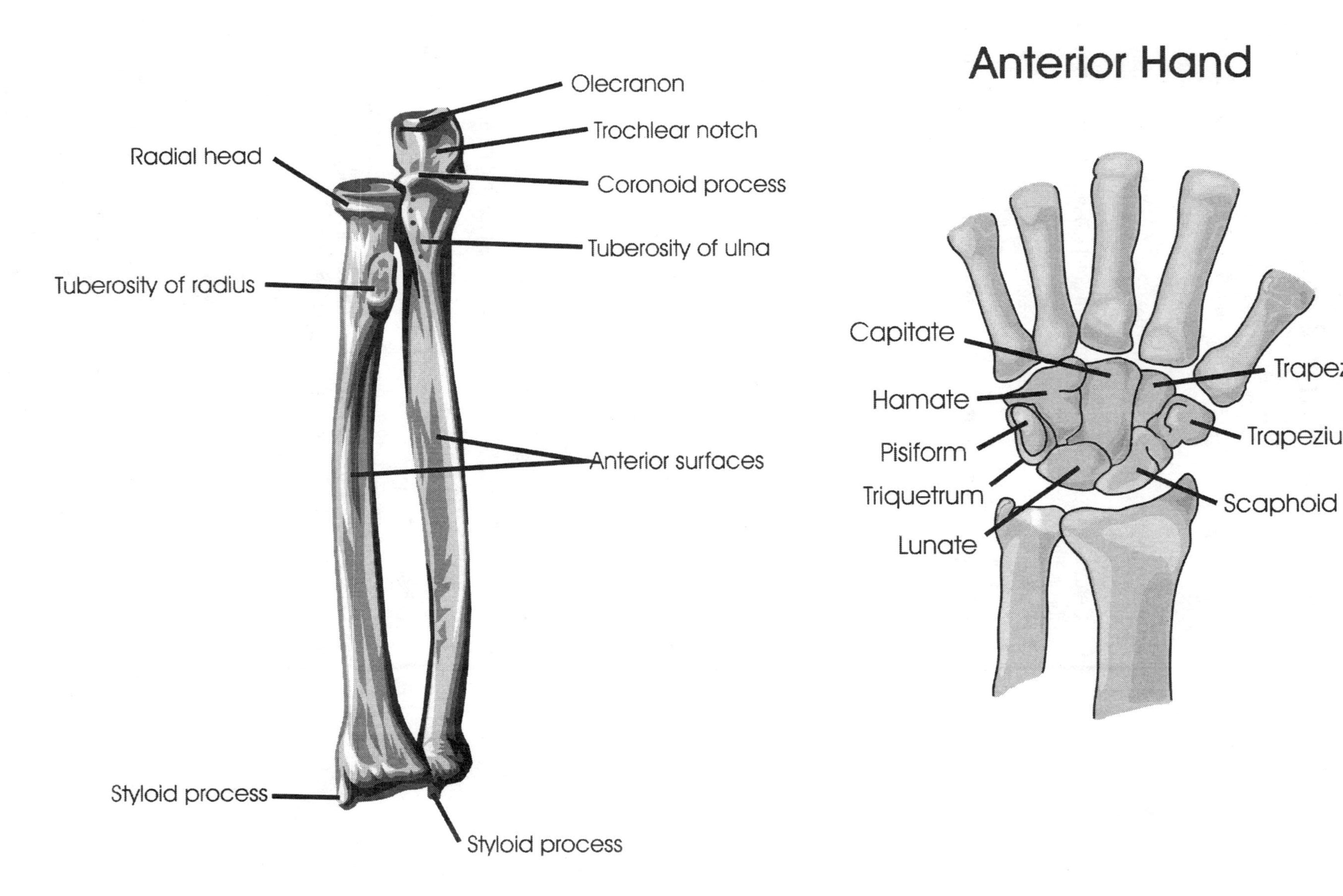
Anterior Radius and Ulna
Olecranon
Trochlear notch
Radial head
Coronoid process
Tuberosity of ulna
Tuberosity of radius
Anterior surfaces
Styloid process
Styloid process
Anterior Hand
Capitate
Trapezoid
Hamate
Trapezium
Pisiform
Triquetrum
Scaphoid
Lunate

THE LOWER EXTREMITY (86,87)

Knee

- Biceps Femoris tendon – lateral knee; drag the heel to pop the tendon out
- Semitendinosus tendon -- medial
- Semimembranosus tendon -- medial
- Tibial plateau
- Gerdy's tubercle – superolateral from tibial tuberosity; the insertion of the iliotibial tract
- Patellar ligament – just below the patella
- Quadriceps femoris tendon – just above patella
- Pes Anserine – sartorius, gracilus, semitendinosus insert here on the posteromedial tibial plateau
- Adductor tubercle – posteromedial portion of the medial femoral epicondyle
- Structures in the popliteal fossa from superficial to deep: posterior tibial nerve; popliteal vein; popliteal artery
- Common Peroneal Nerve –around the head of the fibula
- Coronary Ligament – around the medial meniscus

Foot

- Sinus Tarsi – soft tissue depression just anterior to the lateral malleolus
- 1st, 2nd, and 3rd cuneiforms
- Dome of the Talus -- plantar flex the foot to expose more of it
- Medial tubercle of talus – immediately posterior to the distal end of the medial malleolus
- Navicular
- Navicular Tubercle – first bony prominence proximal from the first cuneiform
- Sustentaculum Tali – one finger's width below the medial malleolus on calcaneus
- Deltoid Ligament – medial; connects tibia to talus and calcaneus
- Cuboid – follow the 4th and 5th metatarsals proximally
- Peroneal Tubercle – on the lateral calcaneus

Muscles of the Anterior and Posterior Thigh

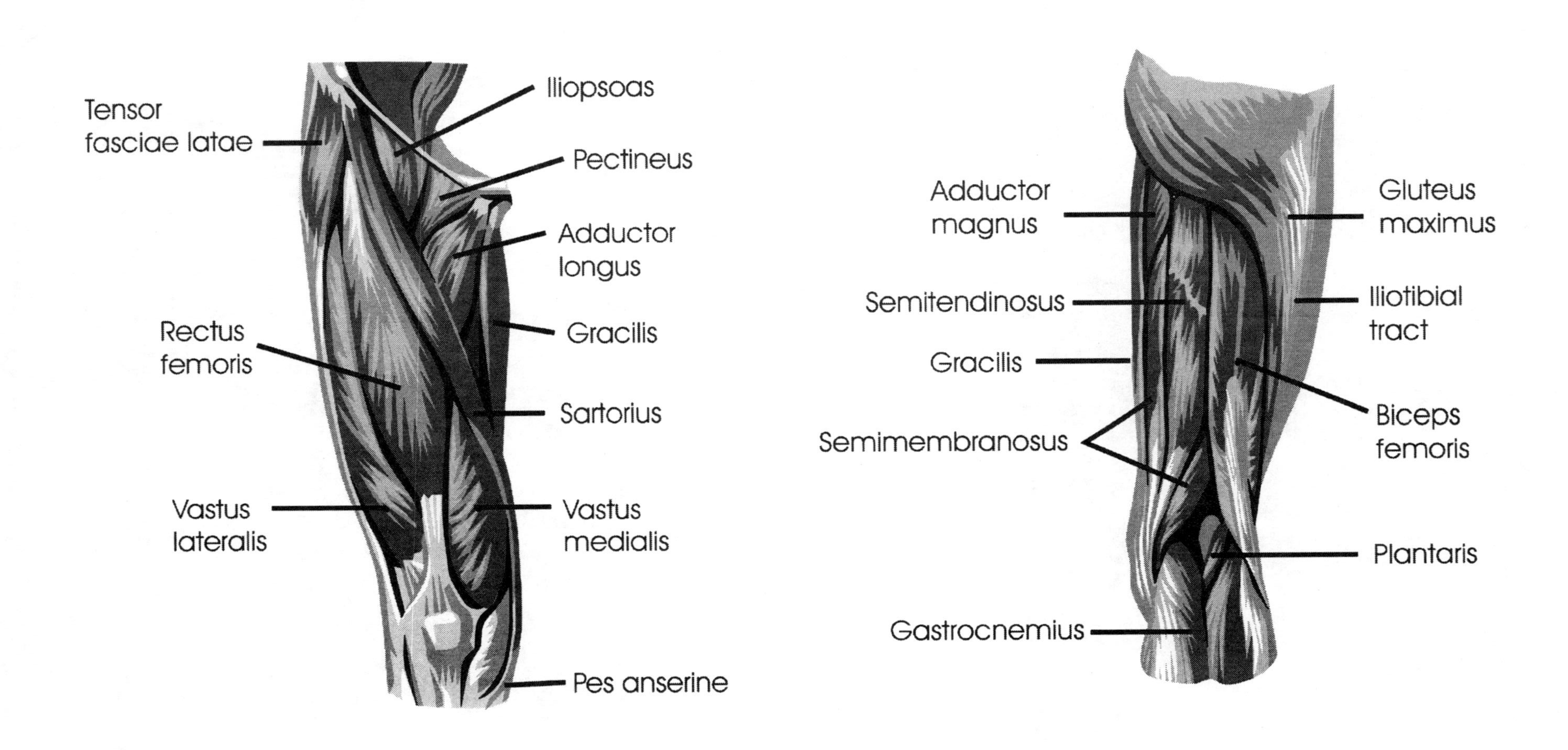

Muscles of the Anterior and Posterior Leg

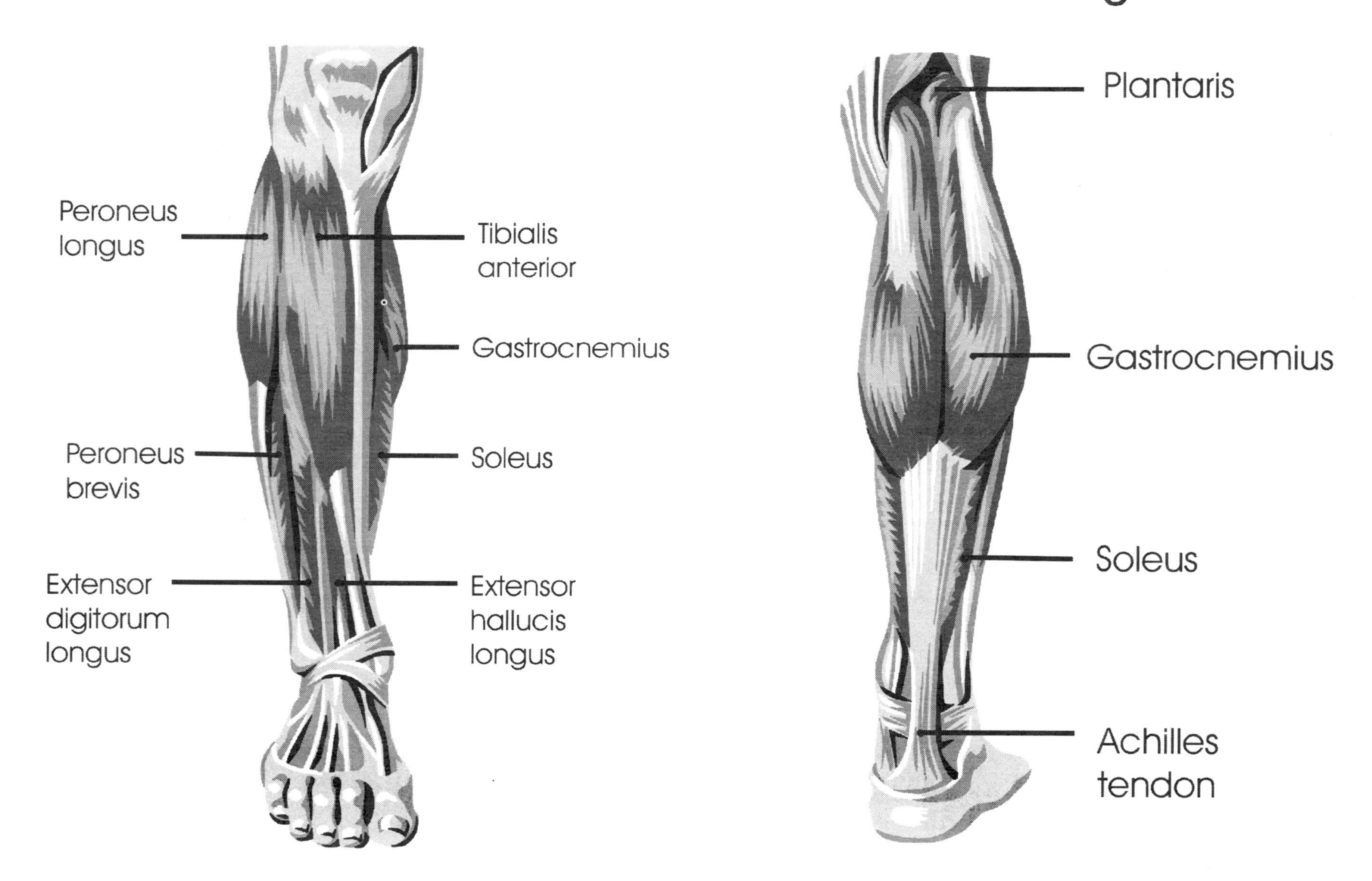

Anterior Views of the Femur, Tibia and Fibula

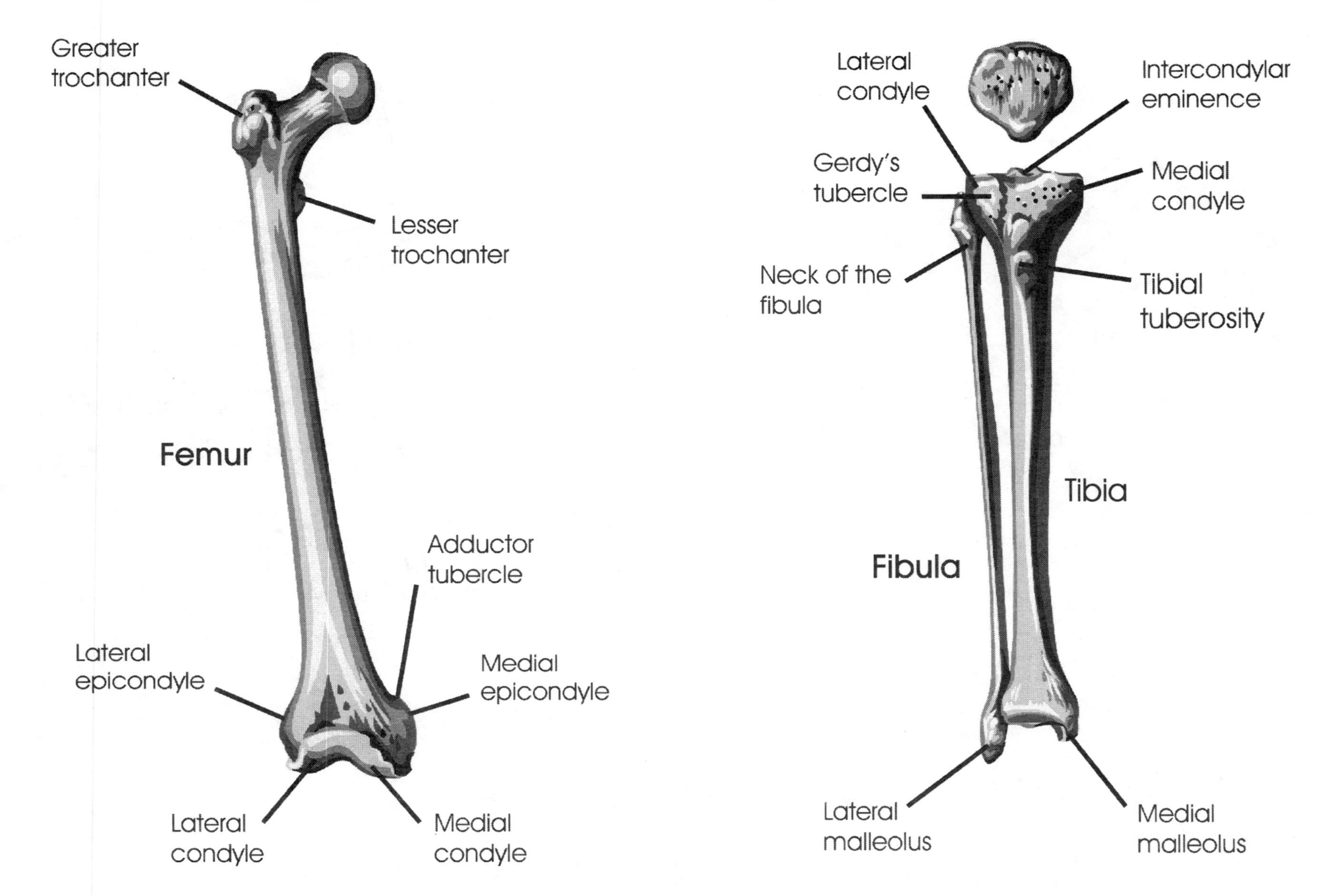

Dorsal and Lateral Views of the Foot

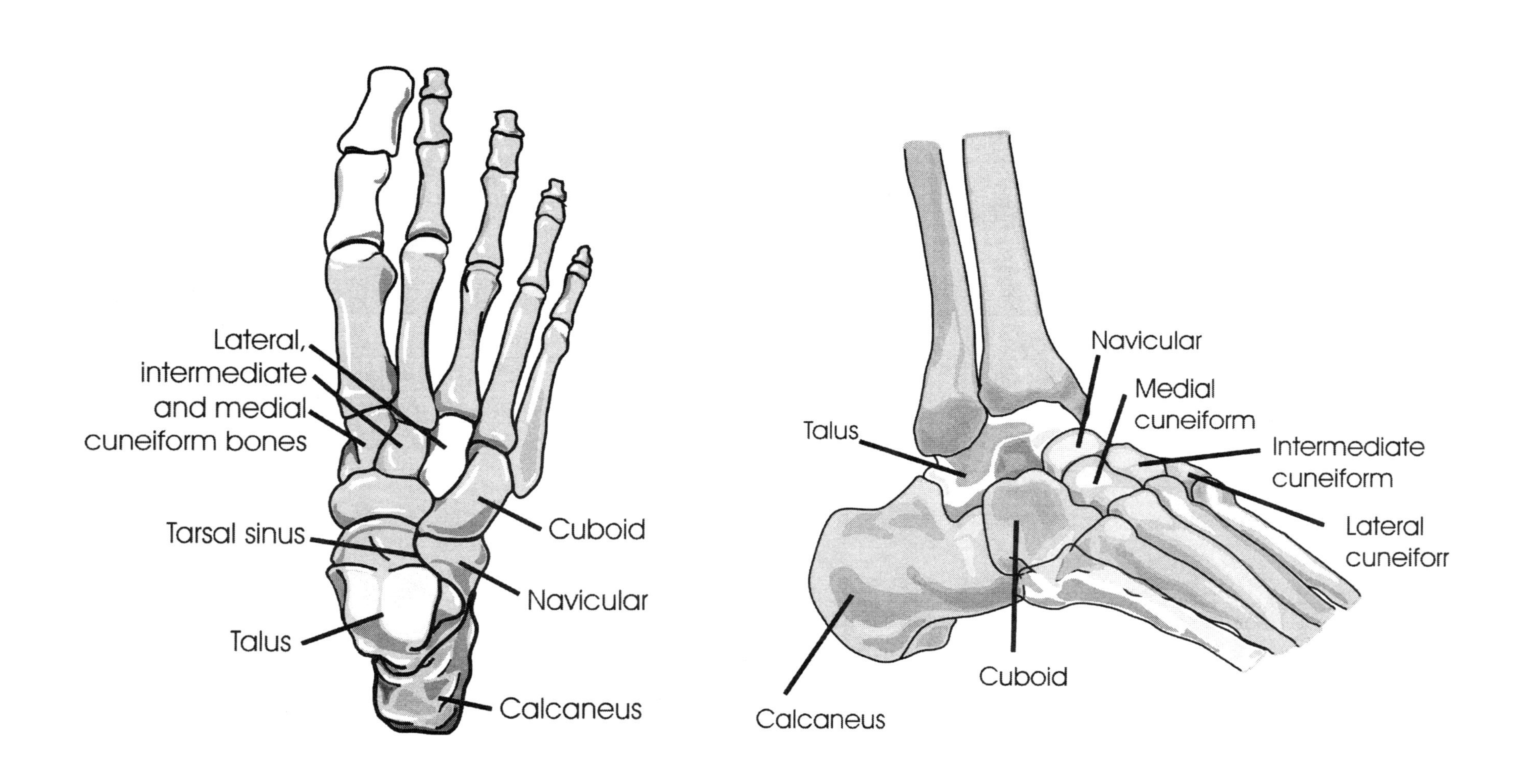

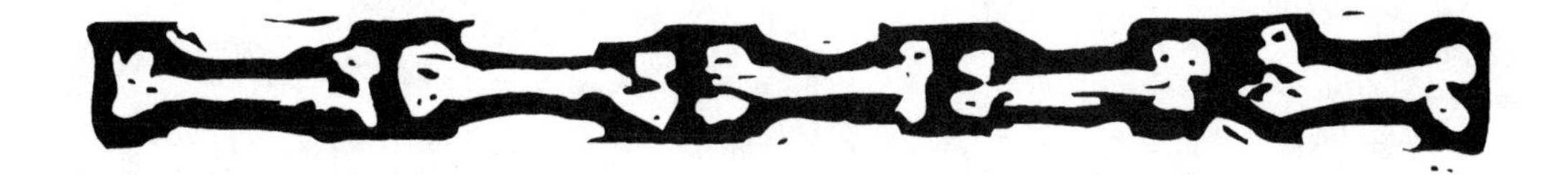

REFERENCES

1 Evans RC. Illustrated Essentials in Orthopedic Physical Assessment. St. Louis: Mosby, 1994: 22-23, 30-31, 34-35, 36-37, 44-45, 48-49, 50-51, 62-63, 64-65, 70-71.

2 Cipriano JJ. Photographic Manual of Regional Orthopaedic and Neurological Tests. 2nd ed. Baltimore: Williams & Wilkins, 1991: 21, 30-33.

3 Evans RC. Illustrated Essentials in Orthopedic Physical Assessment. St. Louis: Mosby, 1994: 26-27, 46-47, 52-61, 288-289.

4 Cipriano JJ. Photographic Manual of Regional Orthopaedic and Neurological Tests. 2nd ed. Baltimore: Williams & Wilkins, 1991: 18-20, 32, 198, 199.

5 Isselbacher KJ, Braunwald E, Wilson JD, Martin JB, Fauci AS, Kasper DL. Harrison's Principles of Internal Medicine. 13th ed. New York: McGraw-Hill, Inc., 1994: 2296.

6 Evans RC. Illustrated Essentials in Orthopedic Physical Assessment. St. Louis: Mosby, 1994: 24-25, 32-33, 38-39, 42-43, 66-69, 72-73.

7 Cipriano JJ. Photographic Manual of Regional Orthopaedic and Neurological Tests. 2nd ed. Baltimore: Williams & Wilkins, 1991: 12-17.

8 Waxman SG, deGroot J. Correlative Neuroanatomy. 22nd ed. Connecticut: Appleton & Lange, 1995: 172.

9 Evans RC. Illustrated Essentials in Orthopedic Physical Assessment. St. Louis: Mosby, 1994: 218-219, 224-227, 232-233, 236-241.

10 Cipriano JJ. Photographic Manual of Regional Orthopaedic and Neurological Tests. 2nd ed. Baltimore: Williams & Wilkins, 1991: 41, 43-45.

11 Evans RC. Illustrated Essentials in Orthopedic Physical Assessment. St. Louis: Mosby, 1994: 258-59, 262-265, 272-279, 592-593.

12 Cipriano JJ. Photographic Manual of Regional Orthopaedic and Neurological Tests. 2nd ed. Baltimore: Williams & Wilkins, 1991: 59, 66.

13 Evans RC. Illustrated Essentials in Orthopedic Physical Assessment. St. Louis: Mosby, 1994: 284-287, 290-293, 296-297, 302-307.

14 Cipriano JJ. Photographic Manual of Regional Orthopaedic and Neurological Tests. 2nd ed. Baltimore: Williams & Wilkins, 1991: 57, 68.

15 Evans RC. Illustrated Essentials in Orthopedic Physical Assessment. St. Louis: Mosby, 1994: 30-31, 50-51, 70-71, 312-315, 318-323, 328-329, 334-335, 338-339.

16 Cipriano JJ. Photographic Manual of Regional Orthopaedic and Neurological Tests. 2nd ed. Baltimore: Williams & Wilkins, 1991: 21, 55, 60, 65, 70.

17 Mazion JM. Illustrated Reference Manual of Ortho/Neuro/Physio Clinical Diagnostic Techniques. 4th ed. Arizona: Imperial Litho/graphics, 1980: 476.

18 Evans RC. Illustrated Essentials in Orthopedic Physical Assessment. St. Louis: Mosby, 1994: 268-269, 276-277, 336-337.

19 Cox JM. Low Back Pain: Mechanism, Diagnosis, and Treatment. 5th ed. Baltimore: Williams & Wilkins, 1990: 381-382.

20 Cox JM. Low Back Pain: Mechanism, Diagnosis, and Treatment. 5th ed. Baltimore: Williams & Wilkins, 1990: 380.

21 Cipriano JJ. Photographic Manual of Regional Orthopaedic and Neurological Tests. 2nd ed. Baltimore: Williams & Wilkins, 1991: 56.

22 Evans RC. Illustrated Essentials in Orthopedic Physical Assessment. St. Louis: Mosby, 1994: 350-355, 358-363, 594.

23 Cipriano JJ. Photographic Manual of Regional Orthopaedic and Neurological Tests. 2nd ed. Baltimore: Williams & Wilkins, 1991: 71, 72, 79, 81.

24 Evans RC. Illustrated Essentials in Orthopedic Physical Assessment. St. Louis: Mosby, 1994: 316-317, 366-369, 376-381.

25 Cipriano JJ. Photographic Manual of Regional Orthopaedic and Neurological Tests. 2nd ed. Baltimore: Williams & Wilkins, 1991: 73, 77, 78, 80.
26 Evans RC. Illustrated Essentials in Orthopedic Physical Assessment. St. Louis: Mosby, 1994: 396-97, 402-403, 412-413, 414-415, 418-419, 420-421.
27 Cipriano JJ. Photographic Manual of Regional Orthopaedic and Neurological Tests. 2nd ed. Baltimore: Williams & Wilkins, 1991: 92-95, 98.
28 Evans RC. Illustrated Essentials in Orthopedic Physical Assessment. St. Louis: Mosby, 1994: 392-95, 398-399.
29 Cipriano JJ. Photographic Manual of Regional Orthopaedic and Neurological Tests. 2nd ed. Baltimore: Williams & Wilkins, 1991: 201.
30 Evans RC. Illustrated Essentials in Orthopedic Physical Assessment. St. Louis: Mosby, 1994: 486-487, 500-501, 508-509.
31 Cipriano JJ. Photographic Manual of Regional Orthopaedic and Neurological Tests. 2nd ed. Baltimore: Williams & Wilkins, 1991: 190, 193.
32 Evans RC. Illustrated Essentials in Orthopedic Physical Assessment. St. Louis: Mosby, 1994: 430-435, 444-445, 450-451, 466-467.
33 Cipriano JJ. Photographic Manual of Regional Orthopaedic and Neurological Tests. 2nd ed. Baltimore: Williams & Wilkins, 1991: 165, 168-171.
34 Evans RC. Illustrated Essentials in Orthopedic Physical Assessment. St. Louis: Mosby, 1994: 434-439, 446-447, 456-457, 460-461.
35 Cipriano JJ. Photographic Manual of Regional Orthopaedic and Neurological Tests. 2nd ed. Baltimore: Williams & Wilkins, 1991: 172-174.
36 Evans RC. Illustrated Essentials in Orthopedic Physical Assessment. St. Louis: Mosby, 1994: 484-485, 494-495, 492-493, 504-505, 514-517.
37 Cipriano JJ. Photographic Manual of Regional Orthopaedic and Neurological Tests. 2nd ed. Baltimore: Williams & Wilkins, 1991: 183-187.
38 Evans RC. Illustrated Essentials in Orthopedic Physical Assessment. St. Louis: Mosby, 1994: 88-91, 102-103, 110-111, 120-123, 134-135, 168-169.
39 Cipriano JJ. Photographic Manual of Regional Orthopaedic and Neurological Tests. 2nd ed. Baltimore: Williams & Wilkins, 1991: 22-29, 192-193.
40 Evans RC. Illustrated Essentials in Orthopedic Physical Assessment. St. Louis: Mosby, 1994: 88.
41 Evans RC. Illustrated Essentials in Orthopedic Physical Assessment. St. Louis: Mosby, 1994: 88, 102, 110, 120, 122, 134, 168.
42 Cipriano JJ. Photographic Manual of Regional Orthopaedic and Neurological Tests. 2nd ed. Baltimore: Williams & Wilkins, 1991: 28.
43 Travell JG, Simons DG. Myofascial Pain and Dysfunction. Vol. 1. Baltimore: Williams & Wilkins, 1983: 346.
44 Evans RC. Illustrated Essentials in Orthopedic Physical Assessment. St. Louis: Mosby, 1994: 86-87, 92-95, 100-101, 104-107, 114-115, 126-127, 136-137.
45 Cipriano JJ. Photographic Manual of Regional Orthopaedic and Neurological Tests. 2nd ed. Baltimore: Williams & Wilkins, 1991: 109, 110, 112, 114, 116, 118, 119.
46 Souza TA. Sports Injuries of the Shoulder: Conservative Management. New York: Churchill Livingstone, 1994: 51.
47 Travell JG, Simons DG. Myofascial Pain and Dysfunction. Vol. 1. Baltimore: Williams & Wilkins, 1983: 368-369,377-380,387-388,410-412.
48 Kelly BT, Kadimas WR, Speer KP. The Manual Examination for Rotator Cuff Strength: An electromygraphic Investigation. AmJSports Med Vol 24, No. 5: 581-588.
49 Souza TA. Sports Injuries of the Shoulder: Conservative Management. New York: Churchill Livingstone, 1994: 167-169, 203.
50 Souza TA. Sports Injuries of the Shoulder: Conservative Management. New York: Churchill Livingstone, 1994: 189-190.
51 Souza TA. Sports Injuries of the Shoulder: Conservative Management. New York: Churchill Livingstone, 1994:190-193.
52 Souza TA. Sports Injuries of the Shoulder: Conservative Management. New York: Churchill Livingstone, 1994:193-196.
53 Souza TA. Sports Injuries of the Shoulder: Conservative Management. New York: Churchill Livingstone, 1994:196-200.
54 Souza TA. Sports Injuries of the Shoulder: Conservative Management. New York: Churchill Livingstone, 1994: 50, 200.
55 Maffet MW, Gartsman GM, Moseley B. Superior Labrum Biceps Tendon Complex. Lesions of the Shoulder 1995; 23(1): 93-98.
56 Souza TA. Sports Injuries of the Shoulder: Conservative Management. New York: Churchill Livingstone, 1994: 11, 51, 189, 207, 371-373.
57 Neer CS. Impingement Lesions. Clinical Orthopaedics and Related Research 1983; 173:70.
58 Souza TA. Sports Injuries of the Shoulder: Conservative Management. New York: Churchill Livingstone, 1994: 200-202.
59 Souza TA. Sports Injuries of the Shoulder: Conservative Management. New York: Churchill Livingstone, 1994: 51, 189.

60 Hammer WI. Functional Soft Tissue Examination and Treatment by Manual Methods: The Extremities. Maryland: Aspen Publishers, 1991: 39.
61 Souza TA. Sports Injuries of the Shoulder: Conservative Management. New York: Churchill Livingstone, 1994: 207.
62 Hammer WI. Functional Soft Tissue Examination and Treatment by Manual Methods: The Extremities. Maryland: Aspen Publishers, 1991:49.
63 Greis PE, Kuhn JE, Schultheis J, Hintermeister R, Hawkins R. Validation of the lift off test and analysis of subscapularis activity during maximal internal rotation. AmJSports Med 1996; 24 (5): 589-593.
64 Gerber C, Krushnell RJ. Isolated rupture of the tendon of the subscapularis muscle: Clincal features in 16 cases. J. Bone and Joint Surgery 1991; 73B: 389-394.
65 Souza TA. Sports Injuries of the Shoulder: Conservative Management. New York: Churchill Livingstone, 1994: 210-211.
66 Evans RC. Illustrated Essentials in Orthopedic Physical Assessment. St. Louis: Mosby, 1994: 146-147, 150-151, 154-159.
67 Cipriano JJ. Photographic Manual of Regional Orthopaedic and Neurological Tests. 2nd ed. Baltimore: Williams & Wilkins, 1991: 130-131, 134-138.
68 Evans RC. Illustrated Essentials in Orthopedic Physical Assessment. St. Louis: Mosby, 1994: 168-171, 180-181, 184-185, 190-191, 198-201.
69 Cipriano JJ. Photographic Manual of Regional Orthopaedic and Neurological Tests. 2nd ed. Baltimore: Williams & Wilkins, 1991: 145-147, 149.
70 Evans RC. Illustrated Essentials in Orthopedic Physical Assessment. St. Louis: Mosby, 1994: 530-534, 536, 537, 540, 543, 567.
71 Hoppenfeld S. Physical Examination of the Spine and Extremities. Connecticut: Appleton & Lange, 1976: 114.
72 Hoppenfeld S. Physical Examination of the Spine and Extremities. Connecticut: Appleton & Lange, 1976: 115.
73 Evans RC. Illustrated Essentials in Orthopedic Physical Assessment. St. Louis: Mosby, 1994: 17-19.
74 Evans RC. Illustrated Essentials in Orthopedic Physical Assessment. St. Louis: Mosby, 1994: 213-214.
75 Evans RC. Illustrated Essentials in Orthopedic Physical Assessment. St. Louis: Mosby, 1994: 251-252.
76 Hoppenfeld S. Physical Examination of the Spine and Extremities. Connecticut: Appleton & Lange, 1976: 23-25.
77 Evans RC. Illustrated Essentials in Orthopedic Physical Assessment. St. Louis: Mosby, 1994: 79-83.
78 Personal communication with Dr. Joseph Miller at New York Chiropractic College.
79 Magee DJ. Orthopedic Physical Assessment. Philadelphia: W.B. Sauders Company, 1992: 6, 42, 12, 13.
80 Hoppenfeld S. Orthopedic Neurology: A Diagnostic Guide to Neurologic Levels. Philadelphia: J.B. Lippincott Company, 1977: 28.
81 Hoppenfeld S. Orthopedic Neurology: A Diagnostic Guide to Neurologic Levels. Philadelphia: J.B. Lippincott Company, 1977: 66-67.
82 Hoppenfeld S. Physical Examination of the Spine and Extremities. Connecticut: Appleton & Lange, 1976: 136-141.
83 Seidel HM, Ball JW, Dains JE, Benedict GW. 3rd ed. Mosby's Guide to Physical Examination. St. Louis: Mosby, 1995: 744.
84 Isselbacher KJ, Braunwald E, Wilson JD, Martin JB, Fauci AS, Kasper DL. Harrison's Principles of Internal Medicine. 13th ed. New York: McGraw-Hill, Inc., 1994: 129.
85 Isselbacher KJ, Braunwald E, Wilson JD, Martin JB, Fauci AS, Kasper DL. Harrison's Principles of Internal Medicine. 13th ed. New York: McGraw-Hill, Inc., 1994: 128.
86 Recommended text for palpation is Hoppenfeld S. Physical Examination of the Spine and Extremities. Connecticut: Appleton & Lange, 1976.
87 Recommended text for anatomy is Netter FH. Atlas of Human Anatomy. New Jersey: CIBA-Geigy corporation, 1989.

CHAPTER 8

Laboratory Diagnosis

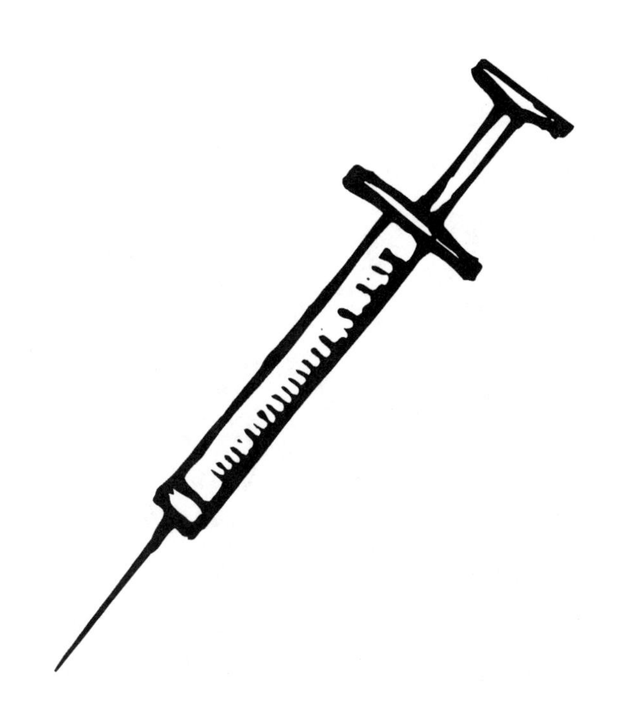

Hematology

Hematology is the study of disorders of cell production (hematopoiesis), synthesis and function and is primarily accomplished through the examination the three cellular elements of blood: RBCs, WBCs and platelets. (1)

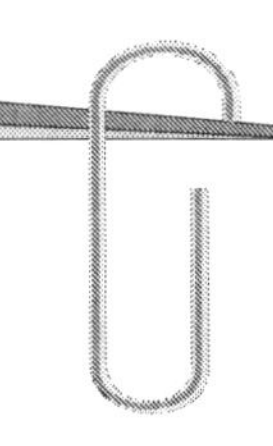

Normal Values for the CBC (2)

Ranges are given for Adults

Important: Ranges will vary between labs

White blood cell count	5-10^3/µl or 5-10^9/L
Red blood cell	Men: 4.2-5.4 x 10^6 / µl (avg. 4.8) Women: 3.6-5.0 x 10^6 / µl (avg. 4.3)
Hematocrit (HCT)	Men: 42-52% Women: 36-48%
Hemoglobin (Hb)	Men: 14.0-17.4 g / dl Women: 12.0-16.0 g / dl
Mean Corpuscular Volume (MCV)	82-98 femto liters (fl) or µm^3 Volume of RBCs is calculated by this formula: MCV = HCT % x 10 / RBC (10^{12} / L)
Mean Corpuscular Hemoglobin (MCH)	26-34 picograms / cell Measure of average weight of hemoglobin per red blood cell
Mean Corpuscular Hemoglobin Concentration (MCHC)	31-37 g / dl Expression of average concentration of hemoglobin in the RBCs
Platelet Count	140-400 x 10^3 / mm^3

The Complete Blood Count (CBC) with Differential (3)

The CBC consists of the following screening tests: white blood cell count, differential white blood cell count, red blood cell count, hematocrit, hemoglobin, red blood cell indices, stained red cell examination and platelet count.

 Fasting is not necessary for the complete blood cell count. Dehydration or overhydration can dramatically alter values.

Test	Test Rationale	Clinical Implications	
White blood cell count ▪ *WBCs produce, transport and distribute antibodies* ▪ *WBCs are the major cellular components of inflammatory and immune responses*	▪ Indicates severity of disease process ▪ Specific patterns of leukocytes indicate different types of disease ▪ Identifies persons with increased susceptibility to infection ▪ Determines WBCs ability to destroy bacteria	**Leukocytosis** **(Increased WBC count**: usually due to an increase of only one type of WBC)	▪ Acute infections ▪ Certain diseases (i.e. measles, pertussis) ▪ Leukemia ▪ Trauma or tissue injury ▪ Malignant neoplasms
		Leukopenia **(Decreased WBC count)**	▪ Viral infections ▪ Some bacterial infections ▪ Primary bone marrow disorders; marrow-occupying diseases
Differential white blood cell count	▪ The relative distribution of the number and type of cells and the degree of increase or decrease is diagnostically significant	▪ The differential count must be interpreted in relation to the total leukocyte count	

White Blood Cells

White Blood Cells	% of Total Leukocyte Count	Functions
Neutrophils	50 to 60%	Primary combatant of microbial invasion by phagocytosis; most numerous of the WBCs
Lymphocytes	20-40%	Source of serum immunoglobulins and cellular immune response; migrate to areas of inflammation
Monocytes	2 to 6%	Combat severe infections by phagocytosis; second line of defense against infection; remove debris
Eosinophils	1 to 4%	Ingest antigen-antibody complexes; increase with allergic disorders and parasitic infections
Basophils	0.5 to 1%	Phagocytic; contain heparin, histamines, and serotonin; function in allergic reactions

Test	Test Rationale	Clinical Implications	
Red blood cell count	▪ Tests the adequacy of red blood cell production; determines the total number of red blood cells (erythrocytes) found in a cubic millimeter of blood	**Decreased RBC count**	▪ Anemia, associated with cell production and destruction, blood loss, insufficiency of iron and certain vitamins ▪ Lymphomas, multiple myeloma, leukemia, Lupus erythematosus, Addison's disease
		Erythrocytosis (increased RBC count)	▪ Primary: polycythemia vera, erythrocytosis-erythemia ▪ Secondary: renal disease, pulmonary disease, cardiovascular disease, others ▪ Relative: due to decreased plasma volume
Hematocrit (HCT)	▪ Test determines red blood concentration expressed as a percentage of packed red cells in a volume of whole blood. The percentage of RBC mass to original whole blood volume is the hematocrit	**Decreased**	▪ Anemia
		Increased	▪ Polycythemia ▪ Shock ▪ Dehydration
Hemoglobin (Hb)	▪ Hemoglobin is a conjugated protein that transports oxygen and carbon dioxide in blood. Test screens for disease associated with anemia, determines the severity of anemia and evaluates polycythemia	**Decreased**	▪ Anemia, hyperthyroidism, cirrhosis of the liver, hemolytic reactions, various systemic diseases
		Increased	▪ Polycythemia, severe burns, chronic obstructive pulmonary disease, congestive heart failure

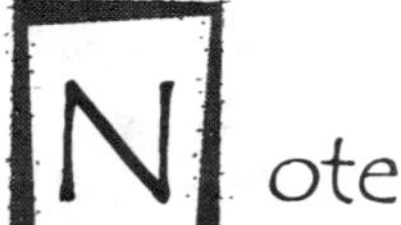

ote

- Polycythemia denotes an abnormal increase in the number of red blood cells. For screening purposes, hematocrit and hemoglobin tests are used to evaluate polycythemia.

Classification of Polycythemia			
Relative	Increase in hemoglobin, hematocrit or RBCs caused by decreased plasma volume		
Absolute / true polycythemia	Primary	Polycythemia vera	
	Secondary	Appropriate	Appropriate bone marrow response to physiological conditions: altitude, cardiopulmonary disorder
		Inappropriate	Overproduction of RBCs not necessary to deliver oxygen to tissues: renal tumor or cyst, hepatoma, cerebellar hemangioblastoma

	Test	Test Rationale	Formula	Clinical Implications	
Red Blood Cell Indices	**Mean Corpuscular Volume (MCV)**	▪ Individual cell size is the best index for classifying anemias; expresses the volume occupied by a single red cell and is measured in cubic microns of the mean volume ▪ Indicates whether the cell is normal in size (normocytic), smaller (microcytic), or larger (macrocytic)	Hematocrit x 10 / RBC count in millions	▪ The MCV results are the basis of classification of anemia; see chart below ▪ Decreases with microcytic anemia ▪ Increases with macrocytic anemia	
	Mean corpuscular hemoglobin (MCH)	▪ Measure of the average weight of hemoglobin per red blood cell; valuable for diagnosing severely anemic patients	HGB in g/100 ml x 10 / RBC count in millions	Decrease	▪ Associated with hypochromia
				Increase	▪ Associated with hyperchromia
	Mean corpuscular hemoglobin concentration (MCHC)	▪ Measures the average concentration of hemoglobin in the red blood cells; most valuable for monitoring therapy for anemia	HGB in g/100 ml x 10 / Hematocrit (%)	Decrease	▪ Iron deficiency, macrocytic anemias, thalassemia
				Increase	▪ Spherocytosis

ote (4)

- Thalassemias: diverse group of congenital disorders in which there is a defect in the synthesis of one or more of the subunits of hemoglobin, causing the red blood cells to be microcytic and hypochromic. Classified as Alpha or Beta depending on which subunit of hemoglobin is abnormally synthesized.
- Spherocytosis: one of four types of inherited abnormalities of the red cell membrane. Affected individuals have congenital hemolysis arising from a defect in one of the proteins in the red cell membrane.

otes on Anemia (5)

- Anemia is characterized by a reduction in the number of circulating red blood cells, in the amount of hemoglobin, or in the volume of packed cells (hematocrit), or a combination of these. The red blood cell indices indicate the size and hemoglobin content of the red blood cell and are used in differentiating anemias.

Classification of Anemia Based on RBC Morphology

Microcytic	**Hypochromic**	▪ Chronic iron deficiency (most frequent cause) ▪ Thalassemia ▪ Occasionally in chronic systems disease
	Normochromic	▪ Some cases of chronic systemic disease
Normocytic	**Hypochromic**	▪ Some cases of chronic systemic disease ▪ Lead poisoning
	Normochromic	▪ Many cases due to systemic disease ▪ Many cases associated with pituitary, thyroid, or adrenal disease ▪ Acute blood loss ▪ Hemolytic anemia
Macrocytic	**Hypochromic**	▪ Some cases of macrocytic anemia with superimposed iron deficiency
	Normochromic	▪ B12 or folic acid deficiency or malabsorption ▪ Chronic alcoholism

Classification of Anemias Based on Pathogenesis

Anemia Classification	Explanation	Most Common Causes
Factor Deficiency Anemia	Deficiency of vital hematopoietic raw material	▪ Iron deficiency ▪ Vitamin B12 or Folic acid deficiency or combination of both
Production-defect Anemia	Failure of blood-forming organs to produce or to deliver mature RBCs to the peripheral blood	▪ Replacement of marrow by fibrosis or by neoplasm ▪ Hypoplasia of the bone marrow ▪ Toxic suppression of marrow production or delivery without actual marrow hypoplasia (e.g. chronic renal disease)
Depletion Anemia	RBC loss from the peripheral blood	▪ Hemorrhage (acute or chronic) ▪ Hemolytic anemia ▪ Hypersplenism

Test	Test Rationale	Clinical Implications	
Stained red cell examination	Determines variations and abnormalities in erythrocyte size, shape, color and intracellular content; useful in diagnosing blood disorders such as anemia, thalassemia, and other hemoglobinopathies	Variations in size, color, shape, and red cell inclusion are indicative of red blood cell abnormalities. Different abnormalities are associated with different diseases	
Platelet count ▪ *Included in a routine CBC*	Helpful for evaluating bleeding disorders that occur with liver disease, thrombocytopenia, uremia, anticoagulant therapy, and following the course of diseases associated with bone marrow failure	**Increased** (Thrombocytosis)	▪ Malignancies ▪ Leukemia ▪ Polycythemia vera ▪ Rheumatoid arthritis; other collagen diseases ▪ Iron-deficiency anemia ▪ Hodgkin's disease, lymphomas ▪ Chronic pancreatitis ▪ Trauma, exercise
		Decreased (Thrombocytopenia)	▪ Pernicious, aplastic, and hemolytic anemias ▪ Viral, bacterial and rickettsial infections ▪ Congestive heart failure ▪ Exposure to chemicals ▪ During cancer chemotherapy and radiation ▪ HIV infection ▪ Lesions of bone marrow ▪ Toxic effects of many drugs

Erythrocyte Sedimentation Rate (ESR) (6)

- Erythrocyte sedimentation is the rate at which erythrocytes clump together (rouleaux formation) and settle out of anticoagulated blood in one hour. Elevated asymmetric protein molecules which increase with certain pathological conditions cause a decrease in the negative charge of erythrocytes that normally keeps them apart. This promotes the formation of rouleaux ("stacks of coins") which sediment more rapidly than single cells.
- The faster the sedimentation rate, the higher the ESR. In other words, the amount of settling is the patient's ESR.
- The sedimentation rate is not diagnostic of any particular disease, but is an indication that a disease process is occurring and should be investigated. The ESR correlates with the severity of the inflammatory process.

 Fasting is not necessary, but a fatty meal may cause plasma alterations.

Test	Test Rationale	Clinical Implications	
Erythrocyte Sedimentation Rate	Inflammatory and necrotic processes cause blood proteins to aggregate, which makes the cells heavier. When placed in a vertical test tube these heavier cells are more likely to fall rapidly.	**Increased**	▪ Inflammatory diseases ▪ Rheumatoid arthritis, gout, arthritis ▪ Non-specific tissue necrosis ▪ Infections, pneumonia, syphilis ▪ All collagen diseases, SLE ▪ Carcinoma, lymphoma, neoplasms ▪ Pregnancy
		Normal or varied	▪ Acute disease ▪ Convalescence ▪ Unruptured acute appendicitis ▪ Malignant diseases ▪ Slightly increased with osteoarthritis ▪ Myocardial infarction ▪ May be decreased with sickle cell and spherocytosis

ote

- Tests are usually performed for bleeding disorders, vascular injury or trauma, and coagulopathies.
- Clotting disorders are divided into two categories: those caused by impaired coagulation, and those caused by hypercoagulability.

Category	Overview	
Impaired Coagulation (Hemorrhagic disorders)	▪ Thrombocytopenia (platelet deficiency) ▪ Liver disease ▪ Uremia ▪ Disseminated Intravascular Coagulation (DIC) ▪ Anticoagulant administration ▪ Hemophilia and other inherited factor deficiencies ▪ Delays in clot formation and premature clot lysis	
Hypercoagulability Unnatural tendency toward thrombosis associated with inappropriate clot activation or localization of the blood coagulation process	**Two general forms**	1. Hyperreactivity of the platelet system resulting in arterial thrombosis 2. Accelerated activity of the clotting system resulting in venous thrombosis
	Conditions	▪ Platelet abnormalities ▪ Clotting system abnormalities ▪ Venous thrombosis

☞ Patient should not take aspirin-based medications for at least seven days before the bleeding time test. Patient should not drink alcohol before the test. The test is postponed in the case of infectious skin disease.

Test	Test Rationale	Clinical Implications
Bleeding Time	▪ Measures the interaction of the platelet with the blood vessel wall and the formation of the hemostatic plug (the primary phase of hemostasis) ▪ A single prolonged bleeding time does not prove the existence of hemorrhagic disease. Another test should be performed and the two results averaged	▪ Prolonged with thrombocytopenia, platelet dysfunction syndromes, decrease or abnormality in plasma factors, abnormalities in walls of small blood vessels and vascular disease, advanced renal failure, leukemia, aplastic anemia, DIC disease, severe liver disease ▪ Bleeding time is normal in the presence of coagulation disorders, with the exception of platelet dysfunction or vascular disease

☞ Patient use of heparin affects interpretation of the test results.

Test	Test Rationale	Clinical Implications	
Partial Thromboplastin Time (PTT)	Screens for coagulation disorders. It can detect deficiencies of the intrinsic and extrinsic pathways of coagulation	**Prolonged**	▪ All congenital deficiencies of intrinsic system coagulation factors, including hemophilia A and B ▪ Vitamin K deficiency ▪ Hypofibrinogenemia ▪ Liver disease ▪ Disseminated Intravascular Coagulation (DIC) ▪ Congenital deficiency of Fitzgerald factor and Fletcher factor ▪ Heparin therapy ▪ Circulating anticoagulants usually occur as inhibitors of a specific factor
		Shortened	▪ Extensive cancer, except when the liver is involved ▪ Immediately after acute hemorrhage ▪ Very early stages of DIC

ote

- DISSEMINATED INTRAVASCULAR COAGULATION (DIC) is usually associated with obstetrical catastrophes, metastatic cancer, massive trauma, and bacterial sepsis. It can be a life-threatening bleeding disorder or a subclinical disorder. Lab findings include thrombocytopenia and presence of schistocytes (fragment of an RBC), and prolonged PT and PTT and thrombin time. The cardinal finding is the plasma fibrinogen level.

☞ Aspirin, acetaminophen, and laxative products should be avoided unless specifically ordered by a physician. Excessive amounts of green, leafy vegetables in the diet will increase vitamin K levels and could interfere with anticoagulant metabolism.

Test	Test Rationale	Clinical Implications	
Prothrombin Time (PT)	Directly measures a potential defect in Stage II of the clotting mechanism. Prothrombin is produced in the liver and will be reduced in patients with liver disease	**Increased**	▪ Prothrombin deficiency (factor II) also factors V, VII, and X ▪ Vitamin K deficiency ▪ Liver disease ▪ Biliary obstruction ▪ Disseminated Intravascular Coagulation (DIC) ▪ Zollinger-Ellison syndrome ▪ SLE ▪ Hypervitaminosis A
		Decreased	▪ Ovarian hyperfunction ▪ Regional enteritis/ileitis

☞ No heparin should be administered for two days before testing thrombin time.

Test	Test Rationale	Clinical Implications	
Thrombin Time (TT)	Detects Stage III fibrinogen defects; measures the time needed for plasma to clot when thrombin is added	**Prolonged**	▪ Hypofibrinogenemia ▪ Therapy with heparin or similar anticoagulants ▪ Disseminated Intravascular Coagulation ▪ Fibrinolysis ▪ Multiple myeloma ▪ Severe liver diseases
		Shortened	▪ Hyperfibrinogenemia ▪ Elevated hematocrit

☞ No special patient preparation.

Test	Test Rationale	Clinical Implications
Coagulant Factors (Factor Assay)	Investigates inherited and acquired bleeding disorders	▪ Inherited deficiencies ▪ Acquired disorders

IMMUNODIAGNOSTIC STUDIES (8)

ote

- Also called serodiagnostic studies, these procedures test for antigen-antibody reactions for diagnosis of infectious disease, autoimmune disorders, allergies and neoplastic disease. The serum is tested for antibodies against a particular antigen.

Patient should fast for 8 to 12 hours before the test (if required). The patient may drink water.

Test	Test Rationale	Clinical Implications	
C-Reactive Protein (CRP) *The most dramatic acute-phase reactant*	CRP is an abnormal protein that rapidly appears in the blood with any inflammatory reaction or injurious stimuli. The test is used the same as an ESR, but is not limited by anemia and is therefore preferred for post-operative diagnosis of infection	**Positive (present)**	▪ Rheumatic fever ▪ Rheumatoid arthritis ▪ Myocardial infarction ▪ Malignancy ▪ Acute bacterial and viral infections

Antibiotic therapy or recent use of antibiotics suppresses the streptococcal antibody response and renders the test impractical.

Test	Test Rationale	Clinical Implications
Streptococcal Antibody Tests; ASO titer (Anti-streptolysin O)	Diagnoses streptococcal infections or illnesses associated with streptococcal infections. Aids in monitoring post-streptococcal sequellae	▪ Streptococcal A infections (e.g. strep pharyngitis, rheumatic fever, glomerulonephritis) ▪ Rising titers over several weeks are more significant than a single result. Increased titers are seen in 80 to 85% of patients with acute rheumatic fever and in 95% with acute glomerulonephritis

Symptoms of infectious mono include fever, fatigue, pharyngitis and lymphadenopathy (especially the posterior cervical nodes).

Test	Test Rationale	Clinical Implications
Infectious Mononucleosis Test; Heterophil antibody Titer Test; Epstein-Barr Virus Antibody Test	Infectious mono causes the formation of abnormal lymphocytes and stimulates increased heterophil antibody formation	▪ Presence of heterophil antibodies (appear by the sixth to tenth day of illness), along with clinical signs and other hematologic findings, is diagnostic for infectious mono

ote (10)

- Primary infection by EBV in older children, adolescents, or young adults produces infectious mono syndrome in up to 50% of cases.
- The Paul Bunnell antibody is not specific for EBV but is seldom found in other disorders.
- 10% of the adult population does not demonstrate a Paul Bunnell heterophil antibody. Heterophil-negative infectious mononucleosis refers to conditions that resemble infectious mono clinically and show a similar Wright-stained peripheral blood smear picture, but without demonstrable elevation of the Paul-Bunnell heterophil antibody.

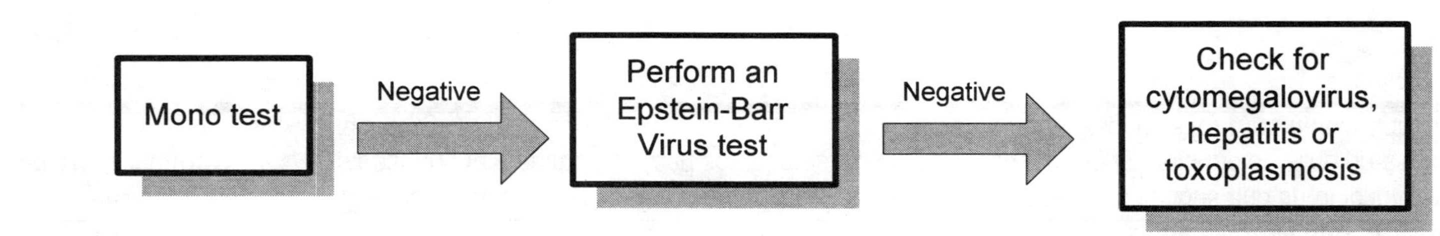

The result is normally higher in older patients and in those who have received multiple vaccinations and transfusions.

Test	Test Rationale	Clinical Implications
Rheumatoid Factor (RF)	The test diagnoses rheumatoid arthritis by measuring IgM antibodies (and sometimes IgG or IgA)	▪ Many rheumatic conditions and chronic inflammatory processes may produce rheumatoid factor. The presence of rheumatoid factor is not a diagnosis for rheumatoid arthritis

ote:

- With increased age, persons with no clinical illness may have rheumatoid factor
- Patients with an increased titer for rheumatoid factor are more likely to have severe systemic involvement.
- Juvenile rheumatoid arthritis is normally RF negative.
- Four of the following criteria must be met to diagnose rheumatoid arthritis: (11)

  1. Morning stiffness for at least six weeks.
  2. Pain on motion or tenderness in at least one joint for at least six weeks.
  3. Swelling in at least one joint for at least six weeks.
  4. Swelling in at least one other joint for at least six weeks.
  5. Symmetrical joint swelling with simultaneous involvement of the same joint on both sides of the body.
  6. Subcutaneous nodules.
  7. X-ray changes, including bony decalcification.

URINE STUDIES

ROUTINE URINALYSIS (12)

Urine Property	Background	Clinical Implications	
Color	Should be pale yellow (indicates low specific gravity) to amber (indicates high specific gravity)	▪ Colors other than normal should be investigated with an appropriate reference	
Turbidity	Should be clear to slightly hazy to the eye	▪ Cloudy urine indicates possible abnormal presence of pus, RBCs or bacteria ▪ Urinary tract infections ▪ Many normal urines can appear cloudy	
Specific gravity	Measures kidneys' ability to concentrate urine; normally a decrease in urine volume = increase in specific gravity	**Normal**	▪ Diabetes causes increased urine volume and increased specific gravity ▪ Hypertension causes normal urine volume and increased specific gravity ▪ Early chronic renal disease causes increased urine volume and decreased specific gravity
		Low	▪ Diabetes insipidus (absence of ADH) ▪ Glomerulonephritis and pyelonephritis ▪ Severe renal damage ▪ Diuretic therapy
		Increased	▪ Diabetes mellitus or nephrosis ▪ Excessive water loss ▪ Increased secretion of Anti-diuretic hormone (ADH)
pH	Average pH falls between 4.6 and 8	**Acidic**	▪ Acidosis, uncontrolled diabetes, pulmonary emphysema, diarrhea ▪ Respiratory diseases in which CO_2 retention occurs
		Alkaline	▪ Urinary tract infections, pyloric obstruction, chronic renal failure ▪ Respiratory diseases that involve hyperventilation
Blood	Urine should be free of red blood cells	**Presence of blood**	▪ Lower urinary tract infections ▪ SLE ▪ Urinary tract or renal cancers ▪ Urinary calculi ▪ Glomerulonephritis ▪ Trauma
Protein	Healthy urine contains no protein	**Presence of protein**	▪ Proteinuria is usually the result of increased glomerular filtration of protein due to glomerular damage ▪ Renal disease: nephritis/glomerulonephritis, nephrosis, malignant hypertension, polycystic kidney disease, others ▪ Can occur following non-renal diseases and conditions: fever/acute infection, trauma, leukemia, multiple myeloma, diabetes mellitus, pre-eclampsia, others

Urine Property	Background	Clinical Implications	
Glucose	Glucose is normally not present in the urine, but is not necessarily abnormal (it may appear after a heavy meal or during emotional stress)	**Increased**	▪ Diabetes mellitus ▪ Pituitary diseases (e.g. Cushing's, acromegaly) ▪ CNS diseases (brain injury) ▪ Renal tubule disease associated with lowered urine threshold
Ketones	Urine should be negative for presence of ketones. Ketosis and kentonuria may occur when increased amounts of fat are metabolized, carbohydrate intake is restricted, or the diet is rich in fats.	**Ketonuria**	▪ Diabetes mellitus ▪ Renal glycosuria ▪ Glycogen storage disease ▪ Starvation, fasting ▪ High fat or low-carbohydrate diet ▪ Hyperthyroidism ▪ Pregnancy or lactation
Bilirubin	Bilirubin (resulting from the breakdown of hemoglobin) should not be detectable in the urine	**Presence of even trace amounts**	▪ Hepatitis and liver diseases caused by infections or exposure to toxic agents ▪ Obstructive biliary tract diseases
Urobilingoen	One of the most sensitive tests available to measure impaired liver function. Increased level is one of the first signs of acute liver cell damage	**Increased**	▪ Hemolytic anemia and pernicious anemia ▪ Malaria ▪ Pulmonary infarction ▪ Excessive bruising ▪ Biliary disease ▪ Cirrhosis ▪ Hepatitis
		Decreased	▪ Cholelithiasis ▪ Severe inflammation of the biliary ducts ▪ Cancer of the head of the pancreas ▪ Antibiotic therapy
Nitrate/ Bacteria	Nitrate is the metabolic end product of bacteria so presence of nitrate indicates presence of bacteria	**Presence of Bacteria**	▪ Urinary tract infection ▪ A negative result does not mean bacteria are absent
Leukocyte Esterase	A positive leukocyte esterase on dipstick detects the presence of leukocytes in the urine	**Presence of WBCs**	▪ Pyuria ▪ Urinary tract infection
Microscopic Examination	Healthy urine contains small amounts of cells and other formed elements from the genitourinary tract. Abnormal sediment components may indicate pathology	▪ Bacteria: Urinary tract infection ▪ Casts: Tubular or glomerular disorders ▪ Epithelial cells: Normal ▪ Erythrocytes: Most renal disorders, trauma, infection, malignancy ▪ Fat bodies: Nephrotic syndrome ▪ Leukocytes: Most renal disorders, urinary tract infection, pyelonephritis	

Chemistry Studies (13)

Biochemical Profiles

☞ *It is often necessary to measure several blood chemicals to establish a pattern of abnormalities, so a wide range of tests may be grouped together to form profiles that screen for certain conditions. Common profiles include cardiac enzymes; kidney function; lipids; liver function; and thyroid function, each comprised of a series of tests to evaluate a certain body system or systems. Components of chemistry studies can include the following (14,15):*

Test	Purpose
Alanine Transaminase (ALT); Serum Glutamic-Pyruvic Transaminase (SGPT)	Primarily used to diagnose liver disease and to monitor the course of treatment of hepatitis, active postnecrotic cirrhosis, and the effects of later drug therapy. Differentiates between hemolytic jaundice and jaundice caused by liver disease
Albumin	Screen for liver dysfunction, protein-losing enteropathies
Alkaline Phosphatase	Used as a tumor marker and an index of liver and bone disease, when correlated with other findings. In liver disease, blood levels rise when biliary tract is obstructed
Aspartate Transaminase (AST) Serum Glutamic-Oxaloacetic Acid (SGOT)	This enzyme, present in tissues of high metabolic activity (liver, heart, and RBCs), is released into the circulation following the injury or death of cells. The test is used to evaluate liver and heart diseases
Total Bilirubin	Measurement of bilirubin (by-product of the breakdown of hemoglobin in the RBCs) evaluates liver function, hemolytic anemias, and hyperbilirubinemia in newborns
Blood Urea Nitrogen (BUN)	Gross index of glomerular function and the production and excretion of urea (end product of protein metabolism)
Calcium	The test measures the concentration of total and ionized calcium in the blood to reflect parathyroid function, calcium metabolism, and malignant activity; hyperparathyroidism and cancer are the most common causes of hypercalcemia and hypoalbuminemia is the most common cause of decreased total calcium
CO_2	Test is a general measure of the alkalinity or acidity of the venous, arterial, or capillary blood
Chloride	Chloride, an extracellular blood anion, is helpful in diagnosing disorders of acid-base and water balance
Cholesterol	Test detects disorders of blood lipids and indicates potential risk for atherosclerotic coronary artery disease. Test can also be part of a thyroid and liver function study
Creatinine	Creatinine is a by-product of energy metabolism removed from the body by the kidneys. The test diagnoses kidney disorders, which result in a reduction of creatinine excretion and increased blood levels
Gamma-Glutamyl Transferase (GGTP)	Used to determine liver cell dysfunction and to detect alcohol-induced liver disease. Screens for the consequences of chronic alcoholism
Glucose	Blood glucose level depends primarily on the liver, and secondarily on tissue utilization of glucose, which is mediated by pancreatic insulin and many other factors. Blood glucose measurement is the mainstay for diagnosis of diabetes
High Density Lipoprotein	Assesses coronary artery disease risk (decreased HDL increases risk) and monitors persons with known low HDL levels
Lactic Acid Dehydrogenase (LDH)	Elevated levels are non-specific, but useful for confirming myocardial or pulmonary infarct when considered in relation to other test findings
Phosphorus	Calcium and phosphorus levels have an inverse relationship. Tests parathyroid hormone function
Potassium	Potassium is the principal cation of intracellular fluid, and is released into the blood by damaged cells. Test evaluates body potassium and diagnoses acid-base and water imbalances. It varies with circulatory volume and other factors
Total Protein	Test can help to diagnose some inflammatory and neoplastic states (multiple myeloma), nephrotic syndromes, liver disease and immune dysfunction (SLE)
Sodium	The most abundant blood cation. The test determines plasma sodium levels to detect gross changes in water and salt balance (**NOTE**: Urinary sodium is a more sensitive indicator of altered sodium balance than blood)
Triglycerides	The test evaluates suspected atherosclerosis and measures the body's ability to metabolize fat. Elevated triglycerides are an atherosclerotic disease risk factor
Uric Acid	Measurement of uric acid (end product of purine metabolism) is used most commonly in the evaluation of renal failure, gout, and leukemia. Also evaluates the prognosis of eclampsia

SERUM PROTEIN ELECTROPHORESIS (16,17)

ote

- Electrophoresis is the separation of ionic solutes based on differences in their rates of migration in an applied electric field. Electrophoresis is the most commonly used screening test for serum protein abnormalities except for measurement of albumin only.
- The test can diagnose some inflammatory states, nephrotic syndrome, liver disease, and immune dysfunctions. It can also evaluate nutritional states and osmotic pressures in edematous and malnourished patients.
- Serum proteins are divided into five groups including albumin, alpha-1 globulins, alpha-2 globulins, beta globulins and gamma globulins (IgA, IgG, IgM, IgD, Ige). Certain predictable changes take place in plasma protein levels in response to acute illness and focal episodes associated with malignant tumors.
- In health, the immunoglobulins are polyclonal instead of monoclonal. Monoclonal bands frequently indicate neoplastic processes.

Serum Protein		Function of protein	Site of production
Albumin		▪ Accounts for about 80% of plasma oncotic pressure ▪ Transport protein	▪ The liver produces most serum albumin
Alpha-1 globulins		▪ Main transport system for certain ions and molecules ▪ Antibody system ▪ Clotting proteins ▪ Complement ▪ Acute reaction proteins	▪ Globulins are produced by the liver, by the reticuloendothelial system and by other means
Alpha-2 globulins			
Beta globulins			
Gamma globulins	IgA		
	IgG		
	IgM		
	IgD		
	IgE		

CLINICAL IMPLICATIONS

	Increase	Decrease
Total serum protein	▪ Dehydration and hemoconcentration due to fluid loss ▪ Liver disease ▪ Multiple myeloma ▪ Collagen disorders ▪ Chronic inflammation states and infection	▪ Starvation or malabsorption ▪ Severe liver disease and alcoholism ▪ Renal disease, nephrotic syndrome ▪ Diarrhea ▪ Heart failure
Serum albumin	▪ Dehydration	▪ Decreased synthesis states (liver disease, alcholoism, protein-losing enteropathies, starvation) ▪ Nephrotic syndrome (albumin loss) ▪ Collagen disease, liver disease, infection, ulcerative colitis
Gamma globulin	▪ Autoimmune diseases ▪ Collagen diseases ▪ Multiple myeloma ▪ Leukemia and other cancers	▪ Nephrotic syndrome

LABORATORY PROFILES (18)

Pathology	Laboratory Profile Test	Background	Interpretation	
Arthritis	▪ Erythrocyte Sedimentation Rate (ESR)	▪ Changes are related to alterations in plasma proteins ▪ Test is a non-specific indicator of infection or inflammation	**Increase**	▪ All collagen diseases, SLE ▪ Infections, pneumonia ▪ Inflammatory diseases ▪ Neoplasia, carcinoma ▪ Cell or tissue destruction
	▪ C-Reactive Protein (CRP)	▪ CRP is an abnormal protein that appears in the blood during inflammatory processes ▪ Non-specific test for evaluating inflammatory disease course and severity in conditions with tissue necrosis	**Increase**	▪ Rheumatic fever ▪ Rheumatoid arthritis ▪ Myocardial infarction ▪ Malignancy ▪ Acute bacterial and viral infections
	▪ Rheumatoid Factor (RF) (AKA RA Factor)	▪ RF is a macroglobulin-type antibody in the blood of some persons with rheumatoid arthritis ▪ The test diagnoses rheumatoid arthritis	**Present**	▪ Rheumatoid arthritis ▪ Results are normally higher in older patients
	▪ Antinuclear Antibody Test (ANA)	▪ ANAs are gamma globulins that react with cell nuclei of all organs ▪ The test is used for differential diagnosis of rheumatic diseases and to detect antinucleoprotein factors and patterns associated with certain autoimmune diseases ▪ Particular antibody patterns are associated with different autoimmune diseases	**Present**	▪ SLE ▪ Scleroderma ▪ Rheumatoid arthritis ▪ Sjogren's disease ▪ Dermatomyositis ▪ Polyarteritis
	▪ Human Leukocyte Antigen B27 (HLA-B27) Test	▪ The HLA complex is a major histocompatibility complex in humans that is responsible for many important immune functions ▪ The test aids in diagnosis of certain rheumatoid diseases, especially ankylosing spondylitis	**Present**	▪ Ankylosing Spondylitis ▪ Multiple Sclerosis ▪ Reiter's Syndrome ▪ Graves disease ▪ Juvenile rheumatoid arthritis
	▪ Uric acid	▪ With gout, there is an overproduction of uric acid occurs when there is excessive cell breakdown and catabolism of nucleonic acids	**Elevated**	▪ Gout

Pathology	Laboratory Profile Test	Background	Interpretation	
Bone Tumor	▪ Calcium	▪ Hyperparathyroidism and cancer are the most common causes of hypercalcemia ▪ Hypoalbuminemia is the most common cause of decreased total calcium ▪ The test measures the concentration of total and ionized calcium in the blood to reflect parathyroid function, calcium metabolism and malignant activity	**Hyper-calcemia**	▪ Metastatic bone cancers ▪ Multiple myeloma ▪ Paget's disease of bone
			Hypo-calcemia	▪ Pseudohypocalcemia (reduced albumin levels) ▪ Hypoparathyroidism ▪ Malabsorption
	▪ Phosphorus	▪ Phosphate levels are always evaluated in relation to calcium levels (there is an inverse relationship between the two) ▪ Controlling factor of phosphorus level is parathyroid hormone	**Hyperphos-phatemia**	▪ Bone disease
			Hypophas-phatemia	▪ Hyperparathyroidism ▪ Rickets and osteomalacia ▪ Hyperinsulinism ▪ Liver disease
	▪ Alkaline Phosphatase (ALP)	▪ ALP is used as a tumor marker and an index of liver and bone disease, when correlated with clinical findings ▪ In bone disease, the enzyme rises in proportion to osteoblastic activity	**Elevated with bone disease**	▪ Paget's disease ▪ Metastatic bone tumor ▪ Osteogenic sarcoma ▪ Osteomalacia (no elevation with osteoporosis)
	▪ Acid Phosphatase (if blastic)	▪ Greatest diagnostic importance is in the prostate gland ▪ Test diagnoses metastatic cancer of the prostate; indicates cancer has spread beyond the capsule to other parts of the body	**Elevated**	▪ Almost always indicative of metastatic cancer of the prostate ▪ Moderately elevated levels occur with Paget's disease, Multiple myeloma, any cancer that has metastasized to bone

Pathology	Laboratory Profile Test	Background	Interpretation	
Kidney Dysfunction	▪ Blood Urea Nitrogen	▪ Urea forms in the liver and is the final product of protein metabolism ▪ Test is a gross index of glomerular function and the production and excretion of urea	**Increased**	▪ Impaired renal function ▪ Congestive heart failure ▪ Shock ▪ Acute myocardial infarct
			Decreased	▪ Liver failure ▪ Nephrotic syndrome (occasional)
	▪ Creatinine	▪ Creatinine is a byproduct of the breakdown of muscle creatine phosphate due to energy metabolism ▪ A disorder of kidney function reduces excretion of creatinine, causing increased blood levels	**Increased**	▪ Impaired renal function ▪ Chronic nephritis ▪ Obstruction of the urinary tract ▪ Muscle disease (myasthenia gravis) ▪ Dehydration
	▪ Albumin	Screen for liver dysfunction, protein-losing enteropathies.	**Increased**	▪ Dehydration
			Decreased	▪ Liver diseases ▪ Alcoholism ▪ Nephrotic syndrome ▪ Low A/G ration
	▪ Urinalysis	▪ Urine is the means of excretion for the end products of metabolism carried out by billions of cells in the renal and urinary systems ▪ Test is one of the most useful indicators for healthy or diseased states	▪ To detect abnormalities in which the kidneys function normally but excrete abnormal amounts of metabolic end products suggesting a particular disease ▪ To detect conditions that may adversely affect the function of the kidneys or urinary tract	
Cardiac Risk	▪ Cholesterol	▪ Test detects disorders of blood lipids and indicates potential risk for atherosclerotic coronary artery disease	▪ Blood cholesterol levels are the basis for classifying coronary heart disease risk	
	▪ Triglycerides	▪ Test evaluates suspected atherosclerosis and measures the body's ability to metabolize fat	▪ Elevated levels indicate atherosclerotic disease risk factor	
	▪ HDL	▪ Test assesses coronary artery disease risk	▪ HDL levels are inversely proportional to coronary heart disease risk	
	▪ LDL	▪ Most serum cholesterol is present in LDL ▪ Test is done specifically to determine coronary heart disease risk	▪ Increased LDLs are closely associated with increased incidence of atherosclerosis and coronary heart disease	

Pathology	Laboratory Profile Test	Background	Interpretation	
Liver Dysfunction	▪ SGPT/ALT	▪ Test is used to diagnose liver disease	**Increased**	▪ Hepatocellular disease ▪ Active cirrhosis ▪ Metastatic liver tumor ▪ Obstructive jaundice or biliary obstruction ▪ Viral, infectious or toxic hepatitis ▪ Invectious mononucleosis
	▪ SGOT/AST	▪ AST is released into the blood due to injury or death of cells of highly metabolic tissue	**Increased**	▪ Always increased with acute myocardial infarct ▪ Liver disease
	▪ LDH	▪ Elevated levels are observed with liver diseases	**Increased**	▪ Liver disease
	▪ Bilirubin	▪ Measurement of liver function, hemolytic anemias, and hyperbilirubinemia in newborns	**Increased with jaundice**	▪ Hepatic, obstructive or hemolytic causes
	▪ Albumin	▪ Screen for liver dysfunction, protein-losing enteropathies	**Increased**	▪ Dehydration
			Decreased	▪ Liver diseases ▪ Alcoholism ▪ Nephrotic syndrome ▪ Low A/G ratio
Pancreatic Dysfunction	▪ Amylase	▪ Amylase enters the blood during inflammation of the pancreas or salivary glands	▪ Tests diagnose acute pancreatitis	
	▪ Lipase	▪ Appears in the blood following damage to the pancreas		

Bilirubin	Description	
Direct / Conjugated Bilirubin	▪ Circulates freely in the blood until it reaches the liver, where it is conjugated and excreted ▪ Increase usually associated with dysfunction or blockage of the liver	**NOTE:** The two are not differentiated unless the total bilirubin is elevated
Indirect / Unconjugated Bilirubin	▪ Protein-bound ▪ Increase usually associated with hemolysis	

Pathology	Laboratory Profile Test	Background	Interpretation	
Autoimmune Disease	▪ Antinuclear Antibody Test (ANA)	▪ The test is used for differential diagnosis of rheumatic diseases and to detect antinucleoprotein factors and patterns associated with certain autoimmune diseases ▪ Particular antibody patterns are associated with different autoimmune diseases	**Present**	▪ SLE ▪ Scleroderma ▪ Rheumatoid arthritis ▪ Sjogren's disease ▪ Dermatomyositis ▪ Polyarteritis
	▪ LE Cell Prep	▪ The LE cell is a neutrophilic leukocyte	**Present**	▪ Seen with SLE and other collagen diseases, chronic hepatitis, drug reactions
Heart Attack	▪ Creatine Phophokinase (CPK)	▪ Test is used in the diagnosis of myocardial infarct and as a measure of skeletal and inflammatory muscle diseases	**Increase**	▪ Myocardial infarct
	▪ SGOT (AST)	▪ AST is released into the blood due to injury or death of cells of highly metabolic tissue	**Increased**	▪ Myocardial infarct ▪ Liver disease
	▪ LDH	▪ Elevated levels are non-specific, but useful for confirming myocardial or pulmonary infarct when considered in relation to other test findings	**Increased**	▪ Myocardial infarct ▪ Congestive heart failure ▪ Pulmonary infarction
Anemia	▪ Hematocrit	▪ Tests the adequacy of red blood cell production; test determines red blood cell mass expressed as a percentage of packed red cells in a volume of blood. The percentage of RBC mass to original whole blood volume is the hematocrit	**Decreased**	▪ Anemia
			Increased	▪ Polycythemia ▪ Heavy smoking ▪ Dehydration
	▪ MCV, MCH	▪ Used to diagnose/classify anemia	**MCH**	▪ Increased with macrocytic anemia ▪ Decreased with microcytic anemia
			MCV	▪ Indicates whether red cell size is normal, smaller or larger than normal
	▪ Hemoglobin	▪ Screens for disease associated with anemia and determines the severity of anemia	**Decreased**	▪ Anemia states
	▪ RBC count	▪ Anemia causes reduction in circulating number of RBCs	**Decreased**	▪ Anemia states
Lymphadenopathy	▪ Mono Spot	▪ Tests for heterophil antibody agglutination	**Positive**	▪ Diagnosis of infectious mononucleosis
	▪ ESR	▪ Changes are related to alterations in plasma proteins ▪ Test is a non-specific indicator of infection or inflammation	**Increase**	▪ All collagen diseases, SLE ▪ Infections, pneumonia ▪ Inflammatory diseases ▪ Neoplasia, carcinoma ▪ Cell or tissue destruction

DIABETES (19,20)

CATEGORIES OF DIABETICS ACCORDING TO THE NATIONAL DIABETES DATA GROUP

Primary	**Diabetes Mellitus** *The most common endocrine disease*	Type I: Insulin dependent diabetes mellitus (IDDM)	▪ Usually begins relatively early in life (before age 40) and is more severe ▪ Patients require insulin for management ▪ Patient is at risk for ketoacidosis in the absence of insulin
		Type II: Non-insulin dependent diabetes mellitus (NIDDM)	▪ Affects about 80% of diabetics ▪ Usually begins in middle age or afterward ▪ Frequently associated with overweight persons ▪ Less severe blood glucose abnormality ▪ Patients do not become ketoacidotic if insulin is withdrawn
Secondary	▪ Associated with various non-idiopathic conditions and syndromes that either destroy pancreatic tissue or produce abnormal glucose tolerance due to various extrapancreatic influences (e.g. hormones or drugs)		
Gestational	▪ Diabetes that begins in pregnancy		

DIABETES INSIPIDUS (21,22)

ote

- Diabetes insipidus is a state of excessive water intake and hypotonic polyuria.
- Diabetes insipidus is not associated with diabetes mellitus, which produces hypertonic polyuria due to over-excretion of glucose.
- The clinical signs almost always include polyuria, excessive thirst and polydipsia.

Three major etiologies of diabetes insipidus	▪ Neurogenic: the hypothalamus is unable to produce vasopressin normally ▪ Renal: kidney cannot respond normally to vasopressin ▪ Temporary overpowering of the vasopressin system

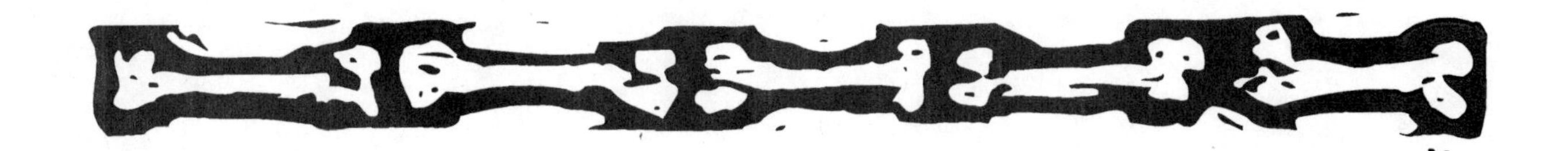

REFERENCES

1 Ravel R. Clinical Laboratory Medicine. 6th ed. St. Louis: Mosby, 1995:9.
2 Fischbach FT. A Manual of Laboratory & Diagnostic Tests. 5th ed. Philadelphia: Lippincott, 1996: 33,51,54,57,61-62, 64-65,118.
3 Fischbach FT. A Manual of Laboratory & Diagnostic Tests. 5th ed. Philadelphia: Lippincott, 1996: 31-38, 42, 44-46, 51-67, 118-120.
4 Isselbacher KJ, Braunwald E, Wilson JD. Harrison's Principles of Internal Medicine. New York: McGraw-Hill, 1994:1741, 1744.
5 Ravel R. Clinical Laboratory Medicine. 6th ed. St. Louis: Mosby, 1995:19-20.
6 Fischbach FT. A Manual of Laboratory & Diagnostic Tests. 5th ed. Philadelphia: Lippincott, 1996:73-74.
7 Fischbach FT. A Manual of Laboratory & Diagnostic Tests. 5th ed. Philadelphia: Lippincott, 1996:102-103, 114-116, 122-133.
8 Fischbach FT. A Manual of Laboratory & Diagnostic Tests. 5th ed. Philadelphia: Lippincott, 1996: 513, 525-527, 551-552, 578-579.
9 Ravel R. Clinical Laboratory Medicine. 6th ed. St. Louis: Mosby, 1995: 263.
10 Ravel R. Clinical Laboratory Medicine. 6th ed. St. Louis: Mosby, 1995: 262-265.
11 Fischbach FT. A Manual of Laboratory & Diagnostic Tests. 5th ed. Philadelphia: Lippincott, 1996:578.
12 Fischbach FT. A Manual of Laboratory & Diagnostic Tests. 5th ed. Philadelphia: Lippincott, 1996:157-161, 163-174, 178-191.
13 Fischbach FT. A Manual of Laboratory & Diagnostic Tests. 5th ed. Philadelphia: Lippincott, 1996:303-304.
14 Fischbach FT. A Manual of Laboratory & Diagnostic Tests. 5th ed. Philadelphia: Lippincott, 1996: 306, 309, 311, 315-316, 320, 331, 348-349, 351, 355-357, 380-382, 389-390, 397, 403, 410-411, 413, 419, 553-555, 917.
15 Ravel R. Clinical Laboratory Medicine. 6th ed. St. Louis: Mosby, 1995:454.
16 Fischbach FT. A Manual of Laboratory & Diagnostic Tests. 5th ed. Philadelphia: Lippincott, 1996: 552-555.
17 Ravel R. Clinical Laboratory Medicine. 6th ed. St. Louis: Mosby, 1995: 342-348.
18 Fischbach FT. A Manual of Laboratory & Diagnostic Tests. 5th ed. Philadelphia: Lippincott, 1996: 40, 55, 57, 61-65, 73-74, 148-149, 306-307,311, 348-352, 355, 356, 378-383, 388-392, 397, 410-411, 413, 415, 419, 527, 551-552, 554, 578-580, 608-609.
19 Ravel R. Clinical Laboratory Medicine. 6th ed. St. Louis: Mosby, 1995:453.
20 Isselbacher KJ, Braunwald E, Wilson JD. Harrison's Principles of Internal Medicine. New York: McGraw-Hill, 1994:1979, 1980.
21 Isselbacher KJ, Braunwald E, Wilson JD. Harrison's Principles of Internal Medicine. New York: McGraw-Hill, 1994:1923, 1925.
22 Ravel R. Clinical Laboratory Medicine. 6th ed. St. Louis: Mosby, 1995:409.

Section 2

Part IV

OVERVIEW

Part IV tests your clinical skills in three major areas:

Case management

- *The test taker is evaluated on his/her ability to perform a case history; perform a physical exam; perform an orthopedic/neurologic exam; choose the most likely diagnosis; choose the most appropriate case management procedures; choose the neurologic signs most likely to be present; and choose the most appropriate orthopedic/neurologic tests to perform.*
- *Patients are provided. These are healthy people who have been trained to simulate certain clinical conditions. Your ability to communicate with "patients" during the test is also evaluated.*

X-ray interpretation and diagnosis

- *X-rays and related clinical data are provided, and the test taker is expected to select x-ray findings that correspond with the clinical data from a multiple-choice list.*

Chiropractic Technique

- *Each required adjustment is listed in both static and motion terminology, and the required patient position, doctor hand contact and segmental contact are provided. The test taker is evaluated on how he or she sets up the patient for the adjustment.*
- *Spinal, pelvic/sacral and extremity adjusting can all be tested.*

ote

- You must demonstrate adequate skills in the allotted time. Effective use of time is a major factor for success on Part IV. Keep this in mind while preparing for the exam.
- Remember to read all the instructions during the exam. Perform those procedures you are asked to perform and speak only when the instructions say to do so.

Case Management

- Review the chapters on x-ray diagnosis and advanced imaging; physical diagnosis; general diagnosis; neurologic exam; orthopedic exam; and laboratory diagnosis.
- Practice with a friend and time yourself. State aloud what procedures you are performing and why (i.e. name the peripheral pulses as you palpate them, and know the implications of absent pulses), but remember not to speak on the actual test unless instructed to do so.

Taking a Chief Complaint and History

The Chief Complaint (1,2)

Mnemonic Letter	Meaning	Explanation
O	**Onset**	▪ Acute vs. chronic
P	**Palliative/ Provocative**	▪ What makes it better ▪ What makes it worse
Q	**Quality**	▪ Achy ▪ Dull ▪ Burning ▪ Throbbing ▪ Stabbing
R	**Radiation/ Referral**	▪ Radiating pain follows the course of a nerve (i.e. sciatica) ▪ Referred pain arises in a region remote from its source
S	**Site / Severity / System**	▪ Body system, bilateral/unilateral ▪ Intensity on a scale of 1 to 10 ▪ Direct source (i.e. gallbladder)
T	**Time**	▪ Temporal factors may be associated with pain ▪ Remittent pain: characterized by periods of abatement of symptoms ▪ Intermittent pain: characterized by appearance and disappearance of symptoms

The General History (1)

The following components of the patient's history should be reviewed with the patient:

- ☞ Allergies
- ☞ Medications
- ☞ Past medical history
- ☞ Family history

ote

- Be thorough when taking histories with the "patients" during Part IV. They may not divulge everything the first time you ask a question. You may have to restate questions, or ask direct yes/no questions to get the information you need.

Proficiency Checklist for the Cranial Nerves

- ❑ Test each cranial nerve individually
- ❑ Test two cranial nerves that are purely motor
- ❑ Test two cranial nerves that are purely sensory
- ❑ Test two cranial nerves that are both sensory and motor
- ❑ Test the cranial nerves involved with speaking
- ❑ Test the cranial nerves which open and close the eyes
- ❑ Test the cranial nerves which are involved with taste
- ❑ Test the cranial nerves which are parasympathetic
- ❑ Describe the extraocular movements, which muscles cause each movement, the cranial nerve innervation of each muscle, and the findings for lesions of Cranial nerves III, IV, and VI
- ❑ Describe and perform the Weber and Rinne tests
- ❑ Differentiate between central and peripheral facial paralysis
- ❑ Describe the pupillary reflexes and the significance of deficiencies

MOTOR, REFLEX, AND SENSORY EVALUATION

Test	Upper Extremity	Lower Extremity
Perform a motor, reflex and sensory evaluation for each of the following nerve root levels individually and in combinations (i.e. L2, 3, 4 and C5, 6, 7) and name the muscles involved	▪ C5 ▪ C6 ▪ C7 ▪ C8	▪ L1 ▪ L2 ▪ L3 ▪ L4 ▪ L5 ▪ S1
Perform a motor, reflex and sensory evaluation for each peripheral nerve	▪ Axillary ▪ Musculocutaneous ▪ Radial ▪ Ulnar ▪ Median	▪ Femoral ▪ Tibial ▪ Obturator ▪ Deep Peroneal ▪ Superficial Peroneal ▪ Inferior Gluteal
Test the strength for each muscle and state the peripheral nerves and nerve roots that supply each muscle	▪ Biceps ▪ Brachioradialis ▪ Triceps ▪ Deltoid ▪ Wrist extensors ▪ Wrist flexors ▪ Finger flexors ▪ Interossei	▪ Iliopsoas ▪ Hip adductors ▪ Quadriceps ▪ Tibialis Anterior ▪ Extensor Digitorum ▪ Extensor Hallucis Longus ▪ Gluteus Medius & Minumus ▪ Peroneus Longus & Brevis ▪ Gluteus Maximus

X-RAY INTERPRETATION AND DIAGNOSIS (3)

- Review the chapters on X-ray diagnosis and advanced imaging; and laboratory diagnosis. Focus on the major pathologies that present to chiropractic offices.

Disorder	Major Radiographic Findings	Laboratory Findings
Rheumatoid Arthritis	▪ Bilateral and symmetric distribution; uniform loss of joint space ▪ Periarticular soft tissue swelling ▪ Juxtaarticular osteoporosis ▪ Marginal erosions	▪ Normocytic, normochromic anemia ▪ Elevated ESR and CRP ▪ Rheumatoid factor present in 70% of cases
Ankylosing Spondylitis	▪ Romanus lesions (erosion of anterior vertebral body; precursor to syndesmophyte formation) ▪ Shiny corner sign ▪ Marginal syndesmophytes ▪ Bamboo spine ▪ Barrel vertebrae	▪ ESR frequently elevated in the active phase of the disease; normalizes once the disease process has resolved or enters remission ▪ HLA-B27 found in up to 90% of patients
Psoriatic Arthritis	▪ Ray pattern in the hands ▪ Mouse ears; pencil-in-cup deformity	▪ Up to 75% of patients with sacroiliac involvement will have the HLA-B27 antigen ▪ Elevated ESR in the acute phase
Metastatic Bone Tumors ▪ *Hot on bone scan*	▪ 75% of lesions are osteolytic; diffuse permeative or motheaten pattern of bone destruction ▪ One-eyed pedicle sign; blind vertebrae ▪ Vertebra plana	▪ Anemia and fever in advanced stages ▪ Elevated ESR often present ▪ Elevation of serum calcium may occur with osteolytic mets ▪ PSA is elevated in patients with cancer of the prostate gland when the tumor capsule has broken
Multiple Myeloma ▪ *Cold on bone scan*	▪ Generalized osteoporosis ▪ Punched-out lesions ▪ Vertebra plana and wrinkled vertebrae ▪ Raindrop skull ▪ Pedicle sign (preservation of pedicles) ▪ Geographic, soap-bubbly, highly expansile lesions	▪ Normocytic, normochromic anemia very common ▪ Elevated ESR ▪ Thrombocytopenia ▪ Hypercalcemia ▪ Hypergammaglobulinemia with a reversal of the albumin-globulin (A/G) ration is common ▪ Bence Jones proteins in the urine (40%)
Paget's Disease ▪ *Hot on bone scan*	▪ Osteoporosis circumscripta of the skull followed by cottonwool appearance ▪ Picture frame vertebrae; ivory vertebra ▪ Cortical thickening and bone expansion; increased trabecular patterns; pseudofractures ▪ Obliteration of Kohler's teardrop in the pelvis (brim sign) ▪ Candle flame appearance in the tibia; saber shin	▪ Anemia with long-standing Paget's disease ▪ Urinary excretion of hydroxyproline ▪ Increased alkaline phosphatase ▪ Hypercalcemia may occur

SERONEGATIVE ARTHROPATHIES (4)

- Seronegative indicates absence of rheumatoid factor.

  - ☞ Ankylosing spondylitis
  - ☞ Enteropathic arthritis
  - ☞ Psoriatic arthritis
  - ☞ Reiter's syndrome

HLA-B27 (5)

- HLA-B27 is a human histocompatibility antigen, responsible for many important immune functions.

  - ☞ Ankylosing spondylitis
  - ☞ Reiter's syndrome
  - ☞ Psoriatic arthritis
  - ☞ Enteropathic arthritis
  - ☞ Juvenile rheumatoid arthritis

IVORY VERTEBRAE (6)

Common causes of solitary ivory vertebrae include:

- ☞ Osteoblastic metastasis
- ☞ Hodgkin's lymphoma
- ☞ Paget's disease

CHIROPRACTIC TECHNIQUE (7)

Motion Listing	Spinous Process Listing	Diagram
Flexion restriction	PI (posterior inferior)	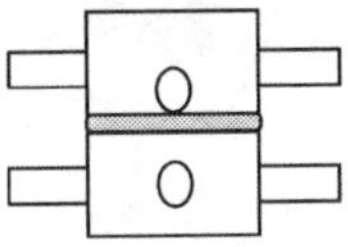
Extension restriction	PS	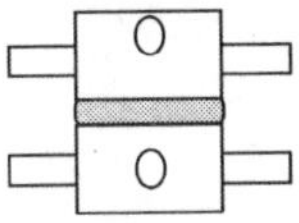
Right lateral flexion restriction	None	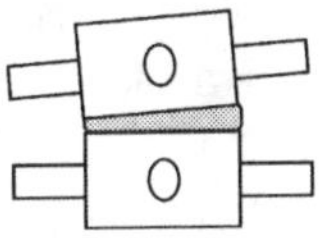
Left lateral flexion restriction	None	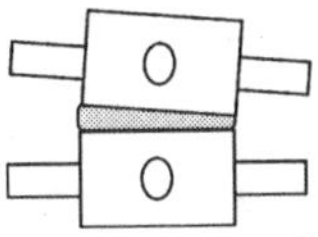
Left rotation restriction	PL (posterior spinous left)	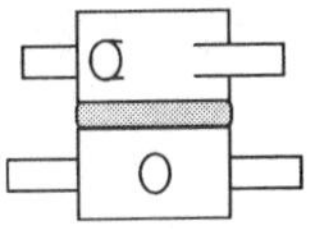
Right rotation restriction	PR (posterior spinous right)	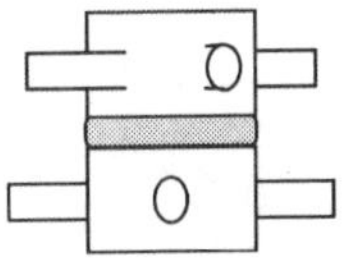
Right rotation and right lateral flexion restriction	PRS (posterior right superior spinous)	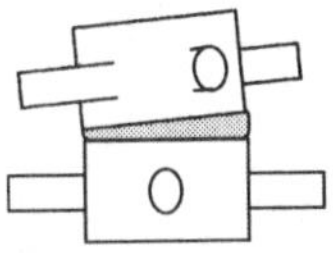
Right rotation and left lateral flexion restriction	PRI (posterior right inferior spinous)	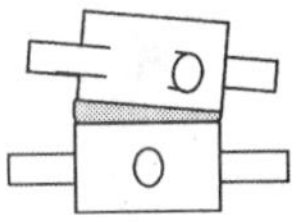
Left rotation and left lateral flexion restriction	PLS (posterior left superior spinous)	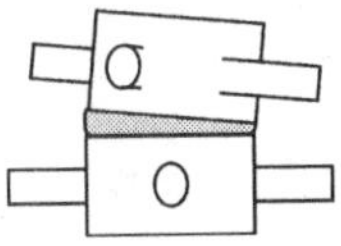
Left rotation and right lateral flexion restriction	PLI (posterior left inferior spinous)	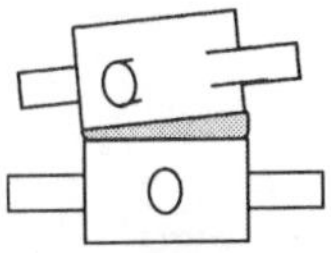

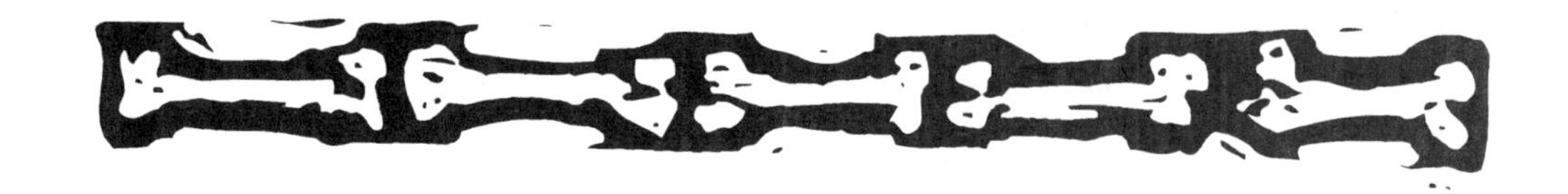

REFERENCES

1 Wyatt LH. Handbook of Clinical Chiropractic. Maryland: Aspen Publishers, Inc., 1992: 28.
2 Travell JG, Simons DG. Myofascial Pain and Dysfunction. Vol. 1. Baltimore: Williams & Wilkins, 1983: 3-4.
3 Yochum TR, Rowe LJ. Essentials of Skeletal Radiology. Vol. One and Two. 2nd Ed. Baltimore: Williams & Wilkins, 1996: 857, 872, 877, 891, 905, 1004-1005, 1019, 1132, 1158.
4 Yochum TR, Rowe LJ. Essentials of Skeletal Radiology. Vol. One and Two. 2nd Ed. Baltimore: Williams & Wilkins, 1996: 895.
5 Fischbach FT. A Manual of Laboratory & Diagnostic Tests. 5th ed. Philadelphia: Lippincott, 1996: 608-609.
6 Yochum TR, Rowe LJ. Essentials of Skeletal Radiology. Vol. One and Two. 2nd Ed. Baltimore: Williams & Wilkins, 1996: 1151.
7 Herbst RW. Gonstead Chiropractic Science & Art. Sci-Chi Publications, 1980: pages 84-85.

A

B

C

F

G

H

I

J

K

L

M

N

O

P

Q

R

S

T

U

V

W

X

Y